Developer Relations Activity Patterns

A Unified Approach to DevRel, DX, and Community Management

Ted Neward
Scott T. McAllister
David Neal
Chris Woodruff

Forewords by Scott Hanselman VP, *Developer Community, Microsoft*

Mary Thengvall *Author, The Business Value of Developer Relations*

Apress®

Developer Relations Activity Patterns: A Unified Approach to DevRel, DX, and Community Management

Ted Neward
Redmond, WA, USA

David Neal
Dalton, GA, USA

Scott T. McAllister
North Bend, WA, USA

Chris Woodruff
Wyoming, MI, USA

ISBN-13 (pbk): 979-8-8688-1894-3
https://doi.org/10.1007/979-8-8688-1895-0

ISBN-13 (electronic): 979-8-8688-1895-0

Copyright © 2026 by Ted Neward, Scott T. McAllister, David Neal, Chris Woodruff

This work is subject to copyright. All rights are reserved by the Publisher, whether the whole or part of the material is concerned, specifically the rights of translation, reprinting, reuse of illustrations, recitation, broadcasting, reproduction on microfilms or in any other physical way, and transmission or information storage and retrieval, electronic adaptation, computer software, or by similar or dissimilar methodology now known or hereafter developed.

Trademarked names, logos, and images may appear in this book. Rather than use a trademark symbol with every occurrence of a trademarked name, logo, or image we use the names, logos, and images only in an editorial fashion and to the benefit of the trademark owner, with no intention of infringement of the trademark.

The use in this publication of trade names, trademarks, service marks, and similar terms, even if they are not identified as such, is not to be taken as an expression of opinion as to whether or not they are subject to proprietary rights.

While the advice and information in this book are believed to be true and accurate at the date of publication, neither the authors nor the editors nor the publisher can accept any legal responsibility for any errors or omissions that may be made. The publisher makes no warranty, express or implied, with respect to the material contained herein.

> Managing Director, Apress Media LLC: Welmoed Spahr
> Acquisitions Editor: James Robinson-Prior
> Development Editor: Jim Markham
> Coordinating Editor: Gryffin Winkler

Cover image and artwork designed by David Neal

Distributed to the book trade worldwide by Springer Science+Business Media New York, 1 New York Plaza, New York, NY 10004. Phone 1-800-SPRINGER, fax (201) 348-4505, e-mail orders-ny@springer-sbm.com, or visit www.springeronline.com. Apress Media, LLC is a Delaware LLC and the sole member (owner) is Springer Science + Business Media Finance Inc (SSBM Finance Inc). SSBM Finance Inc is a **Delaware** corporation.

For information on translations, please e-mail booktranslations@springernature.com; for reprint, paperback, or audio rights, please e-mail bookpermissions@springernature.com.

Apress titles may be purchased in bulk for academic, corporate, or promotional use. eBook versions and licenses are also available for most titles. For more information, reference our Print and eBook Bulk Sales web page at http://www.apress.com/bulk-sales.

Any source code or other supplementary material referenced by the author in this book is available to readers on GitHub. For more detailed information, please visit https://www.apress.com/gp/services/source-code.

If disposing of this product, please recycle the paper

*To developers:
Every language, every platform,
every framework, everywhere.
Because without them, there wouldn't be us.*

*To Charlotte. Always.
—Ted*

*For my sweet wife Amber. My rock. My light.
My inspiration to keep going when things are hard
and the source of my motivation to succeed.
—Scott*

*To Tracy, my steadfast partner and
the light of my life, whose support and love
make everything possible.
—Chris*

*To my sweet wife Tammy, the love of my life.
You are my favorite. For all the coders, creatives,
and community leaders who have inspired me
throughout my journey, I owe you a debt of gratitude.
—David*

Table of Contents

About the Authors xxiii

About the Technical Reviewer xxv

Foreword xxvii

Foreword xxix

Chapter 1: Guide to Readers 1
    What Is a Pattern? 4
    What Is an Activity Pattern? 6
    Activity Pattern Documentation 8
    The Fundamental Triad of Developer Relations 14
    The Building Blocks of Patterns 17
    The Players 20
    The Terminology 20
        Community 21
        Company 21
        Customer 21
        Product/Service 22
    The Catalog of Activity Patterns 22

Chapter 2: A Case Study: Using the DevRel Patterns 23
    Campaigns 24
    Case Study: DCom and Codist 26
        The Executive Team 27

TABLE OF CONTENTS

    The Team 28
    Executive Team H1 Priorities 31
    DevRel Team Q1 Planning 36
    DevRel Team Q2 Planning 41
    Executive Team H2 Priorities 48
    DevRel Team Q3 Planning 58
    Q4 and Beyond 66

Chapter 3: Ambassadors 71
    Also Known As 71
    Intent 72
    Context 72
    Solution 73
    Participants 73
    Implementation 74
    Metrics 79
    Example 81
    Consequences 84
    Variants 88

Chapter 4: Article 89
    Intent 90
    Context 90
    Solution 91
    Participants 91
    Implementation 93
    Metrics 97

TABLE OF CONTENTS

    Example 99

    Consequences 101

    Variants 103

Chapter 5: Blog Post 105

    Also Known As 106

    Intent 106

    Context 106

    Solution 107

    Participants 107

    Implementation 108

    Metrics 112

    Example 115

    Consequences 117

    Variants 119

Chapter 6: Book 121

    Also Known As 122

    Intent 122

    Context 122

    Solution 123

    Participants 123

    Implementation 124

    Metrics 129

    Example 130

    Consequences 134

    Variants 135

TABLE OF CONTENTS

Chapter 7: Booth 137

    Also Known As 138

    Intent 138

    Context 138

    Solution 138

    Participants 139

    Implementation 140

    Metrics 145

    Example 148

    Consequences 149

    Variants 149

Chapter 8: Case Study 151

    Also Known As 152

    Intent 152

    Context 152

    Solution 153

    Participants 155

    Implementation 156

    Metrics 158

    Example 160

    Consequences 163

    Variants 165

Chapter 9: Code Review 167

    Also Known As 168

    Intent 168

    Context 169

TABLE OF CONTENTS

Solution 170

Participants 171

Implementation 172

Metrics 173

Example 175

Consequences 176

Variants 177

Chapter 10: Conference 179

Also Known As 180

Intent 180

Context 181

Solution 181

Participants 181

Implementation 183

Metrics 183

Example 187

Consequences 193

Variants 195

Chapter 11: Conference Session 197

Also Known As 198

Intent 198

Context 199

Solution 199

Participants 200

Implementation 201

Metrics 203

TABLE OF CONTENTS

    Example 205

    Consequences...208

    Variants 209

Chapter 12: Customer Check-In..213

    Also Known As 214

    Intent..214

    Context...214

    Solution 215

    Participants..215

    Implementation 216

    Metrics 217

    Example 218

    Consequences...219

    Variants 221

Chapter 13: Customer Pre-Sale 223

    Also Known As 224

    Intent..224

    Context...224

    Solution 225

    Participants..226

    Implementation 227

    Metrics 228

    Example 228

    Consequences...229

    Variants 231

TABLE OF CONTENTS

Chapter 14: Forums **233**
    Also Known As 233
    Intent 234
    Context 234
    Solution 234
    Participants 236
    Implementation 236
    Metrics 240
    Consequences 241
    Variants 242

Chapter 15: Guide **243**
    Also Known As 244
    Intent 244
    Context 245
    Solution 245
    Participants 246
    Implementation 247
    Metrics 249
    Example 252
    Consequences 253
    Variants 254

Chapter 16: Hackathon **255**
    Also Known As 255
    Intent 256
    Context 256
    Solution 256

TABLE OF CONTENTS

    Participants 257

    Implementation 258

    Metrics 259

    Example 260

    Consequences 261

    Variants 262

Chapter 17: Live Playground 265

    Also Known As 266

    Intent 266

    Context 266

    Solution 266

    Participants 267

    Implementation 268

    Metrics 268

    Example 269

    Consequences 270

    Variants 271

Chapter 18: Live Streaming 273

    Also Known As 274

    Intent 274

    Context 274

    Solution 275

    Participants 275

    Implementation 276

    Metrics 277

    Example: Live Coding 278

Consequences 279

Variants 280

Chapter 19: Newsletter 281

Also Known As 282

Intent 282

Context 282

Solution 282

Participants 283

Implementation 283

Metrics 284

Example 284

Consequences 286

Variants 287

Chapter 20: Office Hours 289

Also Known As 290

Intent 290

Context 290

Solution 290

Participants 291

Implementation 291

Metrics 292

Example 292

Consequences 293

Variants 294

Chapter 21: Open-Source Project 297

- Also Known As 298
- Intent 299
- Context 299
- Solution 300
- Participants 300
- Implementation 301
- Metrics 302
- Example 303
- Consequences 305
- Variants 307

Chapter 22: Partnerships 309

- Also Known As 309
- Intent 309
- Context 310
- Solution 310
- Participants 311
- Implementation 313
- Metrics 316
- Consequences 317

Chapter 23: Party 319

- Also Known As 320
- Intent 320
- Problem 321
- Context 321
- Solution 321

TABLE OF CONTENTS

Participants 322
Implementation 323
Metrics 325
Example 327
Consequences 329
Variants 331

Chapter 24: Podcast 333
Also Known As 334
Intent 334
Problem 334
Context 335
Solution 335
Participants 335
Implementation 338
Metrics 348
Example 351
Consequences 354
Variants 355

Chapter 25: Product/Service Development 357
Also Known As 358
Intent 358
Context 358
Solution 358
Participants 359
Implementation 359
Metrics 360

TABLE OF CONTENTS

Example 360

Consequences.. 361

Variants 362

Chapter 26: Recorded Video 363

Context 364

Solution 364

Participants 364

Implementation 365

Metrics 368

Example 368

Consequences.. 370

Variants 371

Chapter 27: Reference Documentation 373

Also Known As 374

Intent.. 374

Context... 374

Solution 375

Participants 375

Implementation 375

Metrics 376

Example 376

Consequences.. 379

Variants 379

Chapter 28: SDK... 381

Also Known As 382

Intent.. 382

TABLE OF CONTENTS

    Context 382

    Solution 383

    Participants 383

    Implementation 384

    Metrics 384

    Example 385

    Consequences 385

    Variants 385

Chapter 29: Sample/Example 387

    Also Known As 388

    Intent 388

    Context 388

    Solution 388

    Participants 389

    Implementation 390

    Metrics 391

    Example 392

    Consequences 392

    Variants 393

Chapter 30: Social Media 395

    Also Known As 396

    Intent 396

    Context 396

    Solution 397

    Participants 397

    Implementation 398

TABLE OF CONTENTS

Metrics	400
Example	401
Consequences	402
Variants	404

Chapter 31: Sponsorship 405

Also Known As	406
Intent	406
Context	406
Solution	407
Participants	407
Implementation	408
Metrics	409
Example	409
Consequences	410
Variants	411

Chapter 32: Survey 413

Also Known As	414
Intent	414
Context	414
Solution	415
Participants	417
Implementation	418
Metrics	420
Example	422
Consequences	423
Variants	425

Chapter 33: Swag 427

Also Known As 428

Intent 428

Context 428

Solution 428

Participants 429

Implementation 429

Metrics 429

Example 430

Consequences 430

Variants 431

Chapter 34: Technical Support 433

Also Known As 434

Intent 434

Context 434

Solution 435

Participants 435

Implementation 435

Metrics 436

Example 436

Consequences 437

Variants 438

Chapter 35: Training 439

Also Known As 439

Intent 440

Context 440

TABLE OF CONTENTS

　　Solution 441

　　Participants 441

　　Implementation 442

　　Metrics 444

　　Example 446

　　Consequences 446

　　Variants 448

Chapter 36: Tutorial 451

　　Also Known As 451

　　Intent 452

　　Context 452

　　Solution 452

　　Participants 453

　　Implementation 453

　　Metrics 454

　　Example 454

　　Consequences 455

　　Variants 455

Chapter 37: User Group Network 457

　　Also Known As 458

　　Intent 458

　　Context 458

　　Solution 458

　　Participants 459

　　Implementation 460

　　Metrics 462

Example	463
Consequences	465
Variants	466

Chapter 38: Webinar **467**

Also Known As	467
Intent	468
Context	468
Solution	468
Participants	469
Implementation	469
Metrics	470
Example	471
Consequences	471
Variants	473

Chapter 39: Workshop **475**

Also Known As	476
Intent	476
Context	476
Solution	477
Participants	478
Implementation	479
Metrics	481
Example	483
Consequences	485
Variants	486

Index **489**

About the Authors

Ted Neward is a tech consultant, writer, and regular keynote speaker with over 20 years of experience. He has been a part of the DevRel universe since before it had a name, including the creation and development of DevRel teams for several companies. He is an authority in Java and .NET technologies, programming languages of all forms, back-end enterprise software systems, and virtual machine/execution engine plumbing. He is the author and co-author of several books and has been an IBM Champion of Cloud, a Microsoft MVP, an INETA speaker, and a PluralSight course author as well as a member of several Java JSRs. He lives in the Pacific Northwest with his wife, two cats, twelve laptops, seven tablets, nine phones, and a rather large utility bill.

Scott T. McAllister spent more than a decade building software across a variety of industries before moving into Developer Relations. For nearly the past decade, he has worked as a Developer Advocate at multiple companies, helping developers understand complex technologies such as APIs, infrastructure-as-code, network ingress, and Kubernetes. When he's not helping developers solve tough technical challenges, he enjoys spending time with his family, exploring new technologies, and contributing to open source projects.

ABOUT THE AUTHORS

David Neal is a family man, geek, illustrator, musician, international keynote speaker, and seasoned software developer. He has spent the last 12 years passionately engaged in the developer community in Developer Relations roles at organizations such as Okta, Asana, Slack, Plaid, and Pluralsight. Before DevRel, David spent over 15 years building scalable web applications from startups to large corporations. His mission is to empower folks worldwide to be more awesome.

Chris Woodruff has been at the forefront of software development since before the first .COM boom, building a career that spans enterprise web development, cloud solutions, software analytics, and developer relations. His work previously as a Developer Advocate at JetBrains and currently as a Solutions Architect allows him to apply his deep technical knowledge to solving complex challenges, with a focus on API design and scalable architectures. He is a Microsoft MVP in the areas of .NET and Web Development.

About the Technical Reviewer

Richard Seroter is a Senior Director and Chief Evangelist at Google Cloud where he leads a team of developer advocates, developer engineers, and technical writers who inspire and activate the world's developers on Google Cloud. Richard maintains a regularly updated blog (seroter.com) on topics of architecture and cloud computing and can be found on X/Twitter as @rseroter.

Foreword

I've been in developer communities for over 30 years, back before we even called them that. Back when a "network" meant FidoNet, a "post" was on Usenet, and "going viral" meant someone uploaded a Turbo Pascal program to a BBS that lit up enthusiastic nerds across the globe (slowly, remember this was dialup). I built communities in public libraries using Commodore 64s. I've run meetups in gymnasiums, conferences in basements, and blogged for two decades when blogging felt like yelling into the void. I've stood on countless stages around the world, sharing stories, ideas, and code, all in service of one belief: that developers matter, and the non-technical people we build software for matter even more.

That's what this book is about.

Developer Relations has grown up. What started as a loose confederation of folks who "just liked talking to developers" has become a discipline with strategy, rigor, and patterns. Like any real discipline, we've built up enough collective wisdom to need a way to document it. The team behind this book has done exactly that: created a language, a way to name and describe the work of DevRel. Not to make it rigid but to make it understandable, so new advocates, writers, managers, and community builders don't have to reinvent the wheel with every hackathon, office hour, or content campaign.

The structure is familiar. If you ever carried around the Gang of Four's *Design Patterns* book in your backpack, this one will feel like home. Only instead of Singletons and Adapters, you'll find patterns like Office Hours, Partnerships, Newsletters, and Sponsorships. You'll see not just what DevRel teams do, but why they do it and how those efforts connect across a broader campaign. The book gives names to the unspoken knowledge you

FOREWORD

already have if you've lived this life long enough. And if you're just starting out, it gives you a map.

But more than that, this book reflects something essential: that DevRel isn't about tactics, it's about empathy at scale. It's about designing systems that make developers feel heard, seen, supported, and successful. A campaign isn't a checklist. A sponsorship isn't a transaction. A newsletter isn't an email. It's a promise: we're here, we're listening, and you matter.

This book is for those who care deeply. Those who know that good DevRel isn't about heroics, it's about habits. Patterns. Repeatable structures that create space for human connection.

So read it. Use it. Build on it. And then, go do it right.

Scott Hanselman
VP, Developer Community, Microsoft
www.hanselman.com

Foreword

I've spent much of my life building communities—some intentionally, others simply by following curiosity and connection. I've built communities in the tech industry, in my local mountain town, through side projects and shared values, in a pop-up city full of art and intention, and in conference hallways with people who just get it. If there's a common thread in all of that, it's this: community doesn't happen by accident. It takes care, persistence, creativity, and collaboration. And more often than not, it starts by finding your people—and building something together.

When I stepped into my first developer community role in 2012, there were only a handful of us doing this kind of work. I remember meeting my first "kindred spirit" at a conference in London in early 2013. We clicked instantly. Finally, someone else who understood the strange alchemy of technical curiosity, community intuition, and cross-functional diplomacy required to make this role successful. That thrill didn't subside as I continued to seek out more like-minded people over the next year. We weren't competitors or gatekeepers—we were kindred spirits. As community builders, we craved community ourselves. So we created it. And through that shared experience, themes, standards, methodologies, and yes, patterns began to emerge.

That's what makes this book so meaningful. It reflects the kind of collaborative spirit I've seen time and time again in Developer Relations: people coming together to identify what works, share their hard-earned insights, and support one another in doing work that's often hard to define and even harder to measure. Work that sits at the intersection of so many competing priorities—and still insists on keeping *people* at the center.

FOREWORD

This book is a continuation of that effort: an offering of patterns, ideas, and real-world practices from people who have lived the complexity of DevRel. These aren't theories developed in isolation—they've been shaped through late-night DMs, informal hallway-track conversations at conferences, and lessons from flops as well as surprise successes. They reflect not only what DevRel teams do but how they do it: with intention, flexibility, and deep respect for the people they serve.

The best DevRel professionals I know are bridge-builders—not just between the developers who use their product, but within their company itself. They build relationships with the product manager who really gets it and is motivated to create a better experience, the customer success team that knows exactly what users are struggling with, and the engineer who cares deeply about creating exceptional documentation. These internal relationships are just as vital as the external ones. Build them with the same care, and you'll find partners who help your work scale, evolve, and last.

As someone who's spent more than a decade advocating for the business value of Developer Relations, I've learned that our work rarely fits neatly into a single department or job description. Some days, we're product feedback loops. Other days, we're community therapists, trusted technical guides, or liaisons between internal teams with very different goals. We connect, we interpret, we make space for growth. And we do all of this while balancing a deceptively simple truth: *To the community, we represent the company. To the company, we represent the community.* Both sides matter. Both deserve our attention and respect.

Holding that tension with care is the heart of DevRel. It's what makes the work difficult, and also what makes it deeply meaningful.

Even now, working in a role not explicitly tied to Developer Relations, I find myself returning to its core principles every day. Whether I'm building infrastructure for a new taskforce at work, leading a 100-person art car camp at Burning Man, or creating a WhatsApp group to connect my mountain-town neighbors, the same muscle memory kicks in: listen

FOREWORD

deeply, build intentionally, act with compassion, and give people what they need to succeed—and then some. Community building isn't a job description; it's a mindset. And it extends far beyond tech.

The tech landscape looks very different than it did in 2018 when I published *The Business Value of Developer Relations*. But the underlying principles haven't changed. We still rely on trust, relationships, curiosity, and care. And we still need each other—to share what's working, what's not, and what we're learning along the way.

The authors of this book have captured that spirit beautifully. These aren't rigid frameworks. They're insights born of experience—collected, refined, and generously offered to all of us who are navigating this space together.

While not every idea will be a perfect fit for your team, I encourage you to approach it with curiosity. Look for the through-lines. Experiment boldly. Take what resonates, remix what doesn't, and keep building.

After all, the most successful communities aren't built by following a strict formula. They're built by people who care enough to show up, again and again, identify the specific needs of their community members, and help others succeed.

If that's you, you're in the right place.

Mary Thengvall
Author, *The Business Value of Developer Relations*
July 2025

CHAPTER 1

Guide to Readers

Running a developer-facing program is hard.

You need to establish key relationships with the developers that make up your target audience, yet without making explicit moves that alienate you from other developer audiences (or, perhaps more importantly, their managers). You must find topics that will be interesting to your audience, and relevant to your products/services, and then factor them into prose or presentations. Your articles should be interesting to the readers of third-party developer portals or magazines, and your blog posts should feel specific to a given developer's problems, yet general enough to address

CHAPTER 1   GUIDE TO READERS

future problems and concerns (and generate some good SEO traffic for your company's website).

You need to support the marketing department in their efforts to create better brand recognition for your company's products and/or services, yet without crossing the line into "marketecture" or "marketing fluff." You want to support your sales team in closing deals, but you don't want your own efforts to be labeled as "sales," lest you lose the respect of developers (who generally don't like being sold to). You want to be engaged with your developer audience enough to understand their struggles and provide remedies to help them improve their experience with your product/service. You need to keep your own technical skills up to par, both with your own product/service as well as with what the rest of the industry is finding useful and/or interesting.

You also want to avoid building each artifact entirely from scratch, if you can, if only because coming up with new, bespoke topics and entirely new prose or presentations is hard and extremely time-consuming. Experienced developer advocates will tell you that finding the right balance between all the various actions a DevRel team can do is difficult, if not impossible, to get "right" the first time.

If these paragraphs strike you as a bleak indictment of the DevRel space, take heart. In 1994, in the first chapter of the book *Design Patterns*, the authors (known as the "Gang of Four") wrote:

Designing object-oriented software is hard, and designing reusable object-oriented software is even harder. You must find pertinent objects, factor them into classes at the right granularity, define class interfaces and inheritance hierarchies, and establish key relationships among them. Your design should be specific to the problem at hand but also general enough to address future problems and requirements. You also want to avoid redesign, or at least minimize it. Experienced object-oriented designers will tell you that a reusable and flexible design is difficult if not impossible to get "right" the first time. Before a design is finished, they usually try to reuse it several times, modifying it each time.

Close to 30 years later, we find that while the world of software design has embraced (and rejected, then embraced again) the value of the software design pattern, the larger concept of "pattern" has emigrated to other areas of study and interest in our industry. We have process patterns, architecture patterns, cloud patterns, data model patterns, and for a brief shining moment, patterns aficionados even sought to categorize patterns of patterns ("meta-patterns"). While the value of some patterns (or these pattern languages) may be up for debate, the core concept of the pattern—the idea that we can learn from what we have done before and apply it to future engagements—has taken root in our industry and refuses to be shaken loose.

In the early days of object-oriented adoption, understanding just the concept of objects (creating first-class constructs that are the union of state and behavior) was enough to give developers mental fits. But as we got more comfortable with the idea, we began to understand that objects were more than just Boats and Planes or Persons and Students; we began to see how objects also collaborated to create Lists and Iterators or Singletons and Factories. So, too, with Developer Relations: in the beginning, it was enough to simply have a name for those people in that part of the company responsible for connecting to software developers. But now, as DevRel becomes an organization common to many (if not most) companies, the growing need for maturity in the space demands some deeper analysis and rigor.

CHAPTER 1   GUIDE TO READERS

What Is a Pattern?

Patterns come to us, originally, from the world of architecture, where Christopher Alexander wrote a series of books and articles on how the same recurring ideas kept appearing in buildings even though there was no formal design guideline (or legal code) that suggested (or mandated) its appearance. Across a variety of cultures and time periods, we find the idea of a "library" or "study" in a home, for example, often looks the same, regardless of the surrounding cultural style or building material. This prompted Alexandar to write a book entitled *The Timeless Way of Building*.

Alexander used patterns to document successful design practices in the architecture (that is to say, the art-and-science of designing physical buildings) profession. His focus on proven solutions rather than new and unique ones was motivated by his observation that modern day buildings and towns do not approach the beauty of the historical past. His emphasis and impetus was that the vast majority of architecture since the end of World War II has been dehumanizing, of poor quality, and lacking all sense of beauty and human feeling (O'Callaghan, 2001). This created his distaste for simply fashionable architecture and a preoccupation with the search for a design approach that generates beautiful structures (Grabow, 1983).

The state of software development in the late 1980s and early 1990s felt similar: there was a lack of elegance or beauty to what was being produced, and many folks within the space felt that feeling of "something is missing," which echoed Alexander's thoughts about his industry. As is common in software, the similarities, once discovered, led to a desire to draw inspiration and experience out of that space. (This has happened numerous times before: we draw the entire vocabulary of software architecture out of physical building architecture, because that felt like the closest profession to what an architect was doing, at least at the time.)

After discovering it, Alexander's work found soil in which to thrive. Kent Beck and Ward Cunningham wrote their first small pattern language in 1987, specifically around user interface. Beck and Grady Booch later sponsored a retreat in Colorado, which spun up the Hillside Group (which went on to serve as the locus of patterns thinking for decades) in 1993. The Hillside Group's work later led to a slow, building wave of articles, conferences, and research papers, all of which built upon and expanded the concept of a "pattern" to the software space.

In 1994, Erich Gamma and his colleagues known as the Gang of Four (GoF) published the seminal work that served as a direct inspiration for this book; their *Design Patterns: Elements of Reusable Object-Oriented Software* launched the concept of patterns to a broader audience. (It is useful and illustrative to note that in a discipline that is known to experience continual change, these principles are still useful and this book continues to sell more than 20 years after its publication).

But to answer the question that defines this section more specifically, we can turn to the "About Patterns" section on the Hillside Group website: "Patterns are generally defined as a three part construct. First comes the 'context'; under what conditions does this pattern hold. Next are a 'system of forces'. In many ways it is natural to think of this as the 'problem' or 'goal'. The third part is the 'solution'; a configuration that balances the system of forces or solves the problems presented. Alexander explains that a pattern is both a thing and a process for creating that thing. It describes what you have to do to generate the entity which it defines."

We discovered, however, that patterns often do not stand alone. As the GoF book illustrated, while the notion of a Singleton pattern is useful, it is vastly more useful when sitting next to other alternative approaches, like Prototype or Factory Method. When surrounded by other patterns, it becomes easier to see how they all relate to one another within an area of interest. This set of patterns, what Christopher Alexander called a "Pattern Language" in order to emphasize his belief that people had an innate ability for design that paralleled their ability to speak, became the standard norm to document a collection of related patterns. (*A Timeless Way of Building* is the most instructive work describing his notion of a pattern language, particularly via the application of the pattern language to the act of designing and building buildings and towns.)

A pattern language is first a set of patterns, but second it can impose some ordering constraints when the patterns contain pointers to patterns that help complete them. But this is not typically enough. Alexander uses the idea of a "sequence" to teach designers and builders how to construct a coherent artifact. Without some ideas on how to sequence one's design thoughts, the underlying pattern language is likely to be mostly a diagnostic tool. For an extensive example of the application of patterns, see Chris's other book *A Pattern Language*. Here he presents over 250 individual patterns that go into the making of successful towns and buildings (in the context of a western, even North American, environment).

What Is an Activity Pattern?

Novelists and playwrights rarely design their plots from scratch. Instead, they follow patterns like "Tragically Flawed Hero" (Macbeth, Hamlet, etc.) or "The Romantic Novel" (countless romance novels). Beginning authors often are ignorant of these common patterns in fiction, and try to re-invent them from scratch without realizing the commonalities and (slight) differences present in the various portrayals. As an author grows more studied in the genre, though, they often twist subtle elements of these commonalities in order to create different—yet familiar—experiences for their readers and viewers. What the fiction community refers to as "tropes," we call patterns. Once you know the pattern, a lot of decisions follow automatically, until you deliberately choose to twist them, anyway, in order to accomplish a different—yet familiar—result.

We find the same to be true in developer advocacy and relationships. In short, we find that there are numerous recurring approaches—"tropes," if you will—that appear when conducting the business of Developer Relations.

CHAPTER 1 GUIDE TO READERS

When an individual begins their journey down the path of developer relations—whether as developer advocate, technical writer, or community manager—they often begin by attacking each project (presentation, article, blog, whatever) entirely from scratch. In our work with neophyte speakers and authors, we routinely run across people who will create a new presentation for every conference to which they submit a proposal, or look to come up with "entirely brand-new" ideas for articles. When we speak with newly minted "Heads" of DevRel at companies (whether individuals or leaders of a team), we often find individuals who struggle to put together a solid plan for their company's DevRel efforts. More often than not, the individual or team fall back to what they know best, regardless of how it fits in with the company's larger goals or strategy.

Worse, we've seen DevRel engineers and advocates finding themselves struggling to identify "what to do next" when their VP-level management chain tells them they need to "broaden their reach" or "deepen their interactivity." They can see other DevRel teams somehow accomplishing things and becoming the kind of valuable asset they want to be at their own firms, yet success always somehow feels elusive and just out of reach. They struggle to identify something beyond what they know how to do, but in the absence of anyone who can tell them what kinds of activities "broken reach" or "deepen interactivity," they inevitably fall back on what they know. After a few rounds of frustration, they part ways with the company.

The purpose of this book is to record our (and others') experience in executing activities designed to engage with developers (and the wider developer community), and capture them as patterns. Hence the name *activity patterns*. Rather than patterns of software, we have captured what we believe to be foundational activities that members of a developer relations team do. Each activity pattern documented in this book systematically names, explains, and evaluates an important and recurring activity in developer-oriented community activities. In the same way that the Gang-of-Four book sought to capture object-oriented developer experience (DX) in a concrete form, our goal is to capture DevRel experience in a form that people can use effectively to build, run, manage, and grow developer-facing teams whose goal is to connect to developer communities (usually on behalf of a company, though most if not all of these could equally apply to volunteer or non-profit organizations).

To this end we have documented some of what we feel are the most important activity patterns and present them as a catalog for you and your team to be able to use, apply, adapt, and/or extend as your wants and needs demand. As with the software patterns that inspired this book, successful use of these patterns doesn't demand executing the activity exactly the way we've documented it—quite the contrary, in fact. Any time a pattern is applied to a new situation, there's a degree of adaptation required. This is part of the value in pattern documentation—by documenting the pattern, we create a strawman that you can compare against your particular situation, with the intent of making it easier to decide what should or shouldn't be a part of your own implementation.

In short, we have hopefully created a pattern language of developer relations activity patterns in an attempt to help Developer Relations teams better drive their efforts to success.

Activity Pattern Documentation

Although the pattern form has seen many variations and variants, we believe that a pattern fundamentally consists of four elements: the problem, which describes the immediate need facing the team; the context or what the Hillside Group called the "forces," that are necessary to consider when thinking about what to do to solve this problem; the solution, which is a practical series of actions or steps designed to resolve the problem; and the consequences of that solution, which are neither intrinsically positive or negative, except when considered in the context of the company carrying out the solution. (Spending a lot of money, for example, might be a consequence of using a pattern, but that's neither positive or negative in and of itself, until we measure it against the overall size of the DevRel team's budget.) We have found, however, that it's useful to supplement these canonical four pieces with some ancillary supporting pieces, to help the pattern "flesh out" a bit further:

1. The **pattern name** is a handle we can use to describe an activity, its context, its solutions, and its consequences in a word or two. Naming a pattern immediately increases our vocabulary and allows us to think more abstractly and strategically about the larger problem set. In fact, studies of patterns in use at large corporations found this naming to be one of the most valuable aspects of patterns in design conversations. Having a vocabulary for patterns lets us talk about them with our colleagues, in our documentation, and even to ourselves. It makes it easier to think about activities and to communicate them and their trade-offs to others. And, as if to underscore just how valuable these names can be, finding good names (ones that capture both the spirit and right nuance intended) has been one of the hardest parts of developing our catalog. In many cases, because a given pattern may be known by several different names(or, more accurately, because it's hard to universally agree upon a name for a given activity), we tried to select the name that most broadly, yet specifically, captured the essence of what we saw the pattern being, and then included in the pattern description an **also-known-as** section to help readers connect two (or more) terms to the same pattern.

CHAPTER 1   GUIDE TO READERS

2. Each pattern, we found, often was made up of **resources** that went in to the pattern's execution: one or more of *Budget, Code, Presentation, Social,* and/or *Writing* are necessary to carry out the pattern. Startups will often want to eye *Budget* patterns warily, and DevRel management will want to keep an eye on the resources required when discussing tasks for the team—Technical Writers will often be most successful doing *Writing* patterns, for example. We talk more about these in the "Building Blocks" section below.

3. Each pattern carries at its heart an **intent**: What is this activity trying to do? Generally, this is a short description, designed to capture the essence of the pattern in a few words, in order to "frame" the remainder of the discussion appropriately. It will often contain a description of a problem that needs to be solved, or a goal that wants to be reached. (This is, in essence, the "problem" portion of the Hillside Group's three-part tuple.)

4. The **context** describes some of the forces surrounding the problem. Teasing context apart from problem can sometimes be tricky, but often two teams or companies can have the same problems yet be in wildly different contexts. As an example, you may be looking to increase brand recognition of a product as part of its upcoming release. If your team is part of a multi-billion-dollar corporation, it has resources and roadblocks that make certain activities harder and others easier, when compared to being in a scrappy startup. In

this situation, the *problem* is to increase brand recognition; the *context* is the size and resources and policies of the respective companies.

5. The **solution** is a general description of the activity. Here we discuss the activity at a relatively high level, along with some ahead-of-time knowledge about what obstacles can appear and how to (generally) overcome them. These steps will often be relatively generic, owing to the fact that the specifics will be entirely dependent on the specific details involved— we can't write a conference talk for you, nor can we even tell you what topics you should propose! But we can certainly tell you what many conferences are looking for in a proposal, and when they are looking, and how to maximize your chances of being selected. And so on.

6. Each pattern will often involve **participants** beyond the direct members of the DevRel team. Knowing early which people in your company or community that will be involved helps with the planning and scheduling—if getting Accounting to approve purchases is a time-consuming step, it makes selecting a *Budget*—requiring activity a little less spontaneous.

7. The **implementation** describes a lower level of detail around the solution, often diving into a sequence of steps that will need to be taken in order to see the solution through to its completion. Again, the exact steps required or their sequence may differ from instance to instance, even within the

11

same company—the first few times DevRel writes a blog post, the Legal team may demand an editorial pass on the work before it is posted, but after a half-dozen or so efforts, Legal and DevRel have a better sense of what each is concerned with, and the formal review step can often be accelerated to a more informal skim.

8. We often need to know how we know if our activity is successful, and that usually means tracking one or more **metrics**. While we do not advocate that metrics be used as part of employee performance reviews, we do believe that objective data can help identify the best use of limited resources (employee time and company money being the two biggest ones). Some metrics will be automated and quantitative (such as "page views"), whereas other metrics will be more qualitative or more difficult to gather (such as "the Sales team mentioned that the customer read one of our articles in a trade publication"), but all can be useful indicators. And, it should be said, it's likely that hundreds of metrics are possible for any particular pattern; we describe only the ones that we have found useful and/or common.

9. In most pattern documentation, an **example** of how the pattern is applied is often helpful, particularly for those who have not attempted it before. Examples are intended to be illustrative, not normative. Teams' experiences with the actual execution of a pattern may be wildly different than

ours, but we feel like the examples given here are illustrative of what to expect when carrying out the activity.

10. The **consequences** are the results, trade-offs, and experiences that result from application of the activity. Candor compels us to point out that not all consequences are positive. In fact, some consequences could be downright negative—but our experience has taught us that attempts to interpret "positive" and "negative" around a given consequence is extremely difficult and almost entirely dependent on the viewer's perspective. For example, a **Conference Talk (197)** can have the consequence that the speaker gains greater popularity and brand awareness, which can be a positive consequence for that speaker as well as the company, until that speaker leaves the company, taking all that recognition with them! Does that make this a positive or negative consequence? We prefer not to judge, but feel it necessary to point out the consequence regardless. Listing these consequences explicitly helps you understand and evaluate them and their potential effects on you, your team, and/or your business.

11. While patterns are often useful in their own right, sometimes changing one small aspect of the pattern yields something useful but slightly different; these are called **variants** and are documented separately in order to not distract from the main body of the pattern.

CHAPTER 1   GUIDE TO READERS

The Fundamental Triad of Developer Relations

In order to understand the impact a given activity can have, it's useful to think about the entire range of these activities as affecting the developers in the community (and how they affect you in turn). It's been our experience thus far that these effects can be vaguely measured along three lines of thought:

- **Reach:** *How "far" does this activity go?* How many people can see it and/or consume it? Those things done over the Internet tend to have a large reach (particularly if the activity is someplace where Google can find it and pop it up during search results), whereas those things done in person (such as the hands-on workshop) will have a very short reach, since participation requires physical presence. For example, a **Blog Post (105)** can echo across the entire world within minutes, and even across time itself—certain blog posts just keep getting rediscovered by new readers. That kind of reach is just not possible with an in-person workshop done at a conference event, even if the workshop has a thousand people in it (which, by the way, is categorically impossible to do—a group that size isn't doing a hands-on workshop, they're watching you lecture).

- **Interactivity:** *How "conversational" is the activity?* This reflects the fidelity of two-way communication in the activity, and, in many cases, is in inverse proportion to reach. The **Blog Post (105)** doesn't really allow for great conversation (yes, you can open up comments on the blog, but we all know what happens when you do, and nobody wants that kind of content to appear on their blog), whereas a **Workshop (477)** really requires a high degree of interactivity with the attendees. The blog post author doesn't learn much from their audience when posting the blog—the workshop facilitator, however, can learn all kinds of things from the attendees via the questions they ask, the problems they run into, the questions they don't ask, and so on. High-interactivity activities will also lend themselves to gathering feedback, which can (and must) be funneled back inside to Engineering and/or Product for consideration and/or inspiration on future revisions. Without that feedback, the company will remain dangerously ignorant of their customers' real opinions, struggles, and perception of the company and its products and services.

- **Direction:** *To whom is the activity directed?* Traditionally, the view of the DevRel team is that developer advocates talk to the company's engineering, product, and marketing teams, then carry those ideas and messages out to developers outside the company. However, what's often not clearly explained is the other half of that circle: the developer advocates then take the feedback they gather from the outside and bring it back to the engineering, product, and marketing teams, in order to give those teams the feedback they desperately need to ensure their work is being effective. Even that is only half the story, though; as much as DevRel can be pointed "outside," it can also just as easily (and importantly) be pointed "inside," wherein a DevRel team connects to the developers that operate inside the company. Particularly for those companies who are emphasizing "inner sourcing," in which internal projects are run in an open-source fashion, have an internal DevRel team to socialize, train, and gather feedback about those internal projects can be every bit as valuable, if not more, than one doing it to the outside world.

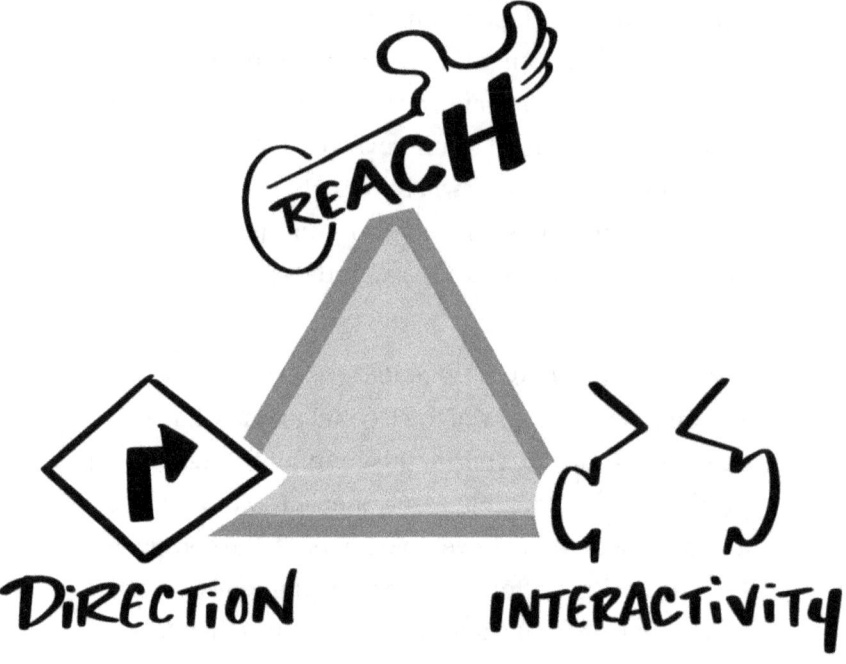

It must be noted that these are not either/or sorts of discussions—a **Blog Post (105)** may be high on Reach and low on Interactivity, but we can take steps to help improve the Interactivity, say by adding moderated comments, then by ensuring that the author of the post spends time during the week answering those comments. A **Conference Talk (197)** is generally extremely high on Interactivity and low on Reach, but if the talk is recorded and posted (particularly if it's posted to YouTube or other **Recorded Video (363)** platform), the Reach extends a great deal. A **Workshop (477)** can be held for developers either internal or external to the company. And so on.

The Building Blocks of Patterns

Lastly, we have found that nearly all of the DevRel activity patterns are made up of one or more of five fundamental kinds of activity:

- **Budget:** It's often the elephant in the room, but candor compels us to admit it: Some activities require budget (cash) to carry out. The **Conference Talk (197)**, for example, will often be held in a part of the world that's not the same part of the world in which you reside, and as of this writing, airlines refuse to transport people in exchange for "positive referrals." Thus, Budget will be required for this activity—but whether that comes from the company, the conference, the speaker's own pocket, or a GoFundMe is actually irrelevant (except maybe to the person writing the check).

- **Code:** The activity contains a degree of creation of a technical artifact, such as code, a database, or similar sort of software construct. It is precisely because of this Code component in so many DevRel activities that many DevRel teams have a requirement that team members have at least some facility with programming (or databases or system infrastructure or...). The depth of this experience need not be vast, and in many cases, it's better to be broad than deep, because the actual Code component can be a variety of different things (language code, database instances, cloud configurations, or combinations of all of these). Because the target audience of a developer relations program uses Code for a significant part of their daily activities, in order to reach developers you generally have to know or at least be conversant with Code.

- **Presentation:** This describes those activities that involve standing in front of a crowd (figuratively or literally) and capture their attention for a period of time. Typically these presentations are around a topic, and many will come with demonstrations of some form. Some presentations may be more informal than others, but the commonality here is that the activity will likely require some preparation: slides, perhaps, or at least an outline, along with whatever materials are needed for any demos (code, for example).

- **Social:** Given that DevRel is about connecting with (and creating a circular flow of information to and from) the developer community, it stands to reason that some of these activities will be Social, across all the different channels we socialize in. Twitter, Facebook, Instagram, in-person meetups, all of these are examples of social interaction activities, with pretty significant differences within them despite that commonality. While social media is not the sum total of the Social component, the history of the technology industry of the past decade makes it very clear that the "social" in "social media" is a component that is here to stay as a part of many DevRel activities.

- **Writing:** When we capture words into a long-term (dare we say permanent) medium, we are said to be writing. This writing can either be entirely factual, or the author can inject some opinion into the piece where appropriate. Writing is often a component of other activities—for example, while video recordings are certainly popular on social media, much of the content produced for, and consumed on, social media sites is written.

We document these at the top of the pattern description as a way of providing a "quick reference" for potential use—if you work for a scrappy startup, for example, you will probably want (need!) to steer away from *Budget*-based patterns, because scrappy startups typically have less of that than they would like. If your DevRel team is made up of a collection of ex-Sales and ex-Marketing folks, you probably want to steer clear of *Code*-based patterns, while a team that is primarily ex-engineers may want to avoid *Writing* and *Presentation*, and so on.

CHAPTER 1   GUIDE TO READERS

The Players

It's important to note that within these pages, we really don't spend a great deal of time thinking about the different kinds of people and/or roles that can be found in a Developer Relations team. Many words have been spent in other places talking about the differences between "developer advocates," "community managers," "technology influencers," and other titles. We choose, deliberately, to leave those words outside this book except in the most general usage cases.

That said, we do periodically need to refer to the people on the DevRel team. Where we do, we tend to use the term "developer advocate" as the term of choice, but we do so without a job description attached. In some places, we may want to be more specific, referring to a "technical writer" so as to emphasize the writing skills, for example.

Just as the original Gang-of-Four patterns could be applied in any reasonably object-oriented programming language, and just as the concepts of patterns themselves could be applied to any reasonably well-defined category of human activity, we feel that the patterns described in here are not exclusive to any particular job title or category. In fact, it's entirely reasonable that these patterns could be of help to people working in Marketing, Sales, Product or even Engineering, if they work at a company that sells directly to developers.

The Terminology

In any language (spoken or written), it's important to establish clear and firm definitions for the terms being used frequently, in order to avoid miscommunication or lost nuance, and a pattern language such as this one is no different. In this book, we use the following terms regularly, and so proffer the following definitions to make clear how we use them.

Community

The collection of developers who are outside the DevRel team. This is often synonymous with "customer," but collective, while "customer" is generally thought to be more individual. A community is often centered around the "product/service," but there may be sub-communities or other filtering criteria, such as by tech stack or platform; an API product/service may have a Java community, a .NET community, a Python community, each of which have different interests and outlook.

Company

Who the DevRel team works for and represents. Basically, if you're on the DevRel team, this is the larger organization around that team. This is most often a company, but could also be a volunteer organization, non-profit, or even open-source community or foundation. The constant here is that the "company" makes "product/services" that the DevRel team is responsible for supporting, promoting, and demonstrating.

Customer

Anybody outside the "company," whether they are a paying entity or not. DevRel teams will often want to segment this further (between open-source customers and paying customers, for example) in order to draw certain distinctions, but for the majority of these patterns, it's sufficient to simply call anybody outside the company a customer. Note that based on the *direction* of the activity, the "customer" could very well be another team or developers inside the same company, so some nuance and flexibility in this definition is going to be needed. Basically, if you're on the DevRel team, this is everybody that's "not us" but is using our "product/service." (Sometimes it helps to draw a distinction between "developers" as "all developers in the world" and "customers" as "those developers using our product/service.")

CHAPTER 1   GUIDE TO READERS

Product/Service

What the DevRel team is looking to talk about. This can be a tool (such as an IDE or database), a library or set of libraries, a web service accessed over HTTP (commonly called an "API," "Web API" or "HTTP API"), some other kind of service (anything that ends with "-as-a-service" is a strong candidate), and so on. It need not be a formal artifact that is "sold"—open source projects around/about which the company sells services would be referred here as "product/service." Note that the company may have many product/services available, and a single DevRel team may support all of them, a few of them, or only one of them, but the distinction between one product/service or many product/services is largely irrelevant to the pattern catalog below.

The Catalog of Activity Patterns

The catalog beginning on page 71 contains 37 activity patterns. Their names and intents are listed next to give you an overview. The number in parentheses after each pattern name gives the page number for the pattern in this book (a convention we follow throughout the book).

CHAPTER 2

A Case Study: Using the DevRel Patterns

This book can be used in a variety of ways.

CHAPTER 2   A CASE STUDY: USING THE DEVREL PATTERNS

For starters, and most obviously, this book can be utilized solely as a reference work, read front to back, as a means by which teams can establish a common lexicon and vocabulary for conducting their work. "I'm thinking that next quarter we need to budget and hire to allow the team to do four **Customer Check-Ins (213)**, eight **Blog Posts (105)**, and a couple of **Conference Sessions (197)**" is a useful way to communicate what the team is thinking in terms of its immediate goals and the means by which the team achieves those goals. This would be a well-used approach to software patterns, as a means of allowing those with some significant experience in the industry to be able to communicate quickly and unambiguously to one another: "I'm thinking we need a Singleton that in turn starts as a Façade over the Chain of Responsibility—made up of a collection of Prototype objects—that handles the actual details of the request." If you know the GoF pattern language, you can already see the software design in your mind's eye.

Of course, the drawback to that approach is the obvious follow-up: If you *don't* know the GoF pattern language, you're completely mystified by that second-to-last sentence in the previous paragraph. This is where this chapter comes in.

Campaigns

Like the GoF book (which, as already noted, is this book's spiritual ancestor), we present this chapter as a more comprehensive and fleshed-out example of how to use the patterns. In this chapter, we will discuss how the patterns combine in various ways to conduct a developer relations *campaign*: a series of activities that are all undertaken together as part of an explicit strategy to support the company's overall strategic goals in turn. Not all software development companies will need to formalize their activities in a specific strategy or campaign. For example, it is easy to assume that a company like Microsoft would "just keep selling Outlook"

CHAPTER 2   A CASE STUDY: USING THE DEVREL PATTERNS

as a strategy for their Office-specific developer relations orgs. However, it often serves the company well to have specific campaigns that have well-defined starting and ending dates, usually along with metrics to determine the success or failure of that campaign. We see this in popular marketing schemes—every year, around the holidays, we know that a popular drink company will begin to run their holiday-themed commercials (actually, several do, one with polar bears and another with a team of horses) in order to convey general feelings of "home" and "celebration," which hopefully connect in their audience's minds with the product whose logo appears.

Within the developer relations space, particularly at smaller companies, we often find that specific company events (usually product or service releases) are useful guideposts to drive starting- and ending-points for a developer relations campaign. The release can be either the release of a new product, or the release of a significant version of an existing product, but since much of the company's internal scheduling and focus is around that release schedule, it helps to begin thinking about doing the same for the developer relations activities, as well.

Foundationally, a DevRel campaign is a discrete set of interrelated activities that are planned and executed in such a way as to support not only a larger goal but also each other. The campaign is often planned at a strategic level in conjunction with other activities being conducted by the company's Sales and/or Marketing organizations, but Product will often want to tap into DevRel activities as well, in order to maximize opportunities to harvest feedback on different Product decisions (and potentially help identify sources for more Product-centric decision-making).

CHAPTER 2   A CASE STUDY: USING THE DEVREL PATTERNS

Case Study: DCom and Codist

In the remainder of this chapter, we examine a **Case Study (151)** (in the meta sense) in the execution of a DevRel campaign. In order to avoid violating any non-disclosure agreements, we choose to describe a fictionalized case, a DevRel team of five people built to support the release of a new artificial intelligence-powered coding assistant called "Codist" by the fictitious software company "DCom." We'll see how the activity patterns capture solutions to various problems getting developer attention around the product, and how the DevRel team can also support the product itself by "closing the loop" for feedback to the Codist Product team. By the end of this chapter, you will have seen roughly a dozen or so of the patterns "in action," some more than others, which is typical for any given campaign, hopefully making it easier to see how each one contributes to the larger perspective and strategic discussion around supporting the product release.

Our mechanism for doing this will be to be a "fly on the wall" during several discussions between the various players among the DCom executive team as they wrestle with the problem of how to meet the overall company goals with respect to Codist. Our primary perspective will be that of Jeremy, the VP of Developer Relations for DCom, who just joined the company a few months prior, and we will follow Jeremy as he engages in various meetings both with his peers (Pam, the VP of Engineering; Li, the VP of Product; Caleb, the VP of Sales; Kimberly, the VP of Marketing; and Gerald, the CEO) as well as his team (Mikaela, Curt, Nkema, Fred, and Janessa).

CHAPTER 2   A CASE STUDY: USING THE DEVREL PATTERNS

The Executive Team

When Jeremy was hired to run the DevRel team, Gerald made it clear that at least initially, their focus would be on the upcoming Codist release, though DCom does have a few other products that may require some DevRel support. (For example, DCom has mobile application frameworks for both iOS and Android that they still do a modest business with, as well as some legacy C++ libraries.) "We're slowly trying to get out of the legacy market," Gerald explained, "But we haven't found a buyer to take them off our hands, and the customers we have still using the legacy libraries are also customers for other of our products, which means we don't want to just drop them and leave them high-and-dry with no support. So, we still have some customers we'll need to support if that comes up. Mostly, though, the Board of Directors is betting big on the Codist release, so we'll want DevRel aimed in that space most of all."

When Jeremy talked to Pam, she was excited that Sales and Marketing would have a partner to help push Codist out into the market. "Beyond that, though, I don't know that I really have much for you, to be honest. I've never worked closely with a DevRel team before, so I'm not sure what more we do together besides provide you some support around building out demos and stuff." When Jeremy began explaining that various DevRel activities can be aimed at the internal developers—particularly the ones on her team—for activities like **Conference Sessions (197)**, though, Pam got very intrigued. "Wait, so you mean like giving talks to my team? Sort of like informal training? That... wow, OK, that's giving me something more to think about. I'll have to get back to you on that one."

Meanwhile, the emphasis in priority was echoed by both Kimberly and Li. "Codist is where we're putting all of our Marketing budget this year," Kimberly said when she and Jeremy met to discuss her team's goals and efforts. "We can see how developers using AI would be good in this market right now, so we're going to put most of our energy there." Li nodded along with Kimberly's assessment, although added that Product would love to get feedback from external developers.

When Jeremy asked Caleb, he got a similar yet slightly different perspective. "Obviously over here in Sales we're never going to turn away a customer expressing interest in any of our products—I think we even had a few TLP (the legacy C++ product suite) sales last year—but we definitely think most of the upcoming interest will be around Codist. And, to be clear, my folks are not super-technical, and then we had to let go of our two Technical Sales folks two years ago during the layoffs, so we're running pretty low on people who can meet with our customers' developers and walk them through demos and answer questions and all that. I'm going to need as much of that technical stuff from your team as you can give me in order to close deals, Codist or otherwise."

The Team

Jeremy's first two weeks at DCom was spent getting to know his team in more detail and reviewing their skills, current assignments, and goals. Part of this was the "getting to know you" that every new manager goes through with their new team, but Jeremy also knew that Coding, Writing, Speaking, and Socializing are all key inputs into the various DevRel activities, and he wanted to know which of his people were interested in which of those kinds of activities.

Mikaela, the most senior of his developer advocates, had been at DCom for ten years and was the definite "go-to" person for anything related to either the C++ legacy libraries or the mobile app frameworks. "I spent 10 years writing C++," she explained when they first met, "And actually got into DevRel when one of the sales folks needed somebody to help them support a customer question." She found that she enjoyed that work so much, she pivoted to one of those Technical Sales roles before moving over to Marketing just before the layoffs Li mentioned. "This was before we even knew that DevRel was a thing," she said, "And I was just out

CHAPTER 2   A CASE STUDY: USING THE DEVREL PATTERNS

there doing this, floating somewhere between Engineering and Marketing until we finally formed a DevRel team." When asked about her skills and preferences, she said, "I really still like Coding, but I'm finding I really enjoy Presentations as well. It's why I've been doing more conferences the last few years. I love getting out there and talking about our stuff and meeting new developers trying to do interesting things with it. Writing isn't my strong suit, though."

Curt, meanwhile, was a 5-year developer advocate who came to DCom three years ago. "I've been doing DevRel for about five years, I'd say, at least officially. I've had a personal blog for way longer than that, and a few folks follow me there, but I didn't start doing DevRel as a job until I was at TechMo, the DevOps startup I worked at before here." Like Mikaela, he found he enjoyed it once he was doing it. "TechMo being a startup, we didn't do much in the way of conferences or really anything that required spending money, but they definitely had me doing a bunch of different things. I wrote docs, I created samples, I built out tutorials, I kinda did everything. Being a team of one means you're really on the hook for anything that vaguely presents itself in the DevRel space, and TechMo really leaned into that." Curt didn't say as much, but Jeremy picked up on the vibe that it had burned him out somewhat. When asked about skills and preferences, Curt shrugged. "Having done all of it before, I can't think of anything I couldn't do, but I don't know that I'm great at any of it. I'm hoping to get a better sense of how each of my skills are, comparatively. As for preferences, I don't know that I have any, but I don't really want to be assigned fifteen things simultaneously. That was one frustration at TechMo—everybody wanted everything yesterday, and all the juggling really meant it felt like I was never getting any movement on anything."

Nkema, meanwhile, was a recent hire, hired the same week Jeremy was, in fact. "This is my first real job out of college, and I'm super-excited to be here," she said. "My degree was in Informatics, so I know how to write code and build applications—I have a few mobile apps that started as homework assignments that I expanded to things I could put on the

CHAPTER 2   A CASE STUDY: USING THE DEVREL PATTERNS

App Store—but I'm definitely interested in doing more public-facing kinds of things. I think that DevRel definitely needs to be lots of online activities, like podcasts, a YouTube channel, all that." When asked about skills and preferences, she responded with all the energy and vigor found in the recently graduated: "I'm down for anything, and I will knock it out of the park."

Fred, however, was a 25-year veteran technical writer. "I've worked as a contractor at companies all over the Silicon Valley before deciding to look for something more full-time and stable." He'd ghost-written articles for several major publications, as well as documentation for several of the FAANG companies on their cloud products before joining DCom as a technical writer. "Originally I was going to be part of Engineering, working on documentation, but then Marketing wanted some copy, and Product was interested in some blog posts, and next thing I know, we're forming a developer relations team—which I'd never heard of before I was a part of it—and here I am." When asked about skills and preferences, Fred simply shrugged. "I'm a good technical writer, but I won't claim that I have any sort of deep development chops, and I definitely don't like getting up in front of an audience. Truth is, I'd rather get a root canal than give a presentation. Brr." He mock-shivered. "I know enough programming to recognize the different programming syntaxes, and I've learned enough about development to be able to sanity-check programs."

The last member of Jeremy's team was Janessa, a Technology Community Manager who'd done stints at Microsoft and Google as a developer-facing program manager. "Basically, I would 'own' the relationship between the company and a particular developer community. When I was at Microsoft, I was a part of their MVP program administration for a while, and while I was at Google, I was in the GDE program. I came to DCom because it was a nice financial jump and I got to set my own title, but to be honest, before this DevRel team was formed, I was starting to think it was a mistake to jump here. I'm excited to see what we can do." When asked about her skills and preferences, Janessa said, "Well, I can't really say I'm familiar with programming, though after being around it so much I can probably fake my way through an interview if I wanted to. I've programmed before, though, and I can definitely manage social activities and events. I often managed a lot of the logistics for our speakers at conferences, for example, when I was working at other companies."

Before long, it was time for Jeremy's first executive team planning meeting.

Executive Team H1 Priorities

As the first half of the year came around the corner, Jeremy sat with the executive team to ascertain their goals and the overall company direction. Gerald opened the H1 planning meeting pretty directly. "Codist is looking good for its initial release on May 1, Pam, correct? No slips?"

Pam nodded. "So far, all signs are good. The team is reporting that the three main IDE integrations we've aimed for are pretty solid—there's some bugs, but most of them look like they're not of the "crash the IDE" variety—and our own developers are starting to use it internally for some of their work, which means dogfooding is working out well."

Jeremy jumped in. "Dogfooding?"

"I know this one!" Kimberly piped up. "That's when the developers use the thing they're building, so that they can feel how solid the product is."

Pam grinned. "Yup. That was an important milestone for us in Engineering, and the fact that we are using it every day for our own development gives us a good feeling about the overall solidity of it."

"That's pretty solid," Jeremy agreed. "Pardon my asking, but what languages or platforms are we targeting with this initial release?"

Li jumped in before anyone else. "We figured our best bet will be to target Java, Python, and Javascript developers in this first release. New platforms can come online later, but with Microsoft doing their own AI thing—and Oracle wasn't—and Python and Javascript not being deeply dominated by a large corporation, we felt this was the best place to get some traction."

CHAPTER 2   A CASE STUDY: USING THE DEVREL PATTERNS

In his notes, Jeremy wrote *Java/Python/Javascript*. "So I'm guessing JetBrains was a principal IDE target?" At Li's and Pam's nods, he notes, *JetBrains (IDEA, PyCharm, WebStorm)*. "What about Visual Studio Code?"

Gerald jumped in. "We wanted to avoid Microsoft."

Before Jeremy could explain, Li jumped in again. "No, Jeremy means the open-source editor with all the plugins that Microsoft ships. It's not Visual Studio proper." She turned to Jeremy. "That was actually our first IDE integration choice, and if I understand it correctly, Pam's team got that one done pretty fast." At Pam's nod, Li continued. "So we have integrations in Code that can assist for Java, Javascript, and Python in VSCode, but no other languages."

In his notes, Jeremy adds, *VSCode integration—Java/Python/Javascript*. "So it's safe to assume that any developer communities we're targeting are the ones from those three languages?" At the nods around the table, Jeremy continues, "And are we going after any particular part of the stack in those communities? Does Codist help more with front-end, back-end, database migrations, …?" As he trailed off, everybody turned toward Pam, who grinned.

"That's the nice thing about Codist—it's a full-stack assistant, fully capable of analyzing both front-end and back-end code." Pam's grin got even bigger. "We call it providing support all the way from the browser to the database." Jeremy notes, *From the browser to the database*. That felt like a phrase that was going to come up again.

It was then that Caleb jumped in. "Since we're there," he said, shifting in his seat some, "I want to double-click on that topic up for a bit. Generally, in Sales, we're trying to focus on some particular pain points that companies have when we're trying to convince people to buy. You know, something like, 'Building your front end takes 65% of your budget, but we make that front end for free' sort of thing. Are we saying that Codist can do all the development itself and customers could fire their entire development team?"

CHAPTER 2   A CASE STUDY: USING THE DEVREL PATTERNS

"No," Pam said. "Codist can help developers be more productive, but it's not going to replace developers. They still have to be hands-on-keyboards. All Codist is going to do is make it easier for them to get the code written—it's not going to be able to write it itself."

Jeremy noted, *Aids developers. Not a replacement,* and underlined that last sentence a few times for emphasis, knowing already that this was going to be something the DevRel team would need to nuance and message carefully.

Meanwhile, Caleb continued. "It's hard for us to go into a company with that broad a mandate, though. We've found it helpful to target some particular aspect of the development stack or pipeline, and focus on that as part of our pre-sales technique."

Gerald frowned. "I don't understand."

"Like with the CI/CD movement a few years ago, the emphasis was really around the build pipeline and all the steps that a company had to do to get ready for pushing code to Production. The big cloud-build vendors could go in saying, 'Are your builds taking more than a few hours? We can reduce that to seconds.' As a sales tactic, having a focus like that let us qualify leads pretty quickly so we don't go barking up trees that were never going to listen."

Meanwhile, Jeremy scribbled, *Sales wants more focus in the pitch; qualified leads over broad-spectrum.* Already he could see that, at least from Sales' perspective, they were going to lean more toward Interactive activities over Reach activities—that the Sales folks were going to want to connect more deeply with specific customers rather than try to follow up on leads from "just anyone."

The executive meeting continued on for a while after that before Jeremy had a chance to broach one final topic he needed. "Before we break, I had one more topic: What sort of metrics are we tracking before, during, and after Codist's launch?" Looking at Kimberly, he said, "I'm

CHAPTER 2   A CASE STUDY: USING THE DEVREL PATTERNS

assuming you're going to be running some broad-spectrum media ads, yes?" At her nod, he continued, "And what are you looking to get out of those ads in terms of results?"

Gerald responded first. "Well, most of all, sales. We are looking for Codist's launch to generate 10,000 signups in the first week of its public availability, and obviously the more of those that are paid signups, the better."

Jeremy nodded, then looked to Pam and Li. "What's the beta program look like at the moment? How many people are using it already?"

They looked at each other for a long moment before Li turned to Jeremy and said, "Well, we don't have a beta program up and running yet. Pam and I have each been trying to figure out who should own it."

Jeremy tried to unobtrusively scribble *No beta* in his notes.

Pam interrupted. "Truthfully, we're both so slammed that we were trying to get Caleb's team to take ownership of it." At Caleb's snort, Pam grimaced. "And you can see how well that conversation was going, to boot. Short story is, we don't have one yet, and we weren't sure how we were going to run one. I think Li and I had actually gotten to the point where we were going to just make do without one."

Gerald scowled. "I thought we had resolved this last quarter."

Li looked away as Pam said, "Frankly, Gerald, we had put money in the budget for it, but we never came to a final decision on the headcount to own it. Remember, we tried to run a beta with the mobile frameworks a few years ago, but my group ran out of energy and the whole thing languished. And Li doesn't have nearly enough bandwidth to run it, particularly if she's still needing to run the user feedback seminars you insisted on."

Before Gerald could respond, Jeremy piped up. "Hey, if it's all right with everyone else, I think DevRel could own it." Already he was noting down Janessa's name after the *No beta* note in his notes. "I'll need to talk to the team to make sure I'm not overpromising and underdelivering, but particularly if we can get the budget"—he glanced over at Pam, who nodded—"then I suspect we can probably run at least the start of one until

CHAPTER 2   A CASE STUDY: USING THE DEVREL PATTERNS

we can figure out a better home for it." He glanced at the calendar on the wall, then said, "We're a little more than five months out from the May 1 date, and it's not uncommon to start a beta three to six months before release, so we won't be looking weird for not having brought it up before now. How tightly confidential do we want to run it, and do we have people on a mailing list or otherwise identified to be the beta crowd?"

Pam shrugged uncomfortably. "I honestly don't know. The person I had a few years ago who was running the mobile beta left us, which was why the program collapsed. I put one of our other program managers on it, but it was always a side effort for him, and when he left a year ago, the whole thing was back-burnered. I don't know if we even have the records of who was on it back then."

Jeremy looked at Caleb. "Do you have some existing customers we're really friendly with that would have some interest in Codist?"

Caleb thought for a long minute, then said, "Probably? I'll check with a few of my folks and see what they say. How many people are you thinking for the beta?"

"I don't know exactly yet, but I'm guessing somewhere between 20 and 50. I would think getting feedback from those folks would be of paramount importance over the next quarter"—at which both Pam and Li nodded emphatically—"and I would want to make sure we keep a close pulse on them."

Gerald spoke up. "Make sure you get Francis in Legal to draw up a confidentiality agreement on this—I do not want anyone thinking they can leak something before the announcement. I want a big splash when we go live with it." Jeremy noted that: *Strong confidentiality; big splash at launch.*

Jeremy asked, "What about pre-release tech press coverage? Is that something you're going after?" He looked at Kimberly. "I'm assuming you're pushing some embargoed press releases?"

Kimberly nodded. "Yes, definitely. But we're holding them until just a day or two before the actual release, so as to minimize the opportunity for leaks or 'accidental' pre-release stories." She glanced at Gerald who nodded in confirmation.

CHAPTER 2   A CASE STUDY: USING THE DEVREL PATTERNS

Jeremy underlined *Strong confidentiality* in his notes several times.

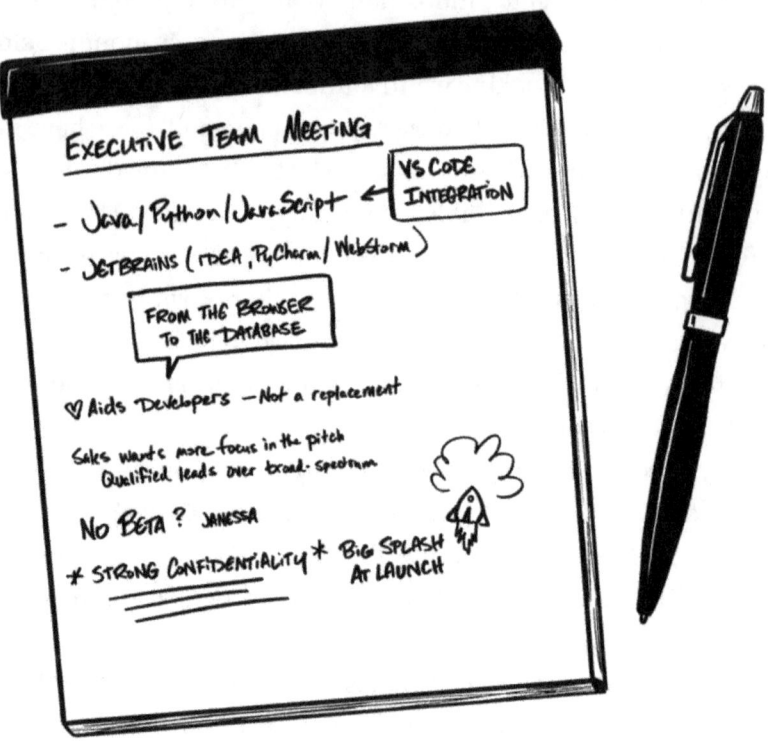

DevRel Team Q1 Planning

Later that same week, Jeremy held his team's Q1 planning meeting.

After a few minutes of chitchat while everybody was assembling, Jeremy launched into it. "Obviously the big news here is the upcoming Codist release on May 1. Engineering confirms that they're on pace to have it ready then, so everybody is operating off of that date as a given. First thing to know: Gerald is *strongly* insisting that this be a surprise. No leaks. No whispers. No nothing—he's dead serious on this."

CHAPTER 2   A CASE STUDY: USING THE DEVREL PATTERNS

"Wow," Mikaela said. "I'd heard he likes to make 'big splash' kinds of moves, but this seems a little counterproductive to me—lots of products benefit from some pre-release buzz and momentum-building. Pre-release signups and all that."

"Which..." Jeremy added before others could comment on Mikaela's statements. "Brings me to my next point on this: There's no beta program set up yet, nor are there any plans in the works to set one up." As the rest of the team gaped, Jeremy explained. "Pam, Li, and I talked about it at the H1 Planning meeting. Engineering and Product are both swamped, so I volunteered us to head it up."

Curt looked thoughtful. "OK, but boss, how are we going to do our thing before the release? If nobody can talk about it before May 1, how are we going to talk about it?"

Jeremy grinned. "Well, first off, if we're owning the beta program—which I'm thinking we'll run along similar lines to an **Ambassador (71)** program—then we'll know exactly who is in the know and who isn't. That means that to those folks who have signed the NDA, we can do a couple of high-interactivity kinds of things." He looked at Janessa. "I was thinking you'd run that. It's probably going to soak up a good chunk of your time, but it's clearly going to be the highest-priority thing we can do, and it'd be a good win for us if we can pick up where Engineering and Product don't have the bandwidth. You down for it?"

Janessa gave him a thumbs-up gesture. "I was going to volunteer if you didn't ask. How many people were we thinking and—"

Jeremy held up a hand. "I suggested 20 to 50, so a bit more than the typical **Ambassador (71)** starting size, and we don't know exactly who, to start. You'll need to work with Caleb and his Sales team to figure out who likely customers with an interest in the beta would be, and you'll need to work with Legal to get everything set up before you reach out to anyone. I'm literally going to dump the entire program in your lap to set up and operate—you've got experience running a program, so it's all in your hands." Then Jeremy thought of something else. "Gerald is probably going to be another step in the setup process—he gets more than a little agitated whenever the idea of Codist leaking to the public comes up."

"Ugh." Janessa sighed. "OK, I'll make sure to keep his admin in the loop."

"Good call." Jeremy then glanced around at the others. "What that means for the rest of us is that any activities we take will likely be setup work for things we can just 'flip the switch' on when May 1 comes around." He looked at Fred. "First up, I'm thinking a **Newsletter (281)** on Codist specifically for the beta members. I'll talk to Pam about getting a few of her engineers to help write and tech-review pieces for it."

Fred was already nodding. "I like it. When the announcement goes public, we can recycle some of those articles into **Blog Posts (105)** for the public website, particularly if we make sure to keep revisions current with any changes between now and May 1." He looked around at Mikaela, Curt, and Nkema. "Can I count on you three for some writing?"

Jeremy jumped in. "Curt and Nkema, yes, but let's not count on Mikaela up front for that. There's a few other things in the works too."

Curt said, "What about turning some of the newsletter pieces into a public **Article (89)**, for broader reach?"

"Not at first, at least until after the release, and maybe not even yet then. Sales, it sounds like, is going to look for some direct engagement with some of our friendlier customers to start, which will probably mean some **Customer Pre-Sales (223)** meetings for us, and that'll probably be a higher priority than more reach-based activities like **Articles (89)** or **Webinars (469)**. That said, though, I think we can prep a few for release on May 1."

Nkema jumped in. "Like a **Podcast (333)**?"

Jeremy nodded. "Yup, though I'm thinking **Recorded Video (363)** episodes, rather than audio-only, so we can do a little screen-sharing demo sorts of things. But whatever podcasts we do, we'll need to embargo them until May 1, and then we can 'drip' those out every other week or so, as a way to build some buzz around Codist after its release. You'll have

CHAPTER 2   A CASE STUDY: USING THE DEVREL PATTERNS

to make sure that your guests are either our people, like Engineering or Product, or else people who've signed the NDA, if you want to go over Codist."

Nkema looked thoughtful. "What about getting a few guests to talk about some of the AI space in general? Sort of like laying some groundwork, building up the audience and so on?"

Jeremy took a few moments to think about it before responding. "That one I may have to run past Gerald first. He's super-sensitive on anything that would ruin the 'pop' of the big release announcement, so if he thinks that talking about any AI at all would give people hints as to what's coming, he'll probably nix it, and this is a big enough deal to him that this is probably not 'better to ask forgiveness than permission' territory. We'll want permission."

Nkema looked a little disappointed at that, but Jeremy was still thinking out loud. "Now, what if you spun up a podcast next week talking about the mobile space?" Nkema's glum turned to grin as Jeremy went on. "The first couple episodes of a podcast are always a learning experience anyway, and we're going to want to get the rough spots ironed out beforehand. I have a feeling that if you get any kind of traction whatsoever, Marketing is going to want to jump in, and it'll be better to have all that sorted out ahead of time."

Mikaela said, "You said you had some other things in mind, too."

"When Codist ships, we're going to want to have some good content out for people to browse and for Marketing to be able to link to and so on. That, to me, means we want to have at least a few **Tutorials (451)** that are ready to go live on May 1. Those take more time to get right, and we'll want them reviewed by Engineering more than once. At the very least, we'll want a 'Getting Started' for each of the three languages, as well as maybe two common scenarios, like refactoring a database or introducing a new front-end form, and we'll want those in each of the three languages Codist supports.

"The other thing that I think will keep us more busy than we expected will be supporting the Sales team with **Customer Pre-Sales (223)** meetings.

CHAPTER 2   A CASE STUDY: USING THE DEVREL PATTERNS

Caleb really wants to go after existing mobile or legacy customers to start, it seems like, so we'll probably need to make holes in our schedule for those meetings. I can pick up some of them—in fact, I want to, so that I can hear what customers are saying—but it may pretty quickly exhaust my availability."

Mikaela nodded, then said, "OK, but what about **Conference Sessions (197)**? CFPs are open already for shows in the middle of the year."

"Yeah, I've been mulling that one over for a bit. Do you have any commitments already?" Mikaela shook her head. "OK. What shows are later than May 1?"

"I think KCDC runs in June, and there's a few after that."

Nkema looked confused. "KCDC?"

"Kansas City Developer Conference. It's a pretty big show."

Jeremy began to grin. "OK, that could work out well. I know the folks who run KCDC, and I have an idea. Let's submit a proposal to talk about Codist at KCDC, but we'll have to ask them to embargo the abstract from appearing on the website until after the release. I can probably talk them into it, particularly if we get Marketing and Sales to help us sponsor the show and get a **Booth (137)** there."

Janessa's face suddenly lit up. "Wait, what if we make KCDC our 'coming-out' party to the developer community? Like, a **Party (319)** to go along with it?"

Faces began to grin all around the team as Jeremy said, "I like it, but let's save some of that for next quarter's planning. For now, we focus on the **Customer Pre-Sales (223)** work, the **Ambassador (71)**-slash-beta program and the **Newsletter (281)** to go along with it, and getting **Tutorials (451)** ready for May 1."

Nkema frowned. "That doesn't feel like that's going to keep us busy."

Jeremy's grin grew wider. "That's because you're forgetting that you three"—he gestured specifically to Nkema, Curt, and Mikaela—"are also going to be spending a significant amount of time learning Codist. I want each of you to be spending a quarter of your time writing some throwaway apps to get to know it better. I don't care what they do—heck, write a video game with it for all I care—but I want to make sure that each of you is comfortable answering questions about it when the veil finally lifts. You are going to be the foremost Codist experts in the world for a few months, at least as far as the outside world is concerned."

Nkema's eyes widened. "Yikes! Pressure!"

DevRel Team Q2 Planning

"Gooooood morning DevRel team!" In his best Robin Williams imitation, Jeremy opened the DevRel team's Q2 planning meeting.

"Jeez, tell a guy once that he sometimes sounds like Robin Williams, and look what he does with it," Fred stage-whispered to the rest of the team, all of whom grinned or chuckled, including Jeremy himself.

"First things first, let's go around and catch up on some metrics from our activities last quarter," Jeremy said. "I'll need a summary of them for the H2 planning in three months, and I want to get 'em while it's all still relatively fresh." He turned to Janessa. "Where are we with the beta program?"

Janessa's grin was a mile wide. "Fan-TAS-tic.

"As you already know, we've currently got a count of 37 people in the program. Turnover rate has been low—we've only lost 2 people over the three months since we started it, both of those due to layoffs at different companies. Both have expressed interest in remaining part of the program, but because Legal insisted that the NDAs were with companies rather than individuals, we had to remove them from the mailing list and rescind their logins."

Jeremy coughed. "Yeah, I followed up with Gerald on that one, and he's going to get Legal to change the wording on that. He hadn't realized we might have individual consultant-types who would want to be on the beta, but it'll be moot in a month anyway, so..."

CHAPTER 2   A CASE STUDY: USING THE DEVREL PATTERNS

Janessa continued. "As far as participation goes, we've had quite a strong response rate. Every time Fred sends out a **Newsletter (281)** to the beta mailing list, we get a close-to-100% open rate, which is unheard of."

Fred's grin was ear-to-ear. "What's really cool is that the decision to make the newsletter email *not* to be a no-response email was great. We've actually had some email traffic in response to each newsletter, which in turn created some interesting conversations between beta users and Product. Li was right in insisting her three Product Managers be a part of the mailing list—they've been pretty active in responding to user feedback, both explaining some of the decisions and in capturing ideas and feedback from them. Plus, I've seen some messages between users that were copied to the list that complimented us—DCom, I mean—in our responsiveness to user feedback. I think when Codist goes live, we'll have a group of **Ambassadors (71)** that will be ready to jump-start our user community."

Jeremy gently interrupted. "Any signs of the beta users abusing the direct connection to the Product Managers?"

Fred looked at Janessa, who shook her head, prompting Fred to answer aloud. "Not that we've been able to spot, no." Then he paused. "Well, we did have one person that was pretty quick to reach out directly to one of Li's people, but we found out later that was because the project manager in question had asked for it—literally. So we left that to the two of them to figure out on their own." Fred shrugged. "Honestly that question would probably be better answered by Li and her team. Most of the folks on the list seem pretty respectful of our time and energy, though of course there's a few folks that love to write lengthy posts—"

"Ugh, Sam." Janessa rolled her eyes.

"—about what they think we should be doing differently," Fred finished up.

Curt grimaced. "There's always one of those, on every mailing list."

Janessa finished out her metrics. "So 37 current members, 2 alumni that have expressed interest in re-joining as soon as possible, and I've

CHAPTER 2   A CASE STUDY: USING THE DEVREL PATTERNS

already had a few queries about expanding the participation at a few of the customer sites. I think Li is following up on that."

Jeremy finished his notes, then turned to Fred. "Any other metrics from you?"

Fred nodded. "Putting the **Newsletter (281)** pieces onto the website behind that restricted beta-user-login was a good idea—we're getting some great metrics from it. Time on each page is measured in double-digit minutes on average, suggesting that the beta users are reading each of those articles all the way to the end, which is a great sign."

Jeremy grinned. "Any signs our articles are doing better than Engineering's?"

Fred laughed. "Actually, the most-read article from the newsletter is the one that Pam wrote, talking about how Codist is built to scale up. That one gets about twice the number of reads as any other, and I wouldn't be surprised if people start linking to it once it's public. She really knocked that one out of the park."

Jeremy was quietly pleased—Pam had agonized over writing that, and it had taken quite a bit of effort to get her to hand off the draft copy for Fred to edit and polish. He made a note to forward Pam the metrics so she could bask in it for a bit, then turned to Curt. "Curt?"

Curt pulled up some notes of his own. "OK, let's see here. Over the last three months, I've completed the Python **Tutorial (451)**, the Python refactoring **Examples (387)**, and I've sat in on twenty **Customer Pre-Sales (223)** meetings."

Jeremy whistled. "Wow. That was way more than I thought."

Curt sighed. "Yeah, more than I thought, too. But when that one meeting turned into two more meetings that led to the big sale, Caleb's folks kinda went all-in on trying to get more and more of my time."

"Do you happen to know how big that contract was, by any chance?"

Curt grinned. "I don't know the exact number, but I heard it was ten digits and is the largest sale to date. Those guys went *nuts* for Codist once they saw it in action." Then he shrugged. "I can't even say that I was all

43

that eloquent or amazing; I think it was that I had just written the Python database refactoring example that quite literally lined up with their problem exactly."

Fred laughed. "Maybe you should've charged them consulting fees."

Once the laughter quieted some, Jeremy said, "You laugh, but I heard Gerald noodling the other day about the idea of spinning up a professional services team, to help customers use Codist better and/or just expand into doing consulting work with Codist at the center. Maybe…"

Curt shook his head. "Nope. I'm happy right here, thank you very much."

Still, Jeremy made a note to talk with Caleb about Curt's availability for **Customer Pre-Sales (223)** meetings; the last thing Curt needed was to be needing to protect his schedule from overeager salespeople. Out loud, he said, "Any metrics on the tutorials or examples?"

Curt spread his hands in a "no idea" gesture. "I haven't followed up with the Ops team to get the numbers, but I can't imagine it would be all that much, since they're not public yet."

Fred coughed gently. "Actually your Python tutorial is #2 behind Pam's article. Most of the referrer links are coming from your sales friends' big sale." He looked over at Jeremy. "I'll include the numbers when I send you the full report later."

Nkema went next. "OK, so I have eight CodistCast episodes in the can, just waiting for the release to go live. Four are with Codist Engineering, and four are with folks that Janessa set me up with from the beta."

"Fred helped me find a dozen or so folks who were pretty active on the mailing list and seemed to be using Codist for interesting things," Janessa explained. "We three figured they'd make good interview candidates."

Nkema nodded enthusiastically. "They've been great, J. Solid stuff. Lots of lessons-learned, lots of insights that'll be useful when to newbies when the thing finally ships." She turned back to Jeremy. "I've got another half-dozen external interviews lined up, and Pam promised me a new batch of Engineers to talk to after the release."

CHAPTER 2   A CASE STUDY: USING THE DEVREL PATTERNS

"All of the recordings have run past Legal?" Jeremy asked.

Nkema nodded again. "And they've agreed that the last few are pretty much rubber stamps from their side of things now. Once we got past the initial unpleasantness"—everybody on the team remembered the near-brawl Nkema had gotten into with the representative from Legal over all the things Legal had wanted to censor out, which in turn Jeremy had needed to get Gerald's sign-off on—"we managed to smooth out the review process and get a three-day turnaround on them. That'll mean we can record, edit, and post within a week."

"Cool! What about the rest?"

"Well, the Javascript **Tutorial (451)** is set, and I did seven of those **Customer Pre-Sales (223)** things." She made a face. "I am definitely not good at Sales, that's for sure."

"Did any of your customer meetings turn into sales?"

Nkema shook her head. "Not that I'm aware of, but the last two were just last week, so... maybe?"

Jeremy made a note to check with Caleb to see if any of Nkema's meetings had led to successful buys. Then he turned to Mikaela. "OK, Miki, you're up last."

"Well, the Java **Tutorial (451)** is done, and I managed to crank out four more **Samples/Examples (387)** from playing around with Codist, and those were pretty well-received by the customers I met when I did the eleven **Customer Pre-Sales (223)** meetings for the Sales team. I can definitely say that they're getting some traction, because I got a couple of direct emails from people in the beta program with questions about the Java tutorial." Even as Jeremy opened his mouth, Mikaela went on. "Yes, I forwarded them to Li and her team, and I think there's already a new feature on the board for a future release." Jeremy grinned and stayed silent while Mikaela continued. "Also, after our conversation with Marketing, I submitted a few sessions on mobile development to about a half-dozen conferences that are taking place in June or later, and I've gotten acceptance notices from three of them. Once Codist ships, I'm planning to contact the organizers and offer to pivot from mobile dev to Codist-specific talks, and see how they respond."

"Are these all Java shows?"

"Two Java, one Python, though all of them are starting to go more 'multi-platform' it seems like."

Janessa eagerly leaned in. "And what about KCDC?"

Jeremy held up a hand. "Let's make sure we've got metrics rounded out before we get into next-quarter planning. Fred, you're going to get me that website report on the activity for the tutorials, right?" Fred nodded. "OK. Hard to have much more by way of sales numbers and web clicks for something that isn't publicly released, so we'll go with that.

"So, let's talk KCDC now. I spoke with the organizers, they're definitely on-board with keeping Mikaela's session entirely 'TBA' until May 1st, which will make Gerald happy, and they were definitely curious about what we're going to announce. I think they're looking forward to being in on something, and I've already told Marketing that we should look for some cross-promotional we can do with them over it." He then turned to Janessa. "The other thing I want to bring up is the idea of a **Party (319)** at KCDC for Codist."

Nkema did a little happy dance. "Party! Yes!"

The team laughed for a moment, then Janessa said, "Well, we'll have to avoid anything KCDC is running that week."

Jeremy nodded. "I talked with them already—they have the attendee shindig on the second night, and a speaker party the first night, but that's it so far."

Mikaela frowned. "That's not leaving a whole lot of room here for our own party—the whole event is only, what, two days? Three days?"

Jeremy nodded. "Two days last year, yup. I think it's still two days this year, too."

Curt raised a hand. "What if instead of a public **Party (319)** for everyone, we go for **Sponsorship (405)** for the public angle, then move the **Party (319)** to a beta-only thank-you dinner or something?"

CHAPTER 2   A CASE STUDY: USING THE DEVREL PATTERNS

Janessa grew thoughtful. "Actually, I like it. We can schedule the dinner for the night of the attendee thing, and make sure we get finished up before the attendee party starts, and that'll give everybody a chance to get to go, *plus* it gives us a chance to give some serious love to these folks. I like it a LOT."

Jeremy held up a hand. "OK, but before we make any decisions, let's talk budget for these. What would we spend to sponsor, and what would we spend on dinner?"

Janessa nodded. "Fair. I'll put those two numbers in your hands by the end of the day? I'm guessing it'd probably be $1k for dinner, since it's a small number of folks, at least so far, but sponsorship for the attendee party—*if* they haven't already sold it to somebody else—sometimes goes for $10k. I'll have to reach out."

Jeremy made a note. "OK, and I'll reach out as well, and whichever of us gets a response first, we go with that. If it's $10k, though, we can swing that, so I'd be game for it.

"By the way, in case I hadn't said it out loud, once Codist is announced, we'll want to transition the beta program over to a more traditional **Ambassador (71)** program."

Janessa nodded, then said, "Is there budget for some **Swag (427)** for the betas? I'd like to get them something unique as a keepsake, send it out at the end of April."

"37 people? Hmm, maybe something not too expensive? I can probably find $5k in the budget for something, particularly if I get Li or Pam to chip in."

Janessa thought for a moment. "I'd probably want to get some extras, like say around 50. Hoodie, shirt, something with the Codist beta logo on it, that they can wear at conferences. As a matter of fact, I found out that four or five of them will be at KCDC, and I'd love to get something to them ahead of time so they could be showing off to people there." She grinned an impish grin. "Nothing like a little FOMO to get peoples' attention, you know?"

Jeremy grinned back.

CHAPTER 2   A CASE STUDY: USING THE DEVREL PATTERNS

Executive Team H2 Priorities

"Allow me, first of all, to offer a round of congratulations to everyone in this room for a wildly successful Codist launch," Gerald said, opening the executive team's H2 review and planning. "In the three months since Codist's announcement, we've crossed the million-user threshold for free signups, and the Board is exceedingly pleased with the paid subscription numbers. We're well on track to hit our annual bonus numbers, and I couldn't be prouder of the work we're doing." Beaming a smile to each of his executive team members all around the room, Gerald continued. "As we begin our second-half planning, let's keep the ball rolling and hit our next million users by the end of the year!" Gerald's smile continued to beam, but his teams' faded slightly.

Turning to Caleb, Gerald said, "Let's start with sales numbers—how are things looking?"

Caleb straightened up. "Well, as you said, we passed a million free-tier signups, and of those, we've had roughly a tenth of that—100,000 users—convert to paid plans, either individually or as part of a company's group-license plan. That nets us some great revenue for the foreseeable future, for sure."

Jeremy raised a hand. "If I may?"

Caleb nodded. "Sure, go ahead."

"Do you have a breakdown of the company-vs-individual license numbers? I ask because it helps us in DevRel understand what our paid community looks like, as opposed to the free-tier community."

Caleb nodded. "Yeah, that makes sense, and as a matter of fact, Sales cares about that a great deal, too. Right now we're showing an 80/20 split, with the 80 coming from corporate users."

The room was silent for a bit, before Gerald asked, "Wait, is that good or bad?"

Caleb shrugged. "Well, it's hard to say definitively. It could mean that developers see Codist entirely as a company-only sort of thing, like it's

CHAPTER 2   A CASE STUDY: USING THE DEVREL PATTERNS

too expensive for them individually, or it could mean that individuals are waiting to see if their company will buy it before pulling the trigger themselves, or," he glanced over at Jeremy with a nod, "It could mean that the DevRel presence in our **Customer Pre-Sales (223)** meetings made all the difference." Turning back to Gerald, he concluded, "We really won't know until we see more of a trend over time."

Gerald looked a little discomfited at that, but then turned to Kimberly. "What's on the docket for Marketing for the rest of the year?"

Kimberly ran through some numbers from the Marketing campaigns, then turned to Jeremy. "DevRel's podcast is getting some good numbers, it seems, and we'd like to look for ways to tap into that. We have some ideas of putting her videos 'on blast' to reach more corners, but there's a few topics we'd love for her to cover as part of it."

Jeremy hesitated slightly before answering. "I won't speak for Nkema—she's been pretty picky about her topics and guests—but I can definitely say that DevRel would love to have some Marketing weight behind the podcast. Her numbers this past month plateaued, and we've been trying to brainstorm some ideas—your jumping in could be what we need."

Kimberly nodded, then clacked away at her laptop keyboard for a moment. "I've told Jasmine"—her admin—"to set up some time together to figure that out."

Jeremy made a note to himself. *Podcast/Marketing pairing, possible Marketing topics for it?*

"As for other activities in the past six months, we put some money into AI-related podcasts and YouTube channels in Q2, to go along with the initial Codist release, and they hit max saturation in July, and—"

"So *that's* what that was." Jeremy was surprised when everyone looked at him, and he realized he'd said that out loud. "Sorry, Kimberly, but we noticed something of a spike on our tutorials pages in July, and we couldn't for the life of us figure out what caused it. We'd thought initially maybe a conference's recorded videos went online around then, but the traffic spike was way larger than what would've been reasonable from the

CHAPTER 2   A CASE STUDY: USING THE DEVREL PATTERNS

viewing numbers on the videos. But if you were running a bunch of ads alongside AI-related things, that would account for it." He made notes to himself to pass on to the team later. "Sorry to interrupt."

Kimberly continued on. "Meanwhile, we're also thinking about making a major media push effort in Q4, looking to give us a big push before the end of the year as a way to help make sure we cross the finish line with the free user signups."

Jeremy thought, *Uh oh, that's not*—but Pam was already speaking. "Kim, wait, when are you planning that push?"

"The usual mid-November, early-December time frame."

Pam shook her head. "I don't want to cut you off at the knees, but that's not a great time. Developers aren't really thinking about work as we roll into the holidays, and if what Caleb said is true about the individual subscriptions, we're not going to get much uptake on your efforts. Individual developers won't convert, and no company I've ever been at has made any major purchasing decisions anywhere after October 1." She looked over at Jeremy for confirmation, and he nodded. Turning back to Kimberly, Pam finished up, "I worry that doing a big media blitz is going to fall on deaf ears, if it falls on any ears at all."

Kimberly's look was a little frosty. "We were thinking that it would give developers and CTOs something to think about and ponder over the holiday."

Jeremy asked, "What if you push it back by a couple of weeks?"

Both Pam and Kimberly looked over, but Pam was quicker to ask. "Why? What are you thinking?"

"Well, first off, we can time a few things—one or two **Blog Posts (105)**, and maybe an **Article (89)** on a major tech-publication site—to drop at the start of your media push, which would give some technical push to go along with the blitz. But," he mused, "What I'm really thinking is that Kimberly's right—giving CTOs and VPs something to think about over the holiday is a good idea. What I think we want, though, is for them to come back from the holiday with a 'bright idea' for the developer team to

CHAPTER 2   A CASE STUDY: USING THE DEVREL PATTERNS

examine and validate—namely, that this 'Codist' thing they heard about over the holidays might be worth checking out."

Pam looked dubious, but Kimberly was warming. "Laying some groundwork for next year, you mean?"

Jeremy nodded, but it was Caleb who spoke up. "That actually tracks better with my group anyway. We generally consider Q4 a 'dead zone' of activity in the sales cycle, so I'd rather we build momentum to hit January running, as it were. Speaking of which, Jeremy, Curt's efforts were amazing last quarter; I think half of the customers he visited with my team all converted."

Jeremy blinked. *Wow*, he thought, "Can you get me the numbers for that? I kinda want to put that in our end-of-year report to the CEO." He glanced at Gerald as he said it, grinning, and Gerald grinned back, acknowledging the point with a slight dip of his head. Then Jeremy turned back to Caleb and continued, "But more importantly, I want to show it to Curt so he gets the satisfaction."

Caleb nodded enthusiastically. "Hey, if it gets him fired up to do more of them, I'll buy him an iPad or something to say thanks."

Jeremy blinked again. "You know, how about I get you a short list of ideas for him? I know he already has an iPad, but there's a particular monitor I know he's been eyeing for his home setup...." Caleb flashed a "thumbs-up" at Jeremy as Kimberly picked up going over her Marketing efforts again.

When she was finished, Gerald turned to Li. "What's Product got cooking up for us?"

Li brought up some metrics and charts. "Let me walk through some of our usage metrics. Thanks to Engineering's observability metrics, we can see that 73% of our users are spending significant time using Codist to write code, with an even breakdown across all three languages so far...."

Jeremy made some idle notes here and there as Li's metrics went on, then suddenly a thought occurred to him, and he raised his hand as she was finishing up a particular set of points. She nodded to him, and he

51

asked, "Can you tell me how many users are firing it up once, then never getting back into it again?"

Li's voice was triumphant. "That was going to be my next point. Within the free tier, we see those numbers at around 50% for each language."

The room was silent, then Gerald was the first to speak. "50 percent?" The tone of his voice was incredulous. "Half of all of them are never coming back?"

Li blinked. "Yes. Actually, these are better numbers than normal."

Pam nodded, supporting Li. "Usually in the developer tools space the number of abandoned subscriptions is much higher. Devs try it out once, find out what they want to find out about it, then bail and never come back."

Gerald blinked but held his tongue.

Jeremy used the silence to ask, "So we had a million signups, 10% of which converted to paid subscriptions, and of the remaining 900k, we lose half of them after a month. Am I seeing that right?"

Li nodded, and Kimberly asked, "We know who those people are, right? Like, we have their emails?" Li nodded again, and Kimberly looked at Jeremy. "What's your best article?"

Jeremy coughed slightly. "Well, if we're going by the numbers, it's still Pam's architecture piece she wrote before the release." Pam blushed slightly, but sat a little taller. "Why do you ask?"

Kimberly turned back to Gerald. "What if we shoot out an email blast to all those who gave up and included something tasty as a part of it? Technical, I mean? Something that gets them to read it and think, 'Maybe I should try this thing again'?"

Pam shook her head. "No, not my article." She looked at Kimberly. "I like the idea, but I don't think my piece is what they're going to want. That's more architect-level, CTO-level kinds of stuff; I think you want something that's an exciting demo to lure them back in."

"Like what?"

CHAPTER 2   A CASE STUDY: USING THE DEVREL PATTERNS

Pam looked at Jeremy, who shrugged but grinned at the same time. "I dunno, but I'll bet Mikaela or Curt can put something together that pleases the tongue," he said, "Since it needs to be tasty and all."

Kimberly grinned in acknowledgement, then turned back to Gerald. "So that could help bring that conversion rate back up," she offered.

Gerald considered. "But it won't get us new signups."

Kimberly shook her head.

Gerald sighed. "The Board was really concentrating on new signups." The rest of his team kept looking at him, and Gerald held his hands up in surrender. "OK, OK, I get it. I'll talk to the Board."

"Don't forget to mention that it's the paid subscribers that actually give us money, so conversions are actually a better thing than new signups," Caleb offered.

Pam coughed. "Make sure the Board understands that the numbers right after launch are the exception, not the rule, too. We're probably never going to get as many new signups in a month like we did in May."

Li, however, was looking at Jeremy. "Can I ask you something?" At his nod, she went on. "The documentation pages—do you track the time people spend on a page?"

Jeremy nodded again. "Sure, we track that. It's not always super-accurate, since browsers don't natively tell us when a user leaves a page, but we get some notion of the numbers in a rough sense."

"Can you tell me the average time somebody spends on our documentation?"

"Yup." He consulted his notes. "According to our web stats, people spend roughly twenty-three minutes on any given page in our docs."

Li looked at him blankly. "Twenty-three?" She looked a little unsure of herself. "Is that good or bad?"

Jeremy shrugged, but grinned. "For a new product like Codist, I'm thinking good, maybe? People need to figure out deeper concepts, so they're reading the docs more than an established product like a mobile platform."

53

CHAPTER 2　A CASE STUDY: USING THE DEVREL PATTERNS

Gerald looked thoughtful as Pam grinned and said, "That tracks with me; whenever I dive into something new, I spend some time reading up on it before getting really started with it."

Li, meanwhile, had taken on a thoughtful look. "What about your tutorials? How'd they do?"

"Well, according to our web stats, we had about 50,000 run-throughs of the Javascript tutorial in June, roughly the same for Python, and Java got about half that, 25,000."

Caleb looked a little shocked. "125,000 tutorial run-throughs?"

"In June alone. May had some really spiked numbers, but we also had some problems with the metrics-tracking software so we can't be sure of the accuracy of them." Jeremy looked a little embarrassed. "Sorry. We messed up the tracking cookies when we got things set up and didn't notice the problem until after the release."

Pam coughed. "That wasn't entirely your fault, Jeremy, we agreed on that."

Gerald waved his hands in a "forget it" gesture. "Never mind that. We have the tracking all set up and working now, though, right?" At Jeremy's nod, Gerald continued, "Good. So we had, how many tutorial numbers?"

"125k."

"So we had a million signups, 125k tutorial-takers, and 100k paid subscriptions?" Gerald looked around at the others for confirmation, and at everybody's nod, he sat back. "OK. So we have a baseline for our first month. That gives us a baseline. I see the rest of this meeting being two things: What do we want the rest of this year's strategy to look like, and how do we want to make it happen?"

Caleb looked around at the others for a moment, then shrugged, a little surprised. "Seems to me like the thing here is to do two things: Get more signups, and get more of them to convert to paid subscriptions. What am I missing?"

Pam started to answer, but Gerald beat her to it. "We don't have an unlimited budget or infinite people, so we want to set priorities to our

CHAPTER 2   A CASE STUDY: USING THE DEVREL PATTERNS

overall strategy." Gerald looked around at everyone. "I do expect each of you to come up with key objectives for your teams, but things generally flow better when we're all going in the same direction."

Everybody was quiet for a moment, then Jeremy chose to break the silence. "So, that begs the question, what are we going after?"

Everyone looked at Gerald, but surprisingly Caleb answered first. "Well, let's look at it this way: Is every programmer in the world using Codist?"

Jeremy shook his head, a little unsure where Caleb was going with this. "No, and we can't even remotely pretend otherwise. There's something like 10 million Python developers in the world, last time anybody did a census, and Java and C# developers are something like 7 or 8 million each. Even if we allow for developers to be counted multiple times because they write code in multiple languages..."

Caleb was grinning as he gestured for Jeremy to stop. "My point, you're proving my point. We only have a million user signups, and we can probably assume that a good number of those are 'throwaway' signups, like people just playing around with it before their company adopts it and they become part of an enterprise license or something." He looked at Gerald for a moment, then turned back to the rest. "From my perspective, we need to push Codist out to the world more. Get more people using it, even if it's just for a short period of time, so they can come to love it like we do." He grinned at Pam enthusiastically. "The more people who use it, the more who'll sign up for it and convert to a paid subscription. After all, who wouldn't want 'AI' on their resume somewhere?"

Li looked uncomfortable. "While I appreciate the nudge of faith in our developer marketing, as it happens I have something of the opposite opinion. I've worked at a lot of companies where we spent millions on advertising and making a product a household name, and frankly it didn't move the needle on the company's bottom line. No offense, Caleb, but I think we need to focus more on getting conversions in our freemium signups—we need to get developers to go from 'trying it out' to 'paying for

55

CHAPTER 2 A CASE STUDY: USING THE DEVREL PATTERNS

it', or we're going to get buried under the avalanche of all the other AI-related developer tools out there." She looked at Gerald, then shrugged. "Unless you want to convince the Board to give me a marketing budget that's roughly the size of the US GDP, of course."

Pam, however, was shaking her head. "Honestly, I don't see the sales conversion thing being our biggest 'win' just yet." Li looked at her, surprised, and Pam held up a placating hand. "History shows that the first version or two are never exactly what the market wants. Look at Internet search, for example—the early players were all focused on creating a perfect ontology of everything on the Web, creating all these categories and hand-maintaining links, and then Google came along and realized what people really want when they go looking for something isn't a card catalog, but an easy-input mode allowing Google to do the hard work of figuring out what's relevant." She shrugged. "We can argue that the Google algorithm is or isn't working the way it should, but the overall takeaway is that search providers didn't know what the market wanted at first. Music players—remember 'MP3 players'?—were the same way, and then Apple came along with the iPod." She took a moment to think, then said, "I think we want to save our big 'push' for when we have a few iterations of Codist under our belt."

Gerald was looking at Pam intently. "So we do nothing?"

Pam looked as uncomfortable as Jeremy felt. "I wouldn't say nothing, but I wouldn't break the bank on anything, either. Remember, our launch numbers are, in all probability, the biggest surge of signups we're going to see for the foreseeable future. Conversions will come as people figure out what our feature set does for them that they actually need, not what we think they need or even they think they need. What does Codist do that makes an actual difference in their professional lives? I argue that we don't know—we only think we know—and we won't know until we get more of that sweet, sweet feedback." She looked at Jeremy. "Right?"

Suddenly Jeremy found himself the target of everyone's gaze, and he felt his face grow flush with the scrutiny. "Yes," he said, drawing it out for a

CHAPTER 2   A CASE STUDY: USING THE DEVREL PATTERNS

second so he could think, "Iterations help, but I also find myself agreeing more with both Li and Caleb."

Gerald's face was carefully neutral as he said, "Go on."

Jeremy paused for a moment to collect his thoughts. "OK, let me put it this way. We obviously need to get the word out more—what DevRel calls 'reach' activities—because if we can get even a tenth of all the programmers in the world to try Codist, it's a huge PR coup and something that Li can shout from the mountaintops for years to come." Li grinned at the image. "But we also can't just go for 'clicks' because we've seen that doesn't work either, not on its own—way too many Internet startups over the last twenty years have demonstrated that just having a billion people signed up for your free service doesn't mean much when it comes to paying the bills. We need conversions, too, or we'll all be looking for new work in a few years." He looked Gerald squarely in the eyes. "I think that there's a healthy 'split' here, probably something like a two-thirds/one-third between 'reach' activities and 'interactive' activities, assuming Kimberly's focusing on the 'reach' and Caleb on the 'interactive.'" He glanced down at his notes again, then looked back up. "One number I'd love for us to track on a daily basis is signups-to-conversions, kind of like how a 'burn-down' chart tracks both newly entered defects and bug-fixes on the same graph, so we can see the gap between them." He suddenly grinned. "I guess that's two numbers, actually, but—"

"But that's a good idea," Gerald interrupted. "I like it. Gives us a good clear picture of both the 'reach' and the conversions." He looked around the room. "I think that's our north star for the next six months, folks—we want to close the gap between signups and sales while not letting the growth of either drop below... hmm." He looked around the room for a bit. "What's a good growth number for us for the next six months?"

Caleb looked skittish. "Are you going to hold us to it?"

"You mean like, 'All your team is fired' if we don't hit it? No. But I think we need a number to aim for, if only so that we have a number to aim for," Gerald said.

CHAPTER 2   A CASE STUDY: USING THE DEVREL PATTERNS

"I suggest 10%, meaning 10% growth in both numbers as a target for our next meeting," Li piped in. "I don't think it's a huge number, but if we start somewhere, we can see how it plays and adjust."

Pam murmured, "That seems awfully low to me."

But at the same time, Kimberly said, "Wow that's going to be hard."

Gerald looked at each of them, then grinned. "Well, if one of us thinks it's easy and the other hard, then we're probably somewhere in the right ballpark. Let's go with that: 10% growth over the next six months, and a target that the gap between signups and conversions doesn't get bigger, only smaller. Agreed?"

The rest of the table nodded.

"Good. Then, there's one more thing we need to go over before we break for lunch."

DevRel Team Q3 Planning

"Wait, they said *what* now?"

The mood in the DevRel Q3 Planning Meeting was a little confused and slightly acidic as Jeremy repeated Gerald's last item from the Executive Meeting. "He said that the mobile libraries were seeing a huge surge in sales, and that apparently the Board wants to see a renewed 'push' out to the developer community around them." Jeremy looked at Mikaela, feeling out her reaction.

And, as he expected, her reaction was not really all that positive. "Ugh, I thought I was finally 'out' of that space," she muttered.

Jeremy sighed. He'd known this was going to be the hardest part of the planning meeting, which was why he'd led with it. "Look, I know in the past DCom has burned you out doing everything around the mobile toolkit." Then he paused for a moment until Mikaela met his gaze again. "That's not going to happen this time." He gestured to the rest of the team. "This is something we're all going to take on collectively, including me." At her surprised look, he nodded. "Yup. I'm signing myself up first for the first

CHAPTER 2   A CASE STUDY: USING THE DEVREL PATTERNS

few **Customer Check-Ins (213)** that Caleb wants to run. I may need to lean on you for a few things from time to time, but that's going to be so we can make sure that I'm up to speed just as much as you are."

Mikaela looked a little skeptical still, but nodded. "OK. So besides the sudden resurgence of interest in the mobile toolkit, what other surprises did you all cook up in there?"

"Kimberly, Caleb, and Pam are spinning up a dashboard that's going to show a real-time graph of the Codist signups as one line graph, with a second line graph tracking the sales conversions. The goal for Q3 and Q4 is to grow each of those graph lines by at least 10%, with the caveat that the signups-to-conversions gap can't grow larger than it is now."

Curt leaned forward quickly. "Relative or absolute terms?"

"A little bit of both, actually—Gerald would like it to be in absolute terms, meaning we never have more free subscribers than we do now, but he gets that trying to hit that would be a really hard target, so he's willing to accept it totally in relative terms."

Nkema said, "I'm not sure I understand."

Curt glanced at Jeremy for permission, and at Jeremy's nod, he turned to Nkema. "Well, currently Codist has a million subscribers, and only 100k paid users, right? That's a 10:1 ratio, which means our conversion rate is roughly 10% of the total user base. In relative terms, that means we have to maintain that ratio, 10 to 1. If we get another million subscribers, another 100k have to be paid users." Nkema nodded that she understood that, and Curt continued. "If we use absolute terms, though, that means that no matter how many free users we get, we can't have more than 900k free users, no matter what. So if we sign up a million users, we need to convert another million to paid so the gap never exceeds 900k."

Nkema looked a little shocked. "Wow."

Curt nodded. "Yup. That's why I asked."

59

CHAPTER 2   A CASE STUDY: USING THE DEVREL PATTERNS

Jeremy cut in. "Keep in mind, folks, paid users are what pay our salaries, so in the end, we do need to think about how to make those conversions. Giving everything away for free is not a long-term viable strategy if we want to stay in business."

Mikaela said sourly, "Unless, of course, everybody turns around and gives up on AI and goes back to writing mobile apps by hand again."

"Let's cross that bridge when we get to it," Jeremy said gently. "I don't want to assume too much about that until we see how it plays out. In the meantime," he continued, "Let's talk about what we do this upcoming quarter. Janessa?"

Janessa nodded. "Well, the **Ambassador (71)** program's been moved into the public, and the Ambassadors we have are pretty happy, it seems. The forums are operating pretty smoothly, no issues there, to the point where I've got a few folks I can lean on online to help squash problems before they get out of hand."

Jeremy's ears perked up at that. "Future Ambassadors?"

"One's actually a current Ambassador, and because she's got some serious reputation cred on StackOverflow, when she suggests people take a conversation offline, she gets their attention." Janessa grinned. "It's kinda nice not having to be the bad cop."

"Any issues getting Pam's people to answer the thorny technical questions?"

Janessa shook her head. "No, she's been great, and honestly there's been a bit of a drop-off in need—most of the obvious ones have answers now, so we can just point people to existing answers. Or," she grinned at Fred, "We point them to the website for stuff there." Fred pantomimed a tip of the hat back at her.

"What about events?"

"We're still doing **Sponsorships (405)** around one a quarter, so unless the budget suddenly doubled, we're probably still running at that level. Why?"

Jeremy nodded, then said, "So are you up for a new challenge?"

Janessa gave him a little side-eye. "What do you have in mind?"

CHAPTER 2   A CASE STUDY: USING THE DEVREL PATTERNS

"I told Gerald I thought it was time we spun up a **User Group Network (457)** for Codist. Feels like we have some momentum in the marketplace, like there's enough critical mass of people interested in it to get something going, at least in some of the more tech-centric cities. Seattle, San Jose, New York, London, maybe a few others if we see a large customer there." He gestured to his notes. "Apparently there's a large insurance company in Des Moines, Iowa, that has a pretty sizable investment in Codist."

Curt almost fell out of his chair laughing. "Des Moines? The corn capital of the country? Are you kidding me? That's awesome."

Jeremy's grin was ear-to-ear when he said, "And, of course, I volunteered you up front for the **Customer Check-Ins (213)** for those folks, Curt."

The team roared at the look on Curt's face, and Fred said, "Tell us how the corn is, Curt!"

Jeremy took that as a sign to switch to Fred. "How's the cadence of **Blog Posts (105)** coming?"

Fred needed a second to stop laughing. "We're still good, though now I'm having to go deeper with Pam's people over in Engineering on topics and subjects, since we've gotten some of the easier ones out of the way. We're still getting them out at least one a week, but between that, the **Newsletter (281)**, keeping an eye on the **Reference Documentation (373)**, and trying to make sure the **Training (439)** materials are moving along, I gotta admit, boss, I'm kinda full-up-to-here with stuff to do."

Jeremy nodded. "Duly noted. Let's take a look at the schedule and see if we can free up some of your time—"

"That'd be great, man, thanks," Fred sighed.

"Oh, you didn't let me finish, Fred," Jeremy cautioned. "That large insurance company in Des Moines? I've been talking with Kimberly and Li about candidates for a **Case Study (151)**, and they check a bunch of boxes. You and Curt may both end up working on that one together there." He grinned at Fred's face. "You can both tell us how the corn is. Which, by the way, is delicious—I have a cousin that lives out there, and when we go visit

CHAPTER 2 A CASE STUDY: USING THE DEVREL PATTERNS

in the summer, he takes us to a diner that does the best corn-on-the-cob you've ever tasted. You never know, you might want to move there. Work from home and all that!"

Mikaela's eyes narrowed as the rest of the team laughed. "Hey Jeremy?"

"Yeah, Mikaela?"

"We seem to be doing a bunch of Reach activities and a bunch of Interactive activities at the same time. Is that deliberate?"

Jeremy nodded. "Yup. Reach helps us get more of those free signups, but interactivity is what's going to get people to flip the switch to paid. At least, that's my working theory, anyway."

"Is Gerald on board with this?"

Jeremy nodded. "Pretty much. Our conversation in the Executive Meeting was one of 'We don't know what we don't know', since this is fairly early in the Codist release cycle. Gerald obviously wants everything, but he's not blind to the fact that we don't have infinite money, time, or people. We came up with the signup/converted chart as a simple—and it may be oversimplified, we don't know yet—way to try and keep an eye on things overall." Jeremy shrugged. "If things go well, we may keep it, if they go poorly, we may tweak it, or we may tweak it or replace it regardless of how things go, but it's a start."

Mikaela didn't look convinced. "Hm."

"Why the doubt?"

"Gerald's not always been known for being all that comfortable with splitting our efforts across multiple things. He's generally tried to go all-in on something, then uproot and go all-in on something different later."

Jeremy nodded. "Yeah, he was leaning a little bit that way during the meeting, but the rest of us were split enough in our opinions that he could see the value in multitasking a little." He paused for a moment. "I suppose there's always the chance that he'll still do that to us, but that's mine to wrestle with now. In the meantime, Mikaela, what's on your commitment list for this upcoming quarter?"

CHAPTER 2   A CASE STUDY: USING THE DEVREL PATTERNS

"I've gotten some traction with my **Conference Sessions (197)**, so I've gotten confirmation from four conferences in Q3 so far, with a few more outstanding."

Jeremy grinned. "That's not a bad number. What're the chances the others are going to accept?"

Mikaela waggled her hands in a "maybe-yes-maybe-no" gesture. "I'm not counting on them—one is a more Microsoft-leaning show that a friend tells me is pretty good, but none of my material is really geared to that crowd, so I'm not expecting much there." She made a face. "I kinda submitted just to get my friend off my back, to be honest."

Nkema asked, "You mostly do Java stuff, right?" At Mikaela's nod, Nkema said, "What about doing some talks at a Java User Group? One of my podcast guests a few weeks ago said there's some speaker in that space who does a bunch of those all over the world, like one a week or something."

Curt let out a low whistle. "Wow. That's like some serious travel."

Jeremy smoothly interrupted. "The Java User Group idea isn't a terrible one, but there is no way I'm going to sign off on 52 weeks of travel for anyone in this group. That's a recipe for completely burning somebody out, and that's a real 'not on my watch' hot-button topic for me."

"Does that apply to **Customer Pre-Sales (223)** visits, too?" Curt asked playfully.

Jeremy offered a mock-scolding finger back. "Don't you push it, buddy. Caleb's apparently your biggest fan, and definitely wants you to pair up with a couple of his salespeople in Q3 again, maybe land a few more accounts, convert a few more folks, that sort of thing."

Curt started to scowl, then sighed. "Yeah, yeah, gotta get the conversions, I get it. It's just... some of the places we end up, it makes Des Moines look like an urban wonderland by comparison." He looked at the others. "One of them took me on a sales call to Warsaw, for crying out loud."

CHAPTER 2   A CASE STUDY: USING THE DEVREL PATTERNS

Nkema looked incredulous. "Poland?"

"No. Indiana. It's a real place. Look it up." Then his eyes got a faraway look in them. "It takes forever to get there from the Indianapolis airport, but I will say the people there are nice... all five of them."

The team laughed again, and Jeremy turned to Nkema. "How's the podcast?"

She beamed. "Great! The Marketing team has been having me do a few two- and three-minute short **Recorded Videos (363)** to show off some of Codist's more interesting features, and those are getting some serious traction. Simone, the woman who runs the DCom **Social Media (395)** accounts, says I'm getting some serious hits and bumping their follower count."

Jeremy made a note. "Get Simone to send me those numbers?" As she nodded, he continued. "Do they do referral links from the video to the site or something? Can we track from your videos to signups?"

Nkema's smile got even wider. "We were talking about that! Simone said you'd probably ask for something like that. There's some codes they can embed in the URL when it lands on the signup page."

"Awesome. That'll help us get a better picture of the impact of your videos, maybe help get you a bigger podcast budget or something."

She clapped her hands and offered a high-pitched "yay" in response.

"Meanwhile, in between your Internet fame, what's the chance we can get some longer-form Javascript **Samples/Examples (387)** going?"

Her smile fell off. "Well, like what?"

"Curt's done some interesting Python examples that I think would make for a fairly easy port to Javascript, and we definitely want to make sure our JS coverage is as good as our Python coverage." She nodded, though not as enthusiastically. Jeremy continued. "And, now that the Javascript course is ready, I'm going to start talking to Caleb and Kimberly about getting an instance scheduled."

Nkema's eyes widened. "Really?"

CHAPTER 2   A CASE STUDY: USING THE DEVREL PATTERNS

Curt snorted. "If you're not careful, you'll end up teaching it in Des Moines."

The team laughed, but Jeremy carefully kept the smile off of his face. "Actually…"

"No!" Nkema was incredulous. "Really?"

"Apparently, according to Caleb, they have a lot of people looking to use it, and several engineering managers there want to get their folks started with it as quickly as possible. I told Caleb the course was ready, and he sold it."

Janessa was scribbling furiously in her bullet journal. "I think I know where the first Codist User Group is gonna be…" She said to herself in a singsong voice.

Mikaela suddenly snapped her fingers. "Wait! Before we go, I had a question for you," she said, looking at Jeremy.

"Fire away."

"What's the company's feeling on us doing podcasts?"

Jeremy looked at Nkema, then back at her. "You mean, you want to start one yourself?"

Mikaela shook her head. "No, no, I mean being guests on them. I've had a few folks at conferences ask me to join them on theirs, and they know some podcasts in the Python and Javascript spaces, too," she added, looking at Curt and Nkema before looking back at Jeremy. "So can we, in official DCom capacity, do these podcasts?"

Jeremy thought about it. "We'll probably want Legal to have a chance to tell you all the things you can't say and all that, but I don't see any reason why not."

Mikaela smiled. "Good. Should I reach out to the Legal folks, or …?"

Jeremy thought for another second, then said, "Actually, let me do it and I'll connect you. Legal has a funny way of de-prioritizing things that don't come from a VP, it seems, so you could be waiting a while if it doesn't come from me. I'll CC you on the message, though, hopefully that'll cut me out as the middle-man quickly enough." Then he took a deep breath, and said, "Oh, and before we break, one last announcement to all of you."

He deliberately held their attention for a few extra beats before saying, "Gerald's in agreement that we have a lot on our plate, and quite probably too much, given the plans and growth curve that everyone's expecting for Codist after the end of the year. So I have the approval to hire two more folks for our team." He grinned. "Anybody know somebody they'd like to work with?"

The grin was infectious.

Q4 and Beyond

As the team concludes their Q3 planning meeting, we've reached that point in the tale where we pan the camera back away from the DCom Developer Relations team and their efforts to support Codist and the mobile libraries. The DCom team certainly has their work cut out for them, particularly if Codist grows the way DCom hopes it will, and (hopefully) begins gathering awards from the various industry groups that love to hand out awards.

It is fair, however, to ask at a high level, how exactly does one use this pattern catalog? While the DCom experience is a useful fable, sometimes the lessons found in a fable are subtle and/or hard to extract. And this book is clearly a **Reference (373)** and not a **Guide (243)**, so how should readers use the patterns documented herein?

This was one of the great weaknesses of the original design patterns movement: for all that it sought to catalog and document all the various patterns in the world, it failed to "close the gap" between the assembly of these pattern languages (as a collection of patterns came to be known) and an understanding of application of those patterns in a real-world setting. In other words, they covered the "what" and the "why" but completely whiffed on the "how."

Thus, in the interests of clarity, let's revisit how the DCom team was able to use the patterns documented herein:

- **As a lexicon:** One of the great benefits of patterns is that they create a shared glossary of terms whose definition and meaning is clear, and whose nuances are already established. As the authors of this book can tell you, for example, working out the specific details and differences between a **Hands-On Lab (477)** and a **Workshop (477)** and a **Hackathon (255)** was not always clear, even between us. If the terms themselves are not clear—and more importantly, how each is different from the other—then the benefits and costs and utility of each is also just as muddled. By creating a shared glossary, a team begins to see clearly where and how each activity becomes useful in which situations.

- **As abstractions:** It seems weird, as developers, to talk about abstractions when we're not talking about code, but several times during the development of this pattern language, we started by speaking of a particular scenario—"Let's create a channel on YouTube"—and found that what we were actually speaking of had nothing to do with the actual website, but the idea (the abstraction) of creating a collection of **Recorded Videos (363)** that could be easily discovered and consumed. This simultaneously makes it easier to understand when and how the pattern applies, as well as creates some areas of variability and flexibility, which can be important when a company has certain restrictions against using a particular vendor or provider.

- **As a filter:** Each pattern's "tags" (Budget, Social, etc.) were our way of trying to help teams (including our own teams) sort through all the various activities that a team could do yet remain within the constraints of a team's budget, skillsets, and target goals. For example, if the goal is a high-reach push, Social activities will tend to be less of an immediate selection, whereas high-interactivity will find that Social activities strongly meet the goal. Budget, of course, is always a factor, but even as we saw with the DCom team, Coding also becomes a useful criterion, as well.

- **As an exemplar:** While most of these patterns will generate (as one reviewer noted) "No duh" kinds of responses from experienced developer advocates, those who are newer to the industry are often unfamiliar with some or even all of these activities as discrete actions. (One of us once interviewed a DevRel candidate who, when asked what sort of activities they would imagine the role would entail, responded with, "I dunno, you just go out there and talk about what you like to program and stuff.") While most developer advocates will find most of these patterns as things they've already done, most will also find that one or two are entirely new, and others are refinement of a more nebulous idea. This, too, has a history in the design patterns movement as a whole; when the original Gang-of-Four book was published, many senior engineers at the time brushed the book off as "twenty ways to use a pointer." For many of us who were newer to the industry, however, that book opened up a world of thinking about object-oriented design differently, and gave us a set of working designs to start from.

CHAPTER 2 A CASE STUDY: USING THE DEVREL PATTERNS

- **As a starting point:** Lastly, it's important to realize that patterns are never solutions, but solutions within a context that yield particular consequences. Since the context at any given company (or time!) is ever the same twice, it stands to reason that many, if not most, of the implementation of these activities will require a certain amount of "tweaking" in order to yield the kind of consequences the team is comfortable with. A given **Blog Post (105)** might need to be longer, or shorter, in order to accomplish a desired result. Some book authors (including one of this book's authors) have actually posted whole chapters for a forthcoming **Book (121)** as **Blog Posts (105)**, in order to help generate some reach for their book. While we certainly wouldn't recommend every **Blog Post (105)** be tens of thousands of words long, sometimes it makes sense to do it that way. As with any pattern language, these patterns only work well if they create favorable consequences for your problem/context pairing. Each of the patterns is just an abstraction over an idea—take them and make them yours as you need.

We can see elements of each of these bullets in the story above:

- Throughout the story, the team was able to use the pattern names as nouns, making it much easier to understand more precisely what was being discussed or proposed.

- In several places, the team was able to implicitly filter out patterns that wouldn't suit a particular goal by applying the filter criteria as part of their discussions and/or suggestions. In many cases, that filtering occurred entirely internally, where we as observers weren't able to see it.

CHAPTER 2 A CASE STUDY: USING THE DEVREL PATTERNS

- The team used patterns as a starting point, but "tweaked" as needed, such as when the beta program was viewed as an **Ambassadors (71)** but with limited visibility and reach.

Lastly, it's important to point out that as authors of a work of fiction (even if it's just a fable inside a work of non-fiction), it's entirely easy to make sure that the actors' decisions turn out a particular way. (It's our world, we get to decide what happens in it!) Moreover, undoubtedly, some readers will have read the fable and felt that certain decisions were incorrect for the problem/context at hand. That's an entirely fair conclusion to reach. Our goal here is not to say, "DCom's decisions were decisions that each of you should slavishly follow," but instead, "We hope that watching DCom wrestle with their problems and context help you wrestle with your own."

In the remaining pages, we document the patterns. We hope it's useful.

CHAPTER 3

Ambassadors

Topics: *Social*

Individuals outside of the company (that is, not employed by the company) who represent the company or (more often) the product/service in a variety of situations—at conferences, online, videos, or in written articles or books. Ambassadors are often self-taught experts on the product/service, and provide that expertise and enthusiasm to others within the community.

Also Known As

Advocates, Champions; MVPs; Experts; Heroes; Insiders; Rangers

CHAPTER 3   AMBASSADORS

Intent

Developer Relations teams, big or small, need to scale through the efforts of others outside their organization if they hope to reach global audiences online or in-person. In particular, you want potential customers to find evidence that people outside the company are using the product/service, and that there are "unbiased" (that is, opinions that aren't coming from your Sales or Marketing team) users of the product/service out in the world.

Context

You want additional content created around your product/service, but you lack the budget and/or bandwidth to create that content. Turning to Ambassadors to create that content (often in exchange for non-monetary compensation, like **Swag (427)** or opportunities to be co-branded at **Conference Sessions (197)** provides additional effective bandwidth without having to increase your team size.

Popularizing/promoting external users of the product/service also creates a deeper sense of legitimacy and increases the comfort level of potential customers. While you might have one or two **Case Studies (151)** available for consumption, many developers recognize that these are cherry-picked and almost always canonical uses, heavily edited, and no case study ever seems to end in anything other than a rousing success for the implementing company. Having third-party users of the product/service out in the world, raw and unfiltered, means that your product/service is "real-world ready" (because otherwise, there wouldn't be people in the real world using it and willing to show the world they're doing so).

Lastly, Ambassadors also help create a "friendly" set of developers who have already demonstrated their commitment to the product/service, and are thus easier to trust when they provide feedback about the product/service, whether that be in the form of bug reports, product suggestions, or even marketing or sales messages. Ambassadors can even sometimes act as internal champions within their company for your product/service, making it much easier to support Sales efforts.

Solution

Find people within your existing community (by examining your **Forums (233)** or by speaking with interested parties at your **Conference Booth (137)** who are active, well-informed on your product/service, and eager to be more active. Create a program by which they will have certain identity ("Ambassadors," "Heroes," etc.) and offer benefits to being a part of the program.

Participants

The most obvious participants will be the external developers who will become the Ambassadors. Less obviously, you will likely need to engage with other divisions within your company, most notably the Engineering team, since the Ambassadors will undoubtedly want to connect with them to ask questions, provide feedback, describe bugs (or possible bugs), and so on. The Marketing team will likely also need to get involved at some point, since part of the benefit to the Ambassador is to be recognized as such publicly, increasing the Ambassador's brand (and salability) within the community.

CHAPTER 3   AMBASSADORS

Implementation

Creating an Ambassadors program will require several steps:

1. **Work out a budget, goals, and "organizational access" to the organization:** It may seem counter-intuitive to work on this even before the formation or announcement of the program, but having conversations internally about where and how Ambassadors will fit within the larger organization will be helpful when recruiting them. If, for example, the Engineering team is absolutely open to having candid conversations with Ambassadors, this will help "sell" the benefits of the program to the community. Knowing this ahead of time will save a great deal of time and potential embarrassment if it turns out differently than you'd imagined. One of the most important questions to answer will be whether the Ambassadors will have access to sensitive information about the company's plans, activities, or upcoming features—if so, you will want/need to get Legal to draft a non-disclosure agreement (NDA) that Ambassadors will need to sign in order to have access to that material.

2. **Decide on Ambassador activities:** What do you want the Ambassadors to do, either for your company directly, or indirectly through their actions in the community? What level of commitment to these activities will be sufficient to "earn" the position of Ambassador? Ideally, the Ambassador's efforts here should align closely with things they are already doing—for example, if you have **forums (233)**,

CHAPTER 3   AMBASSADORS

requiring Ambassadors to be posting on them regularly is something that they're already doing, so it's literally no additional work on their part to earn this distinction.

3. **Work out benefits:** What will the Ambassador earn in return for their efforts on your company's behalf? Possibly create custom Ambassador-themed swag, for example, or work with the team that is hosting your company's conference booth to "reserve" a few speaking slots for Ambassadors.

4. **Announce the program:** Find the places where your developer-users are most likely to see your message, such as your **Developer Forums (233)** and/or **Social Media(395)** channels, and announce the formation of the program. Have a clearly defined set of acceptance criteria (how many years' experience with your product/service does someone have to have in order to be considered for the program, or what degree of knowledge do they have to have demonstrated) in the announcement, as well as a means by which individuals (or companies) can apply. Put a cutoff date for applications, so as to create a sense of "FOMO" (Fear Of Missing Out) and foster urgency in

75

individuals to apply. Put an "announcement date" describing when candidates would find out the results of their application; not only does this create a targeted deadline for yourselves, it also implicitly creates a sense of when the community can expect to see the results.

5. **Identify your potential Ambassadors:** After the announcement goes out, examine the applications received. If the number of applicants is smaller than desired, or if the applicants do not include particular individuals identified as vocal and supportive, try reaching out directly—it's always possible they didn't see the announcement, or may not imagine themselves as meeting the criteria. Ideally, you will want a number of candidates at least twice to three times the number of actual Ambassadors you're planning to invite. It's often best to start with a small number (3 to 5) of Ambassadors, so getting ten to fifteen candidates is a good starting pool.

6. **Evaluate your candidates internally:** The additional criteria here will often be more subjective and "based on feel," but fundamentally you are looking for candidates that appear to be genuinely interested in the product/service and committed to being involved. Keep in mind that Ambassadors will be acting in a capacity that, while not legally representing the company, will at least be doing so in a brand or public-opinion capacity. Look for signs that could create problems down the road. Does the candidate like to stoke controversy? Does the

CHAPTER 3   AMBASSADORS

candidate try to reason with disagreements, or shout them down? Do they have any strongly held beliefs that would run counter to the company's publicly stated goals and values?

7. **Announce the new Ambassadors:** Ask for "head shots," as well as possibly a short introductory paragraph, of each Ambassador. Announce them over **Social Media (395)**. Include their new status in your **Newsletter (281)**. Bring them up on stage at your **Conference (179)**. Any place your company has an ability to promote the Ambassadors in front of your larger community, take it.

Once the program is established, there will be additional implementation work, for as long as the program remains in existence:

- **Periodically review and call for new Ambassadors:** The list of Ambassadors will never remain constant, as developers find themselves leaving positions that embraced their Ambassadorial work, retire, move away from direct work into management, and/or find themselves less enthusiastic about the product/service simply because individual (or corporate) tastes change. Establish a regular cadence on which you will review the existing list of Ambassadors (pruning those who appear to be no longer active) and call for new Ambassadors, and go through the cycle. Annually is a good bet, quarterly is aggressive but often appreciated by those who "just missed" the last cutoff. Note that it's certainly possible to accept new applications constantly, but you will probably find it easier organizationally to "batch up" the applications for review all at once, rather than reviewing them constantly.

CHAPTER 3   AMBASSADORS

- **Review the Ambassador program size:** Do you have too few Ambassadors? Depending on the popularity of your product/service, and in particular the third-party consulting/advising opportunities around your product/service, you may want to grow the Ambassador pool. If the product/service is approaching its end-of-life, one way to signal its eventual retirement is to deliberately shrink the Ambassador program (although this can result in some uncomfortable conversations with Ambassadors who will feel their loyalty has been disregarded and unrewarded when they are "cut" from the program).

- **Keep a steady "heartbeat" of news and information flowing to the Ambassadors:** This needs to be above and beyond the flow of information that is going out publicly to the rest of the community—this is going to be one of the most direct benefits of being an Ambassador in the first place. Present them with opportunities to volunteer for beta-tests, look to connect them with Marketing for testimonials or endorsements, and (if appropriate) loop them into potential Sales opportunities that benefit both your company and the Ambassador. If the Ambassadors are all under NDA, include announcements about upcoming alpha tests, design reviews, or new features under consideration. In some cases, major company announcements (such as opening new regional SaaS server clusters) are also entirely appropriate to pre-announce to the Ambassadors, as it will allow the Ambassadors to time their own marketing/branding messages to coincide with your company's announcement.

- **Keep a healthy feedback loop from the Ambassadors:** Ambassadors are going to be one of the best sources of feedback on your product/service, but all of that feedback will be useless if it doesn't reach the appropriate eyeballs inside your company. Either build direct channels for the Ambassadors to communicate with the Product or Engineering teams, or engage in regular "feedback sharing" meetings with the relevant teams internally in which you provide the raw and unfiltered feedback. Where doable, encourage those teams to connect directly with the Ambassadors, so less of the message is lost in transmission.

Consider, also, feeding Ambassadors with some opportunities that your own team cannot (or will not) take upon themselves to do. For example, if a conference brings together a relatively large number of your Ambassadors into one place, but you have no plans to exhibit there or sponsor, consider asking one or more of your Ambassadors to put a small event together themselves, with your backing (monetary, branding, or any other forms of support).

Metrics

There are several ways to judge the efficacy and reach of an Ambassadors program:

Turnover. How often do Ambassadors leave the program? While it's not reasonable to expect that an Ambassador will want to be one for the rest of their careers, a scenario where Ambassadors become one for a year or two and then choose to quit or opt out is concerning—it indicates they may not be seeing the program's benefits to be worth the time spent earning it or joining it.

CHAPTER 3   AMBASSADORS

Waiting List. How many people have asked to be an Ambassador but your program is already full? This gives you an indication of how desirable the prestige and/or benefits of the program are. If you find you have an opening and nobody clamoring to fill it, you may want or need to do a little refactoring of the program and/or do a little "brand promotion" of the program so that more people in your community become aware of it.

Activities. How many activities are your Ambassadors participating in as your Ambassador? Whether it's hosting meetups, giving talks, creating videos, or writing articles, you should have Ambassadors track their efforts and the results. You could have them also measure traffic to their content or attendance at their in-person events. Or, encourage Ambassadors to provide calls to action (CTAs) that direct users back to your site. That way you see those who were inspired enough by the Ambassador to take action and investigate more about your product.

However, be very careful with this—Ambassadors are not your employees, and your program has to offer benefits enough (in quantity and/or quality) to justify the time they will need to spend gathering and reporting this data. (Make sure it's as simple as possible to report the data, as well—every hour you force your Ambassadors to create pivot tables in Excel to put data into its proper format is hours they will grumble to themselves as to whether the program is worth the time.)

"Touch" Rate. How often does the Ambassador get out into a crowd of developers or in front of developers? If you count the number of developers who see or hear your Ambassador talk, it's a metric of reach; if you count the amount of time each developer gets to spend with the Ambassador, it's a metric of interactivity. Trying to track both simultaneously can be difficult, so pick one and stick with it.

CHAPTER 3   AMBASSADORS

Example

Darryl runs the Developer Relations team at DCom, a developer tools company. Recently DCom has found that their developer community has grown to (by one rough count) several thousand individuals, and Darryl has discovered that a small number (about a half-dozen) of those developers are earning sizable reputation scores by answering questions on StackOverflow. In addition to that, Darryl has also begun to notice that several popular developer conferences are accepting talks on DCom's products from non-DCom individuals (and it seems like it's always the same three speakers that are doing the talks), and his Google Alerts are letting him know that every so often a new article on DCom's software keeps showing up on a couple of blogs.

Realizing that these individuals are currently doing all of this without any formal company support, Darryl wants to spin up the "DCom Champions," an Ambassadors program. He approaches his boss, Tammy, with a modest budget to support an early-stage Ambassadors program: some **Swag (427)**, four quarterly virtual meetings, and a **Party (319)** at the upcoming Kansas City Developers Conference, where several DCom talks are already scheduled. After Darryl's pitch, Tammy notes that the Champions could be a great help in the upcoming (as yet publicly unknown) rollout of DCom's latest programming language assistant, and asks Darryl to make that a primary focus to start.

Darryl agrees, but asks Tammy to make sure the Champions will have access to early-access releases of the assistant, as well as a "point of contact" for any feedback or questions. Tammy suggests Darryl be the first point of contact, but also agrees to set up email intros to three team leads in Engineering that are working on the assistant, with the clear expectation that Darryl can rely on them for support for questions coming from the Champions. Tammy also states that Legal will probably want the Champions to sign something that lays clear the relationship between the

CHAPTER 3   AMBASSADORS

Champions and DCom, as well as expectations. The budget is approved, and the Swag ordered.

Next, Darryl sits down to determine what the "acceptance criteria" should be to become considered for Champion status, and comes to a relatively simple formula: Any individual that does twelve "public" DCom-related activities in a calendar year, where "public" means something that can be (online) discovered by Google or (physical world) attended in person. Although it's certainly possible that someone looking to "game the system" could claim twelve Twitter/X posts were public, the program is small enough that Darryl doesn't think this is going to be much of a problem to start.

Now, Darryl needs to think about administrative overhead, and realizes that given the size of his team, and the fact that he can't hire someone to manage the program full-time (yet), he really can't afford to have too many Champions, lest he drown in administrative coordination (getting legal documents to each of the Champions, shipping **Swag (427)**, and so on). The simplest thing to do, then, is to keep it small, perhaps no more than six Champions.

Darryl then reaches out privately, over email, to six folks that seem most active across all the different places (StackOverflow, conferences, and so on), introducing himself and establishing the desire to spin up the DCom Champions. (He notes three more names, just in case some of the six choose not to participate.) Noting that four of the six are on the schedule to be speaking at KCDC, he asks if any of the others are planning to be in or near Kansas City during that time, and invites them to join him in Kansas City for a nice dinner at a local upscale restaurant, where he wants to present the details of the program, get signatures on the necessary documents required by Legal, and flesh out some of the details of what's coming. All six agree whole-heartedly, with the two non-speakers readily agreeing to meet in Kansas City. (Darryl offers to cover flight and hotel costs for them, but both work for companies that can cover their T&E.)

CHAPTER 3   AMBASSADORS

On the night of the get-together, after introductions, Darryl thanks each of them for their contributions to the developer community. He then lays out the broad vision for the Champions program, and asks them to sign the document in front of them if they wish to participate. As might be expected, all six are "all in" and are willing to sign. Once they have done so, Darryl goes on to establish some particulars up front: continuing their contributions, connecting them to some of the relevant employees inside DCom, opportunities for DCom and the individual Champions to work together (conference talks, etc.), and most of all, early access to the upcoming release. He hands out the "DCom Champions" swag, which includes stickers and T-shirts, and takes careful note of the email addresses, social media handles, and physical shipping addresses for each of them for the future.

Unbeknownst to the six, Darryl has also connected with the organizers of the KCDC conference, and the next evening, during the conference's closing ceremonies, the organizers offer the stage to Darryl for a "special exclusive to KCDC announcement." Darryl takes the stage, announces the formation of the DCom Champions, and asks the six to join him on stage to applause and cheers. Afterwards, several speakers are seen talking to the Champions, who later report that there was great interest in finding out how to become one.

For the next six months, a portion of Darryl's time is spent connecting the Champions to the engineering teams responsible for the upcoming assistant and periodically checking in on their community contributions. He spins up a spreadsheet to take note of what public activities of theirs that he can find, and pays close attention to their blog posts, articles, and social media posts, as he is first of all, making sure they aren't commenting publicly on the forthcoming (still-embargoed) release, and second of all, looking to see if their audience is growing; Tammy has already made it clear that when the coding assistant goes public, DCom wants to get as much reach as possible with the announcement and details.

CHAPTER 3   AMBASSADORS

At the nine-month mark, the assistant launches, and Darryl is pleased to note that the Champions all take great effort to broadcast and re-share the announcement with their own audiences. He's also quite pleased to note that two announce virtual training seminars on how to use the assistant the day the announcement goes out. He makes a note to himself to talk to Tammy about potential **Training (439)** scenarios that those two might be able to help with.

One year after the announcement of the DCom Champions, Darryl takes stock as part of his annual review of the program to Tammy and the CxO suite. He gathers up metrics on the responsiveness of the community to his Ambassadors' posts and the rough audience sizes they've reported for their **Conference Sessions (197)** and **User Group (457)** talks, and takes careful note to point out that one of the Ambassadors has since gone on to start a consulting company that specializes in helping companies better utilize DCom's tools—a clear opening for a **Partnership (309)** relationship. He also notes that he currently has close to two-dozen people interested in becoming Champions, including two who have started a developer **Podcast (333)**, something his team had been mulling over for a while. It's pretty clear the program has been a success, and Darryl realizes he has to ask for more budget (for more **Swag (427)** and another **Party (319)** for the Ambassadors) as well as additional headcount to run the program, as it's starting to get a little complicated!

Consequences

Creating an extension of your DevRel team like this will almost certainly necessitate one of your team to the care-and-feeding (management) of the Ambassadors, including managing communications with them and setting expectations. These "community managers" will be the face of the company to the Ambassadors, and often a first-point-of-contact for the Ambassadors into the rest of the company.

Make sure to keep the "direct channels" open and flowing. If promised access to the Engineering team, for example, set up monthly or quarterly or annual meetings with Engineers and the Ambassadors. Make some of the channel content be formal and scripted (à la a presentation or demo), but also ensure that some of the channel content is informal and unscripted (a hosted Q&A or "Ask Me Anything" session, for example) so that the Ambassadors feel like they are receiving "raw" and/or "unfiltered" communication, not to mention having the ability to provide feedback in a more direct manner. Ambassadors who do not feel like they are getting enough "face time" with the internal organization will not remain Ambassadors for long. The "community manager(s)" will likely own the responsibility for creating these meetings and these opportunities, and ensuring the internal organizations (Engineering, Product, etc.) are "bought in" to the concept.

If the community is large enough, Ambassadors will often want to have a "private space" in which they can have more candid conversations among themselves and/or your team about topics that may not be appropriate to discuss in a more open environment. Consider providing a **Forum (233)** or private **Social Media (395)** connection that is exclusive to your Ambassadors, and consider inviting some of the company's employees (engineers, marketing, etc.) into that forum in order to give the Ambassadors those direct channels. You may also want to consider a yearly "Ambassadors-only" **Conference (179)** to facilitate the highest levels of interactivity with them.

Once created, Ambassadors are often excellent authors for your **Newsletter (281)** and/or to publish to your **Blog (105)**. Provide opportunities for Ambassadors to update the **Reference Documentation (373)**, since this will both give them a sense of accomplishment and contribution, as well as provide a near-constant state of review of those same docs. For those Ambassadors that are not keen to write prose, offer them opportunities to show off their coding skills by incorporating

CHAPTER 3   AMBASSADORS

Samples (387) they've written into the "official" company-sponsored/-owned set of samples/examples.

When looking to bootstrap a **User Group Network (457)**, Ambassadors are often natural individuals to lead or create the individual groups. You may choose to emphasize that the creation and management of a user group network could, in and of itself, satisfy the criteria for remaining in the Ambassador program. (Keep in mind that running a user group is a non-trivial amount of work, and running a user group, for all its benefits, decreases the amount of bandwidth the individual has for doing other Ambassadorial activities!)

Assist Ambassadors in finding **Conference Sessions (197)** at third-party conferences, particularly ones at which your company is sponsoring or at which you will have a **Booth (137)**. In some cases, this can be as simple as just announcing the events at which your company will be present, and offering to connect the Ambassador with the conference organizers—or even just echoing the conference's CFP (Call for Proposals) date (and submission link) so your Ambassadors are aware.

When possible, work to assist Ambassadors in the writing of a **Book (121)** about your product/service. This can be as simple as creating mutual introductions between the Ambassador and a book publisher, by offering to buy a certain number of copies of the book from the publisher to give away as **Swag (427)**, or (at a minimum) offering to have the CEO or CTO (or other similarly distinguished individual) of your company write an endorsement or Foreword to the book. In the more supportive case, have members of your Engineering team review the book for technical accuracy, or members of the Product or Marketing teams review the book's messaging to ensure it aligns (or at least isn't contradictory).

It will be extremely difficult to find metrics to the activities of the Ambassadors, so it's strongly likely that at some point after their foundation there will be a call to shut the program down in order to save money if there aren't obvious and visible benefits to doing so. Make strong efforts to keep the Ambassadors' activities front-and-center to the rest of the company, so that anyone can see the positives of the program without having to see numbers.

Alternatively, you can ask your Ambassadors to provide some metrics around their activities within the program as a post-invitation requirement to remain within the program, so that it's easier to provide metrics about the success of the program. Keep in mind, however, that Ambassadors are (by definition) outside the company and, as volunteers, will only be interested (or even able) to do a limited amount of work on your behalf—the more they are required to fill out reports and forms, the less bandwidth they will have to go out and be Ambassadors.

It's rare, but periodically an Ambassador will be unable or unwilling to sign the NDA to have access to the company's sensitive information. You may want to decide ahead of time what your program's reaction will be to this situation—will you "uninvite" them from the program, or will you take care to screen all the NDA-requiring material away from those non-NDA-signed individuals? The former runs the risk of creating some bad PR for the company, but the latter will require a non-trivial amount of work on your program's part (with potentially significant risk if NDA material ends up in the hands of non-NDA-signatories).

Sad as it may seem, not all of the Ambassadors will agree with one another, and it is almost certain that as the longevity of the program increases, and/or its size, two Ambassadors will disagree—publicly. It is also very possible that an Ambassador will, at some point, say something derogatory, discriminatory, or just outright inflammatory, prompting calls from your company to censure or disavow the Ambassador. Your brand will suffer the longer this drama continues, so connecting with the Legal team ahead of time is strongly advised. Create a Code of Conduct early, describing what is and is not tolerated, and enforce it when violations occur, either by gentle admonishment, stern warning, or outright removal from the program. Make it clear (as part of the paperwork signed by individuals when they join the Ambassador program) what the rules are, and articulate the steps the company will take in response to individuals who do not abide by the rules and requirements of the program. When an individual does violate these rules, move quickly to enforce them—failure to do so will create ill will and foster frustration on the part of the other Ambassadors, or worse, lead the Ambassadors to conclude that the rules and requirements are just "suggestions" and hold no real weight of enforcement.

Variants

Marketing Ambassadors, **Sales Ambassadors:** In many companies, it's useful to have an Ambassadors program that is tied more closely to the Marketing and Sales departments. In this scenario, the Ambassadors program may be more centrally managed, perhaps even in conjunction with the company's **Partnership (309)** efforts, and the DevRel team is one of several departments to which Ambassadors connect. This has the obvious advantage of reducing the amount of administrative overhead the DevRel team needs to absorb in order to manage the program, but comes with the downside that the Ambassadors will often be "distracted" away from DevRel activities by their engagements with Marketing and Sales.

CHAPTER 4

Article

Topics: *Writing, Code*

Written piece published by a third party, whether that's a website (like a developer portal) or a print publication (the few that are left). Intended to be a stand-alone entity without referencing liberally elsewhere (although multi-part articles are certainly doable and can reference each other).

CHAPTER 4   ARTICLE

Intent

You want to present a written piece that will convey some concept or idea or insight to a curated audience that you do not engage or manage directly. This can be to your existing technology community, in order to reinforce, refine, or introduce ideas about your product, with which they are (likely) already familiar.

However, often you will want to reach an audience that isn't already familiar with your product or company, perhaps because they are a different tech stack than your target technology demographic has been, or perhaps because they have historically not seen that your product is something that is accessible to them. For example, you may find that certain developers are in a market that you don't reach—if your company is known for .NET yet you want to reach JavaScript developers, for example, or vice versa—and you want to reach them with a written piece that will have some "stickiness" to them.

Alternatively, your product may be introducing a new feature that is not immediately self-explanatory, or will have implications beyond the obvious, particularly to a new crowd. Perhaps your product is a database, and a new version of it is being scaled down to a "mobile edition" suitable for use on a mobile device, and you want to reach a mobile audience, which is different from your traditional "big iron" server database crowd.

Context

You're looking for high reach from a single work effort (that of writing the article). You want code to be able to accompany the article, often in the form of a **Sample/Example (387)**, but the main effort is in the written prose, with code providing clarity to certain points, rather than laying out all the code and leaving developers to understand it on their own. You want this piece to "stand alone" from other works you create, so that the readers will not need to reference other works in order to understand it.

Solution

Write an article (generally 1500 words minimum, 4000 words maximum) that addresses the needs of that audience in a semi-direct, if abstract, fashion, submitted to a third-party publisher who will distribute it to their audience.

Participants

Besides the author of the article, an article will often involve an **article editor** of some form (either from your organization, the publisher's organization, or often both), who will be responsible for making sure the article is coherent, consistent, logically structured, and engaging to read (among other things). They will often make structural suggestions about the article, focusing more on the topic and/or how the article addresses the topic.

In addition to the article editor, the publisher will often have a **copy editor** whose purpose is to focus on grammar and spelling and proper punctuation. In some organizations, they are one and the same, but even then they will often take these two editing tasks separately, usually first addressing the strategic (content) before tackling the tactical (grammar and punctuation).

Depending on the degree of formality at your organization, you may also require approval/sign-off from the Engineering, Marketing, and/or Legal teams.

- Engineering will want to make sure that your article is technically accurate, particularly with respect to upcoming features that may (or may not) be announced yet.

CHAPTER 4   ARTICLE

- Marketing will want to make sure that the article doesn't disagree or appear to undercut the company's current or upcoming marketing plans.

- Legal will want to make sure that nothing in the article's content will undercut, disagree, circumvent, or otherwise disrupt any current or future legal standing the organization will undertake. Legal will often also be on the lookout for any sort of discriminatory, potentially discriminatory, or allegedly discriminatory statements that might land the company in a lawsuit down the road. Expect that any of these teams could potentially introduce significant delays in the publication process, and that they can (and often will) demand edits to the article before they approve it for publication. (Keep in mind that deliberately attempting to circumvent any of these groups can often be a "career-limiting move," and potentially even lead to job termination.)

One common point of friction with publishers is that of the "final edit"—which party (the author or the publisher) has the final editing pass before the article is published? Publishers will often insist/demand on this, since the article will live on their website, but if your company insists on having that right, this will need to be spelled out in the contract between the parties. For this reason, it is common contractual language to have a "cancellation clause," in which either party reserves the right to cancel the article if one side or the other disagrees with edits made to the source material. Your company's Legal Team will usually be responsible for establishing or negotiating this, but make sure to bring it up if it doesn't otherwise get discussed.

Implementation

Writing an article involves a fair amount of planning and iteration, along with decent fluency in the target language; if the author lacks the time or ability to plan, iterate, or fluency, make some kind of accommodations either by obtaining a co-author and/or a translator.

Articles should have a number of things decided up front:

Length: 1500 words is generally a "short piece," usually two or three printed pages, that can be consumed in a relatively short period of time, such as on a lunch break or perhaps during the reader's daily commute. Longer-form pieces, such as 4000 to 8000 words, are more "feature-length" articles, and will take a longer period of time for readers to work through, particularly since longer pieces will generally have deeper, broader, or more complex topics, and therefore require more time and energy from the reader to understand. Consider, too, that a long-form (8000+ words) article might be more consumable to your audience if it is broken up (into two 5000 word pieces, or perhaps five 2000-word pieces, and so on) and released one after another as a "series" or a "column."

Deadline: When is it due? More specifically, when is it due to the publisher's hands for review, copyedit, and other processes that happen once you are "done" with it? Just as code isn't "done" until it's been reviewed, tested, and/or put through a QA cycle, an article isn't "done" just because you've stopped writing. Knowing the deadlines ahead of time is important for your own planning, but it's also important to recognize that there are people downstream in the process that will be affected by your missed deadline, as well.

Target audience: Before writing, consider carefully the target audience. Is the assumed reader somebody familiar with the basics of your product/service? Are they experts? Are they new to your product, but familiar with other (perhaps competitor) products? Flesh out a more detailed view of what sort of technical prerequisites they would satisfy once you know their background—for example, a reader of an article on NoSQL databases may or may not have some familiarity with SQL databases, but it's reasonable to assume they know what the (general) concept of a database is and the kinds of behavior one provides. Where the audience has familiarity, don't explain; where they don't have familiarity, go into some (or a lot) of depth on a concept as necessary. As you write more articles and get feedback on the audience's reaction to your articles, refine your understanding of the target audience, so that your writing can be tuned to be appealing to that audience. (How to do this is well beyond the scope of this book, and arguably an intuitive process to boot.)

"Voice": Do you want your prose to sound formal, or informal? Will you speak with the first-person voice ("I want to build this app, so I...") or in the third person ("When developers want to build an app, they need to..."), or will you look to the second-person voice, as this book does? Do you want to try to incorporate humor, or keep it "professional"? As part of your target audience consideration, consider some demographic information as well, and how that might affect your voice; in the 2020s, for example, references to terms like "sus" and "lit" will be recognizable to the 20-somethings in your audience, but terms like "super bad" and "groovy" may only feel comfortable to the 50-somethings, or even 60-somethings. Likewise, consider avoiding turns-of-phrase that are regional or cultural (such as the infamous British "Bob's your uncle"), as they may not translate well into other cultures or if/when your article is translated into foreign languages. Keep in mind, it may take several articles before you find a "voice" that you are comfortable with.

Outline or story: Most professionals who have been through primary education have had the experience of writing an essay that required an outline first. The purpose, we are told, is that this outline will help provide structure and clarity to the essay, so that the essay can be sharp and crisp and focused on the topic at hand. Sometimes, however, primary education loses sight of the forest through the trees: the goal is to have a clear picture in the author's mind of what is being written, and the actual format or structure of the outline is irrelevant, so long as it creates clarity in the author's mind. To this end, "mind maps" are another technique for structuring thought, as are "stories" or "storytelling"; frankly, the possibilities here are endless. As an author, you will want to experiment with different mechanisms until you find one that resonates with you, always with the goal of clarity firmly in mind. When in doubt, fall back to the Aristotelian form that was taught in school: "Introduce the topic, declare a thesis or a "hook" that details why the topic matters, provide three different interesting things about the topic, conclude by explaining how these three things combine."

Iterate: Although some authors can produce a fully copyedit-ready copy of an article in a single pass, usually that is a skill that only comes with years of hard-earned, bitter experience, much like writing code correctly the first time. You should expect that your first draft will have weak areas and places where the message or the idea does not come through clearly; more importantly, it will be nearly impossible for you, as the author, to recognize where those weak spots are, because you know in your mind what you were trying to say, making it hard for you to see what is actually on paper (or on the screen) as opposed to what's in your head. This is where a reviewer—formal or informal—can be invaluable. When the draft feels ready, provide a copy to someone who has some familiarity (though they need not be an expert) in the topic, and ask them for feedback. Keep in mind that many colleagues and co-workers will want to be supportive, and believe that doing so means offering up positive affirmations; this is not what you need. You are looking for places where the prose is unclear, makes jumps in logic, or doesn't adequately explain some aspect of the code that your article is building around. Encourage your reviewers to provide some level of detail about what they liked or found clear, and what they didn't like or found unclear. The ideal reviewer will be able to take your copy and provide comments directly on the piece—most word processing programs have the ability to provide "comments," usually as a blob of colored text off to the side at (roughly) the place where the offending text appears. Raw text files (such as Markdown) can be harder to comment in place, but easier to "diff" to see where reviewers made comments inline.

Submit for Review: Merely because your reviewers have given the thumbs-up on your article does not mean it is ready to publish—most publishers will have their own, formal, editorial step, wherein someone associated with the publication will go over your article with a sharp eye. Early authors often resent this step, feeling like their prose is "perfect the way it is"; early programmers often feel the same way during a code review. Keep in mind that the goals of both code reviews and article edits are identical: Make the work stronger and clearer and more in line with the works surrounding it. Certain publishers will have standards around how acronyms are introduced or reference, for example, or will suggest how some of the other articles they have published have covered portions of the topic and therefore could be referenced or linked directly, reducing the need for your article to go into such depth on that portion of the topic. (This is a benefit, by the way—most of the time authors find they have more content than space, and struggle to find ways to cram it all in.) Some publications also have standards that are designed to help create a unified reader experience—the use of a particular perspective (first-person, second-person, or third-person), for example.

Copyedit Review: If the editor accepts the article, it will often go to a copyeditor, who will often do some formatting and layout, and a last pass on punctuation, spelling, and grammar. Because technical publications are always concerned with a misplaced comma changing the entire meaning of a sentence, however, the copyedited article will come back to you for a "final review"; your job at this point is to re-read your article, looking solely to make sure that no sentence was accidentally inverted or cut off. Having a pre-edited copy of your article handy when you do this is helpful.

Metrics

Given that articles are, by definition, published with third parties (rather than on your company's website), you will often be at the mercy of that publisher's metrics to know how your article is doing. Depending on where the article is published, one or more metrics will be available to gauge its success:

Web views: If the publisher is online, then they will almost certainly have some kind of tracking cookie or "click counter" that can tell you how often the page has been served up to browsers. This is often an overly optimistic metric, as it cannot track whether the user actually *read* the article, only whether the server was requested to send it. It may not be tracking unique views, either, meaning if the user clicks on the link several times, each one will be tracked as a "web view." However, it is one of the simplest metrics to track, and is thus often the easiest one for a publisher to provide.

Time on Page: Some content-management systems are able to track how long the page, once served, remains visible in the browser.

Click-through Rate: If the published article is linked from a **Newsletter (281)**, the publisher may have some data around how often this article's link was clicked on in the newsletter (which indicates, presumably, that the user is interested in this topic and clicked on it to read it).

Outside of the publisher, there are a few other metrics you want or might be able to track:

Reference Rate: How often does the article get mentioned, either in spoken conversation with developers or customers? How often does it appear in written prose elsewhere on the Internet? (A search-engine alert can often provide the latter statistic.)

Citation Rate: In some circles, the article may appear as a citation in academic papers/publishing, and certain systems track how often it is cited in other works. It may be useful to create a relationship with these citation websites in order to obtain the citation rate for your article.

Lastly, look for ways to identify how many "new-to-you" readers are reading your Articles; in other words, how many unique readers can your metrics systems identify that have read the Article but had never read anything on (or even visited!) your company's website prior to reading the Article?

Call-to-Action: A CTA appearing somewhere in the Article (if appropriate) offering an easy way to get started or a link to a **Tutorial (451)** for more information can each be ways to capture numbers of new readers interested in your product/service. Although the click-through rate (through the CTA) will typically be low, it is a firm indication of interest, as it is entirely "opt-in" and specifically providing more information about your product/service, company, or related topics.

Free trials: One of the classic Marketing techniques, a variation of the Call-to-Action is to offer a free trial (of a paid service) or a one-click-download link for readers in the Article. Instead of tracking the clicks on the link, however, the link itself has a code embedded within it that is tied to the Article and indicates specifically the download came from the Article in question. Keep a close eye on your SEO, however—if the Article becomes the first link on Google, recurring visitors to your download pages may find themselves clicking through the "free trial" link as a shortcut way to download the product/service, rather than navigating through your website to find the "official" link(s).

Cross-system reader tracking: Setting up a "shared tracker" between the publisher's site and your web properties is tricky, but can yield exactly the desired result: People who read the Article on the publisher's site and then came to your website. This will probably require some cross-corporate sharing of metrics data, and it won't be entirely accurate, but it can give you a good sense of how well the intended purpose of the Article (reaching new audience) is working.

CHAPTER 4 ARTICLE

Example

An online magazine publisher has approached Dave with an opportunity to write an article for their audience. Dave asks about length, and is told, "This is the Web, we don't really care about length." Dave asks again, to get some guidance on what length to target, and is told, "We're looking for something that will explore a topic in some depth, while being short enough to consume quickly." Dave decides that 4000 words seems to be a reasonable target, since that will allow him to dive deep enough into a topic to walk through some code, but is still short enough to be read in a lunch or on both halves (going in and going home) of a commute.

Dave then considers his topic. The magazine is a "DevOps"-branded publication, but flipping through a few back issues online, Dave notices that there seems to be more "Dev" than "Ops" in the articles that have been published beforehand. Dave asks the publisher, "What's your target audience? More developer-centric, or ops-centric?" The publisher replies that the magazine shifted its focus about five years ago, from a "full-stack Web" orientation to something "more DevOps-ish," which tells Dave that the audience is probably made up primarily of developers with knowledge in JavaScript, both client- and server-side. Additionally, it's entirely likely that these developers were building applications using NodeJS and some of the web-development tools from five to ten years ago, including tools like Webpack. He asks the publisher if an article explaining how Webpack works to combine all of a web application's assets into a single download would be interesting to their audience, and is given an enthusiastic nod.

From here, Dave is on the hook to produce a first draft. Sitting down with his favorite caffeinated beverage and a scratch pad of paper, Dave starts to brainstorm and come up with his "story arc" for the article. He decides that the best approach to take is to assume that the reader has used Webpack before, but really has no idea of what the internals look like. Beginning from a simple example, Dave crafts an outline that takes

CHAPTER 4   ARTICLE

the reader through a few internals steps—backed by examples of what happens at various stages in the pipeline.

Knowing that he wants to iterate, Dave sends a rough draft over to an Engineering colleague of his, Miranda, who's been instrumental in the build pipeline for the web application their company builds. Miranda reads it, and finds that the details Dave is highlighting aren't really ones she had to learn when she was building the pipeline; she suggests instead a few other details that aren't quite as interesting to Dave. But when another of their coworkers, Sam, offers up similar feedback as Miranda's, Dave realizes that it's solid feedback, incorporates those details into the article, and puts an introduction paragraph and summary paragraph on it.

While in conversation with his boss, Dave mentions the article, and the boss worries that there could be some internal blowback from the Marketing department, since they were planning to do a strong "push" around the product in a month. The boss tells Dave to run it past Marketing, "just to be safe," and muttering a bit under his breath, Dave complies. The Marketing folks are delighted, however, and ask for more details about the publication date so that they can include it in their push. A little elated that the Marketing folks liked it, Dave obtains the details from the publisher and makes an intro, which makes both the Marketing team and the publisher happy, since now there's possibly other ways the two would like to collaborate (such as spending money on ads).

Finally, internal notifications satisfied, Dave sends it off to the publisher for copyedit and review. The copyeditor comes back with a few edits, and in one case Dave feels the change obscures the intent of his sentence rather than clarifies. After a brief back-and-forth with the copyeditor, they arrive at a mutually acceptable phrasing, and it's off.

The following week, Dave gets an email from the publisher, talking about the number of views his article is receiving, and asking when they can get another one from him, maybe something on "the DevOps of NextJS," maybe next month?

Consequences

One of the key outcomes of an Article is that of gaining mindshare with new audiences—after all, why publish with a third party online if their audience is no different than those who are already coming to your website on a regular basis? This should guide everything about the Article, from the topic selected (make sure to select something that isn't niche and/or only recognizable to those who already know your product/service) to the publishing platform selected (take care not to publish an "introductory" article to a website filled with developers who are already wildly familiar with your product/service).

Ensure that the Article takes great care to adhere to at least some level of vendor neutrality; that is, the Article should cover a particular technical topic, and not serve as a sales piece exhorting the great features of your company's product/service. Like a **Conference Session (197)**, developers read Articles not to be persuaded to buy a particular product, but to learn something new about a topic in which they have interest (or a need) to learn. Heavy-handed sales tactics will have the opposite of the desired effect (scarring your brand with your intended audience), and even light sales tactics can trigger the same reaction. If the topic is one that is core to your product/service, use your product/service solely as a vehicle for demonstrations, and make sure the demo highlights the concept, not the product/service. If unsure, do a mental rewrite of the Article with a competitor's product/service instead—does the Article still hold up? Certainly, it might be that your Article is discussing a feature that no competitor's product/service currently has, but in that case, could the Article be written to describe how one might build that feature using the competitor's product/service? It's a crude test, but it can help to avoid writing inauthentic "clickbait" articles that intend nothing more than to lead the reader to your product/service (and annoy them along the way).

CHAPTER 4   ARTICLE

The publisher will often want either exclusive ownership or shared ownership (with an exclusivity clause) that could prevent the use of the article in other scenarios, such as a **Blog Post (105)** or **Book (121)**. Some publishers will provide a clause that allows the company to re-publish the article on their own web properties after a certain period of time has passed (1–3 months is common) but often will not provide this unless asked. Most publishers will also look for some form of contract to be signed, which may require legal review.

When the article is published, make sure to provide traffic to the publisher's site by using **Social Media (395)** to advertise its publication to your known audience, as they may have interests in that area as well. It is reasonable to ask the publisher for metrics around your article, such as common Web metrics like page views or time-on-page, or current distribution for print media. Most publishers will be very willing to share what metrics and demographic data they have, particularly if they see an opportunity to sell some advertising space.

Once written, the article may atrophy over time as the product/service deviates from what was written about it at the time of the article's publication; ideally, the publisher will be willing to allow for edits to the article to bring it up to date, but this will be effort that is entirely up to the company to provide. Because of this atrophy risk, articles should always be prominently dated so readers can get a sense of how "stale" the code or details described in the article are. **Blog Posts (105)** can also often be used to describe the changes between the article's publication and current-state, although finding ways to get the article and the blog post "connected" can be tricky.

The topic, if large enough, can often be the centerpiece of a **Conference Session (197)**, though typically an article will be too short to fill a 45–50 minute session, and will need expansion.

Variants

White Paper: If the article is written by somebody at the company and used as part of the company's marketing or sales efforts, it is often called a "white paper." White Papers will often be longer, more detailed, and convey a larger point than a typical Article, and are often written with a much more technical voice than a (typically) more casual Article.

CHAPTER 5

Blog Post

Topics: *Writing, Code*

A blog post, a written piece of content published on a website, is a powerful tool for the Developer Relations team to connect with the developer community. It's a platform where we share technical insights, tutorials, updates on products or technologies, and opinions on industry trends.

Blog posts are not just about educating and informing, they are about engaging our readers, providing developers with detailed explanations, examples, and valuable resources. They are an accessible way to reach a broad audience, offering short, timely updates and in-depth explorations of complex subjects. More than that, they are a means to connect and involve the developer community in a shared journey of innovation and learning.

CHAPTER 5   BLOG POST

Also Known As

Blog posts are often deemed synonymous with articles, tutorials, technical write-ups, developer updates, knowledge base entries, tech notes, insights, posts, developer guides, and documentation entries. These terms can be used interchangeably (outside of this book, anyway), as all of them serve the purpose of sharing valuable content with the developer community.

Intent

A blog post aims to communicate complex technical concepts in an accessible and digestible format, helping developers understand and apply new tools, technologies, or best practices. It also builds and strengthens community relationships by addressing their needs, answering common questions, and sparking discussions around emerging trends and challenges. Additionally, blog posts can be used to showcase the expertise of the company or its developer advocates, positioning them as thought leaders in the industry. Consistent and well-crafted blog posts aim to enhance the community's knowledge, foster trust, and encourage deeper interaction with the company's products and services.

Context

The author of a blog post must understand the current industry landscape, technological advancements, and common challenges developers face. They should also be aware of the target audience's specific pain points, questions, and interests.

Blog posts are often written in response to new product releases, updates, or trends, providing timely information that helps developers stay informed and make the most of the tools and technologies available. The content is technical in nature, but crafted in a way that balances depth with clarity, ensuring it is helpful to both seasoned developers and those who are newer to the field. In this context, the blog post bridges the company and the developer community, facilitating knowledge sharing and ongoing engagement.

Solution

Create well-researched, clear, and engaging content that effectively addresses the specific needs and interests of the developer community. The content should provide actionable insights, practical solutions, and in-depth explanations that help developers solve problems, learn new skills, or understand complex concepts. This involves structuring the post logically, with a clear introduction that sets the context, a detailed body that explores the topic, and a conclusion that summarizes crucial takeaways or provides further resources. The tone should be informative and approachable, balancing technical accuracy with readability. Visual aids like code snippets, diagrams, screenshots, or videos can enhance understanding and engagement. The blog post should also include clear calls to action, encouraging readers to try out a product feature, participate in a discussion, or explore additional resources. By delivering valuable content consistently, the blog post helps build trust, foster community engagement, and position the company as a thought leader in the industry. Consistency is key. It's better to publish good content often, than amazing content periodically.

Participants

The participants in a blog post for the Blog Post pattern include the **article author(s)**, **copy editor(s)**, **developer community**, and the author's/team's **company or organization**.

The **Article Editor(s)**, who are typically developer advocates, technical writers, or subject matter experts, bring their deep knowledge and expertise to create the content. They interact with the topic by researching, writing, and structuring the post to address specific issues or interests of the developer community.

The **Copy Editor(s)** review the content to ensure clarity, accuracy, and alignment with the company's tone and messaging. They provide feedback and may suggest revisions to improve the post's quality and effectiveness.

The **Developer Community**, as the primary audience for the blog post, is not just a passive reader. They are the heart of the process, actively engaging with the content, reading, sharing, and applying the information provided. Their interaction often extends to comments or discussions, where they ask questions, provide feedback, or share their own insights, contributing to a vibrant dialogue around the topic. This feedback loop is instrumental in helping the author(s) understand the community's needs and refine future content.

The **company or organization**, as the platform provider, has clear and strategic goals for the blog post. These goals could range from promoting a new product, driving traffic to the website, or enhancing brand visibility. They interact by publishing the post on their blog or developer portal, promoting it through various channels like social media, newsletters, or developer forums, and monitoring its performance to measure engagement and impact.

Implementation

The process begins with **topic selection**, where the author (or some other stakeholder) identifies a relevant subject—this can be based on current industry trends, common challenges developers face, or new updates related to the company's products or services. This stage often involves researching popular queries, feedback from the developer community, and internal discussions with product teams to determine the most timely and impactful topics.

Successful blog strategies establish a regular **cadence** for posts. Publishing blog posts on a consistent schedule, such as once a week, creates predictability for the audience, keeping them engaged and returning for more content. This predictability not only keeps the audience engaged but also makes them feel secure in knowing when to expect new content. Frequent posts also help maintain the blog's visibility and improve search engine optimization (SEO), as regularly updated content is more likely to rank higher in search results. A steady cadence shows that the Developer Relations team is active and committed to providing value to the developer community, fostering trust and ongoing engagement.

Once the topic is selected, the next step is **content planning**. This involves outlining the key points to be covered in the blog post, determining the structure of the content, and deciding on the most effective way to present the information. The author should consider the target audience's technical proficiency, ensuring the content is appropriately detailed and straightforward. At this stage, the author may also gather resources such as data, code snippets, diagrams, or screenshots that will be used to support the content.

To enhance the impact of regular content, organizing **blog posts around thematic periods** is also beneficial. This approach not only provides a cohesive narrative but also keeps the audience informed and engaged. For example, the team might focus on a specific monthly theme, such as "Optimizing Cloud Infrastructure" or "Modern DevOps Practices." This thematic approach encourages readers to follow along, knowing the content will build on previous posts within the same theme. Additionally, having a theme allows the team to explore topics in greater depth, offering tutorials, case studies, interviews, and insights that all contribute to a broader understanding of the subject. It creates a more immersive experience for the audience, who can expect a comprehensive exploration of each theme over the designated period.

CHAPTER 5   BLOG POST

Following the planning stage, the **writing phase** begins. The author drafts the blog post with an engaging introduction that sets the context and explains the topic's relevance. The body of the post should be well-organized, with clear headings and subheadings that guide the reader through the content. Practical examples, such as code snippets or case studies, should accompany technical explanations to illustrate key concepts. Visual aids like diagrams, flowcharts, or videos can be integrated to enhance understanding. The writing should be clear and concise, and jargon should be avoided unless it's clearly explained, ensuring the post is accessible to a broad audience.

Once the draft is complete, it enters the **editing and review** phase. During this stage, the post is reviewed by editors or peer reviewers who check for clarity, accuracy, and coherence. They may suggest revisions to improve the post's readability or to ensure it aligns with the company's messaging and tone. Technical accuracy is critical in developer-focused content, so the review may also involve validating code examples or technical claims. The editing process might include refining the language, tightening the structure, and ensuring that the post flows logically from one point to the next. Editors should also ensure the Blog Post has a strong Call to Action for the readers.

After the content has been finalized, the next step is **publishing and promotion**. The post is uploaded to the company's blog platform, where it is formatted according to the site's standards with appropriate metadata, tags, and links to related content. SEO best practices are applied to the title, headings, and body content to improve the post's visibility in search engines. Once published, the blog post is promoted through various channels such as social media, email newsletters, and developer forums. This promotion is essential for driving traffic to the post and ensuring it reaches the intended audience.

Finally, the **post-publication engagement** phase involves monitoring the blog post's performance and interacting with the developer community. This includes tracking metrics such as page views, time on the page, social shares, and comments. The author or other developer relations team members should actively engage with readers who leave comments or questions, fostering a dialogue that can enhance the value of the post. Feedback gathered from comments or social media can also inform future content creation, helping the team continuously improve their blogging approach.

In addition to contributing to the company's main blog, creating blog posts for an individual member of the DevRel team's personal blog can be highly beneficial. Personal blogs offer a platform for DevRel team members to build their personal brand and establish themselves as thought leaders within the developer community. By writing on topics of personal interest, sharing unique experiences, and offering insights from their career journey, DevRel team members can foster more authentic and direct connections with readers. This not only enhances their credibility but also reflects positively on the company, as readers associate the individual's expertise with the organization they represent. Personal blogs also allow more content style, tone, and focus flexibility, encouraging creativity and a more conversational approach that can resonate deeply with the audience. Furthermore, the personal reach of DevRel members extends the company's influence, attracting different segments of the developer community who may not be reached through the company's official channels, ultimately building a more diverse and engaged following.

Throughout this process, the focus should remain on delivering value to the developer community by providing high-quality, informative, and engaging content that addresses their needs and interests. By following these detailed steps, the blog post can effectively contribute to the company's developer relations strategy, building trust and fostering long-term engagement with the audience.

CHAPTER 5   BLOG POST

Metrics

Since the blog post appears on your own web property, gathering metrics for a blog post will typically be much simpler than doing so for a third-party-published **Article (89)**. However, as much as it may be easier, your choice of metrics will often be smaller, since your blog site will often not have the same level of investment in infrastructure that a publisher's website will want/need.

When documenting the metrics for a blog post created by a developer relations team, it's crucial to track a variety of data points that measure the post's reach, engagement, and overall impact on the target audience. Some of the metrics to consider tracking include

Page views: Most web servers and/or content-management systems (CMS) offer the ability to set up a tracking cookie or "click counter" that can tell you how often the page has been served up to browsers. This is often an overly optimistic metric, as it cannot track whether the user actually *read* the article, only whether the server was requested to send it. It may not be tracking unique views, either, meaning if the user clicks on the link several times, each one will be tracked as a "web view." However, it is one of the simplest metrics to track, and thus often used first before any of the others.

Equally important is tracking the **unique visitors** metric, which offers insight into the number of individual users who have read the post, thereby informing us about the audience size and keeping us well-informed about the blog post's reach.

Time on Page: Some content-management systems are able to track how long the page, once served, remains visible in the browser.

Click-through Rate: If the blog post is linked from a **Newsletter (281)**, you'll want to institute some infrastructure to have some data around how often this article's link was clicked on in the newsletter (which indicates, presumably, that the user is interested in this topic and clicked on it to read it).

Reference Rate: How often does the article get mentioned, either in spoken conversation with developers or customers? How often does it appear in written prose elsewhere on the Internet? A search-engine alert can often provide the latter statistic, and since you are in full control of the server, you can also examine HTTP headers to know "from where" the article was accessed by accessing the HTTP "referrer" header. This will help differentiate between "external" and "internal" referrals, where "external" referrals are those coming from someplace other than your website(s), and worth their weight in gold since they indicate that your blog is gaining some traction/notoriety in the world. The referral doesn't carry any context to it, however, so dedicate some time to following these referrals back to their source so you can see what is being said around the link—not everyone will say nice things, and you may want or need to take steps if the not-nice things being said are serious or grounds for legal action.

Time on page is another important metric, as it reveals how long readers spend on the blog post. A higher average time on the page suggests that readers engage with the content, while a low time on the page might indicate that the content isn't holding their attention. **Bounce rate** should also be monitored; it measures the percentage of visitors who leave the site after viewing the blog post without engaging further. A high bounce rate might suggest that the post's content didn't meet the readers' expectations or needed more compelling calls to action.

Social shares and **referral traffic** are critical metrics for understanding how the blog post is being distributed and discussed across different platforms. Tracking the number of shares on social media platforms like Twitter, LinkedIn, or Facebook can indicate how well the content resonates with the community, making us feel connected to a larger audience. Referral traffic from these platforms can further show how many readers are coming to the blog post from these social shares. **Comments and discussions** on the blog or associated social media posts also provide valuable qualitative insights into how the content is being received and what topics are sparking interest or debate. (They can also be a source of opportunities for terrible people to say terrible things; keep a close eye on these.)

Search engine rankings (SEO) and **click-through rates (CTR)** are vital for understanding the post's visibility in search engines. Monitoring the keywords for which the blog post ranks and the corresponding CTRs helps evaluate the effectiveness of the post's SEO strategy. A high ranking and CTR indicate that the blog post is well-optimized and relevant to the searched queries.

The **conversion rate** is a critical metric if the blog post has specific calls to action, such as encouraging readers to sign up for a newsletter, download a white paper, or try a product demo. Tracking how many readers follow through with these actions provides insight into the post's effectiveness in driving desired outcomes, instilling confidence in the blog post's impact and the success of our strategy.

Analytics tools can gather **audience demographics** such as location, job roles, and industry. This data helps understand whether the blog post reaches the intended audience. It can also inform future content strategies by highlighting the most engaged audience segments.

Backlinks are another valuable metric, representing how many external sites link back to the blog post. This helps with SEO and indicates that other sources find the content credible and valuable enough to reference.

Finally, **post-publication engagement** should be tracked, including follow-up interactions like email responses, further social media discussions, or increased traffic to related blog posts or resources. This metric can provide insight into the long-term impact of the blog post on audience engagement and the overall developer relations strategy.

Citation Rate In some circles, the article may appear as a citation in academic papers/publishing, and certain systems track how often it is cited in other works. It may be useful to create a relationship with these citation websites in order to obtain the citation rate for your article.

All these metrics should be systematically documented in a report that includes quantitative data and qualitative insights. Visualizations like charts and graphs can illustrate trends and key findings. The report should also include a section for analysis, where the metrics are interpreted in the context of the blog post's goals, and recommendations for future content strategies are provided based on the collected data. This comprehensive documentation will enable the developer relations team to evaluate the success of their blog posts, refine their content strategy, and better engage with their target audience.

Example

CodeFlow, specializing in DevOps tools, decides to create a blog post to educate their developer community about a new feature in their continuous integration (CI) platform. The "Smart Build Optimizer" feature is designed to significantly reduce build times by intelligently caching and reusing code segments that haven't changed between builds. The team knows that time efficiency is a critical concern for their audience, so they want to craft a blog post that explains the feature and demonstrates its real-world benefits.

The **blog post's author**, a developer advocate named Sarah, begins by delving deep into the most common challenges developers face with long build times. She meticulously gathers insights from customer feedback, online developer forums, and internal discussions with the product team. Based on this comprehensive research, Sarah decides that the blog post will focus on how the Smart Build Optimizer can help developers save time and resources, making them more productive.

CHAPTER 5   BLOG POST

Sarah then moves into the **content planning** phase. She outlines the blog post with a clear structure: an introduction that discusses the problem of long build times, a section explaining the technical details of the Smart Build Optimizer, a real-world example or case study showing the feature in action, and a conclusion that summarizes the benefits and encourages readers to try the feature themselves. She plans to include code snippets, diagrams, and screenshots to make the explanation as clear and engaging as possible.

With the plan in place, Sarah begins the **writing phase.** She starts with an introduction that immediately connects with the readers by acknowledging the frustration of slow build times and its impact on productivity. She then transitions into a technical explanation of how the Smart Build Optimizer works, breaking down complex concepts into digestible parts. To make the post more engaging, Sarah includes a case study of a development team that reduced their build times by 40% using the new feature. She carefully selects code snippets that illustrate how easy it is to implement the feature, and she includes a diagram showing the optimization process in a visual format. The team's commitment to providing a clear and engaging explanation ensures that the developers feel informed and interested.

Once the initial draft is complete, Sarah sends it to the **editor** for review. The editor, James, goes through the content to ensure that it's clear, accurate, and aligns with the company's tone and messaging. James suggests a few revisions to simplify some of the more technical explanations and to make the call-to-action more prominent. Sarah revises the blog post accordingly, and it goes through a final round of edits before being approved for publication.

The **publishing phase** involves uploading the blog post to CodeFlow's developer blog. Sarah formats the content, ensuring that the images and code snippets are correctly displayed and that the SEO elements, such as the title, meta description, and tags, are optimized for search engines. Once the post is live, the team promotes it through CodeFlow's social media channels, email newsletters, and developer forums.

In the **post-publication phase**, the team closely monitors the blog post's performance. They track metrics such as page views, time on the page, bounce rate, social shares, and comments. They notice that the post has been shared widely on Twitter/X and LinkedIn, and they receive positive feedback from developers who found the case study particularly helpful. Sarah and the team immediately engage with the community by responding to blog and social media comments, answering questions, and thanking readers for their feedback. This responsiveness to feedback ensures that the developers feel heard and respected.

Over the next few weeks, the team sees an increase in the number of users trying out the Smart Build Optimizer, and they attribute much of this success to the blog post. The metrics and community feedback are compiled into a report highlighting the blog post's impact. This report is shared with the product and marketing teams to show the value of content in driving product adoption.

In this example, the blog post is an effective tool for educating the developer community, driving engagement, and encouraging the adoption of a new feature. The success of the post is a result of careful planning, clear communication, and ongoing interaction with the audience, making it a valuable part of CodeFlow's developer relations strategy.

Consequences

If the blog posts are accredited to the author (also known as a "byline"), the community gets the opportunity to get to know the author more directly, creating some brand recognition and familiarity, which in turn helps make the DevRel team more recognizable and approachable to customers and the community. (This will also help with **Conference Session (197)** submissions and can be amplified by highlighting the posts on **Social Media (395)**).

CHAPTER 5   BLOG POST

For the **author**, a well-crafted blog post can enhance their reputation as a knowledgeable and reliable source within the developer community. It can lead to increased visibility, professional recognition, and opportunities to engage further with the community, such as invitations to **Conference Sessions (197)** or contribute to other industry publications like **Books (121)**. However, if the blog post is poorly researched or contains inaccuracies, it can damage the author's credibility and diminish their influence within the community.

For the **Developer Relations team**, a successful blog post can strengthen relationships with the developer audience by providing valuable content that addresses their needs and interests. It can increase engagement with the company's products or services, driving adoption and fostering a loyal user base. The team can also use the blog post as a touchpoint to gather feedback, insights, and ideas from the community, which can inform future content and product development. On the flip side, if the blog post fails to resonate with the audience, it could lead to missed opportunities for engagement or even alienate developers who feel their needs or concerns are not being adequately addressed.

For the **company or organization**, the impact of a blog post extends to brand perception and market positioning. A well-received blog post can enhance the company's reputation as a thought leader and innovator, setting it apart from competitors and building trust with the developer community. It can also contribute to increased traffic to the company's website, improved SEO rankings, and a more substantial online presence. This can translate into tangible business outcomes, such as higher sales, increased customer retention, and stronger partnerships. Conversely, suppose the blog post is poorly executed or perceived as out of touch. In that case, it can harm the company's brand image, losing trust and credibility within the developer community. Additionally, if the content is seen as overly promotional or lacking in value, it could result in decreased engagement and a negative perception of the company's intentions.

CHAPTER 5   BLOG POST

In summary, the consequences of a blog post are far-reaching. They can significantly impact the author's standing, the effectiveness of the Developer Relations team, and the overall reputation and success of the company or organization. The key is to create content that is well-researched, valuable, and aligned with the developer community's needs to ensure positive outcomes for all involved.

Variants

In the **technical tutorial**, this type of blog post provides step-by-step instructions on how to use a specific tool, technology, or feature, often including code snippets, screenshots, and detailed explanations. Tutorials are designed to help developers solve specific problems or learn how to implement new technologies in their projects. If your technical tutorial becomes longer than a blog post, it would be wise to consider making it a full **Tutorial (451)**.

The **Product Announcement**, is a blog post that introduces a new product, feature, or update. These posts typically outline the key benefits, provide an overview of new functionalities, and may include links to further resources, such as documentation or demos. Product announcements are often timed with releases meant to inform and excite the community about what's new.

Thought leadership posts are another variant, where the content focuses on broader industry trends, challenges, or insights. These posts are less about specific products and more about offering expert opinions or predictions on where the industry is headed. Thought leadership posts position the author or company as a forward-thinking leader in the field, helping to build credibility and influence within the developer community.

Interview, "Ask me Anything," or Q&A blog posts are also a popular variant. In these posts, the author interviews an expert, influencer, or key team member, providing readers with insights from experienced voices

CHAPTER 5   BLOG POST

in the industry. These posts can help humanize the brand, share diverse perspectives, and directly offer valuable advice or knowledge from thought leaders.

Roundup posts, another variant, are a time-saving resource. They aggregate and summarize resources, tools, or articles on a particular topic, providing readers with a curated list of the best or most relevant information available. This saves them time and effort in their research, making their reading experience more efficient and productive.

Lastly, **opinion pieces** are blog posts where the author shares their personal views on a specific topic, issue, or trend. These posts are more subjective and can spark discussion or debate within the community. Opinion pieces can generate engagement and encourage readers to think critically about the subject matter.

CHAPTER 6

Book

Topics: *Writing, Code*

A written piece that covers a large subject expansively, usually published through one of the "traditional" tech publishers (Addison-Wesley, O'Reilly, Manning, Apress, and others in this sector). Books typically run 150 to 400 pages in length, though much larger textbooks and shorter, more-focused, books on specific topics are often popular as well.

CHAPTER 6   BOOK

Also Known As

Handbook; Playbook; Manual

Intent

Your product/service is a complex (or deceptively complex—simple to start but complicated beyond the basics) subject and customers are overwhelmed with the options and features listed in your **Reference Documentation (373)**. They are looking for something more comprehensive than a **Guide (243)** or article, with broader scope and depth. You need to get a vast amount of information out into customers' (and potential customers) hands.

Context

The material is relatively stable (requiring less updates due to changes), and the principal aim is to educate and/or explain, with little interactivity or feedback required or needed.

In some cases, the material is complex enough that supporting code samples, in line with the prose, are provided, and need to be larger than a "snippet" in order to get a complex concept across. (For example, explaining the concept of "middleware" in an HTTP stack usually requires demonstrating several files and separate and distinct "middleware agents" to get the concept across.) This means that it may be too complex to get across in a single **Article (89)** or **Blog (105)**, and spreading it across multiples of either will break the flow of understanding for the reader.

Solution

Identify one or two people on the DevRel team who are comfortable with long-form writing, and have them write material to form a book. (Alternatively, the material can come together from a variety of sources, such as internal engineers, but then the one or two people will be editors, rather than authors, bringing all the material together to feel like it is written in one style, and ensuring material does not substantively overlap.) This book can either be self-published (often in electronic form only) by the company, or published through an established publisher for greater reach.

Participants

Writing a book is primarily the responsibility of the **author(s)**, who develop the topics, outline, and chapter breakdown for the book. They may be assisted by one or more **developmental editors** (either at the publisher, your company, or both) who bring some expertise in both the writing and selling of books, but the final responsibility always rests with the author(s). The publisher will typically want or need (or assign) a schedule or timeline for the authoring, typically with several milestones, to ensure the book's development remains on track.

Once the book has reached a point of "written," usually somewhere between 50% and 75%, the publisher may bring in **technical reviewers** to begin to assess the book from both a technical and/or content-approach perspective. Technical reviewers are typically unpaid volunteers who often receive either name recognition in the acknowledgments of the book, and/or free copies of the publisher's other books in exchange for reading the draft manuscript and offering up suggestions to the author about ways to improve the book. Publishers typically welcome additional reviewers suggested by the author, but author(s) should be careful to make sure they suggest reviewers who will work to make the book better—this is not a time to get validation or "feel-good" statements like "Great read!" or "Loving it!" regardless of how good it might feel in the moment. These technical reviewers serve the same purpose as code reviewers do in pull requests, so feedback should be concrete, specific, targeted, and widespread.

Once the manuscript has reached a "100% draft" state, it is submitted to **copyeditors** for an editorial pass to correct for any grammatical or structural mistakes, and from there to **layout** for preparation for printing. (Books that are laid out are often referred to as "camera-ready" for historical purposes.) Author(s) typically are required to do a quick validation of the post-edited manuscript to ensure that the copyeditors haven't accidentally changed the meaning of a sentence, but most professional copyeditors are very good at what they do, and such scenarios are rare.

Implementation

Most books begin with a proposal, which is submitted to the publisher for consideration. Most publishers have a specific template they like to use for creating a book proposal, which is similar but not exactly the same, so each proposal is essentially a publisher-specific exercise. Fortunately, most proposals are one or two pages at most, and intended to not only communicate the author's vision of the book to the publisher, but also ensure that the author has thought through the details to at least some degree.

As part of the proposal, the prospective author must generally sort out several things, either ahead of time (in the proposal) or interactively, in conversation with the publisher. This includes questions about compensation and licensing: Who retains the rights to the book, the author or the company they work for? Is the author allowed to receive royalties directly, or will the company expect to collect the proceeds, especially if the book is written during work hours? These matters often require input from both legal and management teams to determine whether the project is personal, professional, or a mix of both, and to clarify expectations regarding intellectual property ownership, time allocation, and financial benefits.

- **Length:** Books are generally measured in terms of "page count," the number of printed pages in the book. (A printed page is one side of a physical page, so a 400-page book is usually a little bit more than 200 physical pages.) Publishers are generally looking for a book to be between 300 and 500 pages—too short, and it doesn't justify the overhead of printing physical copies, whereas too long means the cost-per-page puts the printed book cost too high for most consumers. While e-books may not have this physical limitation, most publishers still seem to be looking for books of about this same range even for electronic-only publications.

- **Deadline:** Typically the publisher will have some input on this, but in general, this is up to the author(s) to decide. Keep in mind that writing a book is a marathon, not a sprint, and that writing a book is not just the time spent with "fingers on keyboard" but also the time spent staring at the empty screen and feeling zero levels of inspiration. Like most software projects, it's safe to assume that the book will take two-and-a-half times longer than expected.

- **Target audience:** Before writing, consider carefully the target audience. Is the assumed reader somebody familiar with the basics of your product/service? Are they experts? Are they new to your product but familiar with other (perhaps competitor) products? Flesh out a more detailed view of what sort of technical prerequisites they would satisfy once you know their background—for example, a reader of an article on NoSQL databases may or may not have some familiarity with SQL databases, but it's reasonable to assume they know what the (general) concept of a database is and the kinds of behavior one provides. Where the audience has familiarity, don't explain; where they don't have familiarity, go into some (or a lot of) depth on a concept as necessary. As you write more articles and get feedback on the audience's reaction to your articles, refine your understanding of the target audience, so that your writing can be tuned to be appealing to that audience. (How to do this is well beyond the scope of this book, and arguably an intuitive process to boot.)

- **"Voice":** Do you want your prose to sound formal, or informal? Will you speak with the first-person voice ("I want to build this app, so I...") or in the third person ("When developers want to build an app, they need to..."), or will you look to the second-person voice, as this book does? Do you want to try to incorporate humor, or keep it "professional"? As part of your target audience consideration, consider some demographic information as well, and how that might affect your voice; in the 2020s, for example, references to terms like "sus" and "lit" will be recognizable to the 20-somethings in your audience, but terms like "super bad" and "groovy" may only feel comfortable to the 50-somethings, or even 60-somethings. Likewise, consider avoiding turns-of-phrase that are regional or cultural (such as the infamous British "Bob's your uncle"), as they may not translate well into other cultures or if/when your article is translated into foreign languages. Note also that if there are multiple authors on the book, the authors must try to "unify" their voices somewhat, or it will be jarring to readers. (Good editors can help a great deal with this, but the closer the authors can be to one another, the easier it will be to smooth over the rough edges.)

- **Outline or story:** Most professionals who have been through primary education have had the experience of writing an essay that required an outline first. The purpose, we are told, is that this outline will help provide structure and clarity to the essay, so that the essay can be sharp and crisp and focused on the topic at hand. Sometimes, however, primary education loses sight of the forest for the trees: the goal is to have a clear picture in the author's mind of what is being written, and the actual format or structure of the outline is irrelevant, so long as it creates clarity in the author's mind. To this end, "mind maps" are another technique for structuring thought, as are "stories" or "storytelling"; frankly, the possibilities here are endless. As an author, you will want to experiment with different mechanisms until you find one that resonates with you, always with the goal of clarity firmly in mind. When in doubt, fall back to the Aristotelian form that was taught in school: "Introduce the topic, provide three different interesting things about the topic, conclude by explaining how these three things combine." In the case of a book, it becomes even more critical to keep a sharp eye on what the book is about, as it will be (very) easy to keep adding things into the book and "lose" the original point or direction. Creating a solid outline and focus for the book will be extremely helpful later when deciding what material can or should be cut.

If accepted, the publisher and author negotiate a contract around royalties and such. Depending on how much the company is involved in the effort, the publisher may wish to extract some guarantees about book sales (in terms of the company purchasing a set number of books up front, usually for **Swag (427)** purposes), and/or the company may have some concerns about author(s) receiving money for work being done on company time. Those will likely be details that need to be worked out by management and your company's legal team.

Once the contract is signed, the author(s) are more or less on their own to produce the manuscript. Some publishers will have a predefined process or set of tools to use for submitting the manuscript, but much of the time any decisions around which tools to use to author (Markdown, GitBook, Microsoft Word, etc.) are up to the author(s) so long as the submitted content is in the publisher-preferred format. (This book, by way of example, was authored entirely in Markdown using Git and VS Code until it was poured into Word .DOCX files for submission.)

The publisher will often have milestone checkpoints along the way to ensure that the work continues, but for the most part the publisher typically "stays out of the way" of the author(s) until either a manuscript is ready or the publisher is worried the effort is being abandoned.

Once the manuscript is "draft ready," the author(s) hand it off to the publisher for technical review and copyedit. This is typically done either one right after the other or in parallel, after which the author(s) receive an edited copy of the manuscript requiring author examination. Author(s) will need to go through the manuscript and for any changes made directly to the prose, either approve or disapprove (and refactor) the change, taking into account any notes from reviewers or copyeditors. Many changes will be grammatical and/or structural, in keeping with publisher style standards, but it is not uncommon for reviewers to have questions or suggest clarifications that will require deeper consideration.

Once the author(s) have handed back the review copy, the process is almost entirely in the publisher's hands at that point. The manuscript will get laid out, printed, and shipped. Typically the author(s) will get some number of copies ("author copies") to give away to friends and/or family, which is the first sign author(s) have that the book is about to "hit the shelves."

Metrics

By far and away, the biggest book metric is that of sales—how many copies are sold? After all, this is what drives the New York Times Bestseller list, and most book metrics tend to follow this trend.

Beyond this, however, depending on what you're doing with the book, other metrics can be applicable.

- **Downloads:** For example, many books are self-published and hosted on your company's website, so download numbers can provide a sense of the interest in the book, particularly if there's a means by which your company can track unique downloads. That is, if a particular individual downloads the book ten times, you want to know that rather than thinking that ten different people are all interested in the book. This helps avoid drawing incorrect inference from your download numbers.

- **Mentions:** Once the book is out (or just before it comes out), set up a search engine alert for particular phrases from the book, the author's name(s), or links back to the download page for the book. This will help track the number of times the book is brought up in "casual conversation" across the Internet, which helps identify the degree to which the material is permeating the community.

- **Giveaways:** Grab a number of copies and take them with you to **User Group (457)** meetings, **Conference Sessions (197)**, and/or the **Booth (137)** when the author is speaking there. Watch how quickly you can give the books away, and if recipients look to have the book autographed by the author. Some conferences will even look to set up book signings by the author, if the book is popular enough.

Example

After his success writing several **Articles (89)**, Dave has gotten "the itch" to write a book on his company's new service, particularly since he keeps getting questions about how to get started with it when he is out doing **Conference Sessions (197)** and **Workshops (477)**. He sits down to work out a proposal for a roughly 450-page book—he thinks it will be roughly 18 chapters, taking readers who are brand new to the service through the basics (part 1), into some commonly used features (part 2), and then into some interesting "advanced" capabilities that not every company will be interested in (part 3). Feeling pretty excited, he contacts several publishers (Apress, Manning, O'Reilly, and Pragmatic Bookshelf to name a few) using contact information he finds on each company's website.

Thus, he is beyond elated with two of the publishers respond to his proposal with requests for meetings. In meeting with both, he finds that one publisher somewhat misunderstood his general vision for the book, and although they have a pleasant conversation ("Keep us in mind for any future projects!") they mutually decide to part ways. The second conversation goes much more smoothly, as the publisher has been idly wondering about publishing a book on his company's service, and they like where Dave is going with this. The acquisition editor agrees to take the proposal before their internal review board, and get back to him within a week or two with a response. Dave spends the next ten days somewhat "on edge" while waiting for a response, which comes in the form of an email expressing acceptance and a request to set up a meeting to go over more details and get a contract signed.

From here, Dave is on the hook to produce a first draft. Knowing that this is not going to come in a short period of time, Dave and his manager Keisha have a long conversation about how to structure his time so that the book can be "draft-ready" in the six months he and the publisher discussed. (An author herself, Keisha is a little doubtful that six months is even close to realistic, but chooses not to try and talk Dave out of it, knowing that publishers sometimes agree to aggressive delivery dates but expect some slippage.) They agree that Dave will take Mondays and Fridays as "book time," and will continue to focus on his other team-centric duties on Tuesdays through Thursdays. He has permission to refuse any meetings on Mondays and Fridays, and Keisha works out a plan where Dave will provide drafts of chapters to the team as a whole, so that he can get some feedback from a friendly audience (and allows Keisha to follow his progress and potentially adjust expectations, both Dave's and the company's, as the realities of book-writing become more clear).

At first, Dave is over the moon, and dives into writing with gusto and enthusiasm. The team is supportive, moving to cover Dave's absence during any Monday or Friday meetings, and he in turn is quick to share what he's working on, even going so far as to invite his teammates and Keisha into his private GitHub repository where he's working on the book. (Dave read somewhere that using Markdown to write the early drafts and using a version control system like GitHub makes it much easier than trying to write in Word.) He gets some good feedback—in the form of pull requests, of course—and the first month or two fly by. First one chapter, then another, and he sends both off to the publisher (after getting the feedback from the team and Keisha) for good measure.

After that, however, Dave begins to struggle, finding the energy and willpower to write is a lot harder to maintain over time. His friends and family begin to tease him about how he's always unavailable for concerts or family outings, and he finds himself often staring at the empty editor screen trying to figure out how to get started on a chapter without sounding too abrupt, too terse, or too… lame. He falls behind his self-imposed cadence of chapter writing, and after a month with little to no progress, he reaches out to Keisha for a 1-on-1 on the book.

When they meet, Keisha is both sympathetic and ruthless. "I understand where you're coming from, I've been there. But I also know that writer's block is something you have to force yourself through—there's really nothing anybody can do to help you get past it." She does offer some tips—"Remember that you don't always have to write a chapter in the same order people read it; write the introduction or opening paragraphs later, after you've written the rest of the chapter, if you have to" particularly strikes him as profound yet obvious—and they decide to meet once every other week in a 1-on-1 that's specific to the book. Armed with this new surge of engagement, Dave jumps back into the writing with more determination, and finds a few of Keisha's tips incredibly helpful in breaking through the writer's block.

Despite that, though, Dave finds that he's only about halfway done with the book when he hits the six-month target date, and sheepishly has to inform the publisher that he hasn't hit his goal. The publisher is not surprised at all—"We thought six months was a little on the aggressive side"—and they are pleased with the eight chapters he's provided so far. They agree to another three-to-six months (Dave thinks three, the publisher six) and Dave goes back to writing.

As the five-month-mark approaches, Dave finds himself figuratively running uphill, devoting weekends and late nights to furiously pounding away at the keyboard. The book has progressed from exciting to frustrating to overwhelming to grim determination, and Dave marvels at the idea that anyone would ever actually do this twice. Finally, though, just two weeks shy of the one-year anniversary of the contract signing, Dave sends off the final chapter to the publisher, and Keisha takes Dave and his team out to the local brew pub to celebrate.

At one point in the evening, when Dave remarks how he's "glad to be done with the whole thing," Keisha laughs. "Oh, you're not done, Dave, not yet." When he looks on in surprise, she smiles. "Well, now the publisher's going to copyedit it, but you've got to find some reviewers, go over the copyedited manuscript to make sure their edits didn't accidentally change a sentence's meaning, make sure your code samples are accessible, approve any graphics the publisher comes up with for the diagrams in the book, and then," she clinks her glass to his, "You can write the Acknowledgements in the front matter and wait for the printed copies to show up at your doorstep."

Dave sighs. "Now I understand why every book's Introduction is filled with all these gratitude statements to everybody around the author. I used to think it was just polite, but…" He shakes his head, then looks up at Keisha. "And you've done three of these?", he asks in wonder.

Keisha laughs. "Four. I just signed a contract to do another one. Maybe you want to co-author?" she asks with a twinkle in her eye.

CHAPTER 6 BOOK

Consequences

The cost of writing a book is extremely high to the author, often requiring a full-time effort for many months, leaving zero bandwidth to participate in many of the other activities. The author's brand recognition and credibility will improve after the book's publication, however, and being a named author on a book often opens doors for the author and the company due solely to its existence.

The publication of a book on a topic is often considered a mark of maturity on that topic, as it implies that the topic has remained relevant (and useful) enough to merit the time, energy, and financial commitments necessary to the creation of a book on the topic. As such, many new technologies often seek to "bootstrap" the maturity of their new offering by having project core committers put documentation together into a collection that becomes known as "The Book" to its early adherents.

Customer commitment to consuming a book is non-trivial, as most books require days to read, even without distractions, and most will require weeks or months given a typical day and commitments. The content must be worth the investment, or the reputation will be negative rather than positive. For this reason, books should be reviewed by subject-matter-experts to ensure its accuracy, and the book should be written to have some "longevity" beyond the current product/service release.

Books written by the DevRel team act as a much broader and deeper **Guide (243)** and can go into depth and detail that is often not possible otherwise.

Books written by **Ambassadors (71)** instead of the DevRel team members can be very beneficial to both company and Ambassador; the Ambassador improves their own branding within the community (which is good for them), and the company sees deeper technical content distributed to the community without requiring a large time investment from their DevRel team or internal engineers. Usually the DevRel team and/or internal engineers will need (and want!) to be a part of the editing team, however, to ensure that the material is correct and/or in line with the company's messaging and future plans.

Books are popular as **Swag (427)**. Book excerpts can be used as **Articles (89)** and/or **Blog Posts (105)**. Books are also highly eye-catching and credibility-building when displayed at the **Booth (137)** and/or used in **Customer Pre-Sale Meetings (223)**, particularly if written by somebody on the DevRel team. (On a related note, when challenged on a particular point within the topic, nothing is more satisfying than to pull out a copy of the book, toss it on the table, and say, "Why should you believe me? Because I wrote the book on the subject.") To make the most of these opportunities, ensure that your employer has a designated budget for purchasing copies to distribute. Securing this support ahead of time helps avoid the common frustration of having to manage and fund giveaways on your own. This way, you can use books strategically as part of your outreach and advocacy efforts.

Variants

- **E-book:** As phones (and later, tablets) became more ubiquitous devices in the hands of consumers, Amazon and other booksellers pushed harder on the notion of digital-only copies of published works. As a result, it has become more fashionable for digital-only works, known as "electronic books" or "e-books," to be available. These are much more likely to be available as free downloads, often as a reward for signing up for a webinar. They typically run much shorter (though still much longer than an **Article (89)** or **Blog Post (105)**) but still go through much the same publication process as their analog cousins, and several publishers have "joined forces" with companies to produce company-specific publisher-processed books that are used by both publisher and company as digital **Swag (427)**.

- **Internal book:** Although less common, some books are written for internal consumption within the company, rather than put through a formal publishing process for external use. As an example, during the early days of .NET, Microsoft developers working on the virtual machine (the Common Language Runtime) began collecting documentation together into what came to be known as "the Book of the Runtime" (or BotR, for short). This became a deeply valuable resource for new developers joining the CLR team, as well as those .NET developers outside the company (after .NET became open-sourced) who wanted to learn more about the CLR's inner workings.

CHAPTER 7

Booth

Topics: *Budget, Presentation*

Purchase space on an event's "vendor floor" where you can "pitch a tent" for attendees to wander by and be engaged.

CHAPTER 7   BOOTH

Also Known As

Conference Booth, Floor Presence, Tech Expo Stand

Intent

To create an engaging and informative space at developer conferences that allows attendees to interact with company representatives, get firsthand information about products/services, and strengthen the bond between the brand and the developer community.

Context

The company wants to be present at an event that brings many people together under the umbrella of a particular identity (i.e., a tech-stack-centric conference) or region (i.e., a community event run for the immediate surrounding geographic area) or brand (i.e., a "destination" conference held in a popular city, like Las Vegas or Orlando), to connect with current and potential customers in a more interactive way.

Solution

You purchase booth space at a conference (or other event), and send a team to staff the booth during the conference's run. During that time, the booth team answers questions, hands out **Swag (427)**, potentially obtains the email or other contact information of possible buyers, and in general tries to leave a positive impression of the company and its product/service in the minds of those who attend the conference.

Participants

Successful booth runs will involve a number of different participants:

- The **booth staff** are the frontline representatives of the company, trained to engage effectively with attendees, answer their questions, and provide a welcoming and informative experience. They are pivotal in creating a positive impression of the brand. They will often be a mix of several different groups within the company: Marketing folks (who can help design and operate the booth itself—the signage, a table covering, and so on), Sales folks (many of whom will be operating the booth and answering questions), Engineering folks (who will often be operating the booth and answering questions), and/or Product folks (who will be able to speak to the features and direction of the product/service).

- **demo presenters** are subject matter experts (often from Engineering, though not always) who are tasked with conducting live demonstrations of the company's products or services. Their expertise not only showcases the technical merits of the offerings but also educates and excites the audience about the potential applications.

- The **logistics team** is the backbone of the booth's physical presence, handling the setup, teardown, and ensuring that everything operates smoothly throughout the event. This includes managing the technical equipment, ensuring the booth is well-stocked with materials, and addressing any unforeseen issues that may arise.

- Outside your company, the **attendees** are the conference-goers who visit the booth, engaging with the staff, participating in demos, and providing the feedback and interactions that are vital for the company to understand its market presence and user expectations.

It's highly likely that a given physical individual at the booth will occupy multiple roles, particularly in smaller organizations, as its very common for booth staff to also be demo presenters, and often the logistical team is in fact a single individual who is part of the booth staff during the conference.

Implementation

Participation in a conference event will often require somebody to be a point of contact for the conference; materials (such as the booth itself, printed handouts, any **Swag (427)**, and so on) will need to be shipped to the event, schedules will need to be coordinated, and so on. This is a non-trivial commitment of time and energy, particularly so as the conference gets bigger (it's a much larger commitment of time to have a booth at AWS re:Invent than at a 250-person local community conference). It will often be useful or necessary to have a single person serve as the "event coordinator" for that particular event instance, and this is often a full-time position within firms that run booths at multiple events per year.

Start with **booth design**, focusing on solid branding elements like banners and handouts, and incorporate interactive features such as screens and hands-on stations to facilitate attendee engagement. The decision on booth size—large for significant presence and high traffic at major events or small for intimate, quality interactions at niche gatherings—should align with the company's event goals, budget, and target audience. A well-designed booth, irrespective of size, should

CHAPTER 7   BOOTH

be inviting, reflect the brand identity, and facilitate interactions that strengthen community ties and enhance market penetration. Effective booths encourage meaningful conversations and feature engaging, interactive elements that resonate with developers, providing a memorable experience that can significantly impact developer relations and market positioning.

The **booth position** on the floor of the event impacts the success of the **sponsoring (405)** purpose and is inherently tied to the conference's foot traffic and relevance; if the booth does not attract the right audience or suffers from low attendance, its effectiveness and potential return on investment may significantly diminish.

Logistically, **booth setup and teardown** involves transportation, setup, and possibly dismantling hurdles, which can be resource-intensive and require meticulous planning. This process demands careful allocation of financial, human, and material resources to ensure a successful presence.

booth demonstrations deserve dedicated focus as one of the most powerful tools for drawing interest and delivering value in a short span of time. A strong demo not only showcases what the product does but also tells a compelling story, explaining why it matters, how it solves real-world problems, and what makes it unique. Ideally, demos should be short, engaging, and tailored to the audience at the event, whether it's developers, decision-makers, or curious passersby. Consider scripting the demo with checkpoints for live interaction, questions, or even surprise outcomes. Rehearsals are critical; the demo should run smoothly and be ready for anything from dropped Wi-Fi to skeptical attendees. Having a simplified "starter" version available for hands-on exploration after the demo can also invite deeper engagement. Ensure the demo presenter possesses both technical expertise and the ability to engage a crowd. A great booth demo can spark memorable conversations and turn casual interest into real leads.

CHAPTER 7   BOOTH

engagement activities at event booths are pivotal in capturing and maintaining the interest of attendees, comprising diverse, interactive elements such as product demos, gaming stations, and pre-recorded videos. Product demos offer hands-on experiences with new or existing products, allowing attendees to see the practical application of technologies firsthand. Gaming systems can provide a fun, competitive atmosphere, often related to the company's industry or products, engaging attendees in a memorable way. Pre-recorded videos are useful for demonstrating product features or company milestones in a visually engaging format, especially when live presentations aren't feasible. Additionally, celebrity appearances or talks by industry influencers can draw larger crowds, adding a unique appeal and potentially increasing booth traffic significantly (but often at greater cost). Each of these activities is designed to enhance visitor engagement, making the booth a dynamic and must-visit location within the event.

Event booth **feedback mechanism** are essential for gathering actionable insights from attendees, utilizing tools such as digital surveys, feedback forms, and interactive kiosks. Organizers often encourage visitors to provide real-time feedback on their experience, discussions at the booth, and product interactions by offering incentives such as giveaways or entry into a prize draw. Questions typically focus on the user's experience with the booth activities, their perception of the product demos, and general impressions of the brand. Collecting contact information allows for follow-up discussions and continued engagement. After the event, the marketing and product development teams should systematically compile and analyze this data to evaluate the booth's effectiveness and refine future strategies and product enhancements based on attendee feedback. This continuous feedback loop and improvement are crucial for evolving the company's offerings and enhancing customer satisfaction.

Capturing **attendee information** is one of the most critical aspects of the booth, since this will be how the company generates "leads" of potential buyers/consumers of your product/service. Many booths will operate on a quasi-formal "barter/swap" system: Company **Swag (427)** in exchange for attendee information. This information will need to be gathered swiftly from attendees during their time at the booth, since attendees often are in a very "low-tolerance-to-delay" mindset while visiting. Keep in mind, too, that many conferences will have some form of automation (such as QR codes on the printed conference badges) and/or provide a list of all registered attendees to vendors, so make sure to check with the conference staff before deciding on how your company will engage with attendees on this.

Lastly, **staff training** is paramount to ensure that your team can effectively discuss product details and engage with booth visitors. Staff should possess deep product knowledge and be trained in engagement practices, ensuring that every attendee interaction is positive and informative. This holistic approach ensures that your conference booth captivates attention and fosters meaningful connections with the developer community. Above all, staff should be prepared to be polite and courteous, even in the face of disinterest or ambivalence to the product—often developers "cruise" the expo/vendor floor simply as a way to see what's going on or being released (or sometimes just to collect swag), and have no direct interest in the product itself. This is normal, and if the interest isn't there, shouldn't be forced.

Operating the booth is a non-trivial time commitment; ideally, there should never be fewer than two people at the booth while the "vendor floor" is open (typically a 12-hour time frame), so three or four people will be needed during each day of the conference. This number will go up as the size of the booth goes up, just to make sure that there are "eyes open" all over the booth to pick up on any visitors to the booth who might have questions but don't want to interrupt someone if they look like they are busy with something else.

Additionally, while **Swag (427)** will often be of help to draw initial interest to the booth, do not be surprised when developers stop by just for the swag. In fact, some developers have been known to collect T-shirts and other clothing from conferences solely to avoid having to go shopping for clothes.

When the event is over, materials (such as the booth frame and/or branded table covering, as well as any remaining handout materials) must be shipped back to the company—venue staff will not take care of that for you. Many of these materials and/or their packaging will be quite large and bulky or heavy, so expectations of "the booth staff can just bring it home with them on the plane" are quite impossible and/or unreasonable.

The **post-event report** for a booth at a conference or event should capture the positive and negative feedback about the company's products and services. On the positive side, the report should highlight areas where attendees showed strong interest, such as specific features or solutions that resonated with the audience, leading to meaningful discussions or potential leads. It should also document successful demonstrations or engagements that boosted the company's reputation. On the negative side, the report must address any recurring concerns or challenges that attendees raised, such as difficulties in understanding certain functionalities, perceived gaps in the product, or areas where competitors were favored. This feedback provides valuable insights the company can use to refine its offerings and approach. It's crucial to ensure that future booth engagements and product development align more closely with the audience's needs, as this will make the company's offerings more relevant and competitive.

The booth team should always **act professional and approachable**, staying off their phones and avoiding standing in huddles with peers that could appear unwelcoming to visitors. Smiling and maintaining open body language helps draw people in, creating an inviting atmosphere. Each team member should have a solid opening line, such as "Can I show you a quick demo of something I'm loving right now?" to initiate conversations in an engaging manner. In the event they encounter questions they cannot answer, they should feel confident in redirecting visitors to the appropriate person or resource, ensuring that the visitor feels their inquiry is valued and will be addressed effectively. This approach encourages interaction, fosters connections, and leaves a positive impression of the company.

Metrics

Booth metrics are a combination of immediate and delayed numbers: immediate, in that you can track some of them in real time as time at the conference passes, and delayed, in that some of them will take months to resolve.

Immediate metrics include

- **Visitor Count:** One of the simplest/easiest metrics to track is a simple count of people who've come to the booth. You can track this metric as either "people who've stopped to at least look," "people who've stopped to ask a question," or "people who've agreed to give us their email or other contact information," depending on the degree of interactivity you're interested in from the metric. Be careful, however, to keep the number in mind compared to the total attendance of the conference (500 visitors at a show of 1,000 attendees is a great number; 500 visitors at a show of 10,000 attendees, not so much), and keep in mind that some number of those might be repeat visits. Most conferences give attendees a QR code on their badge that you can scan (with the attendee's permission, of course), which is not only a means to avoid duplicates, but also a good way to let attendees "opt-in" to receiving more information about your company's product/service.

CHAPTER 7   BOOTH

- **Swag Count:** Because your booth will often have **Swag (427)** that you want to give away to attendees, one way to informally track the degree of interest in your booth is to keep an eye on the piles of swag—the faster those go away, the more you have people coming by your booth (and taking the swag away with them).

- In addition to traditional metrics such as visitor scans and swag distribution, it's valuable to track the number of **live product demos** performed during the event, as well as the **number of attendees who watch each demo**. This metric provides a more meaningful indicator of genuine product interest, especially when compared to high-level traffic counts that may be skewed by individuals seeking swag. A simple manual tally, clicker, or even a spreadsheet can be used to log demo sessions and estimated viewership throughout each day. Over time, this data can reveal which demo formats, times of day, or messaging strategies resonate most with your audience. They can help you optimize future booth setups and staff training accordingly. Unlike passive visits, demo engagement reflects active curiosity and often signals a higher likelihood of post-event follow-up or conversion.

- **Follow-up Count:** One trailing metric that you can keep an eye on for months after the event is the number of attendees from the show that later come to the website and browse or download the product or sign up for the trial for your service. Tracking this will usually require either the attendee to self-identify, or else go through a link that you've prepared for them which is exclusive to those who were at that conference.

This, in some ways, is a much more meaningful metric, since it tracks not just the people who stopped by your booth to get your snazzy swag but were interested enough to take the time and visit your website and/or explore your product/service after the fact. If you can personalize the links they use, even better, since now you have direct evidence of an individual's interest. (One way to do this is to take all of the opt-in scanned contact information from attendees and create a short **Newsletter (281)** specific to the conference with an auto-generated ID the link to the product/service or website.)

- **Adoption Count:** The final trailing metric is that of the attendee who ends up adopting (as in, paying for) the product/service. Again, tracking this requires no small degree of logistics infrastructure, most notably at the company's CRM (customer relationship management) level—knowing that this customer was at the conference, that they downloaded/signed up from the link provided to them after the conference, and then tracking them all the way through the sales cycle to the final signature. It's powerful information, since it will help correlate conference attendance directly to sales numbers, but it will likely require a deep partnership with both the Sales and Marketing team to coordinate effectively.

CHAPTER 7   BOOTH

Example

DevTech designs its booth with bold branding, featuring large, eye-catching banners with its logo and cloud solution themes. The booth is divided into zones, each dedicated to different aspects of their cloud services—from storage solutions to computing power. Interactive touch screens are placed throughout, allowing attendees to explore DevTech's offerings through videos, tutorials, and live demos. A hands-on station is set up for visitors to try DevTech's cloud services in real time, guided by experts.

Engagement Activities: DevTech schedules hourly live demos, showcasing how their cloud solutions can optimize workflows, enhance data security, and reduce costs. These demos are interactive, with a Q&A segment to engage the audience further. Attendees visiting the booth also receive DevTech-branded swag, including eco-friendly tote bags, reusable water bottles, and USB drives preloaded with trial versions of their software and exclusive access to cloud resources.

Feedback Mechanism: DevTech sets up several tablets around the booth, inviting attendees to complete quick surveys about their cloud service needs and feedback on the demos. These stations are prominently displayed, with signs encouraging visitors to share their thoughts.

Near or inside the booth, a beautifully designed feedback box invites attendees to drop in business cards or feedback cards with their thoughts, suggestions, or contact information for further engagement.

Attendee Information: DevTech encouraged booth visitors to participate in a digital survey accessible via tablets stationed around the booth. Participants are asked about their experiences with the demos, the relevance of the products to their needs, and their overall impression of DevTech. To incentivize participation, they were offered a chance to win a premium software subscription.

Staff Training: DevTech's booth staff undergoes intensive training sessions on the latest cloud solutions and updates to the company's

CHAPTER 7   BOOTH

offerings in the weeks leading up to the conference. They learn to navigate the interactive demos flawlessly and are equipped to answer deep technical questions. Staff are also trained in customer service excellence, learning how to engage booth visitors positively, manage crowded situations gracefully, and tailor their communication style to different types of attendees, from novices to seasoned developers.

Consequences

Note that a company's booth presence does not prevent or assume the company is engaged in **Sponsorship (405)** of the conference; where sponsorship flexes on reach, the booth focuses on interactivity.

A booth allows for direct interaction with the target audience, facilitating personal connections and deeper understanding of user needs. This setting is ideal for gathering real-time feedback and troubleshooting specific user issues, enhancing product understanding and customer satisfaction. Additionally, a well-designed booth can create a lasting visual impact, reinforcing brand identity and product memory among attendees.

Variants

Pit Crew: If the company or the product/service doesn't directly fit the audience of the conference, but you still want a strong "presence" at the event, consider spending the Booth budget on sending some company employees to the event (as attendees) with the intent of "taking the field by storm": simply be out and around, milling on the floor, attending talks and absolutely being present at any **Conference Session (197)** being given by the DevRel team or other company employees. Pit Crew can carry **Swag (427)** around with them (if it's small) and hand it out as they move about the conference, or toss it out during the DevRel's talks

149

CHAPTER 7   BOOTH

("Free T-shirt to anyone who asks a question!"). Be careful not to be too obnoxious about this, though, or the conference organizers (or the vendors that paid for a booth) may get annoyed and want to have a chat.

The pit crew need not (and arguably shouldn't be) members of the DevRel team: sales, recruiters, marketing folks, and anyone who is looking to start speaking at events and/or considering a role as DevRel make for a great Pit Crew, as it allows them to "feel the vibe" of a conference event. Associate Developer Advocates (or anyone at the company who are unfamiliar with developer events) should do a stint or two as Pit Crew before being sent on their own to a conference event.

CHAPTER 8

Case Study

Topics: *Writing, Code*

A case study is a detailed examination of how a specific user, team, or organization successfully implemented a product, service, or technology to achieve their goals. In Developer Relations, a case study focuses on real-world applications, enlightening the audience about the practical benefits and outcomes of using a particular tool or solution. It typically includes background information on the problem or challenge faced, the solution provided, the implementation process, and the results or impact achieved. A case study serves as a powerful narrative that demonstrates the product or service's value, providing other developers or potential customers with insights into how they might achieve similar success.

CHAPTER 8   CASE STUDY

Also Known As

Success story, customer story, use case, implementation story, project profile, application narrative, user story, real-world example, deployment report, and practical example.

Intent

A case study aims to showcase the real-world application and impact of a product, service, or technology by illustrating how a specific user, team, or organization successfully implemented it. The primary goal is to provide concrete evidence of the value and effectiveness of the solution, helping other developers, potential customers, or stakeholders understand its practical benefits and how it can solve similar challenges they may face. A case study aims to build credibility and trust by demonstrating actual results, such as improved efficiency, cost savings, enhanced performance, or successful project outcomes. It also serves as a powerful marketing tool by highlighting the positive experiences of current users, which can influence decision-making and drive adoption among prospective users. By providing detailed insights into the problem-solving process, a case study educates the audience about the product or service, inspires confidence in its capabilities, and encourages others to explore its use in their own contexts.

Context

A case study aims to provide a detailed narrative highlighting how a specific product, service, or technology was utilized to address a particular challenge or achieve a set of goals. Case studies are typically created after a solution has been successfully implemented. They are used to document and share the experience with a broader audience, particularly developers, technical decision-makers, and potential customers.

The context involves selecting a real-world example where the product or service had a significant impact, ideally with measurable outcomes. The focus is on practical application, demonstrating how the solution was integrated into existing workflows, how it solved specific pain points, and what benefits were realized. This practical approach is designed to keep the audience engaged and interested in the case study. The case study often includes background information on the company or team involved, their challenges before implementing the solution, and the decision-making process that led them to choose the product or service.

This context is also shaped by the need to provide credible, relatable, and detailed information that resonates with the target audience. It involves understanding the audience's everyday challenges, needs, and interests and framing the case study to speak directly to those aspects. The case study is presented as a success story that highlights the effectiveness of the product or service and provides detailed, actionable insights for others considering similar solutions. The ultimate goal is to create an informative and persuasive narrative, helping to build trust in the product or service and encouraging adoption among the broader developer community.

Solution

The solution for a case study in the Case Study pattern is to create a detailed and structured account that illustrates the power of a specific product, service, or technology in overcoming a real-world challenge or achieving a particular objective. This involves selecting a relevant example where the solution played a pivotal role in overcoming obstacles or enhancing performance and then documenting the entire process, from problem identification to the final results.

CHAPTER 8 CASE STUDY

At the outset, the case study should meticulously define the problem or challenge faced by the user or organization. This step is crucial as it not only sets the context for the solution but also helps the reader understand the significance of the challenge and the limitations or inefficiencies that existed before the solution was implemented. The narrative should then describe the selection process, detailing why the chosen product or service was considered the best fit for the task. This includes highlighting key features, functionalities, or advantages that made the solution stand out as the ideal choice.

The implementation phase is crucial, where the case study outlines how the solution was integrated into the existing environment. This part should cover any steps taken to adapt the solution to specific needs, how it was deployed, and any technical or organizational challenges encountered during the process. The case study should also document how these challenges were addressed, providing insights into the flexibility and support offered by the solution and its provider.

The results section of the case study is where the effectiveness of the solution is demonstrated. This should include quantitative data, such as performance improvements, cost reductions, time savings, or other measurable outcomes resulting from the implementation. Qualitative outcomes should also be highlighted, such as increased user satisfaction, improved workflow efficiency, or strategic advantages gained. The case study shows that the solution delivered real value by providing concrete evidence of success.

Throughout the case study, the narrative should remain clear, focused, and relevant to the target audience, emphasizing the aspects of the solution that are most likely to resonate with other potential users. More than just a collection of facts, the case study should tell a compelling story that showcases the solution's success in a specific context. This narrative approach helps the reader connect with the solution and understand its practical benefits. The case study acts as both an educational tool and a promotional piece, demonstrating the product's or service's practical benefits and encouraging others to consider it for their own needs.

Participants

The participants in a case study include the **customer**, the **developer relations team**, the **product or service team**, and the **audience or readers**. The **customer** is the organization, team, or individual implementing the product or service to address a specific challenge. They provide the real-world example that forms the basis of the case study, sharing details about their problem, the solution they chose, how it was implemented, and the results they achieved. Their experience and feedback are crucial in illustrating the practical application and effectiveness of the solution.

The **developer relations team** is responsible for creating and documenting the case study. They interact with the customer or user to gather information, conduct interviews, and collect data. The team then organizes this information into a coherent narrative, highlighting the key aspects of the solution's success. The developer relations team also collaborates with the **product or service team**, which provides insights into the technical details, features, and capabilities of the product or service used. The product or service team may also help verify the accuracy of the technical content and ensure that the case study aligns with the product's value proposition.

Finally, the **audience or readers** are the potential users, developers, or decision-makers who engage with the case study. They interact with the content by reading and analyzing the case study to understand how the product or service could be applied to their challenges or needs. The case study is a persuasive tool for the audience, offering them a relatable example and compelling evidence of the product's effectiveness. The interaction between the case study and the audience may also lead to further engagement, such as inquiries, product trials, or purchases, based on the confidence and understanding gained from the case study.

Overall, these participants interact in a collaborative process that begins with the customer or user's real-world experience, is documented and communicated by the developer relations and product teams, and is ultimately consumed by the audience, who may be inspired to take action based on the insights provided.

Implementation

Implementing a case study involves several key steps that ensure the case study is thorough, engaging, and effective in showcasing the value of a product, service, or technology. The process begins with **identifying a suitable candidate** for the case study. This could be a customer, team, or organization that has a compelling story of success, having used the product or service to solve a significant problem or achieve a noteworthy result. The selection process involves considering the use case's relevance, the solution's impact, and the target audience's potential interest, inspiring them with a real-life success story.

Once a candidate is identified, the next step is to **initiate contact** and secure their participation. The developer relations team reaches out to the customer or user, explaining the purpose of the case study and how it will be used. It's essential to ensure that the participant is willing to share detailed information and that confidentiality concerns are addressed, often through a formal agreement. This collaborative approach ensures that everyone involved feels part of the team.

The **information gathering** phase follows, during which the developer relations team interviews key stakeholders from the customer's organization. These interviews are designed to extract detailed insights about the challenges faced before implementing the solution, the decision-making process that led to choosing the product or service, the steps taken during implementation, and the results achieved. The team may also collect supporting materials such as data, metrics, screenshots, and any relevant documentation that can help illustrate the story.

After gathering all the necessary information, the developer relations team moves into the **content creation** phase. The case study is structured into several key sections: an introduction that provides background on the customer and the problem they faced, a detailed account of the solution selection and implementation process, and a results section that highlights the benefits and outcomes achieved. The narrative should be clear, concise, and focused on the relevant aspects to the target audience. It's important to include qualitative and quantitative results, such as performance improvements, cost savings, or user satisfaction metrics, to provide a well-rounded picture of the solution's impact.

The **visual design** of the case study is also crucial. The developer relations team collaborates with designers to create a visually appealing layout that incorporates charts, diagrams, and images, complementing the text and making the information more accessible. Visual elements should highlight key points, illustrate complex processes, and summarize the text to maintain reader engagement.

Once the case study is drafted, it undergoes a **review and approval** process. The customer or user reviews the content to ensure accuracy and approves the use of their name and information. The product or service team may also review the technical details to ensure they are correctly represented. Based on this feedback, revisions are made, and the final version is prepared for publication.

The **publication and distribution** phase involves making the case study available to the target audience. It is typically published on the company's website, blog, or developer portal and may be featured in newsletters, social media posts, and other marketing channels. The developer relations team may also create different case study formats, such as a downloadable PDF, a video version, or an infographic, to reach different audience segments.

Finally, the case study's performance is **monitored and evaluated**. The developer relations team tracks metrics such as page views, downloads, social shares, and engagement rates to assess the effectiveness of the case study. Feedback from readers, such as comments or inquiries, is also gathered to understand the case study's impact on the audience. This data helps the team refine their approach to future case studies and provides insights into the types of content that resonate most with the developer community, making the audience feel valued and integral to the process.

Throughout this process, the goal is to create a compelling narrative that showcases the customer or user's success and clearly demonstrates the product or service's value and effectiveness. Following these detailed steps, the case study becomes a powerful tool for building credibility, fostering trust, and driving adoption within the target audience.

Metrics

The metrics for a case study that a developer relations team creates and publishes are essential to track and measure the case study's reach, engagement, effectiveness, and overall impact on the target audience. The first metric to track is **page views** or **downloads**, depending on how the case study is made available. This metric indicates how often the case study has been accessed, providing a baseline for understanding its visibility and interest level among the audience.

Another important metric is **engagement time**, which measures how long readers spend on the case study web page. Higher engagement time suggests that readers thoroughly consume the content, indicating that the case study is relevant and engaging. **Bounce rate** is also crucial if the case study is published on a webpage. This metric shows the percentage of visitors leaving the page without interacting further, which can help determine if the content meets expectations.

Conversion rates are essential for understanding the effectiveness of the case study in driving specific actions. This could include the number of readers who sign up for a product demo, download additional resources, or contact the sales team after reading the case study. Tracking these conversions helps gauge the case study's influence on the customer journey and its role in generating leads or sales.

Social shares and referral traffic provide insights into how widely the case study is distributed and discussed across different platforms. Tracking the number of shares on social media and the referral traffic generated from these platforms can reveal how well the case study resonates with the community and how effectively readers promote it.

Backlinks to the case study from other websites or publications can also be a valuable metric. These indicate that external sources find the content credible and valuable enough to reference, boosting SEO and increasing the case study's authority and reach.

Feedback and interactions from the audience, such as comments, emails, or inquiries, should be documented to understand how the case study is being received. Positive feedback and engagement suggest the content is valuable, while any criticisms or suggestions can provide insights for future improvements.

If the case study is used in presentations or sales pitches, **internal feedback** from the teams using it can be another metric. This feedback can reveal how compelling the case study is as a tool for communication and persuasion within the company's sales and marketing efforts.

Lead generation is another critical metric if the case study is part of a broader content marketing strategy. Tracking the number of leads generated directly from the case study and their progression through the sales funnel provides a precise measure of its business impact.

Finally, **overall ROI (Return on Investment)** should be calculated by comparing the costs of creating and promoting the case study (such as time, resources, and any promotional expenses) against the benefits gained, including lead generation, sales, and brand exposure. This metric helps assess the financial efficiency of the case study as a marketing tool.

These metrics should be systematically documented in a detailed report that includes quantitative data and qualitative insights. Visualizations such as graphs and charts can illustrate key trends and performance indicators. The report should also include an analysis section where the metrics are interpreted in the context of the case study's goals, and recommendations for future case studies are provided based on the collected data. This documentation enables the developer relations team to evaluate the success of their case studies, refine their strategies, and better understand their impact on the audience and the business.

Example

A developer relations team at DataForge, specializing in big data analytics solutions, decides to create and publish a case study. The goal is to showcase how one of their customers, a leading e-commerce platform named ShopEase, used DataForge's analytics platform to optimize their recommendation engine, leading to increased sales and customer satisfaction. The developer relations team recognizes that this story could resonate well with other e-commerce businesses looking to enhance their customer experience through data-driven insights.

The **story begins** with the developer relations team identifying ShopEase as an ideal candidate for the case study. ShopEase recently implemented DataForge's analytics solution and significantly improved its recommendation system. The team contacts the ShopEase data science team to discuss the possibility of creating a case study. After securing their agreement, the developer relations team arranges interviews with key stakeholders at ShopEase, including the lead data scientist, the head of customer experience, and the CTO.

During these **interviews**, the developer relations team gathers detailed information about the challenges ShopEase faced before implementing DataForge's solution. ShopEase had struggled with outdated algorithms that provided generic recommendations, leading to low engagement and missed sales opportunities. They explain how they evaluated several analytics platforms before choosing DataForge for its unique selling points: scalability, advanced machine-learning capabilities, and ease of integration.

The interviews also provide insights into the **implementation process**. ShopEase shares how they integrated DataForge's platform with their existing infrastructure, the steps they took to customize the recommendation algorithms, and how they overcame initial challenges, such as data quality issues and the need for real-time processing. The developer relations team documents these details, emphasizing the collaborative effort between ShopEase and DataForge's support team, which is a hallmark of our customer service.

Next, the **results** section of the case study is crafted. ShopEase provides quantitative data showing a 20% increase in recommendation-driven sales and a 15% improvement in customer retention rates after implementing the new system. They also share qualitative feedback from customers who have noticed and appreciated the more personalized shopping experience. The developer relations team carefully documents these outcomes, highlighting DataForge's platform's significant impact on ShopEase's business.

With all the information gathered, the developer relations team moves into the **content creation** phase. They draft the case study, structuring it with a clear narrative flow: the introduction provides background on ShopEase and its initial challenges, followed by a detailed account of the solution selection and implementation process, and concluding with the impressive results achieved. Visual elements such as graphs showing the increase in sales, screenshots of the recommendation engine in action, and a flowchart of the integration process are included to make the case study more engaging and accessible.

CHAPTER 8   CASE STUDY

After the first draft is complete, the case study goes through a thorough **review process**. ShopEase reviews the content to ensure accuracy and approves using their name and data. The product team at DataForge also reviews the technical aspects to ensure they are correctly represented. Based on the feedback, the developer relations team makes necessary revisions and prepares the final version of the case study, ensuring its accuracy and quality.

The **publication** phase involves making the case study available on DataForge's website and featuring it on the homepage and resources section. The team also creates a downloadable PDF version for distribution. The case study is promoted through DataForge's social media channels, email newsletters, and targeted ads aimed at other e-commerce businesses to maximize reach. The developer relations team also collaborates with the sales team to use the case study in pitches to prospective clients in the e-commerce sector.

After publication, the team closely monitors the case study's **performance**. They track metrics such as page views, download numbers, and social shares to assess how widely the case study is accessed and shared. They also pay attention to conversion rates, noting how many leads or inquiries are generated by the case study. Feedback from the sales team indicates that the case study has been particularly effective in demonstrating the value of DataForge's platform to potential clients, making it a key resource in their sales toolkit.

The developer relations team analyzes the case study's overall impact in the following months. They find that it helped generate new business opportunities and strengthened DataForge's reputation as a leader in big data analytics. The team documents these findings in a report, which includes detailed metrics, insights from the feedback received, and recommendations for future case studies, fostering a sense of achievement and growth.

Through this example, the case study proves it is a powerful tool for demonstrating the real-world application and value of DataForge's analytics platform. By meticulously documenting each process step, from identifying the candidate to publishing and analyzing the results, the developer relations team ensures that the case study effectively communicates the success story and resonates with the target audience, ultimately contributing to the company's growth and industry standing, fostering a sense of thoroughness and professionalism.

Consequences

The consequences of a case study in the Developer Relations Case Study pattern can have significant implications for both the Developer Relations team and the company or organization. The Developer Relations team plays a crucial role in this process, from identifying potential case study subjects to gathering data and crafting the narrative. For the Developer Relations team, a well-executed case study can enhance their credibility and establish them as effective communicators of the company's value propositions. The team can build stronger relationships with the developer community, potential customers, and industry influencers by demonstrating real-world successes. This success can lead to increased demand for similar content, positioning the team as a vital resource within the organization for producing high-impact, persuasive materials. However, if the case study is poorly executed—lacking depth and accuracy or failing to resonate with the audience—it can harm the team's reputation. It may also result in missed opportunities to engage with the target audience or to influence potential customers, ultimately diminishing the perceived value of the Developer Relations team's efforts.

For the company or organization, a successful case study can significantly boost its market presence and reputation. By highlighting how its products or services have delivered tangible results for a customer, the company can build trust and credibility with potential customers, leading to increased sales and customer acquisition. The case study serves as a powerful marketing tool that can be used across various channels, such as sales pitches, website content, social media, and industry events, amplifying the company's message and showcasing its capabilities. Moreover, case studies can help differentiate the company from competitors by providing concrete examples of success, making it easier for prospects to envision the benefits of choosing its solutions. This strategic advantage can inspire a sense of competition and drive for success within the company.

On the other hand, if a case study fails to deliver a compelling story or is perceived as biased or unconvincing, it can have negative consequences for the company. A weak case study may fail to generate interest or credibility, leading to a lack of engagement from the intended audience. In some cases, it could even backfire, raising doubts about the product or service's effectiveness and potentially damaging the company's reputation. Additionally, suppose the case study is seen as too promotional or insufficiently informative. In that case, it might be disregarded by the audience, leading to wasted resources and effort without achieving the desired impact.

Overall, the consequences of a case study extend beyond just the immediate content creation process. They influence how the Developer Relations team is perceived within the company, how the company is viewed by its target audience, and, ultimately, the effectiveness of its broader marketing and sales efforts. A well-crafted case study can be more than just a piece of content. It can be a cornerstone of the company's communication strategy, demonstrating the team's value and impact. Moreover, it can serve as a powerful tool for internal communication, helping different departments understand the company's value propositions and successes. Conversely, a poorly executed one can undermine trust and credibility, highlighting the importance of their work.

Variants

The variants of a case study in the Developer Relations Case Study pattern include several different formats and approaches that can be tailored to specific audiences, objectives, and contexts.

One common variant is the **success story**, which focuses on highlighting a particularly positive outcome achieved by a customer using the product or service. This variant often emphasizes the transformative impact of the solution and is designed to inspire and persuade potential customers by showcasing a clear win.

Another variant is the **technical deep dive**. This type of case study is geared toward a more technically savvy audience. It provides an in-depth look at the implementation process, including challenges, technical details, and how specific features or tools were utilized to achieve the desired outcomes. This variant is ideal for developers, engineers, or technical decision-makers looking for detailed information on how to apply the solution in their environments.

A **comparative case study** is another variant that focuses on comparing the results before and after implementing the solution or comparing the chosen solution against other considered alternatives. This type of case study helps to highlight the unique benefits of the product or service and provides a clear rationale for why it was selected over other options.

The **industry-specific case study** is tailored to resonate with a particular industry or sector. This variant emphasizes how the solution addresses the industry's unique challenges and needs, using industry-specific language, metrics, and examples. It's particularly effective for demonstrating the product's relevance and effectiveness within a particular market segment.

Another variant is the **multi-customer case study**, which combines the experiences of multiple customers into a single narrative. This approach can be helpful when illustrating a broader trend or common challenge that the product or service addresses across different organizations. It allows the developer relations team to show the solution's versatility and wide applicability.

Another variant that focuses heavily on the customer's problem before using the product or service is a **problem–solution case study**. It provides a detailed analysis of the issue, explores the negative impacts of not addressing it, and then explains how the solution was applied to resolve the problem. This variant is particularly effective for customers currently facing similar challenges and looking for a proven way to overcome them.

Lastly, the **video case study** is a multimedia variant that uses video content to tell the story. This format can include interviews with key stakeholders, footage of the product in use, and visual data representations. Video case studies are engaging and can be easily shared across digital platforms, making them an effective tool for reaching a broader audience.

Each of these variants serves different purposes and appeals to different audiences, allowing the Developer Relations team to tailor their case studies to specific contexts and goals. Whether the aim is to provide technical insights, showcase industry relevance, or inspire potential customers with success stories, these variants offer flexible approaches to communicate the value of the product or service effectively.

CHAPTER 9

Code Review

Topics: *Code, Writing*

Code reviews are a collaborative process where developers examine each other's code to ensure quality, maintainability, and alignment with best practices. For Developer Relations (DevRel) teams, code reviews extend beyond internal collaboration to engaging with the broader developer community. By participating in or facilitating community-driven code reviews, DevRel professionals improve the quality of their organization's open-source projects and foster trust, mentorship, and learning among developers. This process can help identify pain points, such as inefficient code or unclear documentation, share expertise, and introduce developers to the company's tools or technologies in an authentic, value-driven manner.

When positioned strategically, community-focused code reviews become a powerful tool to enhance a company's reputation and drive the adoption of its products. The company can establish itself as a trusted leader in the developer ecosystem by demonstrating technical excellence, transparency, and a commitment to community growth. This goodwill can translate into greater adoption of the company's tools and services, driving business growth. Through code reviews, DevRel teams play a crucial role in bridging the gap between technical advocacy and business objectives, making their work impactful and integral to the company's success.

Note: Organizations should carefully consider the legal implications of reviewing or "sanctioning" customer code. In some cases, offering

CHAPTER 9 CODE REVIEW

official guidance on external codebases could introduce liability if that code later causes issues in production. To mitigate this risk, DevRel teams should clearly define the scope of their reviews (e.g., educational, advisory, or best-practices guidance only) and coordinate with Legal on policies that strike a balance between community support and responsible risk management.

Also Known As

Collaborative code reviews, peer-to-peer code audits, open-source contributions reviews, developer feedback sessions, pull request reviews, external code evaluations, community-driven quality assessments, and partner collaboration reviews.

Intent

The intent of a community or customer code review in the context of Developer Relations is to create a meaningful touchpoint between the company and its developer audience, fostering collaboration, trust, and shared growth. By engaging developers in the review process—whether through open-source contributions, pull requests, or direct feedback sessions—DevRel teams can showcase the company's commitment to quality, transparency, and developer success. This engagement not only improves the quality and usability of the codebase but also provides an opportunity to highlight how the company's tools, frameworks, or platforms can solve real-world challenges. Furthermore, these reviews position the company as a leader in the developer ecosystem, enhancing its reputation as a partner that listens and values its community's input. Over time, this builds brand loyalty and trust, directly influencing product adoption, customer retention, and ultimately, sales growth. Developer Relations transforms a routine practice into a strategic driver of both relationship and business outcomes through this intentional alignment of technical excellence and community engagement.

Context

The context for a community or customer code review lies in the intersection of technical collaboration, developer advocacy, and business strategy. Developer Relations teams operate in a space where fostering solid and authentic relationships with developers is as important as promoting the company's tools and services. Community and customer code reviews provide a practical avenue for engaging directly with developers, addressing their needs, and demonstrating the company's commitment to supporting and empowering them. However, it's essential to acknowledge the legal implications of "sanctioning" customer code, as this could potentially make the vendor or advocate liable for issues arising from the use of that code. These reviews often occur in open-source projects, user feedback loops, or technical forums, where developers actively contribute ideas and code. By creating a collaborative and constructive review process while carefully navigating these legal considerations, DevRel teams can improve the quality of shared codebases and position the company as a trusted leader in the developer ecosystem. This active engagement serves a dual purpose: it strengthens the sense of community among developers while simultaneously showcasing the company's expertise, transparency, and dedication to developer success, which in turn enhances reputation and can drive product adoption and sales.

Solution

The solution for a community or customer code review is not just a process but a valuable opportunity to establish a structured, inclusive, and value-driven review process that actively engages developers and aligns with the company's goals. Developer Relations teams can implement this by creating clear guidelines for participation, fostering a welcoming and collaborative environment, and prioritizing constructive feedback. This can be open-source contribution reviews, customer feedback sessions on SDKs or APIs, or collaborative pull request evaluations for shared projects. By facilitating these reviews, DevRel teams can address developer challenges, provide actionable insights, and demonstrate the effectiveness of the company's tools or platforms in solving real-world problems.

To maximize impact, the review process should be transparent and emphasize mutual learning. This would allow developers to gain valuable knowledge while showcasing the company's unwavering commitment to technical expertise and quality. Regularly highlighting successful collaborations—through blog posts, social media, or case studies—further amplifies the company's reputation as a trusted partner in the developer ecosystem. Over time, this consistent engagement improves code quality, deepens relationships with the developer community, increases trust in the company's brand, and fosters adoption of its products and services.

CHAPTER 9   CODE REVIEW

Participants

The community or customer code review participants include external developers and engineers, Developer Relations team members, internal software engineers, and product owners. **External developers and engineers** are the primary contributors, submitting code to integrate or use the company's products, such as SDKs, APIs, or platforms. These participants bring diverse use cases and real-world challenges to the table, which can highlight areas for improvement or new opportunities for the company's offerings. **Developer Relations team members** act as facilitators, ensuring the code review process is smooth, constructive, and inclusive. They provide technical feedback, share best practices, and guide external contributors in maximizing the potential of the company's products.

Internal software engineers play a supporting role by offering deeper technical insights, particularly on how the company's products function and how they can be optimally used. They can clarify edge cases, troubleshoot integration issues, and recommend design patterns that align with the company's tools. **Product owners** participate to understand how customers and community members use the products in their projects. They gather usability feedback, identify features gaps, and assess how well the company's offerings meet customer needs. This cross-functional interaction creates a feedback loop, where external developers receive valuable guidance, internal teams gain actionable insights, and the company strengthens its reputation as a collaborative and customer-focused organization. By focusing the reviews on community or customer's software that uses the company's products, these interactions ensure the company remains relevant, responsive, and trusted in the developer ecosystem, ultimately driving product adoption and sales.

CHAPTER 9   CODE REVIEW

Implementation

Implementing a community or customer code review requires a well-structured and intentional process that facilitates collaboration, fosters trust, and highlights the value of the company's products. The first step is establishing clear participation guidelines and ensuring the review process is accessible and inclusive. This involves creating documentation outlining how community members can submit their code for review, the most beneficial contributions, and the expected etiquette during discussions. Platforms like GitHub, GitLab, or similar tools are ideal for hosting these reviews, as they provide a familiar environment for developers to share and discuss their work. Developer Relations (DevRel) team members play a central role in moderating these interactions, ensuring feedback is constructive and aligned with the community's goals while reinforcing the company's position as a trusted and knowledgeable partner.

The review process not only evaluates the integration, efficiency, and proper usage of the company's products within the external developers' code but also carries significant legal implications. DevRel professionals, in collaboration with internal and legal experts when necessary, assess submissions for adherence to best practices while offering clear guidance on when, how, and who should be involved in this process. It's crucial to approach feedback with care to avoid any advice that might adversely affect the source company, as such actions could lead to liability. The review team identifies areas for improvement and provides actionable suggestions, highlighting how the company's tools can be used more effectively. This addresses developers' challenges and offers insights into advanced features or alternative approaches. Maintaining a balance between critical evaluation and encouragement, feedback should recognize the contributors' efforts and emphasize learning opportunities. Publicly recognizing high-quality contributions or innovative implementations through social media, blogs, or case studies can motivate participation and showcase real-world success stories involving the company's products.

To ensure long-term success, the DevRel team can host periodic events like live code review sessions or webinars to foster deeper engagement. These events allow contributors to receive real-time feedback and connect with the DevRel team and peers in the community. The company demonstrates its commitment to developer success and continuous learning by consistently engaging with the community through structured code reviews. Over time, this improves the quality of the software ecosystem around the company's products and builds a reputation for technical excellence, fostering trust and loyalty. This strategic approach can drive increased adoption of the company's tools, expand its developer base, and contribute directly to business growth.

Metrics

To document metrics for a community or customer code review, the focus should be on evaluating the qualitative and quantitative impact of the reviews, aligning them with the goals of Developer Relations and the company's broader objectives. Key metrics should capture the code review process's engagement, technical outcomes, and business impact. These metrics can be organized into participation, quality improvement, community engagement, and business influence.

- **Participation metrics** should track the number of external developers and engineers submitting code for review, the diversity of contributors (e.g., geographic location, industry, or expertise), and the volume of reviewed contributions over time. These metrics provide insights into how actively the developer community engages with the company's products and the review process.

- **Quality improvement metrics** should measure the number of issues identified and resolved during reviews, the enhancements made to the contributors' code as a result of feedback, and the alignment of the reviewed code with best practices for using the company's tools. This demonstrates how the reviews directly improve the usability and reliability of the company's products in real-world scenarios.

- **Community engagement metrics** should reflect the level of interaction during the code review process, such as the number of comments exchanged, the ratio of feedback adopted by contributors, and any follow-up activities, such as discussions or collaborations inspired by the reviews. These metrics showcase how effectively the reviews foster relationships and build trust with the developer community.

- **Business influence metrics** should include tracking how many reviewed projects lead to increased adoption of the company's tools, how often contributors publicly share positive feedback about the review process, and any resulting case studies or testimonials that enhance the company's reputation. Additionally, the impact on product sales or subscription renewals can be assessed by correlating code review participation with product usage patterns or purchasing behavior.

By systematically documenting and analyzing these metrics, Developer Relations teams can refine their code review practices, clearly demonstrate their value to the organization, and strategically align their efforts with the company's goals of enhancing reputation, driving product adoption, and increasing sales. This structured approach ensures that code reviews are a tool for technical improvement and a strategic asset for growth and engagement.

CHAPTER 9   CODE REVIEW

Example

A strong example of a community or customer code review involves a Developer Relations (DevRel) team hosting a virtual or in-person "Code Review Workshop" tailored for external developers and engineers who use the company's products. Imagine a scenario where a customer has developed a machine learning application leveraging the company's cloud-based AI API. The customer faces challenges optimizing their implementation to reduce latency and costs while maintaining accuracy. The DevRel team organizes a one-on-one session with the customer involving DevRel engineers, a product owner, and an internal software engineer specializing in the AI API.

During the session, the customer presents their code and explains its functionality and challenges. The DevRel engineer facilitates the conversation by asking questions to understand the context better and offering initial suggestions for improvement. The internal software engineer provides deeper insights into the API's performance characteristics and shares advanced techniques to optimize calls and manage resources effectively. The product owner listens actively, noting usability challenges and feature gaps that the customer highlights during the discussion. Together, the group identifies critical areas for improvement in the customer's implementation, such as restructuring API calls to batch requests for efficiency or fine-tuning specific model parameters to enhance performance.

Throughout the review, the DevRel team ensures the feedback is actionable and supportive, helping the customer solve their immediate issues and learn best practices for using the API. After the session, the DevRel team follows up with a summary of the recommendations, additional resources, and an invitation to showcase the improved application in an upcoming webinar or case study. The customer feels supported and valued, and their application now demonstrates the full potential of the company's product.

This example highlights how a direct, personalized code review process connects the company with its customers or community members. It showcases the company's technical expertise and commitment to customer success, strengthening its reputation. By empowering the customer to achieve better outcomes and promoting their success story, the company indirectly drives product adoption and builds loyalty, translating into tangible business benefits.

Consequences

The direct consequences of a community or customer code review include improved quality and functionality of the customer's software that integrates with the company's products. These reviews provide immediate value to the developers by identifying bugs, inefficiencies, and potential improvements in their code while introducing best practices for using the company's tools or platforms. This technical guidance helps customers optimize their implementation, ensuring a better user experience, reduced errors, and enhanced performance. Additionally, these reviews create a sense of trust and reliability, as developers feel supported and valued by the company. Customers are more likely to adopt or continue using the company's products when they see direct evidence of its commitment to their success.

The indirect consequences are equally impactful. Through regular and constructive code reviews, the company strengthens its reputation as a thought leader and a trusted partner in the developer ecosystem. Positive interactions during reviews often lead to word-of-mouth recommendations, increased loyalty, and the willingness of external developers to promote the company's tools within their networks. Furthermore, these engagements give the company valuable insights into how its products are used in real-world scenarios, uncovering feature gaps, usability challenges, or new use cases that can inform product development. Such insights can drive innovation and ensure the company's offerings remain competitive and relevant.

Over time, these code reviews build a stronger developer community around the company's ecosystem. This fosters advocacy, where developers become enthusiastic about the products and share their success stories through **Case Studies (151)**, testimonials, or **Conference Sessions (197)**. In some cases, if the issue appears often enough, it may warrant creation of **Blog Posts (105)** with accompanying **Samples/Examples (387)**, and/or trigger a refactoring of the **SDK (381)**. These indirect effects translate into greater visibility, adoption, and sales of the company's tools or services while improving customer retention rates. By aligning the technical benefits of code reviews with broader strategic objectives, Developer Relations teams turn these reviews into a powerful mechanism for community growth and business success.

Variants

- **Internal code review:** In some cases, it can be helpful to the DevRel team to better understand the product/service if they are used as reviewers of the code that make up the product/service (if it is not open-sourced already). While the DevRel team may not find any bugs or issues, the act of walking through the code can help Engineers think through some edge cases that might not be already covered, and the DevRel team will gain greater insight into how the product/service works "under the hood."

CHAPTER 10

Conference

Topics: *Budget, Presentation, Social, Code*

A conference is a large formal gathering where individuals, typically from a specific industry or professional field, come together to share knowledge, discuss trends, and network. In the context of Developer Relations, a conference is organized by a company or organization to engage directly with developers, users, and partners. It typically features a series of sessions, workshops, keynotes, and networking opportunities, all aimed at educating attendees, showcasing new products or technologies, and fostering a sense of community within the developer ecosystem. Conferences provide a platform for in-depth learning, collaboration, and exchanging ideas in a focused environment.

CHAPTER 10   CONFERENCE

Also Known As

Developer Days (or DevDays), Tech Conference (or TechCon), Developer Conference (or DevCon), User Summit, User Conference

Intent

Create a high-interactivity event that showcases your company's technology, innovations, and people, by providing educational content, creating a space that enables the attendees to mingle. This should encourage feedback between your company, your partners, industry experts invited to speak, and attendees interested in and/or that are already customers of your product/service.

CHAPTER 10   CONFERENCE

Context

You want to create some "buzz" around your product/service and/or your company, and use that "buzz" to gain some brand recognition, bootstrap some community activities, and/or persuade developers to take a deeper/harder look at your product/service collectively with their peers. But far from being just a "big announcement," you also want to create a space where the feedback loop between your community and your company is at the shortest it can possibly be, by creating a highly interactive event where your company's people can talk directly to your users/customers and get unfiltered feedback in a relatively safe setting.

And if that "buzz" also creates a sense of "FOMO" (Fear of Missing Out) among those that don't partake of the event, so much the better for when you repeat the exercise again later.

Solution

Create a company-funded conference dedicated to the company and/or the product/service, with high-ranking company executives taking prime slots to address the attendees about the company's successes, future directions, and exciting news. Use breakout sessions to further refine that messaging and further "deep dives" into the details of the product/service. Invite members of the tech press to attend for free, and provide opportunities for exclusive interviews with the company executives for the press to run.

Participants

Creating a conference will require a multi-team effort over a variety of different groups all across the company; in fact, depending on the size of the company and the conference, it may well require the complete attention of everyone in the company for some percentage of their time.

CHAPTER 10   CONFERENCE

Generally the participants involved in a conference will fall into several categories:

The **organizing team** will be the principal group responsible for the logistics, content, and overall management of the conference. This group, which will often segregate much of the work among themselves, will often be made up of people within the company, plus perhaps one or more outside consultants and/or "event organizers" who specialize in logistics and working with venues.

No technical conference can expect to be successful without **speakers**, who will be responsible for presenting the content that attracts the attendees. Depending on the theme and direction of the conference, speakers will often include internal (that is, internal to your company) as well as external experts. Often, depending on the target audience (and the budget available), obtaining a "big name" speaker to provide your conference's keynote will help make the conference more visible and attractive, although it is common for the company's own CEO or CTO to take that slot in order to be able to personally showcase the company's upcoming products and services.

attendees of the conference will often be made up of the people that consume your product or service, either directly or indirectly (depending on the products and services). In other words, the attendees will be your company's users, customers, developers, partners, and other stakeholders.

Conferences are also an excellent time to provide some space for **vendors** and **partners**, external entities that might have integrations or collaborations with the hosting company's products, to connect with the community around your products/services as well. Frequently, these entities will be looking for opportunities both to have a **Booth (137)** on your conferences vendor floor (from which to give away **Swag (427)**), give a **Conference Session (197)** to your audience, and so on. They will also often have the experts you are seeking as speakers for the conference.

CHAPTER 10 CONFERENCE

Implementation

Orchestrating a conference requires meticulous planning across various domains to ensure the event's success and its resonance with the attendees.

content planning is at the heart of the conference, necessitating that sessions, workshops, and keynotes not only cater directly to the user's interests and needs but also encapsulate a broad spectrum of topics to foster inclusivity and diversity among speakers. This lays the groundwork for a rich, engaging learning environment.

On the **logistics** front, selecting a venue accessible and equipped with necessary facilities is crucial, alongside crafting a well-balanced agenda that intersperses educational sessions with ample opportunities for breaks, networking, and significant events, ensuring a dynamic yet comfortable attendee experience.

community engagement strategies, such as establishing robust feedback channels and curating dedicated networking spaces, are essential for fostering a participatory atmosphere and facilitating valuable connections among attendees.

Finally, **post-conference actions** are critical in extending the conference's value beyond its temporal boundaries. By sharing content like recordings and slides and engaging in thorough feedback analysis, organizers can amplify the reach of the conference's insights and refine and enhance future iterations, reinforcing the event's impact and the company's commitment to its community.

Metrics

Documenting the metrics to track a Conference created by a developer relations team, a comprehensive and structured approach should be used to capture the event's quantitative and qualitative aspects.

- **Registration and attendance:** This includes the total number of registrants, the actual number of attendees, and the rate of no-shows. Tracking the number of no-shows is crucial as it provides insights into the accuracy of our registration process and helps in planning for future events. Additionally, analyzing the demographic details of the attendees, such as job roles, industry sectors, geographic distribution, and company size, will provide insights into whether the conference attracted the intended target audience.

- **Session attendance:** This is the number of participants in each session, workshop, or keynote should be tracked. This data not only helps us understand which topics and speakers drew the most interest but also empowers you, our audience, to guide content planning for future events. Furthermore, *engagement during sessions* should be measured by observing the level of participation in Q&A segments, interactive polls, and discussions. This can be quantified by counting the number of questions, the frequency and quality of interactions, and participation rates in interactive elements like polls or live demos.

- **Attendee feedback:** Collected via post-session surveys, feedback forms, and on-site interviews, this is a cornerstone of your evaluation process. This feedback, which should evaluate your satisfaction with the sessions, the relevance of the topics, and the effectiveness of the speakers, is invaluable. It not only highlights the strengths and areas for improvement in the content delivered but also shows that your opinions are highly respected and integral to our process.

CHAPTER 10   CONFERENCE

- **Networking activity:** This metric reflects the conference's effectiveness in fostering connections among attendees. This can be measured by tracking the number of meetings arranged through networking apps, the use of designated networking areas, and the volume of business cards exchanged or connections made on professional networking platforms like LinkedIn.

- **Brand visibility and exposure:** This includes the frequency and reach of mentions on **Social Media (395)**, the number of social media posts related to the conference, the use of event-specific hashtags, and the visibility of the company's branding throughout the venue. Additionally, tracking the distribution and use of branded materials, such as **Swag (427)**, brochures, and digital resources, can provide insights into the event's impact on brand awareness.

- **Return on Investment (ROI):** This involves calculating the total cost of the conference against the tangible outcomes, such as new leads generated, **Partnerships (309)** formed, or direct sales influenced by the event. It's essential also to monitor the post-conference follow-up activity, such as the number of attendees who continue to engage with the company after the event through channels like email **Newsletters (281)**, **Follow-up Meetings (223)**, or other participation in subsequent company initiatives. This follow-up activity plays a significant role in maintaining the momentum and relationship established during the event, thereby contributing to the long-term success of the event.

- At conferences with a strong sales or executive focus, especially those featuring forums, roundtables, or invite-only leadership tracks, it's valuable to track **Deal Acceleration** as a distinct metric. This refers to sales opportunities that progress more quickly through the pipeline due to direct, high-impact interactions at the event. For example, when key decision-makers meet with your executives or product leaders during the conference, they may be more inclined to move forward with a proof-of-concept, pilot agreement, or purchase decision. Tracking these accelerated deals, either through CRM tags or post-event sales team feedback, can help quantify the conference's impact on revenue velocity, not just lead generation. It's especially relevant for enterprise products, partnerships, or multi-stakeholder deals that benefit from face-to-face trust-building and strategic alignment.

- **Sponsorship effectiveness:** The value delivered to **Sponsors (405)** should be evaluated based on their visibility at the event, the traffic to their booths or sessions, and their overall satisfaction with the exposure provided.

- **Overall attendee satisfaction with the event:** This should be captured through a comprehensive post-conference **survey (413)**. This survey should assess various aspects of the conference, including the organization, the value provided, and the likelihood of attendees returning for future events. A comprehensive survey is crucial as it provides detailed feedback that can be analyzed to identify patterns or common areas of concern, thereby guiding future event planning and improving the overall attendee experience.

Each of these metrics should be systematically documented in a detailed report that includes numerical data and qualitative insights, along with data visualizations to clearly communicate the findings. This report will serve as a critical tool for evaluating the conference's success, informing future event planning, and demonstrating the event's value to stakeholders.

Example

CodeStream Solutions is a consulting company in the DevOps space that is growing year-over-year, and wants to make a particularly big "splash" in the DevOps space by throwing their own DevOps conference. Tentatively calling it "StreamCon," they decide they want to aim for a 3-day event, looking to get roughly 250 to 500 developers. It's an audacious target, but one they think is doable given the budget they are willing to put into marketing the event, and the connections they have within the DevOps community. The C-suite greenlights the initiative, and CodeStream forms a "StreamCon Committee" to get the planning under way, with a goal of delivering an event in April of the following year, just under thirteen months away.

To start with, the team needs some dates for the conference, and that's most likely to be affected by what venue space is available when. The team starts with which quarter in the upcoming year they are hoping to run the event, and then begins talking to various venue spaces (hotels, convention centers, and so on) that will be able to accommodate the size crowd they are targeting. After some back and forth, the team chooses a centrally located convention center known for its excellent facilities and ease of

CHAPTER 10   CONFERENCE

access, accommodating both local and international attendees. The venue assigns an "event coordinator" to work directly with the team, handling much of the logistics on the venue's side, including working with local hotels nearby to reserve blocks of rooms at a discounted rate for attendees. The conference team also takes a percentage of the rooms closest to the venue for the conference team itself (they already know they're not going home while the event is in full swing!), as well as the staff that CodeStreams will need to run the event (such as the registration desk), and for all of their speakers.

As part of its preparation, the conference team needs to know how many "slots" it has in its total conference agenda. They'll need this for a variety of reasons, not least of which is how many talks they can accept, and this requires a little bit of ahead-of-time planning around the number of rooms they have available, the number and length of breaks they want to provide (which means some kind of catering service for each break, most likely), and so on. Not all the slots have to be the same length, or start and stop at the same time, but not having them start and stop at uniform times means breaks will be staggered, complicating the catering service, and potentially creates some scheduling conflicts for attendees.

After some fierce debate and discussion, the team decides to keep all the slots at a uniform 50 minutes, with 10-minute breaks, so that each talk can start at the top of the hour, making it easier for attendees (and speakers) to remember the schedule easily. They plan to run each day from 8:30am to 5:30pm, with keynote talks in the first slot on all three days. Lunch is scheduled for 12:30pm, to last for an hour, and the first slot after lunch (the 1:30pm slot) on each day is designated to be "lightning talks," each slot consisting of four ten-minute talks, which they figure can be used to help "shake things up a bit" during that post-lunch doldrum period.

In a status meeting, the CEO asks about "the parties," and the team realizes they have forgotten about anything "extracurricular" like a welcome reception or other evening activities. The keynote ballroom can easily serve as a "welcome reception" space, and the venue is asked about catering for the event. The team decides—after much debate—to avoid serving alcohol at the event, however, as many on the Legal team are worried about liability issues arising out of potential overindulgence. The venue points out that there are four bars within walking distance, and the conference team agrees that they will make sure the welcome reception ends somewhat early in the evening so that those who wish to "keep the party going" have options available to them. They also reserve the last slot on the 3rd day for "closing ceremonies," including a closing speech from CodeStream's CEO and CTO.

One of the conference team mentions that they attended a recent event that had provided a "lounge area" provided with both bean bags, where attendees could relax, as well as small tables with chairs, where developers could cluster and pair-program on whatever had their attention in the moment. They consider using one of their breakout rooms for this "lounge" space before finding an open space near the vendor floor that is otherwise going unused, and target that as the "lounge." One of the team speaks with a friend who works for one of their sponsoring vendors about the idea, and the friend loves it—vendors, it turns out, love being within eyesight of the lounge, because it generally encourages more traffic flow to the vendor floor over the course of the conference.

Another of the conference team points out that it would be good to have a "quiet zone" where attendees with sensory-processing issues (or even those that don't but just get overwhelmed) can go if they are overstimulated. They look around the venue plans for a bit, and realize that there's a patio that is well away from any street traffic, zoned for non-smoking, and still under a roof. They make plans to set up a few tables out there, complete with power strips, and many lounge-style chairs in which to relax, along with signs indicating the "quiet" nature of the space. Another of the team asks about nursing moms, and a quick email to the venue reveals they have a small room next to each women's restroom specifically designed for that. The venue also notes that the catering service that the venue uses for breaks and meals has a full range of options

CHAPTER 10   CONFERENCE

for various dietary preferences, something the conference team hadn't even thought about yet, despite one of them being vegan themselves.

Next, the team begins to flesh out its desired themes and content for the conference, setting up some general categories of topics for speakers to build talks around. If the theme is too broad, the conference runs the risk of being too "all over the map" and attendees interested in a particular set of topics will find times when none of the talks in a particular slot are of interest to them. On the other hand, if the theme is too narrow, the conference may well not draw enough interest from the community and not hit its desired attendee target. After much deliberation, the organizing team settles on topics that are commonly found at DevOps-centered conferences, such as CI/CD, cloud computing advancements, and future directions. They have deliberately chosen to avoid some topics, like blockchain and AI, which are popular but not really in CodeStreams' wheelhouse, or security, which could easily double the amount of material they would want to cover.

Armed with this list of topics, the conference team puts out a "call for proposals" (CFP) using the Sessionize online speaker-management tool, posting the CFP's submission URL through various channels, including **Social Media (395)** and the **Newsletter (281)**, as well as reaching out directly to their **Ambassadors (71)** and **Partners (309)**. They set a closing date two months out, so as to give speakers a chance to think about what topics they'd like to present. Knowing full well that speakers have tendency to postpone sending in proposals, however, the committee periodically sends out reminders of the CfP's closing date over their **Social Media (395)**, and sure enough, fully 50% of the proposals come in 48 hours before the deadline. (A few are submitted post-deadline, and the committee spends a meeting debating whether to allow those proposals in after the deadline or not.)

They then begin the wearying task of sorting through the proposals, looking to balance the agenda appropriately. Some areas got a much larger percentage of the total proposals, and the committee spends some

CHAPTER 10   CONFERENCE

time debating whether they should adjust how many sessions go into each track before agreeing to stick with their original plan—this is their first event, after all, and it's entirely possible that future events will see the percentages shift from one topic to another.

After much deliberation, the organizing team settles on a list of speakers-and-sessions that includes talks on the latest in CI/CD, cloud computing advancements, and the future of DevOps, with a mix of technical deep dives, case studies, and a couple of visionary keynotes. The committee takes a close eye at not just the topic list, but also the speakers themselves—in keeping with their company's stated goals and objectives, they want a diverse collection of speakers from a wide array of backgrounds, including industry veterans, innovative startups, and influential thought leaders, ensuring a rich, inclusive dialogue throughout the event.

As speaker notifications go out, the selected speakers are asked/encouraged to talk about their upcoming session over **Social Media (395)** channels, and the full program is not only made public on the conference website, but also sent out in that month's **Newsletter (281)**.

The conference team, first and foremost, makes sure to be present at the event from before it opens to well after it closes, ensuring (as best they can) that the event is proceeding well. While the team knows that entirely unexpected issues will always arise (one of the conference team talks about the time a tornado alarm went off in the middle of an event he was at), the team also knows there will be many issues that are common to conferences, and briefs various conference staff members on how to handle the common situations (forgotten registration details, one attendee can only attend one day and wants to give their pass to another co-worker, and so on). In particular, all of the staff are carefully briefed on the Code of Conduct the Legal team worked up, and what to do if an attendee brings attention to a potential violation.

CHAPTER 10 CONFERENCE

As part of its desire to close the feedback loop as tightly as possible across all different levels of interaction, the conference team also uses several different solutions in an effort to integrate multiple channels of feedback. This includes a mobile event app, for real-time feedback during sessions, as well as dedicated feedback booths with staff collecting insights, and post-session digital surveys. Each night, the feedback is collected into a large central repository/database, both to anonymize it and to help make it easier to "get the big picture" of all of what's offered.

Certain feedback is sorted out—that which is about the conference itself (the food, the venue, and so on) is separated from the feedback about the speakers, which in turn is separated from feedback about the company's product/service and direction. All of the feedback is useful, but not everyone in the company is the "target" for all of the feedback sent, and much of it is not requiring of immediate action. That which is—namely, feedback about the venue, any violations of the Code of Conduct, or notifications from speakers about travel delays or cancellations—are immediately prioritized and addressed.

In addition, the conference team keeps a close eye on **Social Media (395)** and all relevant **Forums (233)** for discussions of the conference, both good and bad, as additional elements of feedback, and responds with a sense of urgency on the feedback that potentially risks bad PR if it is not addressed directly.

After the closing ceremonies on the third day, the conference team first lets out a roar at having completed their event, and then takes a trip to one of those local bars to celebrate for the evening before getting into the meat of the after-event activities.

First, all sessions, which were recorded, are sent to the group managing the conference website and made available, along with presentation slides and additional resources. An email blast notifies attendees when these materials go live, extending the learning experience beyond the event.

The following week, the "StreamCon" team thoroughly analyzes the collected feedback, identifying key takeaways, areas for improvement, and insights to guide the planning of future events. A summary report is shared with all stakeholders to demonstrate transparency and commitment to continuous improvement.

The conference team also makes sure to send each of the relevant pieces of feedback to each of the relevant groups, sending the venue feedback to their venue liaison, speaker feedback to each of their speakers, and the product feedback to the Product team. After a brief conversation with the CEO and CTO, both of whom are extremely pleased with the results, next year's "StreamCon" is greenlit, and the conference team begins the process of planning next year's event, taking into account the feedback they received and experienced.

Consequences

Running a company conference offers tremendous opportunities to create brand awareness among the community, and it is one of the few activities that can create both high-reach (particularly if the sessions are recorded and made available for later offline consumption) as well as high-interactivity (direct conversations with the very users of your product/service) outcomes.

For example, besides the usual **Conference Sessions (197)**, **Workshops (477)** found at a conference, your conference can offer a number of other opportunities to connect with your audience, such as **Hackathons (255)**, or even in-person **Office Hours (289)**. The opportunity to directly observe and/or engage with developers using your product/service creates an incredibly valuable feedback loop, particularly if you can bring your internal developers into the exercise.

This opportunity for observation is huge, particularly for products/services that are not yet quite out the door (that is to say, those that are "in beta"). Watching developers in person "open the box" on your forthcoming

CHAPTER 10   CONFERENCE

product/service and work through instruction, tutorials, or even just trying to understand the point of the product/service can guide you to weak spots in the **Reference Documentation (373)** and/or make it clear where more **Tutorials (451)** or **Guides (243)** are necessary to reduce the amount of "friction" developers experience at first.

Throwing an event does not have to be exclusively reserved for companies of 10,000 or more; more informal level small companies can do so on a without some of the hoopla and formality. However, proportionally, throwing an event always requires a non-trivial amount of time and almost always requires at least an individual (if not a whole team) dedicated to the task of organizing, scheduling, managing, and monitoring the event.

For those companies that look to host an event (internally facing or external) yet lack the bandwidth to do the logistical work, numerous third-party "event hosting companies" can be retained to provide the logistical support (up to a point—they will likely need company assistance in deciding what sessions to schedule and approve, for example) for running such an event. It will tend to drive the cost of the event up, but doing so will also leverage experts who have several events already "under their belts" and avoid some common beginner mistakes.

The rewards of a successful conference can also be very high. A conference dedicated exclusively to the product/service and/or to the company, particularly if well-attended (even sold out!), can signal that the product/service has "arrived," and if the hallways are packed just enough, it creates a sense of "buzz" that the tech press will be happy to talk about in their articles and reports.

CHAPTER 10   CONFERENCE

Variants

- **TechReady, TechWeek:** Some companies are large enough that it behooves them to hold an internal conference to talk openly about secret projects that cannot be discussed outside the company walls, and/or to conduct a wide variety of training on topics that the company is using. These are often combined with **Hackathons (255)** to give developers a break from their "daily grind," connect with peers across the company they don't normally get to meet and provide opportunities for training without having to explicitly take time away from a feature schedule or disrupt a sprint. (In those companies that run 2-week sprints, for example, it is common to take one week aside once a quarter for activities like this; given that each quarter is 13 weeks, this way, the company gets six sprints per quarter plus one week for internal training and social gathering.)

CHAPTER 11

Conference Session

Topics: *Presentation, Code*

A conference session is a structured presentation or discussion that takes place during a conference, focused on a specific topic or area of interest relevant to the audience. In the context of Developer Relations, these sessions are opportunities for speakers to share insights, demonstrate technologies, or discuss industry trends with attendees. These sessions typically include a formal presentation followed by a Q&A segment, where the audience's questions and feedback play a crucial role in shaping the discussion. The goal of a conference session is to educate, inspire, and involve the audience in the conversation.

CHAPTER 11   CONFERENCE SESSION

Also Known As

Talk, Presentation, Session, Breakout, Panel

Intent

To deliver a concise, impactful, and engaging presentation (such as what might be seen at a developer conference), ensuring that attendees gain valuable insights, learn about products/services, and feel a strengthened connection to the brand.

CHAPTER 11 CONFERENCE SESSION

Context

Complex information, particularly abstract and conceptual information, is often hard to communicate in a purely "visible" spectrum (that is, writing). For whatever reason, humans still seem to learn and understand more effectively when multiple communication channels are engaged simultaneously—that is to say, when they are shown things at the same time they are told things (so long as those things are supporting each other).

Perhaps there are conceptual parts to what the product/service does that are confusing, or the product/service has a large "surface area" of material that is overwhelming. There may be nuances to certain features that aren't visible at first, or advanced features that require some foundational understanding before being able to be used effectively.

Solution

Deliver a technical presentation at a third-party conference (that is, run by a group or company that isn't your own). It can be in a variety of different forms, ranging from an "all-code, no-slides" presentation in which you have the outline memorized in your head and you code-on-the-fly interactively with the audience, to an "all-slides, no-code" presentation in which you talk about concepts and ideas that would be tricky to pull off "on the fly." Most "breakout" presentations are somewhere in the middle, depending on the topic, the presenter, and (sometimes) the culture of the event.

Most conference breakout sessions are just under an hour in length; anything less than 45 minutes is better categorized as a "lightning talk" (see Variants). Some talks can run as long as 90 minutes, but anything longer than that may be leaning into a Workshop or Training.

CHAPTER 11   CONFERENCE SESSION

Participants

Presenters are central figures, typically selected for their deep knowledge of the topic and proficiency in public speaking. They are responsible for delivering engaging and informative talks, demonstrating products, or leading discussions, serving as the face of the company's expertise and commitment to the developer community.

Company stakeholders and management leadership often play an essential behind-the-scenes role in conference sessions, mainly when talks include product announcements, forward-looking statements, or messaging tied to the company's brand. Advocates and speakers may need to coordinate with stakeholders from engineering, marketing, or legal to ensure that the content is accurate, on message, and aligned with the company's priorities. Even when presenting in a personal capacity, it's essential to remember that speakers are still seen as representatives of their employer. As such, maintaining transparency, professionalism, and internal alignment helps avoid surprises and ensures the session supports broader company goals while serving the audience effectively.

The **audience** consists of developers, tech enthusiasts, and other conference attendees who interact with the booth, seeking to learn about new technologies, tools, and practices and to engage directly with the presenting company. Their participation and feedback are critical for the dynamic exchange of ideas and the overall success of the session.

At some conferences, **session moderators** facilitate and/or coordinate and/or "run" the session, ensuring that the session runs smoothly by managing time, orchestrating the Q&A segments, and handling logistical details. They act as a bridge between the presenters and the audience, maintaining order and flow and enhancing the quality of interaction and engagement during the session. Together, these participants create a collaborative and educational environment that benefits the presenting company and the attending community.

event staff are those who are running the event, such as the folks behind the desk at the registration station, checking in attendees as they arrive, or the folks who take care of the audio/video equipment (most often these are the projectors to which one hooks up their laptop for a presentation). Most conference event staff will have a principal **conference organizer**, who is the titular head of the event, and ultimately the "captain of the ship," responsible for making executive-level decisions that no one else feels comfortable or empowered making. Prior to the event, some event staff are the **track chairs**, who evaluate all of the incoming proposals and determine which will be selected to speak at the event.

Implementation

When orchestrating a Conference Session, a strategic and thoughtful approach to content creation, engagement, feedback collection, and rehearsal is paramount to delivering a session that resonates well with the audience.

Content creation, the process of developing the overall narrative of the presentation, is a crucial aspect of engaging the audience. This includes crafting slides, speaking points, and any supporting multimedia, such as videos or live demos. The essence of successful content creation is crafting a compelling, coherent story that resonates with the audience, often consisting of developers and industry professionals. It's essential to avoid canned or marketing-driven content, as these can quickly lose the audience's interest and come across as insincere or salesy. Instead, focus on providing valuable, genuine insights that are relevant to the audience's real-world experiences. This involves clearly outlining the session's objectives, ensuring the content is technically accurate yet accessible, and integrating real-world examples to illustrate key points effectively. Additionally, visually engaging slides and interactive elements can enhance understanding and retention of the material presented, making the session both informative and memorable.

CHAPTER 11   CONFERENCE SESSION

In implementing **engagement strategies** for a conference session aimed at developer relations team members, choosing methods that maximize interaction and learning is vital. Options include live Q&A sessions to address immediate queries, interactive polls to gauge audience opinions and steer the discussion, and hands-on workshops to apply learning in a practical setting. The choice between these strategies depends on the session's goals: live Q&A is best for deep dives into complex topics and real-time engagement; polls are effective for gathering instant feedback and customizing content flow; workshops are ideal for skills enhancement and fostering collaborative learning.

Rehearsing for a conference session is crucial to ensure a smooth delivery and to build confidence. However, the practice of rehearsal must be balanced to avoid over-rehearsing, which can lead to a presentation that feels scripted or needs more spontaneity. It's advisable to memorize only some of the talk (such as particular key points or phrases) word-for-word, leaving the rest of the talk to be delivered extemporaneously, so long as the speaker(s) understand and fully grasp the key points and transitions to maintain a natural flow. To simulate potential issues, practice with the technology you'll use during the session, such as microphones or presentation software, and have contingency plans for common problems like audiovisual failures or disruptions. Rehearsing in front of peers or using video recordings can provide critical feedback for improving delivery and timing while preparing you for unexpected questions or interactions with the audience.

Effective **delivery** of a conference session hinges on clear communication, engaging storytelling, live demonstrations, and responsive interaction with the audience. It's crucial to speak clearly and maintain an enthusiastic tone to engage the audience. Using natural gestures and maintaining eye contact can make the presentation more dynamic and relatable. Implementation notes should include reminders to check and adjust the pace of speech, use technical language appropriately, and ensure that all visual aids, like slides or videos, are synchronized with the talk. Additionally, being prepared to handle live questions with informed and thoughtful responses is essential, as this interaction can significantly enhance the session's impact and audience engagement. These notes serve as guidelines to help speakers deliver their content effectively, ensuring the session is informative and compelling.

Conference sessions come with **financial and logistical requirements** for speakers, travel (both the planning and the cost) being the biggest of the lot. While many DevRel teams handle these themselves, consider making it easier for them to do so: allow them to work with a travel agency (a human one, not an online one) to make it easier to book travel (and get them home in the event of a travel disruption), and consider working with Accounting to streamline and expedite the process of reimbursement; although it is tempting to tell the team "just float it on your credit card," that may not be feasible and/or financially disadvantageous to the team.

Metrics

To document the metrics for a conference session organized by a conference speaker or developer relations team, a detailed approach is necessary to capture both the immediate and long-term impact of the session. The first metric to track is **session attendance**, which includes the total number of attendees in the session relative to the room's capacity. This data helps gauge the session's draw and popularity within the context of the overall conference.

Engagement levels during the session are another crucial metric. This can be measured by the number of questions asked during the Q&A segment, participation in live polls or interactive activities, and the volume of social media mentions or live posts during the session. These indicators reflect how actively the audience interacts with the content, underscoring their pivotal role in the session's success, and can highlight areas where the session resonated or fell flat.

The **quality of content delivery** should be assessed through post-session surveys where attendees rate the content's relevance, the presentation's clarity, and the speaker's effectiveness. Collecting qualitative feedback about what attendees found most valuable or areas they felt needed improvement will provide deeper insights into the session's strengths and areas for enhancement, instilling a sense of optimism for future sessions.

Audience retention is another critical metric that tracks how many attendees stayed for the entire session versus those who left early. High retention rates suggest that the content was engaging and relevant, whereas lower retention rates indicate pacing, content, or delivery issues.

Speaker performance can be evaluated through both attendee feedback and peer reviews. This might include assessing the speaker's ability to engage the audience, handle questions effectively, and maintain a clear and concise delivery. Feedback from other speakers or event organizers can provide additional perspectives on the speaker's effectiveness, ensuring that the audience's voice is heard and respected.

Social media impact is another important metric, measured by the number of social media mentions, shares, and likes related to the session and the use of any session-specific hashtags. This helps understand the session's broader reach beyond the immediate audience and its resonance within the larger community.

Post-session follow-up engagement is crucial for measuring the longer-term impact of the session. This includes tracking how many attendees engage with follow-up materials such as slide decks, video recordings, or related blog posts. Additionally, monitoring the number of attendees who continue interacting with the speaker or company through social media, email newsletters, or other channels provides insight into the session's lasting influence.

Content sharing metrics track how widely the session materials (slides, videos, or handouts) are distributed and accessed post-conference. This includes counting the downloads or views of these materials, which reflects the session's continuing value to attendees.

Finally, the **overall attendee satisfaction** with the session should be documented through comprehensive surveys that assess the content, delivery, and the overall value the session provides. This feedback should be analyzed to identify trends or common themes that could inform future session planning.

All these metrics should be compiled into a detailed report that combines quantitative data with qualitative insights. This report should include visualizations, such as graphs and charts, to communicate the findings clearly. This documentation aims to provide a thorough evaluation of the session's success, guide improvements for future sessions, and demonstrate the session's impact to stakeholders and event organizers.

Example

Beth, a seasoned developer relations manager, is scheduled to present at an upcoming tech conference on "Innovations in Cloud Computing." Her session aims to engage a diverse audience, from industry newcomers to experienced developers, and highlight her company's recent advancements in cloud technology. Where these two needs may conflict, she opts to default to the newcomers, as the conference tends to attract more senior developers than newcomers.

Beth begins planning her session: a brief introduction, in order to warmly greet the audience, and then an agenda, to outline the session's objectives. She will set the stage by sharing intriguing statistics about cloud adoption rates to grab attention. To make her presentation more relatable, she introduces a common scenario many developers face and explains how it ties into the day's discussion. Finally, she'll wrap up with a conclusion designed to leave the audience with some "thinking points" and how to adopt her ideas to their needs.

Before she begins deep work on creating the content, Beth decides to run the outline past a few colleagues on her team for validation. Gagan, another developer advocate with more than a few conferences under his belt, points out that her target audience is a little broad, and suggests she narrow it down a little: "Either do a session for newbies, or do it for the seniors—don't try to do both. You'll annoy everyone if you do." Beth reluctantly agrees, and chooses to build her session for more senior developers, but leaves a note for herself to explore the newbie angle as a separate talk, likely for other conferences (or as the opening pieces of a cloud **Training (439)** effort). Another colleague, Xian, notes that she probably wants to follow the classic Aristotelian outline: Intro, 3 main points, summary. Beth notes that she actually has 5 points she wants to make, at which Xian notes that in a 50-minute session that means less than 10 minutes per point, and that's before allocating time for Intro and Conclusion, and 10 minutes is not a lot of time, particularly since Beth has three demos she wants to do. "Knock it down to three points, Beth, or you're going to go way over time," Xian warns.

After revising her outline appropriately, Beth begins to flesh out the outline into actual slideware. Her presentation content is meticulously planned to provide depth and breadth on cloud innovations. She uses slides to break down complex technologies into digestible segments, incorporating diagrams and simplified metaphors to clarify technical concepts. Each central point is supported by real-world examples of how her company's technology has successfully addressed specific industry challenges. At Xian's urging, she ditches the idea of live demos, and instead prepares a few short videos demonstrating their technology in action, which are embedded within her slide deck.

To keep the audience engaged, Beth incorporates interactive elements throughout her session: She uses live polls to gather audience opinions on key topics, which she then discusses in real time, tailoring her content based on their responses. Beth allocates a few minutes for an explicit Q&A segment for the end of her talk, but also makes a note to tell the audience that she is open for questions at any point during the talk, hopefully encouraging the audience to ask questions verbally or via a conference app. She also makes a note to herself to create a conference proposal for a follow-up workshop where attendees can experience the technology hands-on to foster further interaction.

Beth rehearses her session multiple times, first by herself to refine her timing and transitions and then in front of her colleagues to get feedback. She pays particular attention to mastering the flow of her narrative, ensuring that her transitions between topics are smooth and logical. During rehearsals, she simulates potential technical issues, like slide malfunctions or audio problems, to prepare herself to handle them gracefully during the presentation. Once or twice, she asks her teammates to try and disrupt her talk by doing some of the things that happen during conference sessions, and Xian manages to fluster her by asking a "question" that turns into a five-minute rant about a bug. Beth makes note to work on her "heckler management" strategies, because she found it difficult to step in and resume control of the talk once Xian got going.

On the conference day, despite the nervousness she always gets before a talk, Beth delivers her session with confidence and enthusiasm. She speaks clearly, making sure to pace her presentation to match the audience's engagement and understanding. As she navigates her slides, she seamlessly integrates the responses from the live polls and adjusts her focus based on the audience's interests. Her ability to adapt and interact with the audience in real time makes the session dynamic and memorable. Post-presentation, she remains available to answer additional questions and connect with attendees, reinforcing relationships and providing further value.

CHAPTER 11   CONFERENCE SESSION

The Q&A segment is designed to encourage attendees to ask questions, share their agile experiences, and suggest features, providing immediate feedback and insights to the internal team building the tools she demoed.

Consequences

Conference sessions often pair well with conference **Sponsorship (405)**, including the purchase of **Booth (137)** space and copious amounts of **Swag (427)**. If you have more than one session, or more than one of your team is speaking at the same event, consider bringing a **Pit Crew (137)** and have them visibly present in each of your company's talks, not to act as a cheering section, but to be available for questions that the audience might have but aren't willing to wait very long to ask. In these situations, consider putting somebody in charge of logistics and event coordination for all of those committed to the event (including **Pit Crew (137)**), as doing the event as a team can be a strong emotionally bonding experience to do things as a group (share the same flights, be at the same hotel, coordinate dinners and evening activities, and so on).

A Conference Session offers a direct communication channel with the target audience, allowing presenters to engage personally and address specific interests or concerns. It is an excellent platform for showcasing expertise and establishing thought leadership within the industry, enhancing the presenter's and the company's credibility. Additionally, the interactive Q&A segments provide valuable opportunities for feedback and deeper interaction, facilitating a two-way exchange of ideas and insights.

A Conference Session demands significant time and effort from the presenters, so that presenters can do thorough preparation and rehearsal to ensure the clarity of the message and a smooth flow of information. The session's effectiveness is also constrained by its limited duration, which makes efficient time management essential to cover all intended points without rushing or overshooting the allotted time.

CHAPTER 11   CONFERENCE SESSION

Furthermore, the session's success relies heavily on the presenter's delivery and communication skills; a lack of engaging presentation techniques or clear articulation can diminish the session's impact, regardless of the content's quality.

Variants

- **Beta/Buzz Talk:** Although this is less common in an era of open-source, sometimes the desire is to "build buzz" around an upcoming release of the product/service, and one great way to do that is to do a presentation on the new features of the upcoming release before it is generally available. This way developers and customers can be "ready to go" when the release drops, and the feature set might even help attract new customers because they heard about it at the conference. **Ambassadors (71)** in particular love to give "Upcoming Features" talks, as it positions them and their own branding as being smart and "in the know" when it comes to the product/service.
  This material is also very powerful when used in a **Pre-Sales (223)** meeting.

- **User Group Session. Meetup Session:** A common staple of the **User Group (457)** is to have somebody from the company (or an **Ambassador (71)**) come and speak to the group on some technical topic related to the product/service (more or less). The DevRel team can either help facilitate Ambassadors speaking at the

209

group(s), or have members of the DevRel team do it directly (in which case the DevRel team will need to handle many of the logistics and expense for doing so). Note that because most user group sessions are more informal than other settings, expect that the presenter will spend more time with the attendees than at a conference. (It is common to go out for food and drinks after the event, or to mill in the room both before and after the talk.) It is common for DevRel teams to use user group sessions as an opportunity to practice a talk before it is delivered as a **Conference Session (197)**. Some groups welcome this, but some resent it. If the relationship with the group is strong, ask for feedback on the talk; if it is not, treat it as a formal presentation every bit as "real" as the conference or a **Customer Meeting (223)**.

- **Sponsored Conference Session:** At times, a conference will sell a speaking slot to a **Sponsorship (405)** company, guaranteeing the company will have a speaker at the event without going through the traditional Call-for-Presentations process. Be warned that developers historically have not taken well to these slots, doubly so when the sponsor chooses to do a presentation or talk specifically around their product/service. If your team is sponsoring the slot (perhaps the Marketing or Sales team decided to buy it without consulting you), consider not taking it—let somebody from Marketing or Sales do the presentation, so as to preserve the credibility of the DevRel team with their developer audience. If the

DevRel team *must* do the sponsored presentation, then be up front and respectful of the developer audience: "Hi, my name's Denny, I'm from ToolCorp, and we threw some money at the organizers to get this time slot. What I'd like to do is show you the pros and cons of our tools, and give you some idea of when—and when not—to use our stuff." Don't try to "hide" the fact that this is a sponsored session—most attendees can already tell, owing to the different advertising around sponsored sessions. If metrics are captured for this session, do not compare them to other Conference Sessions, as the surrounding context of each are different enough that it is comparing apples to oranges.

- **Brown Bag. Lunch-n-Learn:** When the direction of the activity is pointed internally, these become known as "brown bags" or "lunch-n-learns," wherein the DevRel team (or other internal employees of the company) deliver the presentation (often over the lunch hour) to other engineers within the company. These can be organized periodically (weekly or monthly), as part of an internal **Hackathon (255)**, or as part of the company's internal **Conference (179)** (or all of the above). If there is no formal internal training team, the DevRel team should take on the organization, logistics, and "acquisition" of speakers (internal or external) for such events; if there is a training team, DevRel can be frequent speakers, and/or help with the acquisition of speakers, and/or help with some of the logistics. Note that if internal employees are interested in speaking, DevRel should (must!) volunteer to assist that employee in the preparation and practice of delivering the presentation, since many developers are not comfortable delivering or preparing presentations. If DevRel is scheduling these, it's often best to start with monthly events, then move to biweekly and weekly as the "pipeline" grows. Let the upcoming pipeline grow to six months' in advance before reducing the timing—for example, if you are doing monthly sessions, and you have six months' speakers/topics in the pipeline, go biweekly (thus reducing your pipeline to three months' worth) and rebuild the pipeline out to six months' worth before going weekly.

- **Lightning Talk:** Any presentation that is 15 minutes or less is generally best considered to be a "lightning talk," and requires very different preparation and delivery considerations. (You will not have time to write code on the fly. You will not have time to take questions. Instead of three things to talk about, focus on one. Scripting the talk is easier when it's shorter like this, particularly if the deadlines are "hard" and no wiggle room.)

CHAPTER 12

Customer Check-In

Topics: *Social*

A customer check-in is a proactive interaction initiated by the Developer Relations team to connect with users of the company's technology or products, providing an opportunity to gather feedback, address challenges, and foster relationships. These check-ins are not just about understanding customer needs and ensuring satisfaction, but also about building a community. Developer Relations professionals play a key role in this, engaging directly with customers to build trust, enhance the company's reputation, and provide actionable insights to engineering and product teams. This helps refine the product and positions the company as responsive and customer-focused, which can lead to increased loyalty, positive word-of-mouth, and, ultimately, improved sales and adoption of the technology.

CHAPTER 12   CUSTOMER CHECK-IN

Also Known As

Temperature Check; "Love" (as in "It's time to give the customer some love")

Intent

A customer check-for a Developer Relations team aims to foster meaningful dialogue with users. By uncovering pain points and celebrating successes, professionals can understand how customers use the company's tools. This process helps identify user behavior trends, anticipate needs, and provide personalized support beyond basic interactions. Additionally, these engagements introduce new features, share best practices, and reinforce that customers are valued. Ultimately, this outreach builds partnership and community, enhancing trust and brand perception, which drives deeper adoption and supports long-term sales growth.

Context

The Developer Relations team plays a crucial bridge between the technical community and the company, balancing technical credibility with strategic advocacy. Customer check-ins are essential for users integrating the company's tools into complex workflows or adopting new features. These interactions go beyond problem-solving; they celebrate successes, identify community champions, and gather in-depth insights often missed in surveys. In today's competitive tech landscape, such check-ins demonstrate a commitment to users, foster long-term partnerships, and ensure a productive feedback loop that aligns customer needs with business objectives.

CHAPTER 12   CUSTOMER CHECK-IN

Solution

To implement effective customer check-ins, Developer Relations teams should establish a consistent and intentional process for meaningful engagement. Start by identifying key customers, such as early adopters and power users, especially those facing challenges. The check-in should be personalized, focusing on building rapport through open-ended questions that explore their experiences and uncover pain points. Emphasizing the customer's goals and achievements makes the interaction feel collaborative rather than transactional.

Active listening and empathy are essential to ensure customers feel heard. After the check-in, document critical takeaways and create actionable follow-ups, such as connecting customers with resources or escalating feedback to internal teams. Sharing these insights internally allows the company to address issues and seize opportunities, demonstrating that customer input is valued and impactful. This structured yet flexible approach creates a feedback loop that builds trust, enhances brand credibility, and drives long-term success by positioning check-ins as strategic tools for improving customer relationships and business growth.

Participants

In a customer check-in, participants typically include a representative from the Developer Relations team, such as a **Developer Advocate** or **Community Manager**, and customer stakeholders like **developers** or **decision-makers** involved with the technology. The roles may vary based on the check-in's objectives, which could range from addressing technical challenges, like API integration, to discussing product roadmap priorities. While a sales representative may not be directly involved, it's often important to provide a heads-up to the account manager or customer success owner to ensure alignment and avoid surprises.

CHAPTER 12   CUSTOMER CHECK-IN

The interaction is collaborative and conversational, with the Developer Relations representative acting as a facilitator and listener. They create an open environment that encourages customers to share their experiences and feedback, fostering a sense of partnership. Throughout the discussion, the representative may share updates, suggest optimizations, and provide insights into upcoming features, ensuring a two-way value exchange. This balance of listening and offering actionable advice strengthens the relationship and promotes long-term collaboration.

Implementation

Customer check-ins can happen for a variety of reasons; in some cases, a salesperson or customer service associate wants to do a regular "drop-in" visit with the customer as part of a regular cadence of contact to help identify trouble spots before they begin. In other cases, tech support or customer feedback may lead the sales or customer service organization to want to make a "special trip" (either figuratively or literally) to the customer to help smooth out a rough patch or address a particular customer concern. Check-ins can also be tied to larger gatherings, such as **Conferences (179)** or community events, where multiple customer stakeholders are present in the same place. In these cases, teams often schedule check-ins en masse, leveraging the efficiency of in-person events to cover a broad set of accounts in a short period of time.

Once identified as necessary, the implementation of a customer check-in often (though not always) begins with the Developer Relations team preparing for the meeting by identifying the interaction's purpose and selecting the appropriate customers to engage, such as frequent users or vocal advocates. Scheduling the check-in is carefully managed to accommodate the customer's availability, fostering a low-pressure environment for meaningful conversations. Representatives review relevant history before the meeting to personalize the experience and set clear goals. During the check-in, the conversation should be structured yet adaptable, initiating with an overview before delving into exploratory discussions. In some cases, this agenda may be driven by the underlying reason for the meeting itself—if this is a drop-in visit, the agenda will likely be very open-ended and exploratory, whereas if this is a "fix-it" meeting, the agenda will likely be tailored around the concern brought to light that necessitated the check-in in the first place. The team guides the dialogue with targeted questions while remaining open to essential topics raised by the customer. Capturing insights in real time through detailed notes or recordings (with consent) ensures no valuable feedback is overlooked.

Following the check-in, the Developer Relations team synthesizes the gathered information into actionable insights, categorizing feedback into themes such as usability, documentation gaps, or feature requests. This feedback is shared with relevant internal teams, including product management and engineering. The team also follows up with customers to address immediate concerns and updates them on how their feedback is utilized, demonstrating accountability and fostering goodwill. Implementing a tracking system for these interactions ensures consistency across future check-ins, identifies trends over time, and creates a comprehensive view of customer sentiment that can inform broader company strategies.

Metrics

To document metrics for customer check-ins, the Developer Relations team should identify qualitative and quantitative indicators that measure interaction success and alignment with company goals. Key metrics include

- **Number of check-ins** conducted over a specific period
- **Diversity of customer profiles** engaged
- **Frequency** of successful follow-ups

CHAPTER 12   CUSTOMER CHECK-IN

- **Resolution tracking** for issues raised, linking feedback to actionable outcomes
- Product feedback collected, including the number of **bugs filed** and **feature requests submitted** as a direct result of the check-in
- Customer sentiment can be gauged through **surveys**, Net Promoter Score (NPS), or direct feedback to assess satisfaction and trust.

Long-term impact metrics should monitor product adoption rates, engagement in the developer community, and advocacy behaviors, such as favorable reviews or participation in case studies. Additionally, the influence of feedback on internal processes—like the percentage of implemented feedback items and cross-department collaboration—should be tracked.

Example

The Developer Relations team at CodeSpark, known for its API management tools, organized a check-in with FlexFinance, a fintech startup that recently adopted its API gateway solution. After noticing several minor issues reported through support tickets but limited engagement in community forums and webinars, Developer Advocate Maya reached out to understand their experience and address any pain points.

During a virtual meeting, Maya met with FlexFinance's lead backend developer, Alex, and head of engineering, Priya. She began by expressing appreciation for their innovative work in financial APIs and asked about their experience with the API gateway. Alex noted that while powerful, they faced challenges integrating custom authentication schemes, and the documentation for advanced use cases needed improvement. Priya added that while the tool's performance was satisfactory, better onboarding materials would have streamlined their implementation process.

Maya acknowledged these challenges and shared that CodeSpark was planning to enhance its documentation. She invited Alex and Priya to review an early draft for feedback and suggested workarounds for their authentication issue, promising to escalate it to the engineering team. She also highlighted upcoming features that aligned with FlexFinance's roadmap, which piqued Priya's interest and led to a proposal for a follow-up meeting with their product team.

After check-in, Maya sent a detailed email summarizing their conversation and the next steps to take while providing helpful resources. She flagged their feedback, resulting in a quick update to the documentation and prioritization of the authentication issue in the next sprint. A month later, Priya praised CodeSpark's responsiveness in a testimonial on their website. FlexFinance also became a beta tester for new features, solidifying their partnership and increasing the adoption of CodeSpark's tools. This proactive check-in transformed a neutral customer experience into one of advocacy, demonstrating the value of Developer Relations efforts.

Consequences

Customer check-ins lead to improved satisfaction and valuable insights that enhance products and services. Through meaningful dialogue, Developer Relations teams can address customer challenges, offer tailored solutions, and demonstrate commitment to user success. These interactions result in faster issue resolution, greater product adoption, and higher retention rates, as customers feel valued. They also elicit critical feedback that informs new features, documentation improvements, and onboarding adjustments, fostering a more user-friendly experience. Immediate visibility into customer needs helps identify trends, allowing for proactive product or strategic adjustments.

CHAPTER 12   CUSTOMER CHECK-IN

Indirectly, customer check-ins enhance brand reputation and increase community engagement. Satisfied customers often advocate for the company by sharing positive experiences and participating in case studies and testimonials, attracting new users and building trust in the developer ecosystem. This goodwill positions the company as approachable and customer-centric. Additionally, these interactions promote a culture of collaboration, driving alignment between Developer Relations, product teams, and marketing. Over time, these benefits lead to higher sales, stronger loyalty, and a more vibrant community that supports the company's growth and innovation.

If not managed properly, a customer check-in can potentially create a new, undeclared "back-channel" support avenue for customers: If they complain, they get priority support! Both the DevRel and the Tech Support teams should keep a close eye on the time allotted to customer check-ins in order to avoid accidentally rewarding customers for being "squeaky wheels" in a manner that will, over time, become unsustainable at scale.

Legal may have some concerns about these conversations unless they are covered by NDA and/or disclaimers, and the DevRel team should take care to connect with Engineering about what is (and what is not) safe to talk about. More than once, a customer has walked away from a check-in with a "promise" that a new feature would be delivered by a certain date that wasn't ever an actual company commitment. (And note that "promise" can range anywhere from an actual promise by the Developer Advocate—which shouldn't happen, since it creates an obligation the company may not or cannot or may want to not uphold—all the way through the customer's imagination, hearing a collection of words as a promise.) It may be advantageous to put a disclaimer at the front of each meeting that explicitly states that any discussions are under the umbrella of "possible" or "exploratory," with no promises implied.

CHAPTER 12   CUSTOMER CHECK-IN

Variants

- **Partner Meeting**: If the company has signed partnerships with other companies, meeting with those customers will have the same benefits as the typical customer check-in. Customer-Partners tend to have a deeper relationship, however, so these meetings may need to happen more often or act as a two-way communication opportunity to discuss future plans or needs. Partner meetings can often bring with them requests from the partner to build some **Product Development (357)**, such as integrations or extensions that either the partner will own after development, or the company will be required to maintain.

CHAPTER 13

Customer Pre-Sale

Topics: *Social*

A customer pre-sale in Developer Relations involves proactive engagement where teams interact with potential customers before finalizing a sale. This interaction focuses on providing technical expertise, addressing concerns, and demonstrating how products or services meet specific needs through personalized demos and consultations. By fostering trust and credibility, Developer Relations professionals build relationships that support sales efforts and enhance the company's reputation for being customer-focused and reliable. This approach can lead to stronger customer satisfaction, increased adoption, and long-term loyalty, ultimately driving growth and success for the company.

CHAPTER 13   CUSTOMER PRE-SALE

Also Known As

Technical Pre-Sales; Pre-Sales Consulting; Pre-Sales Engagement

Intent

A pre-sale approach in Developer Relations aims to connect technical solutions with customer needs, fostering meaningful, trust-based interactions beyond traditional sales tactics. Developer Relations teams utilize their technical expertise and community advocacy to thoroughly understand each customer's unique challenges, providing tailored insights on how the company's technologies can integrate into their workflows or address specific issues. The team ensures customers receive tangible value before purchasing by offering hands-on support—such as developing prototypes, guiding proof-of-concept explorations, and granting early access to features. This strategy positions the company as a dependable partner in innovation, enhancing its reputation for technical proficiency and genuine commitment to customer success while also paving the way for long-term partnerships and repeat business through memorable, solution-oriented pre-sale experiences.

Context

In Developer Relations, customer pre-sales focus on technical advocacy and customer engagement to address the specific challenges faced by developers and technical teams evaluating a product. The Developer Relations team acts as trusted technical advisors, engaging early in the sales cycle to align customer requirements with the company's offerings. This process involves understanding the customer's technical landscape, providing best practice guidance, and showcasing real-world product applications. The team facilitates a smooth adoption process by ensuring customers feel supported and informed. This approach fosters a customer-centric experience, builds trust, and positions the company as a technical innovation and community engagement leader.

However, this is a risky pattern if handled without clear boundaries. Most companies already employ technical sales staff whose role is to guide customers through evaluation and adoption. If DevRel professionals spend significant time in one-on-one pre-sales sessions, they risk becoming a de facto extension of the sales organization and losing the ability to focus on the one-to-many activities (such as content, workshops, and community programs) that uniquely scale their impact.

When approached deliberately, DevRel's role in pre-sales should be occasional and strategic—supporting sales when deep technical credibility or community perspective is needed, but without becoming the primary technical resource for every customer opportunity. This balance allows DevRel teams to contribute meaningfully to customer trust and early adoption while maintaining focus on scalable, community-driven advocacy.

Solution

To effectively engage with potential customers during their evaluation phase, Developer Relations teams should adopt a flexible approach tailored to both technical and business needs. This can be achieved by establishing a framework emphasizing technical expertise, collaborative problem-solving, and community engagement. Key strategies include offering technical workshops, hosting interactive demos, and developing proof-of-concept implementations that align with customer goals.

By being proactive, responsive, and transparent, these teams foster an environment where potential customers feel confident in their decision-making process and view the company as a reliable partner. Integrating feedback from pre-sale interactions into the product development life cycle ensures that offerings evolve to meet real-world challenges, refining products and building goodwill among prospects.

Furthermore, the visibility of these initiatives enhances the company's reputation as a thought leader, as satisfied customers are likely to share their positive experiences. This dual focus on addressing immediate customer needs and contributing to long-term product and brand improvement transforms pre-sales from a transactional process into a strategic investment in the company's growth.

Participants

Sales will typically be heavily involved in the pre-sales cycle, often being the catalyst for the meeting(s) with the customer's stakeholders. Sometimes these meetings will be the first connections with a potential customer after **Marketing** has qualified the lead. Sales may want the Developer Relations team to participate for their technical acuity, giving the sales effort a "push" from a more technical direction and (hopefully) circumnavigating any customer technical obstacles or objections. However, sometimes the DevRel team brings their public brand/reputation to the meeting, providing a tiny bit of "celebrity" status to the discussion. (This will only be applicable for more senior DevRel members who are well-known in the community, either through **Conference Sessions (197)** or perhaps **Recorded Videos (363)**).

Depending on the level of participation desired, the Developer Relations team may become the meeting's central facilitator, bringing technical expertise and community insights to the table while actively listening to the customer's challenges and objectives. They work closely with the customer's technical team to provide hands-on guidance, share best practices, and resolve any initial concerns about the product's implementation or compatibility within the customer's ecosystem.

Product managers' involvement will be to speak to the product and/or its roadmap, again often as a way to work around customer obstacles/objections, and in some cases to build some excitement over forthcoming features. Sales may want a particular demo to show to the customer, which will usually involve a joint effort between product management and developer advocates, and these demos may get polished to a point where making them publicly available is a good return on the time invested.

Implementation

The customer pre-sale typically begins with some amount of research and discovery, whereby the team gathers insights about the customer's technical environment, pain points, and goals. This may involve direct discussions with technical stakeholders, analyzing existing systems, and identifying how the company's product can add value.

The next phase involves designing tailored engagements that showcase the product's practical benefits. These can include proof-of-concept implementations, sample applications, or hands-on workshops to enhance customer experience. Throughout this process, the team maintains open communication, addressing technical concerns and incorporating feedback. Upon completion, detailed documentation—including recommendations, workflows, and integration guides—is provided to facilitate smooth adoption.

Finally, the Developer Relations team ensures continuity by involving post-sale support and customer success teams while sharing insights with product managers for future enhancements. This thorough approach helps convert potential customers into advocates and strengthens the company's reputation for technical excellence and customer-centric innovation.

CHAPTER 13   CUSTOMER PRE-SALE

Metrics

Documenting metrics for customer pre-sales involves defining measurable outcomes aligned with the Developer Relations team's objectives and the company's broader goals. Key metrics to assess the effectiveness of pre-sale activities include the number of successful proof-of-concept deliveries, customer satisfaction scores from interactions, conversion rates from pre-sale to actual sales, and response time for technical inquiries. Engagement levels during pre-sale activities, such as workshop attendance and product demo participation, can also indicate customer commitment.

Beyond immediate sales, metrics should measure long-term impacts on the company's reputation and product improvement. Tracking the volume and quality of feedback gathered during pre-sale engagements can provide insights for product refinement. The number of customers who become advocates or give testimonials post-interaction is also a success indicator. The Developer Relations team should regularly review and share insights with sales, marketing, and product teams to ensure these metrics remain actionable. This continuous feedback loop validates the pre-sale process's effectiveness and highlights areas for improvement, bolstering the company's reputation and future business opportunities.

Example

The sales team approached the Developer Relations team at TechNova, a company specializing in cloud-based AI solutions, with a promising opportunity: a mid-sized financial services firm, FinSecure, was considering adopting TechNova's API for fraud detection. However, FinSecure's engineering team expressed concerns about API integration into their existing systems and performance under high transactional loads. The sales team recognized this as critical and enlisted the DevRel team to lead a customer pre-sale engagement.

The DevRel team began by conducting a code review of FinSecure's existing fraud detection system, focusing on its architecture, coding standards, and API integration patterns. During this review, they identified areas where TechNova's API could provide immediate value, such as improving latency in real-time fraud checks and enhancing anomaly detection capabilities. To address FinSecure's performance concerns, the DevRel team developed a proof-of-concept implementation using sample data provided by FinSecure, demonstrating how the API could seamlessly integrate into their systems while maintaining high performance. They also created custom documentation and scripts to simplify deployment, making the process as frictionless as possible for FinSecure's developers.

Throughout the engagement, the DevRel team maintained close communication with FinSecure's engineers, hosting virtual sessions to discuss findings from the code review and iterating on the proof-of-concept based on their feedback. By the end of the process, the FinSecure team was convinced of the API's capabilities and deeply appreciative of TechNova's hands-on, customer-focused approach. The success of this engagement secured the sale and resulted in FinSecure agreeing to be featured in a case study, enhancing TechNova's reputation as a developer-friendly, technically advanced partner. This story highlights how a thoughtful, well-executed customer pre-sale process can address technical concerns, build trust, and turn a potential customer into a long-term advocate.

Consequences

The direct consequences of a customer pre-sale include increased customer confidence in the product, higher conversion rates from potential leads to paying customers, and faster adoption of the product or solution. By addressing technical concerns and showcasing tailored solutions during the pre-sale process, Developer Relations teams help remove barriers to purchase decisions, leading to quicker deal closures. These engagements also enable smoother implementations post-sale, as customers have already been guided through potential challenges and solutions, reducing onboarding time and effort. Additionally, successful pre-sales can generate immediate revenue and create opportunities for upselling or cross-selling related products and services.

The indirect consequences extend to long-term benefits such as enhanced customer loyalty, positive word-of-mouth referrals, and a stronger brand reputation in the developer community. Customers who experience a well-executed pre-sale process are likelier to become advocates, sharing their experiences with peers and endorsing the company as a trusted partner. This, in turn, helps attract new leads and strengthens the company's position as a thought leader and technical innovator. Moreover, the feedback gathered during pre-sale interactions contributes to continuous product improvement and a better understanding of market needs, enabling the company to stay competitive and relevant. These indirect outcomes amplify the impact of the pre-sale process, creating a virtuous cycle of customer satisfaction, community engagement, and business growth.

However, there is also a **significant risk**: DevRel teams can quickly become perceived as a sales resource. This is an anti-pattern—while occasional involvement can be valuable, scaling DevRel primarily through one-to-one pre-sales work takes them away from the one-to-many activities (such as community programs, content, and education) where their unique strengths lie. Over time, this misalignment can reduce DevRel's broader impact and blur the boundary between advocacy and sales.

Variants

- **Proof-of-Concept (PoC) Pre-Sale**, where the Developer Relations team collaborates with the customer to build a small, functional implementation that directly demonstrates the product's value in the customer's specific use case.

- **Technical Workshop Pre-Sale** focuses on hands-on training for the customer's technical team. It provides deep insights into the product's features and integration points to empower developers and address technical barriers to adoption.

- **Architecture Review Pre-Sale**, where the Developer Relations team evaluates the customer's existing systems and offers strategic advice on how the product can fit into or improve their architecture. This approach is often used for enterprise customers with complex requirements.

CHAPTER 14

Forums

Topics: *Social, Writing*

Easily accessible places online where customers can post questions and receive answers from both company employees and/or the surrounding community.

Also Known As

Support Forums; Bulletin Boards

CHAPTER 14   FORUMS

Intent

Customers want to have a place in which to obtain answers without having to schedule conversations, comb through documentation, or read through lots of tests—in essence, they want to be able to post a question and get an answer (or a confirmation of what they think is a bug).

Context

Customers often want to do this Q-and-A style interaction asynchronously, with the ability to write code to support their question and/or see code in the answer. Developers also like helping other customers who are in similar situations, which helps build a sense of community around the product/service. However, they want some reasonable reassurance that the answers they are receiving are from "people who know," so that they do not have to wade through incorrect or incomplete or untested answers.

Solution

One solution is for the company to host a forums system on the company's domain umbrella (see **Apple Developer Forums** for an example), in which customers can post questions and receive answers from employees or other customers. This ensures that the forums are always available so long as the company is in existence, and provides a measure of "stickiness" in that customers using the forums are still on company web properties while they engage in these conversations.

Another solution is to make use of a third-party-hosted forum system, like Stack Overflow or Reddit, by creating a "channel" or a "tag" that questions from the community on the product/service can be easily identified.

In the case of hosting their own forum, companies can benefit from attracting traffic to their own site. They benefit from the SEO of traffic passing through their own domain. The company can also collect information about each user when they register for the forum. The company can control exactly how the forum is set up, organized, and configured. They can control who is allowed to post and even who is banned from ever posting. Sometimes companies even put the entire forum behind a paywall and only provide access to their forums for customers who pay for the privilege.

The main benefit to adopting a third-party-hosted forum system, like Stack Overflow, is putting the forum functionality where their customers already live. Developers regularly visit sites like Stack Overflow to find answers for a variety of development questions. Creating a tag for the company or product increases the likelihood of discoverability. Users will potentially be more likely to post questions, as well as answer other users questions. That is the ultimate goal of any forum. When the community starts answering each other's questions, the community feels a sense of ownership for the product.

In either case, the DevRel team commits to being a visible presence on the forums, directly answering questions and/or visibly taking questions or issues internally and promising an answer within a reasonable period of time. The team should also reach out to particularly active members of the community who voluntarily answer questions. Send those helpful community members some sort of recognition; this can range from designating those users as **Ambassadors (71)**, to as small a gesture as sending them a unique piece of swag—either physical or digital. Even a personalized note will help them feel a deeper connection with the community surrounding the product.

CHAPTER 14   FORUMS

Participants

Most forums consist of two different kinds of users, **authors** and **readers** (sometimes called "lurkers"). The former are active on the forums posting information, opinions, and sometimes entirely irrelevant or distracting material that often (but not always) is related to the topic of the forum or other posts. Authors often require some form of authentication (login credentials) to the forum in order to be able to post, in order to discourage abuse, but generally a forum sees value in being available for consumption by readers without requiring login. If a reader wants to post a comment or provide some other form of feedback (such as an "upvote"), however, typically the forum requires authentication to, again, discourage abuse.

Other participants on forums include **moderators**, to whom falls the thankless task of deleting harmful or abusive posts, often including the power to remove users from the system. Moderators typically have a public presence to them, partly so that they can have some credibility with the other frequent users of the forum, and partly so that when they threaten a malcontent with accountability to their actions, their threat is deemed credible.

Silently, **operations staff** keep the forums up and running, although the move to the cloud can automate and reduce the work necessary to do this. These typically do not appear on the forums at all, except to post notices of downtime for maintenance, or to post other operational and administrative news.

Implementation

There are several pre-built ("turnkey") packages and services for running a forum, from open source projects that are run and maintained on premises to paid services that run externally. At the time of this writing, many companies have chosen to run public Workspaces on Slack or Discourse to interact with their users. The key is to look over the current options and decide which solution is the easiest for your users to engage with. If they're commonly using Slack, it would be much easier for your users to simply connect to a new Slack Workspace rather than creating an account on your isolated forum that takes extra steps to read, track, and post to. You may also find it useful to create a corporate "presence" on genericized public forums like StackOverflow or Reddit, given their incredibly broad reach, intrinsic search, and copious cross-linking.

If choosing to use public forums (like StackOverflow or Reddit), organizations must first make sure that all of their participants are signed up with accounts in good standing (which may or may not require payment or licensing of some form). Before engaging with a public forum, your team should specifically answer the question of "ownership," as in, are the participants using their personal accounts (and thus any branding/reputation they may have already accumulated), or do you want them to use company-affiliated credentials (email)? The former allows your participants to bring their previous reputation (which may be sizable) to bear on your company's behalf, but you must also then accept that they are representing themselves first, and the company by association, which your Legal team may have concerns about (including, but not limited to, potential Code of Conduct violations). Alternatively, if the company requires employees to use company-affiliated credentials, it will eliminate much of Legal's concerns and allow the company to exert greater control over what is posted using that account, but at the same time fails to take advantage of any social standing (reputation or branding) the employee has built up over time. This can be particularly painful on those forums which require a certain amount of participation (such as StackOverflow's "reputation") to unlock certain features.

If choosing to use private forums, implementing the forum is usually a relatively straightforward exercise to provision, install, and configure, but prior to any of this, the company should have conversations regarding the administration and "ownership" of the forums' instance(s). Who is

CHAPTER 14 FORUMS

responsible for correcting an incident (network outage, database crash, etc.) involving the forums instance? Who is responsible for upgrades and/or patches? In the event there is a report of a violation of the Code of Conduct on the forums, who is responsible for determining its existence and its mitigation? It will be tempting to assume the DevRel team will own all of this, but Legal may have some other ideas (certain posts may need to be preserved in the event of litigation!), and the Marketing team may want to make use of the forums for their own purposes (SEO and links to/from the company main website!), to name two possible complications. On top of that, the IT/Security team may have concerns about where the forum's instance lives, such that a security breach in the forums cannot lead to a breach of other systems hosted in the same cloud provider. And so on.

When setting up a forum, consider how to categorize the conversations. Start with categories, channels, and tags that make sense for your community. But, also be open to making changes as users provide feedback—either with their words or their actions. One other, trivial-seeming at first, consideration is that of "tone" and "signature" when writing posts: Do you want participants to sign their names to their posts, or do you want to have anonymized "company" accounts that do not tie a particular individual to responses? The former "humanizes" the team more with the community, but also runs the risk of creating implicit dependencies ("Thanks, but I'm waiting to here what Tim has to say on this.") or favoritism ("Hey, Tim, I know Biff responded to my post, but can you weigh in please? Biff doesn't always seem to be accurate in what he says.").

Configuring and releasing a new forum can be fun and exciting. However, once it's off the ground it's important to have a strategy for monitoring conversations in the forum. The point of a forum is to provide a platform for users to connect with one another, as well as connect with members of your team. Consider the following options for staying up-to-date with forum conversations:

CHAPTER 14 FORUMS

- Set up notifications that alert when new posts are published, and then act on those notifications.

- Appoint a person or team responsible for monitoring forum posts and make sure posts are responded to in a timely manner. You may even want to set internal standards for post response time. For example, every post should be responded to within 3 business days.

- Monitoring posts should also include watching for any conversation that violates your community's code of conduct. Every forum should be a safe space for all users.

In order to best communicate the "rules" surrounding participation on the forums, it is advisable that a "Code of Conduct" post appear near the top of any entry point into the Forums—most forum systems have the ability to "pin" a topic so that it remains near the top—that describes what is considered acceptable and unacceptable conduct. This should be reviewed by Legal to ensure that the company is covered in the event of any legal action (either between the company and an individual, the company and another company, or even between two entirely unrelated-to-the-company individuals on the forums).

In either case, your company's participants in the forums should not be required to "vet" each of their postings (passing them through to Legal or Marketing before posting), as this will create deep bottlenecks and slow down your ability to reply to community members' questions or comments. However, in order to get that freedom, Legal and/or Marketing will often want to sit down with the company-employed participants and lay out some "ground rules" for what can and cannot be said in a public setting (particularly an online one, where "receipts" are so easy to

239

CHAPTER 14 FORUMS

screenshot and use in other places, such as a courtroom). Make sure all the participants are clear on what the company's guidelines are, including time spent on an "internal" Code of Conduct, complete with clear rules on what happens in the event a participant violates the company's guidelines ("Tim just posted a release date for the next version, which we haven't announced publicly yet!"). Company participants need to be sensitive to the idea that even if it doesn't violate the Code of Conduct on the forum, certain posts could create problems for the company and result in lost sales, angry Marketers, lost jobs, or even legal action.

Metrics

Some metrics worth considering when evaluating forums:

- **Posts:** One natural metric that emerges is the number of posts being posted to the forum. In the early days of the forum, it may be sufficient to simply note the total across the entirety of the forums, but as the number grows (particularly as you surpass different orders of magnitude), you may want to track this a little more granularly, such as "average posts per user," "initial posts vs. reply posts," "posts per topic," and so on. Keep in mind that this metric doesn't attempt to ascertain the quality of each post, merely the volume.

- **Post Views:** This metric tracks the number of times a post has been viewed, presumably by readers who are interested in the topic. Depending on the way the forum is architected, this may be more a reflection of the page views of the web page on which the post appears—Reddit, for example, lays out all posts in a hierarchical reply-based format, so viewing a single page can lead to seeing hundreds of posts.

- **"Upvotes":** StackOverflow popularized the notion of "upvotes" on posts, allowing readers to weigh in with spot votes on a given post, under the theory that the more popular posts would be the ones more likely to be clear, concise, and correct. They also used a mechanism called "reputation" attached to the authors of posts, and granting certain forum privileges to those authors who had reached a certain level of reputation, thus providing incentive for authors to want readers to upvote their posts.

- **Post-response Time:** The ideal situation for a forum is to have the community answer each other's questions. However, your team should remain aware of the community's needs and make sure that questions do get answered. Setting an internal Service Level Object (SLO) for the amount of time a post should be responded to will communicate clear expectations to your team, and will help your users feel seen.

Consequences

Hosting forums requires a commitment to moderation, or the company runs the risk of creating a hostile environment that will alienate customers. Various forums platforms have attempted a wide variety of different mechanisms in an effort to self-police online communities, all with mixed results, none with overwhelming success. For the foreseeable future, some form of human-based moderation should be assumed for any online environment in which people outside of the company can post content or express opinions.

Additionally, hosting forums can have the benefit of being accessible to both internal employees as well as external customers, allowing for a degree of interaction without creating opportunities for customers to bypass traditional company information channels. (Customers having

CHAPTER 14 FORUMS

direct access to internal software engineers, by having their email address for example, can often have the negative side effect of customers using those engineers for tech support purposes, distracting them from their other duties and/or creating issues for the **Tech Support (434)** team.)

Forums make for an easy way to identify potential **Ambassadors (71)** from the community. Forums can also suggest **Samples**, enhancements to **Guides (243)** or **Reference Documentation (373)**, or even **Extensions or Providers (242)** for future development.

Variants

- **Wiki:** A wiki is essentially a forum, with the caveat that the roles are flexible—where traditional forums focus on question-followed-by-answer-and-discussion, a wiki is more free-form and allows for more collaborative interaction.

- **Developer Portals**, like StackOverflow, Reddit, TheServerSide. The traditional developer portal is often more than just a forum—for example, it often aggregates links to developer-centric downloads like **SDKS (381)** or **Samples/Examples (387)**. However, much of the "stickiness" of the portal is its ability to capture developer attention via the question-and-answer forums.

- **GitHub Issues. Jira:** Forums are a natural mechanism to act as intake for **Technical Support (433)**, and most GitHub-hosted projects have an "Issues" page in which customers can file questions that are either answered (and closed) or then used as bug reports that are referenced from pull requests during **Code Reviews (167)**. Jira serves a similar purpose, but usually Jira is behind a company firewall rather than being publicly accessible.

CHAPTER 15

Guide

Topics: *Writing, Code*

A guide serves as a structured and comprehensive resource designed to educate, inform, and assist developers in adopting and succeeding with a company's technology. A guide is often classified as a type of documentation. It provides clear, actionable insights, bridging technical complexities with real-world applications while demonstrating best practices and showcasing the tools or platforms' potential. By offering practical value and addressing developers' challenges, a well-crafted guide not only supports the day-to-day efforts of the Developer Relations team—such as advocacy, community building, and onboarding—but also enhances the company's reputation as a trusted technical partner, ultimately fostering deeper developer engagement and driving product adoption and sales.

CHAPTER 15 GUIDE

Also Known As

Manual; Reference; "How-to" Document; Handbook; FAQ (Frequently Asked Questions)

Intent

A guide empowers developers by offering clear, actionable insights that help them overcome challenges and succeed with the company's tools or platforms. By being tailored to developers' needs and focused on real-world use cases, a guide demonstrates the company's commitment to developer success, fostering trust and loyalty. It enables the Developer Relations team to showcase the value and versatility of the technology, streamline the onboarding process, and address specific pain points, thereby enhancing the developer experience. This trust and utility translate into more robust community engagement, positive word-of-mouth, and increased adoption.

Context

Reference Documentation (373) is more tactical in nature, rather than conceptual, and developers at some point are going to ask questions like, "How does this work?" or "Why is it when I call A, then B, I get a different result than when I call B, then A?"

Customers will often need to understand the concepts behind the product/service in order to be able to understand its nuance, particularly when compared against competitors, or when measured up against something that might be a competitor (but isn't).

This is particularly apparent if the product/service is relatively novel or innovative in its space, as customers will not have much (if any) experience with the novelty or new concepts from other products or services they've used before.

Solution

Write one or more sets of longer-form prose pieces that each tackle the important concepts of the product/service. While precise details aren't necessary, there should be enough information in each one that a developer can build a mental model of how the product/service works "under the hood." For example, if the product/service stores data, some discussion of how the data is stored, how the data is queried, and when/how/if that data is encrypted "at rest" are necessary to give the developer a clear picture in their minds on how to approach using the data store.

Write these docs in a crisp, concise style, devoid of "tone" as much as possible. This is not the place to let the company culture fly or to weigh in with controversial technology opinions (except those that are baked in to the central concept of the product/service; it would be reasonable for a cloud service to weigh in on the advantages of running in the cloud, for example).

Certain guides will be specific to particular domains; popular guide topics include security, performance, scalability, accessibility, observability/monitoring, and reliability (backups), though many more are possible depending on the details and nuance of the product/service.

Participants

A guide, like other writing, is usually performed by an individual **author**, who will be responsible primarily for its outline, prose, and editing. In some cases, a guide will be written by multiple authors, but in this case, the authors must take great care to ensure that each write in a style that is similar to the others, so there is no jarring changes of "voice" to the piece—to readers, it should be absolutely impossible to tell that this was written by multiple individuals. (In fact, most guides are also entirely unattributed—that is to say, no author information appears on the guide—making it impossible to know whether this was written by one or multiple individuals.)

Most guides should be reviewed extensively by a professional **copyeditor**, whose job will be to eliminate any misspellings, grammatical errors, or punctuation issues. It is of utmost importance that the prose be professional and error-free, far more so than with a **Blog Post (105)**, since this is official documentation for the product/service it describes, and thus it represents the company's professionalism and attention to detail.

It is also highly advantageous for a guide to have one or more **editors** examine the prose, to make sure that it reads well, conveys its message well, and describes any new concepts in a clear and comprehensible manner. Sometimes a professional **technical writer** can serve as author, copyeditor, and editor, but it is still advisable that some other party beyond the author review the work, if only because another pair of eyes will help spot mistakes the author will miss.

Another important review for the guide will be a review by Engineering, an individual who will act as a **technical reviewer** to ensure the technical parts, including any code snippets or associated downloadable demos, are correct and consumable (that is to say, they can be compiled/executed without error or additional steps).

Implementation

A guide begins with a clear description or target of something that requires description; this can be "demand-driven" by identifying specific needs and challenges of the target audience, often through developer feedback, user research, or analyzing common support queries. Often, however, the need for a guide is self-evident, particularly if the product/service is novel or innovative—in the early days of object-oriented programming, for example, understanding what the language meant by "object" was an important concept that needed to be clarified and described before potential users of the language could understand how the language worked. In a similar vein, a novel database may need to describe its data model (and, perhaps in a separate guide, how to approach data modeling with this new kind of data model), and so on. Identifying the core concept that drives the guide—even if it is something as modest as "getting started"—is the bedrock upon which the rest of the guide will be built.

From there, the author must flesh out the concept or discussion in a manner that is logical and consistent, drilling into sub-topics as necessary to flesh out details and address nuances or exception cases. Note that unlike a **Tutorial (451)**, a guide will not be looking to take users step-by-step through a sequence of actions geared toward producing a specific kind of outcome, but instead focus on the general topic as a whole.

Once the author has the guide in a draft state, it should be reviewed—ideally repeatedly—for clarity (editor), technical accuracy (technical reviewer), and correct prose (copyeditor). If the guide must be handed back to the author for revision or correction, assume that another review pass is necessary. Some review/correction cycles can be done collaboratively and synchronously, but most of the time these are done in batches and asynchronously, and so some form of version control is often helpful; while tools like "git" immediately spring to mind, most word processing software packages (such as Microsoft Word or Google Docs) also have a mode by which "comments" can be made to a document and/or support some basic (linear) versioning capabilities.

While some guides will want to be accessible as printed material (and/or possibly sold through an online bookstore), most guides will be online-only sorts of material, and therefore they must be easily consumable via web browser. Never lose sight of the fact that even if the guide isn't sold as a book, developers may want an offline copy, and thus download it (or print to PDF through their browser).

Once published, try to get some readers to take a pass through the guide, to help ensure the guide addresses actual developer pain points, is clearly written and understandable, and is free of any ambiguities. Those portions of the document which feel rough should be reviewed and potentially rewritten, repeatedly if necessary, until the meaning is crystal clear—more so than any other documentation, the guide will be the place developers will turn to learn about the product/service, so if it isn't clear, the overall opinion of the product/service will suffer.

However, once the guide reaches a level of acceptable quality, the work isn't finished—because the product/service evolves, the guide will (more than likely) need to evolve with it. Therefore, any published guide must also undergo periodic revisit, to ensure that there are no errors or mistakes due to the evolution (as well as to catch any errors that might have remained undetected from previous reviews). Metrics will also help the team measure the guide's success.

Metrics

Since the guide appears on your own websites, gathering metrics will typically be much simpler than doing so for a third-party-published **Article (89)**. However, as much as it may be easier, your choice of metrics will often be smaller, since your developer portal or documentation site will often not have the same level of investment in infrastructure that a publisher's website will want/need.

When documenting the metrics for a guide, it's crucial to track a variety of data points that measure the post's reach, engagement, and overall impact on the target audience. Some of the metrics to consider tracking include

- **Page views:** Most web servers and/or content-management systems (CMS) offer the ability to set up a tracking cookie or "click counter" that can tell you how often the page has been served up to browsers. This is often an overly optimistic metric, as it cannot track whether the user actually *read* the article, only whether the server was requested to send it. It may not be tracking unique views, either, meaning if the user clicks on the link several times, each one will be tracked as a "web view." However, it is one of the simplest metrics to track and thus often used first before any of the others.

- Equally important is tracking the **unique visitors** metric, which offers insight into the number of individual users who have read the post, thereby informing us about the audience size and keeping us well-informed about the blog post's reach.

- **Time on page:** Some content-management systems are able to track how long the page, once served, remains visible in the browser.

- **Click-through rate:** If the guide is linked from a **newsletter** you'll want to institute some infrastructure to have some data around how often this guide's link was clicked on in the newsletter (which indicates, presumably, that the user is interested in this topic and clicked on it to read it).

- **Reference rate:** How often does the guide get mentioned, either in spoken conversation with developers or customers? How often does it appear in written prose elsewhere on the Internet? A search-engine alert can often provide the latter statistic, and since you are in full control of the server, you can also examine HTTP headers to know "from where" the guide was accessed by accessing the HTTP "referrer" header. This will help differentiate between "external" and "internal" referrals, where "external" referrals are those coming from someplace other than your website(s), and worth their weight in gold since they indicate that your documentation is gaining some traction/notoriety in the world. The referral doesn't carry any context to it, however, so dedicate some time to following these referrals back to their source so you can see what is being said around the link—not everyone will say nice things, and you may want or need to take steps if the not-nice things being said are serious or grounds for legal action.

- **Time on page** is another important metric, as it reveals how long readers spend on the guide. A higher average time on the page suggests that readers engage with the content, while a low time on the page might indicate that the content isn't holding their attention. **Bounce rate** should also be monitored; it measures the percentage of visitors who leave the site after viewing the blog post without engaging further. A high bounce rate might suggest that the post's content didn't meet the readers' expectations or needed more compelling calls to action.

- Analytics tools can gather **audience demographics** such as location, job roles, and industry. This data helps understand whether the guide reaches the intended audience. It can also inform future content strategies by highlighting the most engaged audience segments.

- **Citation rate.** In some circles, the guide may appear as a citation in academic papers/publishing, and certain systems track how often it is cited in other works. It may be useful to create a relationship with these citation websites in order to obtain the citation rate for your guide.

All these metrics should be systematically documented in a report that includes quantitative data and qualitative insights. Visualizations like charts and graphs can illustrate trends and key findings. The report should also include a section for analysis, where the metrics are interpreted in the context of the blog post's goals, and recommendations for future content strategies are provided based on the collected data. This comprehensive documentation will enable the developer relations team to evaluate the success of their prose, refine their content strategy, and better engage with their target audience.

CHAPTER 15   GUIDE

Example

At TechNova, a software company specializing in cloud-based APIs for real-time data processing, the Developer Relations team identified a recurring challenge: developers from prospective customer companies struggled to integrate the API with their existing platforms during pre-sales trials. To address this, the DevRel team, led by Mia, a senior developer advocate, created a comprehensive "Integration Quick Start Guide." The guide walked developers through the setup process, showcased common use cases, and included troubleshooting tips tailored to feedback gathered from the sales team about potential customer pain points.

One of the guide's first uses was with DataStream Corp, a logistics company exploring TechNova's API to optimize their supply chain monitoring. During the trial phase, their lead developer, Raj, was tasked with implementing the API but encountered roadblocks due to legacy system constraints. While working closely with the sales team, Mia shared the Quick Start Guide with Raj, which included a step-by-step example of integrating the API with older infrastructure. Raj followed the guide, completed the integration within two days, and even discovered a previously unknown feature that enhanced their real-time tracking capabilities. Seeing the smooth process, DataStream's CTO praised TechNova for its "developer-first approach" and purchased a premium subscription for their enterprise operations.

The guide's success continued. TechNova's sales team reported a 25% faster trial-to-purchase cycle when customers used the guide. In contrast, the DevRel team noticed a spike in community engagement as developers shared their positive experiences on forums. Mia and her team continued to refine the guide based on user feedback, adding new examples and clarifications. Over time, the guide became a cornerstone of TechNova's pre-sales strategy, strengthening their reputation for excellent developer support and contributing to a 15% increase in revenue from new customers within the first year of its release.

Consequences

Guides will often be the first set of documentation that developers will read when they begin their serious journey to understanding your product/service, and should therefore be something *very* carefully curated and edited. Consider using professional editing services and/or personnel to help ensure the writing is clear, consistent, and easily consumable.

Guides should link to the **Reference Documentation (373)** liberally, relying on the reference docs to describe all of the different permutations and possibilities. This leaves the Guides to focus on the more commonly used aspects of the product/service, and as a result stay streamlined and more easily consumable.

As the product/service becomes more widely used internationally, consider hiring translation services to create native-tongue translations of the guides into languages that represent your customer population; if you find that your product/service has a significant user base growing in Eastern Europe, for example, consider a Polish or Czech translation.

Recognize that in many cases, the ability for an individual in your community to make the transition to **Ambassador (71)** lies in the ability to consume conceptual documentation about your product/service and then utilize that knowledge in **Forums (233)** and to create **Conference Sessions (197)** and **Articles (89)**. Provide opportunities for your **Ambassadors (71)** to collaborate on the authoring and editing of these documents, perhaps even before they become publicly available.

A **Book (121)** often covers the same material covered in Guides, but usually takes a more "high-level" approach to describing the contents, stretching across a greater number of broader topics in ways that Guides typically don't. Books also often don't go into quite the depth of detail that Guides do, and look to be shorter than the full collection of your Guide(s).

CHAPTER 15   GUIDE

Variants

- **Quick Start Guide:** A concise resource focused on getting developers up and running with minimal setup

- **Comprehensive Tutorial:** A detailed, step-by-step guide covering in-depth use cases and advanced features

- **API Integration Guide:** Focused on helping developers integrate specific APIs into their applications

- **Troubleshooting Guide:** A resource for diagnosing and resolving common issues or errors

- **Best Practices Guide:** Offers insights into optimizing usage, including performance, scalability, and security tips

- **Migration Guide:** Assists developers in transitioning from older systems or competitor solutions

CHAPTER 16

Hackathon

Topics: *Code, Social*

Also Known As

CodeFest, HackFest, GiveCamp. Startup Weekend, Innovation Challenge, TechJam, Coding Marathon

CHAPTER 16   HACKATHON

Intent

A community of developers using your product/service helps to generate the feedback and engagement that your DevRel team needs, but there doesn't seem to be as much as you'd like. In some cases, you have a community, but they're using an older version, or aren't using the product/service for certain scenarios.

Context

Developers are a notoriously fickle lot, in that trying to tell them what to build will often generate resistance and/or pushback. The creative aspect to building software is what draws many to the field, and many developers aren't given much opportunity to exercise that creativity in their workplace.

For some products/services, the target audience or customer are those that are entrepreneurs or innovators, particularly those that are in a city well-known for its startup "vibe" (such as the Silicon Valley, New York, Seattle, London, Bangalore, and a few others). These are locations in which developers leave the comforts of corporate life to pursue the statistically risky space of startups and are often looking for products/services that will allow them to get-to-market more quickly and get their product out in the hands of users.

Solution

Create, or sponsor, an event in which developers come together specifically for the purpose of "hacking" code to build an application or system. Usually such events are open to the public, and the teams that are formed are entirely temporary, made up of those who found a pitch idea to be interesting to work on. The events typically last anywhere from 24 hours to 5 days, and the shorter time frame often implies an all-night kind of exercise; many of the original hackathon events were weekend events, beginning with pitches on Friday night, then "hacking" continuously for the next 48 hours and concluding on Sunday evening.

Participants

Hackathon participants in the Developer Relations context typically include developers, designers, product managers, and sometimes technical writers or marketing professionals. These individuals come together with diverse skill sets and levels of expertise, united by a shared goal of solving specific problems or building innovative solutions within a constrained time frame. While developers often focus on coding and technical implementation, designers ensure solutions' usability and aesthetic appeal. Product managers contribute by aligning efforts with user and business needs, and other roles, like technical writers, help document outcomes for broader use and understanding.

Interactions among participants are highly collaborative, driven by shared objectives and a culture of experimentation. Teams are usually formed at the beginning of the hackathon, balancing expertise to ensure complementary skill sets. Throughout the event, participants engage in brainstorming, rapid prototyping, and iterative development, with frequent communication to align on progress and troubleshoot challenges. This dynamic fosters an environment where knowledge sharing is constant, and individuals learn from each other's perspectives and approaches. Mentorship can also play a significant role, as experienced participants or organizers often provide guidance to less experienced team members.

CHAPTER 16   HACKATHON

Implementation

Implementing a Hackathon in the Developer Relations context begins with meticulous planning to align the event's goals with the overarching objectives of engaging and empowering the developer community. Organizers define a central theme or problem statement that resonates with participants while leaving room for creativity and innovation. They also establish a clear structure, including the timeline, deliverables, and criteria for judging. Securing a venue—whether physical or virtual—is another critical step, along with ensuring the availability of tools, platforms, and APIs participants might need. Pre-event communication, such as invitations, announcements, and onboarding materials, helps set expectations and build excitement.

Successful hackathons also require careful attention to infrastructure and sponsorship support. Technical infrastructure, such as reliable Internet connectivity, adequate power supplies, cloud credits, development environments, and collaboration tools, must be planned and stress-tested in advance to avoid disruptions that could frustrate participants. Equally important, securing corporate sponsorships not only helps offset event costs but also provides relevant and motivating prizes. Sponsors may contribute hardware, software licenses, or even direct mentorship that aligns with the hackathon's theme, ensuring rewards feel meaningful to participants' work. Together, solid infrastructure and thoughtful sponsorship transform a hackathon from a coding marathon into a well-supported innovation experience that inspires developers and strengthens community engagement.

During the event, the implementation relies on smooth facilitation and active engagement. Organizers and mentors guide participants through workshops, provide technical support, and foster a collaborative atmosphere. Tools like collaboration platforms, version control systems, and dedicated communication channels are essential for efficiency. Organizers also structure periodic check-ins or milestones to keep teams on track and address challenges as they arise. The event concludes with team presentations or demos, where participants showcase their work to judges or peers. Closing the hackathon with recognition, prizes, or actionable next steps ensures participants feel their efforts are valued, cementing its impact as a meaningful and engaging community experience.

Metrics

To document metrics for a Hackathon in the Developer Relations context, it is essential to track quantitative and qualitative data that reflect the event's impact on community engagement, product adoption, and company reputation. Quantitative metrics include the number of participants, the diversity of their roles or backgrounds, the number of projects submitted, and engagement metrics such as social media mentions or hashtag usage during the event. Tracking the adoption or integration of the company's tools, APIs, or platforms in the submitted projects is particularly important, as it directly ties the hackathon's outcomes to the company's products. Additionally, post-event surveys can provide numerical insights into participant satisfaction, skill improvement, and the likelihood of recommending the company's tools to others.

Qualitative metrics involve analyzing participant feedback about their experience, identifying how the hackathon influenced their perception of the company, and documenting stories of innovation or impactful projects that emerged. These narratives are invaluable for Developer Relations, showcasing how the event enabled developers to solve real-world problems using the company's technology. The team can also analyze changes in developer behavior, such as increased contributions to the company's ecosystem or new advocates emerging from the event. By combining these metrics with a focus on follow-up actions, such as fostering ongoing relationships with participants, the team can

CHAPTER 16   HACKATHON

demonstrate how hackathons build trust, drive technology adoption, and ultimately enhance the company's reputation and sales pipeline.

Example

The fictitious tech company, CloudForge, decided to organize a hackathon to promote their newly launched serverless computing platform, ForgeEdge. The Developer Relations team collaborated closely with the sales team and a key customer, InnovateHealth, a healthcare startup aiming to modernize patient data management. The "Revolutionize Healthcare with ForgeEdge" hackathon invited developers, data scientists, and healthcare IT specialists to build innovative solutions using CloudForge's platform. InnovateHealth sponsored the event and shared a real-world challenge: designing scalable, secure, and cost-efficient tools for managing patient appointments and data.

Over a weekend, teams worked on solutions ranging from intelligent scheduling systems to machine learning-driven patient health insights. The DevRel team ensured participants had all the needed resources, including detailed ForgeEdge documentation, live coding workshops, and 24/7 support via a dedicated chat channel. They also introduced a leaderboard system that encouraged participants to explore advanced features of the platform. Throughout the event, the sales team networked with critical developers and InnovateHealth representatives to understand how ForgeEdge could address broader organizational pain points.

At the end of the hackathon, a team of independent developers presented a solution that integrated ForgeEdge's serverless APIs with secure data encryption, addressing InnovateHealth's compliance needs. The project won first prize and received direct interest from InnovateHealth for further development. The event not only showcased ForgeEdge's capabilities but also positioned CloudForge as a leader in healthcare tech innovation. Post-event, the sales team secured a licensing deal with InnovateHealth, and the DevRel team gained several new advocates who continued building on ForgeEdge. This hackathon became a case study for how collaboration between DevRel and sales could foster innovation, enhance the company's reputation, and drive measurable business outcomes.

Consequences

Many events are public, Sponsorship by various vendors and/or other interested parties, and many offer prizes to teams whose hacked project ranks best in one of a variety of categories. The top prize often depends on the intent of the event—at Startup Weekend, for example, the top prize was an opportunity to meet with VCs and pitch them on the startup idea "hacked" together over the weekend, while at GiveCamp, "prizes" are often more celebratory in nature, offering up rounds of praise for those who "hacked" projects together on behalf of charities.

Company participation in a hackathon can come in many forms: direct sponsorship of the event as a whole, sponsorship by providing one or more of the prizes, sponsorship by providing free licenses or credits of the product/service, providing coaches and expert advice (either around your product/service or across a broader range of topics), and/or your company's employees' participation in the event itself. (Participation in the event is highly suggested for charity-centric hackathons, as it generates good feelings toward the company, gives the developers a good feeling of helping those in need, and generates good PR for the company.)

Some Hackathons provide time and space for presentations by sponsoring companies and/or experts/coaches that are volunteering their time at the event; these are essentially **Conference Sessions (197)** but for the Hackathon audience instead of a conference. Many of the presentation slots are given to **Sponsors (405)**. It is common that less than 10-15% of the attendees will come to a talk, but those that do are often extremely interested in using the topic as part of their hacking project.

CHAPTER 16   HACKATHON

Hackathons are also a great place to hand out **Swag (427)**, and/or have a **Booth (137)** (more like a table) as part of the company's Sponsorship of the event.

If the Hackathon is internally facing, it is often done in conjunction with an internal **Conference (179)**, to help the company foster a culture of training and innovation. "Vendors" in this scenario are often company internal services or platforms, and "coaches" are often the senior developers, architects, and SMEs who assist the ad hoc teams working on ideas that may or may not be company-related.

Logistics management will be important for a Hackathon depending on the degree to which the company chooses to participate: attendance will require physical presence (travel and hotel, if the hackathon is not local to the participants), and sponsorship will require greater work, depending on details. Consider having an individual on the DevRel team serve as "point of contact" for all logistical issues around the Hackathon.

Variants

Code With Us. Open Labs: Rather than holding an event in which many different groups of people come together to hack on something short-term for a short period of time, customers may be looking for opportunities to hack together with experts on the product/service in a more collaborative and focused fashion. (These "open labs" were a popular Apple tactic during the days of OpenDoc.) The customer is free to bring whatever code they have or are working on, and either company engineers or (more often) members of the DevRel team sit and pair (or "mob") to work through a customer's concerns or obstacles for a period of time, usually a day, sometimes two. These can be on-site at the customer's location, on-site at the company's location, or possibly virtual (if the interactivity is good enough—paired editing and/or jumping up over to the whiteboard is very common in these activities, and the virtual experience may not yet quite be up to the task). These are usually scheduled, rather than impromptu, and considered private. Note that, although similar, this is still different from a **Code Review (167)**, in that a **Code Review (167)** is usually *post-facto*, after the customer has written the code, and the Open Labs are usually *pre-facto*, taking place much earlier in the development cycle, sometimes before any code is written at all. Customers might have NDA concerns about bringing their proprietary/closed-source language to be viewed (and hacked on) by developers outside their company (not to mention any IP ownership concerns), so have Legal draft a document that customers and your DevRel team participants can sign so as to allay concerns ahead of time.

CHAPTER 17

Live Playground

Topics: *Code*

A Live Playground is an interactive online environment where developers can explore, test, and experiment with a company's technology in real time, without the need for extensive setup or installation. For Developer Relations teams, it serves as a dynamic tool to engage the developer community, showcasing the capabilities of the technology while addressing real-world use cases and fostering hands-on learning.

CHAPTER 17   LIVE PLAYGROUND

Also Known As

Sandbox, "Try" site, Test Lab, Developer Environment. Code Gym, Prototyping Lab, Safe Zone.

Intent

Developers want to "get their hands dirty" on your product/service but aren't installing it (if it runs locally) or aren't creating accounts (if it is cloud-hosted) to explore it further. You want to reduce the barrier-to-entry as far as possible, so that there is no reason they cannot start "playing" with your product/service as quickly as possible.

Context

Your product/service may have a complex installation process, requiring several distributed system services all configured to find each other, or there is a large amount of configuration to consider. Or your product/service may have a large install footprint and require significant amounts of time to download and install.

Solution

The solution for a Live Playground involves creating a hosted, interactive environment where developers can experiment with the company's tools, frameworks, or APIs directly in their browser without requiring local setup. This environment should include guided tutorials, pre-configured scenarios, and opportunities for open-ended exploration, allowing developers to understand the technology's value and practical applications quickly. Developer Relations teams can use this platform to showcase best practices, highlight new features, and facilitate workshops or live coding sessions, creating an engaging and educational experience that strengthens developer confidence.

Participants

In the Live Playground pattern, the creators, a combination of Developer Relations team members, including developer advocates, engineers, and technical writers, alongside product and engineering teams, play a crucial role in designing and building the playground environment. However, it's the participants, the developers and technical decision-makers, who truly bring the playground to life. Their engagement with the live playground, often as part of evaluations, workshops, or onboarding processes, is what makes the technology exploration interactive and meaningful.

The interaction begins with the creators crafting a dynamic, accessible environment where participants can experiment with actual code, configurations, and use cases without needing to set up their own infrastructure. Developers explore the playground to test features, troubleshoot integration scenarios, or learn the platform's capabilities through guided or open-ended exercises. Feedback loops are a critical component of this interaction. Participants provide feedback on their experience through structured surveys, informal comments, or live Q&A sessions. At the same time, creators observe how users engage with the playground to identify usability issues, common questions, or opportunities for improvement. These interactions not only enhance the playground but also offer valuable insights that directly contribute to refining product features, making the participants' work truly impactful.

CHAPTER 17   LIVE PLAYGROUND

Implementation

Implementing a Live Playground involves building a web-based platform that integrates directly with the company's technology stack, offering an interactive and secure space for developers to experiment. It requires robust infrastructure to handle real-time interactions, such as cloud-based virtual environments or containerized instances that can be spun up and isolated for each user session. To make the experience as user-friendly as possible, the playground should include intuitive interfaces, pre-loaded examples, and contextual documentation, ensuring developers can quickly get started and solve real-world problems. However, it's important to recognize that a Live Playground is a **significant investment**: hosting costs can grow quickly, security vigilance must be constant, and ongoing monitoring is required to prevent abuse (for example, someone spinning up a BITCOIN miner). Teams should plan for clear SLAs around uptime and reliability, as well as dedicate resources to continuous monitoring, feedback collection, and analytics integration. These measures not only safeguard the platform but also ensure the Developer Relations team can measure engagement, refine the playground, and identify opportunities to improve developer satisfaction and product offerings.

Metrics

Metrics for a Live Playground should focus on quantitative and qualitative data to assess its impact on developer engagement, product adoption, and business outcomes. Key metrics include the **number of active users**, **session duration**, and **frequency of use**, which indicate how effectively the playground captures and retains developer interest. Additionally, **tracking completion rates of guided tutorials, feature interactions**, and **transitions from the playground to entire product trials** can reveal how well it drives deeper adoption. Feedback collected through **surveys** or in-session prompts provides qualitative insights into user satisfaction and areas for improvement. To justify the significant investment in hosting and maintaining the sandbox, ROI-focused metrics should also be measured, such as the percentage of playground users who convert to paying customers, the average deal size influenced by playground usage, and the reduction in sales or onboarding time when prospects engage with the sandbox before purchase. These outcomes help demonstrate that the playground not only fosters learning and experimentation but also directly contributes to business growth.

Example

The DevRel team at CodeFusion, a company specializing in real-time data streaming APIs, launched a Live Playground to showcase their flagship product, StreamSync. The playground allowed developers to build, test, and visualize real-time data pipelines directly in their browsers. One of the team's key initiatives was to partner with a fintech company, BrightLedger, whose developers needed a solution for real-time fraud detection. BrightLedger's lead developer, Maya, was skeptical about onboarding yet another API but decided to try the playground during a CodeFusion-hosted webinar. Within minutes, Maya could set up a sample pipeline using StreamSync, simulate incoming transactions, and see real-time alerts for flagged activity—all without writing boilerplate code or setting up local environments.

Impressed by the ease of use and immediate value, Maya shared her experience with her team, which led to a full trial of StreamSync in a production scenario. Over time, the playground's pre-configured examples and guided troubleshooting sessions helped BrightLedger integrate the API seamlessly into their systems. CodeFusion's DevRel team monitored BrightLedger's progress through metrics captured in the playground, offering tailored support and demonstrating new features during

CHAPTER 17   LIVE PLAYGROUND

follow-up sessions. As a result, BrightLedger became a paying customer and an advocate for StreamSync, further boosting CodeFusion's reputation in the fintech space.

Consequences

Operating a Live Playground will most likely require some commitment from your Operations staff, either in the form of direct Site Reliability Engineering support or direct Engineering support. At the very least, you will probably need some sort of budget for the hosting, as well as whatever up-front cost building out the Live Playground might require. This also implies some amount of maintenance, such as keeping the Live Playground up-to-date with whatever the v.Current version is.

The Live Playground makes an excellent basis for conducting **Workshops (477)**, and often provides a convenient backdrop for **Tutorials (451)** and **Guides (243)**. You might even show screenshots from the Live Playground for the **Reference Documentation (373)**.

Some customers may actually find the restrictions of the Live Playground still sufficient for their needs, at least through a prototyping stage, and that means there is a possibility that a customer could "go live" with the Live Playground as their production service/environment. Your company may have strong reactions to this idea, so make sure the ramifications are carefully thought out: this may be the "freemium" tier that your company offers, for example. If this is undesirable, then consider your options to persuade or force customers out of doing this: put Legal text in a frequent reminder to customers that this is not to be used for production purposes, or wipe out the Live Playground on a periodic basis (which will help with abuse, mentioned below), or throttle the Live Playground in some severe way that would dampen its ability to serve in any production capacity to anything but a prototype.

Sadly, making any resource available for free over the Internet—even if it is just comments on a webpage—is target for rampant abuse by malicious or immature actors. Ensure that if your live playground is accessible without some kind of gated entry (account login), you have procedures in place to safeguard it or at the very least reboot/wipe clean the environment periodically. Otherwise you could end up hosting content that may be embarrassing, damaging, or illegal.

Variants

Docker install: The Live Playground will often be slower than executing something locally because of Internet latency and bandwidth restrictions. For some products/services, this will be undesirable, and/or developers sometimes simply prefer to "have it locally" so that they can experiment while in places with little or no network connectivity. (This may be much more necessary for those who work in highly secure or network-isolated environments that do not or cannot have a regular Internet connection.) By providing a version of your product/service that can be installed locally via Docker, you give developers a chance to one-line-install your product/service, explore it for a while, and then one-line-delete it without having to do any additional configuration cleanup. NOTE: Docker installs are copying software down to the developer's machine, so if your product/service contains proprietary/closed-source code, you increase the ease by which malicious actors can obtain your binaries for reverse-engineering.

Third-party sandbox: Another variant is to host your experience inside someone else's sandbox. For example, leveraging a cloud provider's trial environment or a partner's free tier. Instead of building and maintaining your own infrastructure, you piggyback on an existing platform that already has robust security, scalability, and cost management in place. This approach lowers your hosting expenses while still giving developers hands-on access to your framework, plugin,

CHAPTER 17   LIVE PLAYGROUND

or product in a real-world setting. It can also reduce friction for developers who are already familiar with that environment, making it easier for them to integrate your solution into their workflows. The trade-off is that you surrender some control over the user experience and may need to adapt your product's setup or documentation to fit within the host platform's constraints.

CHAPTER 18

Live Streaming

Topics: *Code, Social, Budget*

An online activity that consists of one or more presenters delivering live content in a casual and interactive way.

CHAPTER 18 LIVE STREAMING

Also Known As

Twitch. Vimeo. YouTube. LinkedIn Live

Intent

You want your DevRel team to get more "face time" (a high degree of interactivity) with customers in a coding-related activity but without them having to travel to conferences. You'd like them to do something that has a high degree of Reach, but **Webinars (469)** or **Recorded Videos (363)** are too one-way to generate the interactivity you'd like.

Context

Developers often like seeing the people behind or around a particular technology—more than one company has found some significant value in having a "face" to their brand, creating something of a "developer rock star" that draws a crowd during events (physical or online). Doing so requires developers to be able to see the individual on a regular basis, and feel like there is some kind of emotional connection to them, which usually implies a high degree of interaction.

This high degree of interaction is often more easily facilitated by choosing a setting that is more informal; developers feel more comfortable approaching someone at a **User Group (457)** meeting than approaching the speaker after a **Conference (197)**.

It is also (contrary to most popular beliefs) endearing to developers to see people they respect struggle with certain situations or problems; it makes the observed individual seem more human (and therefore more approachable). It can also be instructive to see how other developers approach problems while still struggling with a solution, rather than seeing the "finished product" that usually appears in a **Sample/Example (387)**.

Solution

Use one of the live streaming platforms (Twitch, Vimeo, YouTube, or LinkedIn Live) to capture and broadcast informal, longer-form video. Live streaming is similar in tooling to the **Webinar (469)**, but the "vibe" is very different—where webinars are more structured presentation-like affairs, often intended to be one-way (with some interactivity in the form of questions from the audience), live streaming often is much more *ad hoc* or free flowing, with streamers often seemingly doing nothing more than "turning on the camera and starting to code something interesting."

Topics for the live stream can range widely; some live streamers have no agenda other than "I'm going to code something today that I've never built before" to show participants their process when building, including mistakes, while other live streamers have a more focused agenda.

That's the beauty of live streaming. There is no expected format, so you're free to make the content as casual or as formal as you like.

Great live streams are the ones that can get the audience involved with the conversation. As a presenter, go out of your way to acknowledge as many comments and questions from the audience as you can, as soon as you can. Encourage the audience to participate by inviting them to comment and ask questions.

Participants

At a minimum, there is a live stream host who is running the stream by talking to the audience, interacting with the attendees, and possibly hacking on some code.

Often times there are guests in addition to the host. Having a guest can create a more natural on-screen conversation that can give the live stream a more natural vibe that encourages the audience to join the conversation between the host and guests.

CHAPTER 18 LIVE STREAMING

Implementation

Live streaming can be as simple as turning on your camera and microphone, signing in to a streaming platform—such as Twitch, and clicking the Go Live button. Audiences of live streams watch because they want to see life unedited. The tolerance for imperfections in show quality or delivery is pretty high. Use that to your advantage by experimenting and trying new things. Don't be afraid of making mistakes on air.

An agenda can help structure a live stream in case there are specific goals to be met or topics to be addressed. But, keep the program flexible. Show yourself and your guests or a screen showing a demo/code. Slideshows are generally more formal and would probably fit in a Webinar.

Stop and talk to the audience as much as possible throughout the live stream. Make them feel part of the show. Live stream audiences want the show to be authentic and interactive. It will give them a sense of connection which will lead them to come back for future live streams.

It takes several minutes for the stream platforms to notify subscribers when streams go live. Because of that, it's recommended to hold each episode as long as possible. Each show should be at least 30 minutes in length. Many go for over an hour. Attendees will likely come and go during the stream and may not stay the whole time. So, it's okay to periodically recap what has happened up to that point in the show. In the case of live streams, it's okay to repeat yourself to catch everyone up on key points.

Be predictable in scheduling and promote each episode. Viewers like repetition. If they know the stream will be live every Wednesday at 10 am PST they will make time for it in their schedule. Use all communication channels to promote live stream episodes. **Social media (395)** posts should go out as soon as the previous episode is complete. Include invitations to join the live stream in **Newsletters (281)** or ask the marketing team to send email invitations to your user base.

Metrics

- **Live Viewers:** The goal of all content is eyeballs. With live streams, the number of live viewers shows how well you're able to get the attention of your community and influence them to action. To get them to interact with your content you need to first get them to attend, and thus live viewers is the north star metric for live streams.

- **Interactions:** Once you get live viewers, the next step is to get them to interact with the host or guests. Whether it's comments or questions, one of the leading indicators of a successful live stream is viewer engagement. The more viewers interact with the hosts and other viewers show they're engaged and interested in the content.

- **Recorded Viewers:** Making recordings of live streams available after the stream is complete allows for viewers to view the session after the fact. This will allow the viewers to consume the content in case they missed it live or if they wanted to review the stream. One drawback is the viewers miss out on interacting with the other participants. From a DevRel perspective it's good to track the number of recorded viewers to gain an understanding of which topics matter to the community.

- **Call to Action**: A live stream should lead the viewer to a specific action—installing or trying the tool being highlighted in the stream, creating an account, signing up for something like a newsletter, or building something new. Measure the number of times this call to action is fulfilled.

CHAPTER 18   LIVE STREAMING

Example: Live Coding

Franklin is a developer advocate for a company with an e-commerce API. The engineering team just released a series of **SDKs (381)** to help developers build integrations with the company's platform. Franklin wants to learn the new **SDKs (381)** and also create content to show developers how the **SDKs (381)** work. He has an idea for an example app to build, and a link to the documentation for the new **Go SDK (381)**. For everything else, he's going to explore and experiment during the live stream. The point of the show will be to show the experience of learning the new **SDK (381)**.

Franklin creates a new live stream in StreamYard, a popular live streaming SaaS, that allows him to stream to multiple services at once. He chooses to stream the session to Twitch, Twitter, and LinkedIn Live. He creates a title and description that lets viewers know he's going to be live coding, and invites everyone to come learn along with him.

When the stream goes live, Franklin begins by introducing himself and describing his task—to learn the new **SDKs (381)** by building a sample application to show how to use the **SDKs (381)**. He briefly explains the API his company provides and introduces the new **SDKs (381)**. Franklin then shares his screen, pulls up the **SDK (381)** documentation, and loads his code editor.

He finds a Quick Start guide in the documentation and copies the code from there. He uses it as a starting point and walks through the guide's steps for building and running the code. Through this process Franklin does all his thinking and reading out loud so the viewers can follow along with what he's doing.

About 10 minutes into the live stream, Franklin notices that he's getting a few viewers. He tries to engage with them by asking them to post any questions or comments in the chat. He also invites the audience to post which city or country they're connecting in from. Franklin ends his comments to the audience by giving a brief recap of what he's doing and the progress he's made up to that point. Then, he dives back into the code.

Franklin continues this pattern of coding while thinking out loud and pausing to address audience comments and questions for over an hour and a half. During the time, he's able to build out a barebones application that works with his company's Go **SDK (381)**.

He closes the live stream by recapping what he accomplished, posts links to the **SDK (381)** and documentation in the chat, and thanks the viewers for their participation.

Consequences

Interactivity in a Live Stream is often very high, as the various streaming platforms allow for comments, as well as "likes" and other emoji-fueled effects to appear on the screen during the stream. Streamers will often take their efforts in different directions based on the commentary and reactions from participants, including suggestions on what to do next, how to solve a particular problem, or even collaborate to solve a bug or other issue. (Note that most streaming platforms only allow the streamer to display their video and audio, so all commentary from participants is done through chat messages to the stream as a whole.)

Because of the nature of displaying both the streamer's screen and the streamer's video simultaneously or side-by-side, streaming requires some investment into equipment and a good Internet connection. This usually means it is difficult to do anywhere except in "the studio" (usually the streamer's home or work office), and will thus conflict with travel schedules somewhat. (Some streamers have worked to make their streaming setups portable so that they can stream from hotels while on the road, but this is yet somewhat rare, at least as of this writing.)

Recordings of the live stream often don't need much by way of editing (although it should be reviewed before publication, in case there is a violation of the company's code-of-conduct to avoid legal liability), but do need to be stored someplace publicly accessible. Live streams and Webinars are often saved on a platform such as YouTube or Vimeo and become part of the **Recorded Video (363)** pattern.

Keep in mind that the live stream is, as the name implies, live, and participants on the stream may turn out to be malicious individuals with goals that differ from yours (and, more importantly, are a violation of your code of conduct or not emblematic of the image your company wants to present). The live streamer will need to be ready to handle those situations, moderating and/or removing those individuals as needed.

Your company may also have certain concerns around the potential liabilities of live streaming and the potential dangers of an "open mic," so you may want or need to run the idea past Legal beforehand.

Variants

The line that defines the difference between a **Webinar (469)** and a live stream is getting more and more murky. As a rule, live streams are more public events that do not require registration. Their content is generally more casual and unscripted and the presenters make a point of including the audience in the conversation and interacting with them.

CHAPTER 19

Newsletter

Topics: *Writing*

A newsletter is a recurring publication that serves as a direct communication channel between a tech company and its developer audience. It provides curated, valuable content such as updates on product features, tutorials, community highlights, and industry insights, helping to build trust, foster engagement, and establish the company as a thought leader.

CHAPTER 19   NEWSLETTER

Also Known As

Zine

Intent

Customers are always surprised to hear of news about the product/service over social media and not from the company itself. You want to find ways to give them better opportunities to hear the news directly from the company, without coming across as "spammy" or "in your face," which could turn customers off.

Context

A newsletter's context lies in its role as a strategic tool to connect with and empower the developer community. By offering a consistent and reliable source of information, a newsletter creates an ongoing dialogue that aligns developers with the company's vision, fosters their success, and keeps them informed about relevant updates, events, and resources. It serves as a touchpoint that amplifies the Developer Relations team's reach and reinforces the company's commitment to supporting developers, bridging the gap between the company's goals and the needs of its technical audience.

Solution

Create a periodic newsletter that is emailed to an opt-in list of customers and/or other developers, consisting of a mix of technical articles about your product/service, news about your product/service, and wider news about the technical domain your product/service is in. (For example, if your product/service is a financial services service/API, then periodically share major news about the larger financial services cloud space.)

Participants

The guide creators of a newsletter pattern are typically Developer Relations team members, including **developer advocates**, **technical writers**, and **community managers**. These individuals are responsible for crafting the content, defining the tone, and curating resources that resonate with the developer audience. They work closely with **product teams**, **marketing**, and **leadership** to ensure the newsletter aligns with company objectives while addressing the needs and interests of the developer community. Their role involves creating compelling and relevant content and analyzing feedback and performance metrics to refine future editions, ensuring the newsletter remains a valuable asset for the audience.

Participants include **developers**, **engineers**, and **technical decision-makers** who subscribe to the newsletter for insights, updates, and resources that support their professional growth and problem-solving needs. These participants interact with the newsletter by reading, sharing, and occasionally responding to the content through feedback forms, community discussions, or direct engagement with the company. This interaction creates a feedback loop, enabling the Developer Relations team to understand the audience's evolving interests and concerns.

Implementation

Creating a newsletter involves establishing a clear purpose, defining the target audience, and creating a structured content creation, distribution, and feedback process. It requires selecting a reliable email platform, designing a visually appealing and accessible layout, and developing a consistent publishing schedule that aligns with the audience's preferences. Content must be carefully curated or authored to provide real value, such as tutorials, updates, and insights, while incorporating feedback mechanisms to gauge effectiveness and refine future editions. Additionally, decide on the suitable tone for your newsletter. It can either be a polished, professional voice with formal sections or a more casual, conversational tone featuring a DevRel advocate's byline. Whatever option you choose, the tone should align with your brand's personality and connect authentically with your developer audience.

Metrics

Metrics for a newsletter focus on quantifiable data that reflects audience engagement, content relevance, and overall impact on the company's goals. Metrics such as **open rates**, **click-through rates**, **subscriber growth**, and **unsubscribe rates** provide insights into how effectively the newsletter captures and retains attention. Tracking the performance of specific content, like links to tutorials or product updates, helps gauge what resonates most with the audience. Additionally, qualitative feedback from surveys or comments can shed light on perceived value. By linking these metrics to broader outcomes, such as increased product adoption or enhanced developer advocacy, the DevRel team can demonstrate how the newsletter improves the company's reputation. These metrics should be analyzed regularly and documented in reports to guide iterative improvements and highlight successes to stakeholders.

Example

The Developer Relations team at CodeSphere, a tech company specializing in cloud-based developer tools, launches a newsletter to engage their growing developer community and highlight their flagship product,

CloudForge. The DevRel team collaborates with the product and marketing teams to outline a clear purpose for the newsletter: educating developers on CloudForge's capabilities, sharing best practices, and fostering a sense of community. The team brainstorms content ideas, such as tutorials for deploying serverless applications, success stories from developers using CloudForge, and previews of upcoming features. They name the newsletter *Forge Focus* and commit to sending it monthly.

The first issue of Forge Focus includes a feature article on optimizing cloud costs using CloudForge, a step-by-step guide on automating CI/CD pipelines, and a spotlight on a small startup, BuildFlow, which reduced deployment time by 70% using CloudForge. The newsletter also includes an exclusive invitation to a live webinar with the product team to discuss future updates and gather feedback. The marketing team ensures the newsletter has a professional yet approachable design, while the DevRel team ensures the tone resonates with developers. The product team provides insights and technical details for accurate and engaging content. When the newsletter goes out, BuildFlow's founder, Alex, reads it and feels valued by the spotlight, sharing it on social media and garnering attention from other startups in their network.

As Forge Focus grows in readership, Alex emails the DevRel team, excited to share that their exposure from the newsletter has led to several new customers. Meanwhile, analytics show a spike in webinar registrations and increased trial sign-ups for CloudForge after the first issue. The DevRel team reviews this data with the product and marketing teams, discussing ways to deepen engagement, such as including more interactive content or adding a Q&A section. Over time, the newsletter becomes a trusted resource for developers, boosting CodeSphere's reputation as a developer-first company while directly contributing to increased adoption of CloudForge.

CHAPTER 19   NEWSLETTER

Consequences

Keeping the rhythm of the newsletter going is crucial, and managing the pipeline of content is a major task. Consider hiring a technical writer to assist with the creation of articles and news, and/or a copyeditor to help with proofreading and "tone" of the articles. In addition, consider hiring an editor to oversee the newsletter full-time, including the process of acquiring new content for the pipeline. Also, start with a period that is far enough apart to allow for steady publication (every other month or quarterly is not unusual as a starting point) until you have enough content for six months' worth of publication, and only then "compress" the period down (quarterly to twice-quarterly, then monthly, then twice-monthly, then weekly, and so on). Regardless of how much content you have, don't go faster than your editorial process can handle.

Finding that content on a regular basis can be difficult, particularly if your DevRel team is occupied with other tasks. Look to other engineers within the company who are interested in growing their individual brands (and make sure to provide them with "bylines"—author credit—on any piece they write), as well as to your **Ambassadors (71)**. Many of the articles written here could be repurposed into (or from) another **Article (89)**, but make sure to check with the third-party publisher for any concerns of exclusivity—many publishers want to be the only source of original content for some period of time before allowing re-publication.

Keep in mind that commitments to publication from employees at your company other than your DevRel team are likely to be secondary commitments (when compared to their "day jobs"), and be prepared for deadlines to be missed. You might be able to get other managers to help their employees keep to their commitments, but remember that they usually have differing goals than your team does, so be flexible.

CHAPTER 19   NEWSLETTER

Newsletters are an excellent way to advertise upcoming **Conference Sessions (197)**, as well as to announce any particularly relevant **Samples/Examples (387)** that relate to the news or articles included in this newsletter. (For this reason, even if you hire an editor, consider strongly having one of your Dev Advocates do a technical-review pass on each newsletter and suggest relevant items.) Make sure to reference your newsletters from your **Social Media (395)**, **Live Streaming (273)**, and/or **Podcast (333)**, and vice versa.

As you build out your **User Group Network (457)**, consider offering opportunities for each user group to put an "advertisement" into a newsletter, as a way of increasing user group attendance, particularly those in major cities.

Variants

One variant is the **developer digest**, a concise and periodic update focusing on the most relevant and actionable content for developers. This format prioritizes brevity and clarity, often highlighting critical product updates, quick tips, and links to in-depth resources such as blogs, training, or tutorials. It is designed for busy developers who want to stay informed without being overwhelmed. The digest approach works well for teams that maintain consistent communication while respecting their audience's time, ensuring critical information reaches developers effectively.

Another variant is the **community roundup**, which curates content generated by the developer community alongside official resources. This format features user-submitted projects, community-driven tutorials, and highlights from forums or social media, creating a sense of inclusivity and collaboration. The community roundup emphasizes peer recognition and celebrates the ecosystem built around the product, encouraging developers to participate and contribute actively. By balancing community-generated content with curated technical insights, this variant strengthens trust and fosters a vibrant, engaged developer audience.

CHAPTER 20

Office Hours

Topics: *Social*

Office hours in Developer Relations provide a dedicated time for developers to engage directly with the DevRel team, fostering an open channel for feedback, troubleshooting, and sharing insights. This collaborative engagement makes you an integral part of our team, strengthening the relationship between the community and the company and uncovering opportunities to improve products and services.

CHAPTER 20 OFFICE HOURS

Also Known As

Drop-ins, Open Hours, Community Hours, Ask Me Anything (AMA) Sessions

Intent

Customers often run into problems that are hard to capture as a stand-alone **Sample/Example (387)** or in a written format for a bug report for Tech Support or a **Forum (233)**. In many cases, they don't have any idea what's going on because the product/service is complex, intimidating, or running in the cloud. The customer doesn't even know how to begin to describe the problem, making it difficult for them to take advantage of some of the other high-reach resources that are available.

Context

This kind of "I have no idea where to start" problem demands a high degree of interactivity from the customer: questions lead to answers that in turn generate more questions before the nature of the problem is even remotely understood. Additionally, you want to be able to see the customer's environment more closely, because often debugging a problem can be something entirely enmeshed in their environment (misconfigured installation, PATH conflicts, "DLL/JAR/Assembly Hell" issues, and so on).

Solution

Provide an "office hours" (similar in concept to what college professors offer students in their classes): a period of time during which customers can "drop in" without scheduling anything ahead of time and use the time for whatever purpose they choose. They can ask questions, do a **Code Review (167)**, do a quick **Customer Check-In (213)**, or (most often) work on something Technical Support.

Participants

The primary participants in office hours are developers from the community and members of the DevRel team and product teams. Developers attending office hours may include beginners seeking guidance, experienced users looking to resolve specific issues, or contributors who want to share feedback or collaborate on ideas. These developers interact by bringing questions, challenges, or insights about the company's tools, frameworks, or platforms. Their role is to drive the conversation with their needs, ensuring the time is productive and focused on real-world concerns.

The DevRel team facilitates these interactions by providing technical expertise, listening actively to feedback, and guiding discussions to meaningful outcomes. Team members may offer solutions, demonstrate features, or note areas where improvements are needed, using this interaction as a two-way channel for building trust and gathering valuable insights. By fostering transparent and collaborative communication, both parties benefit: developers gain direct support and a sense of community, while the DevRel team gathers actionable feedback and strengthens relationships that enhance the company's ecosystem.

Implementation

Executing office hours involves setting up regular sessions where developers can join to ask questions, share feedback, and seek guidance. These sessions are typically held online via video conferencing tools or community platforms to maximize accessibility. Clear communication

CHAPTER 20   OFFICE HOURS

about the time, format, and purpose of the office hours is essential, often shared through developer-focused channels like **Forums (233)**, **Social Media (395)**, or **Newsletters (281)**. The DevRel team prepares by having representatives with deep technical knowledge available and creating a welcoming, inclusive environment to encourage participation. Sessions should be documented to capture critical insights and follow-up actions, ensuring continuous office hours and improvement in the developer experience.

Metrics

Metrics for office hours track quantitative data such as the number of attendees, recurring participants, and questions or issues addressed per session. Include qualitative data like feedback collected during the sessions, common themes in developer concerns, and follow-up actions completed based on discussions. These follow-up actions are crucial in addressing the needs of our developers and should make us all feel responsible and committed to our work. Additionally, monitor indirect impacts such as increased community engagement, improved satisfaction scores from post-session surveys, or an uptick in product adoption or feature usage linked to topics covered during office hours. By combining these insights, the Developer Relations team can demonstrate how office hours foster stronger developer relationships, enhance the company's reputation for responsiveness, and contribute to better-informed product decisions.

Example

The DevRel team at CodeForge, a fictitious company offering a cloud-based development platform, introduced weekly office hours to better connect with their developer community. Their platform was known for its robust APIs and integrations, but developers often needed help with

CHAPTER 20   OFFICE HOURS

configuration and advanced use cases. The DevRel team announced office hours via the **Company Blog (105)**, social media, and **Developer Forums (233)**, emphasizing their availability for live Q&A, feedback, and technical demonstrations. The sessions were held every Wednesday afternoon on Twitch, with the time chosen based on a community survey to accommodate global participants.

In one session, a developer from a mid-sized fintech company joined to discuss performance challenges while scaling one of the platform's APIs for high transaction volumes. A DevRel advocate guided the developer through potential optimizations involving a CodeForge API engineer on standby during office hours. The engineer provided a quick fix and noted the developer's suggestions for improving the documentation and adding a new feature for rate-limit configuration. By the end of the session, the developer left with actionable solutions and a positive impression of CodeForge's commitment to its community. Other developers attending the session learned from the exchange, adding value even to those without direct issues.

Consequences

Office hours are time-consuming, and can often seem like a waste of time if nobody attends. (This is true for university professors, too!) It will be particularly sparse when first getting started, as it is not a common tactic used by a number of teams or companies. Advertise it frequently (on your **Social Media (395)**, in your **Newsletter (281)**, and/or maybe from your **Reference Documentation (373)**), and give it a quarter or two, minimum, before drawing significant conclusions.

Consider recording office hours, both for opportunities for reuse as well as for your own internal improvement purposes (such as evidence of customers asking for particular features or finding particular features). If you do this, however, make sure you are in compliance with legal

CHAPTER 20   OFFICE HOURS

requirements around recording—some places require only to notify participants that they are being recorded, others require consent (which can be captured with a web form before entering into the Zoom/Teams/Discord/whatever video chat). Also be up-front about the use of the recording; if you intend to use it in any public capacity, absolutely make that explicitly clear to the participants.

Office hours are often a great tool combined with **Live Streaming (273)**, and in fact either can be a nice segue into doing the other—office hours can give suggestions on what to live-stream, for example. Keep in mind that Live Streaming tooling prioritizes high-reach more than interactivity, however, so the two are not entirely interchangeable.

Consider capturing any significant code built during office hours as a Gist, or if the code is much bigger, as a **Sample/Example (387)**. Make sure, if you do this, to get the customer's OK, on the off-chance that they are discussing something with you that they consider a secret or competitive advantage.

It's important to be aware of the legal risks that may arise when offering product implementation advice or suggesting solutions during office hours. What starts as casual guidance can sometimes unintentionally evolve into professional services or contractual obligations if not handled properly. To minimize these risks, consider having representatives from professional services or support engineering available during calls. This way, if discussions extend beyond general advice, they can smoothly transition into a formal engagement when needed. This approach protects both the company and the community while ensuring that developers feel supported and valued.

Variants

Variants of office hours include **Developer Clinics** and **Expert Q&A Sessions**, each tailored to specific needs of the developer community. Developer Clinics are focused, problem-solving sessions where developers can bring detailed issues or projects for guidance. These clinics often feature a structured format with pre-submitted questions or use cases, allowing the DevRel team to prepare in advance and provide deeper technical insights. This variant works well for tackling complex challenges or offering hands-on support, making it particularly effective for early adopters or users facing advanced integration hurdles. Creating a conversational setting helps build trust and establishes the company as a thought leader. Both variants cater to different community needs, providing flexibility in engagement while strengthening relationships and improving product experiences.

CHAPTER 21

Open-Source Project

Topics: *Code*

An open-source project is a robust platform that not only empowers the developer community but also fosters innovation and collective problem-solving. It's a collaborative initiative where a software project's source code, designs, or other components are publicly accessible under an open license, allowing anyone to view, use, modify, and distribute the work. These projects thrive on community contributions, maintaining transparency and inclusivity. Open-source initiatives can range from small utility libraries to complex frameworks, often becoming essential tools in the tech ecosystem.

For Developer Relations teams, open-source projects are a powerful avenue to engage with developer communities, build trust, and showcase a company's technical expertise. By contributing to or leading open-source efforts, DevRel teams can highlight the capabilities of their company's tools, provide practical examples of their use, and encourage adoption. This approach not only strengthens the company's reputation as a thought leader but also supports sales by demonstrating real-world applications of its products. Open-source projects also bridge the company and its user base, fostering long-term relationships that drive feedback, loyalty, and advocacy, and make the audience feel connected and engaged.

CHAPTER 21 OPEN-SOURCE PROJECT

Also Known As

Other names for an open-source project include community-driven software, free software, collaborative software, publicly available codebase or shared-source project. These terms reflect the nature of open-source development, emphasizing the collective effort, transparency, and accessibility to the project's source code. In some contexts, open-development projects are also used to highlight the process of collaborative contributions to software development. While some of these names might be used interchangeably, they can sometimes carry different nuances depending on the focus, whether it's on the software's freedom, the process's openness, or the project's collaborative nature.

CHAPTER 21   OPEN-SOURCE PROJECT

Intent

An open-source project's intent, particularly in the context of Developer Relations, is to create a platform that bridges the gap between a tech company and the developer community by providing accessible, high-quality tools or frameworks that solve real-world problems. By fostering collaboration and transparency, open-source projects enable a company to showcase its technical expertise, highlight the practical applications of its products, and most importantly, build trust with developers. These projects serve as living demonstrations of the company's commitment to innovation and support, driving the adoption of its technologies while inviting meaningful feedback and contributions from the community. This collaborative dynamic enhances the company's reputation as a trusted leader in its domain and nurtures relationships that can translate into increased product adoption, customer loyalty, and ultimately, sales growth.

Context

The context for an open-source project in the Developer Relations space revolves around creating accessible, community-driven software solutions that align with a tech company's strategic goals and developer needs. Open-source projects are rooted in transparency, collaboration, and inclusivity, making them an ideal vehicle for engaging with developers authentically. By actively participating in or leading open-source initiatives, a Developer Relations team can demonstrate the practical value of the company's technologies, foster goodwill within the community, and position the company as a trusted partner in solving industry challenges. This context allows the team to build meaningful relationships with developers, gather valuable feedback to improve the company's offerings, and drive organic adoption of its tools.

CHAPTER 21   OPEN-SOURCE PROJECT

Solution

The solution for an open-source project in the Developer Relations context is to create or contribute to projects that directly address the needs and challenges of the developer community while aligning with the company's strategic objectives. This involves identifying gaps in the current ecosystem and leveraging the company's expertise and technologies to deliver tools, frameworks, or libraries that solve real problems. A successful open-source project should be well-documented, actively maintained, and designed to showcase the company's products in action without being overtly promotional. By fostering a collaborative environment, the Developer Relations team can engage with developers, encourage contributions, and establish a vibrant community around the project. This community engagement is not just about the project, but about creating a sense of belonging and shared purpose, which in turn, creates long-term value for both the users and the company.

Participants

Open-source project participants are a diverse group of stakeholders, each playing a critical role in the project's success. **Core contributors**, typically employees of the company or dedicated community members, initiate and maintain the project, ensure code quality, manage releases, and guide its direction. However, it's the **community contributors**, ranging from individual developers to teams from other organizations, who truly add value to the project. They do this by submitting code, reporting issues, proposing features, and offering feedback. Users, who may not directly contribute code, provide crucial insights through their experiences with the project, helping identify pain points and driving its evolution. The **Developer Relations team** orchestrates these interactions, acting as facilitators, educators, and advocates, ensuring all voices are heard and the project remains accessible and welcoming.

CHAPTER 21   OPEN-SOURCE PROJECT

These participants interact through various channels, fostering a collaborative ecosystem. Core contributors and the Developer Relations team engage with community contributors through pull requests, issue discussions, and feedback sessions, often held on platforms like GitHub or GitLab. Regular communication in forums, mailing lists, or dedicated chat groups allows for open dialogue and support. The Developer Relations team also actively creates tutorials, documentation, and webinars to help users and contributors get involved with the project effectively.

Implementation

Implementing an open-source project for a Developer Relations team is a collaborative endeavor that begins with identifying a meaningful project idea. This idea should align with the developer community's needs and the company's strategic goals. To ensure this alignment, the team conducts market research, gathers developer feedback, and identifies gaps in the ecosystem that the project can address. Once the idea is solidified, the team initiates the project by setting up a transparent and collaborative development environment, typically on platforms like GitHub or GitLab, with a clear and permissive open-source license to encourage participation. The repository should include well-structured documentation, such as a detailed README file, a contributing guide, and a code of conduct, to set expectations and provide a welcoming environment for all contributors.

The Developer Relations team ensures the project gains traction by promoting it through **Blogs (105)**, **Social Media (395)**, **Webinars (469)**, and **Conference Sessions (197)** while engaging with the community to encourage contributions and feedback. They actively collaborate with the company's engineering teams to ensure the project integrates seamlessly with its tools and technologies, providing clear use cases and examples. Regularly scheduled updates, such as new releases, changelogs, and

301

progress reports, keep the community informed and engaged. To maintain momentum, the team organizes **Hackathons (255)**, issues triage sessions, or virtual meetups to foster collaboration and increase awareness. However, the team's commitment to ongoing support through **Forums (233)**, chat groups, and direct communication is what truly ensures participants feel valued and connected to the project's success. This approach nurtures a vibrant community around the project. It positions the company as a leader in the space, driving adoption, building trust, and ultimately enhancing its reputation and revenue.

Metrics

Documenting the metrics for an open-source project created and managed by a Developer Relations team involves clearly defining quantitative and qualitative measures that reflect the project's impact, community engagement, and alignment with the company's goals. These metrics should demonstrate how the project significantly enhances the company's reputation, fosters community trust, and drives adoption of the company's products and services.

Key metrics include **community growth**, such as the number of contributors, pull requests and issues submitted, engagement indicators like stars, forks, and discussions on platforms like GitHub. These metrics show how well the project resonates with developers and whether it fosters collaboration and inclusivity.

Additionally, **adoption metrics** are critical, including the number of downloads, integrations, or project usage in other repositories or tools, as these directly correlate to their real-world impact. The role of the developer Relations team in tracking qualitative metrics, such as sentiment analysis from community feedback, mentions in blogs or forums, and participation in events like hackathons or meetups, is crucial.

Additional metrics are related to **business impacts**, such as referrals to the company's products, API usage rates, or customer inquiries generated by the project, help tie the open-source initiative to broader company objectives like sales growth. These metrics should be regularly analyzed and shared with stakeholders through reports, dashboards, or case studies, providing transparency and showing the value of the project.

By demonstrating measurable progress and community influence, the Developer Relations team can validate the importance of open-source projects as a cornerstone of their strategy for improving reputation, fostering trust, and driving business outcomes.

Example

To document an example of an open-source project that a developer relations team would create and publish, the story could begin by describing a real-world problem the project aims to solve. Imagine a developer relations team at a company building a framework to simplify API integrations for developers working with multiple cloud services. The project, called "CloudConnect," was initiated because the team identified that many developers were struggling to manage multiple cloud APIs efficiently, leading to repetitive work and inconsistencies in implementation.

The developer relations team, with a clear strategic plan in mind, would first outline the problem and the motivations behind CloudConnect. They would explain that their goal was to create an open-source library that standardizes API integrations across major cloud providers, making it easier for developers to work seamlessly across AWS, Azure, and Google Cloud without having to write custom code for each service.

After defining the problem, the team would document the project's start. The core developer relations team developed the initial codebase and hosted it on GitHub to provide a solid foundation for the community. They would explain that they chose the MIT License for the project to encourage contributions and allow developers to use and modify the library freely in their projects.

CHAPTER 21 OPEN-SOURCE PROJECT

Next, the story would describe how the team actively invited community participation. They published a blog post introducing CloudConnect, its features, and how developers could contribute. They created detailed documentation to simplify onboarding, including a "Getting Started" **Guide (243)** contribution guidelines, and a code of conduct. They also hosted a live webinar and demo, showing developers how to integrate CloudConnect into their projects.

The team would explain how they continuously improved the project through the invaluable contributions of the community. For example, after the initial release, a contributor suggested a new feature to improve support for multi-region deployments. This feature became a pivotal enhancement to the project. The team documented how the contributor submitted a pull request, which went through a **Code Review (167)** process with the core maintainers before being merged into the main codebase. This interaction not only improved the project but also strengthened community trust and engagement, making every contributor feel valued and integral to the project's success.

The story would also highlight how the developer relations team monitored key metrics, such as the number of active contributors, pull requests merged, and issues resolved. They tracked growth in adoption through GitHub stars, forks, and downloads, which helped gauge the project's impact on the broader developer community. Over the year, they published quarterly reports summarizing these metrics, sharing success stories from developers who had used CloudConnect to streamline their work.

The documentation would describe how the team facilitated ongoing communication within the community. They set up a dedicated Slack channel and GitHub discussions where developers could ask questions, share feedback, and propose new ideas. The team regularly engaged with users, offering support and encouraging contributions from diverse developers, ensuring everyone felt informed and engaged.

CHAPTER 21   OPEN-SOURCE PROJECT

Finally, the story will conclude by reflecting on the project's broader impact. CloudConnect has become a widely adopted tool in the developer ecosystem, and companies use it to simplify their cloud operations. The developer relations team successfully created an open-source project that solved a real problem and fostered a thriving community around it. They would document how the project evolves through ongoing community contributions supported by clear governance, transparent metrics, and an active engagement strategy.

This example showcases the life cycle of an open-source project from inception to growth and how a developer relations team can drive its success through strategic planning, community involvement, and ongoing communication.

Consequences

The consequences of an open-source project can be positive and challenging, affecting the Developer Relations team, the company or organization, and the individuals involved in the project. One key consequence for the Developer Relations team is the need for ongoing community management. Once an open-source project is released, it creates a continuous responsibility to nurture and guide the community, ensuring that contributors are supported and conflicts are managed. This can become resource-intensive, requiring time and effort to maintain open lines of communication, provide clear documentation, and manage contributions, which may concern the team's bandwidth and long-term sustainability.

For the company or organization, open-sourcing a project can affect intellectual property and competition. The organization may lose some control over its competitive advantage by making the source code public. Competitors can use the code to build solutions or improve their offerings. Additionally, maintaining an open-source project may require dedicating company resources to ensure the project remains healthy, which could

305

impact overall resource allocation. However, open sourcing can also lead to positive consequences such as increased innovation through external contributions, wider adoption of the company's technology, and an enhanced reputation as a leader in the developer community.

The open-source project can provide career-building opportunities for individuals, especially contributors, allowing them to showcase their skills and collaborate with other developers globally. On the downside, contributors might face the challenge of managing their time between personal responsibilities and contributions to the project, particularly if the project grows in complexity. Maintainers who are heavily involved in reviewing contributions, fixing bugs, and ensuring the project's success also face the risk of burnout.

For both the Developer Relations team and the organization, one critical consequence is the exposure to public scrutiny. Open-source projects often receive positive and negative feedback on their quality, architecture, and overall management. If the project is poorly maintained or fails to meet community expectations, it could damage the company or organization's reputation. Security risks arise as the source code is publicly accessible, making it a potential target for malicious actors. Ensuring that the project follows the best security and code hygiene practices becomes paramount to avoid vulnerabilities that could impact users and damage trust.

In a broader sense, the open-source project contributes to the overall software ecosystem, which can lead to broader industry impact. If the project is successful, it can become a cornerstone tool that others build upon, leading to widespread adoption and the evolution of standards around the project. For companies, this can reinforce their thought leadership in the industry, while individuals may gain recognition for their contributions.

Ultimately, the consequences of an open-source project—both positive and negative—affect all stakeholders, including the Developer Relations team, the company or organization, and individual contributors.

Managing these consequences requires a thoughtful approach, balancing the benefits of community engagement, transparency, and innovation with sustainability, security, and reputation management challenges.

Variants

An open-source project's variations can differ in scope, governance, and community involvement. One variant is the solo-maintained project, where an individual developer or a small team creates and manages the entire project. This type of project is often smaller in scope and relies heavily on the maintainers' personal efforts. While the community may contribute, the control remains primarily in the hands of the original creators, empowering them with more direct control over the direction of the project, albeit with some limitations on scalability.

A dual-licensed open-source project is a model where the software is released under an open-source license but also has a commercial license available. This variant allows companies to monetize the project by offering enhanced features, support, or other services under the commercial license while still providing a free, open-source version to the community. Companies often use this model to maintain control over some aspects of the project while encouraging community collaboration and innovation.

The open-core project variant involves releasing a project's core functionality as open-source while keeping advanced features proprietary. In this model, the community can use, modify, and contribute to the core project, but additional functionality or services are provided as paid offerings. This variant allows for an open-source foundation while providing a business model for sustaining the project. Examples include projects like GitLab, where the core is open-source, but enterprise-level features require a paid subscription.

CHAPTER 21   OPEN-SOURCE PROJECT

Each variant of an open-source project presents different opportunities and challenges depending on how the project is managed, the level of community engagement, and the goals of the original creators or organizations backing it.

CHAPTER 22

Partnerships

Topics: *Social*

Formal relationships with other companies or projects that mutually benefits both user bases. These can be centered around, but not limited to, a technical integration between the two services. Or, a business-focused relationship that involves collaborative joint-messaging efforts.

Also Known As

Integration partners, collaborations

Intent

Your product or service will likely benefit from connecting to, integrating with, or being used alongside other related products. Create formal relationships with the developers of those products and services that would integrate or go to market well with your own, so as to generate benefit for both parties.

CHAPTER 22 PARTNERSHIPS

Context

Partnerships may be technical, where your software can integrate or interact. Or, it could be entirely a commercial or marketing relationship where you jointly market to your combined user bases. Developer relations is likely to get involved during the former situation, when there is an integration bringing the parties together. Like any other healthy relationship, both sides of the partnership bring some kind of value to the table. Both partners should see the benefit of working with the other. By joining forces both parties are essentially validating one another and endorsing their partner to the community.

It's extremely advantageous, when you're starting out as a smaller company, to partner with larger more established firms to show your value by associating yourself with those firms. This is what drives companies toward partnerships as opposed to simply making references on their website that their software works with these other companies.

Solution

Cultivate a relationship with the technical members of the partnering company. This is done either by assisting with the various stages of writing an integration—discussing possible integration scenarios, providing guidance and resources such as documentation or a **Sample/Example (387)**, possibly writing the integration, or reviewing the integration and documentation.

Outside of building integrations together, there are also opportunities to work with the partnering developer relations teams to jointly produce content—**Blog Posts (105)**, **Samples/Examples (387)**, **Conference Sessions (197)**, **Webinars (469)**, and so on.

Participants

Besides the DevRel team, collaborators around partnerships will often include

- **Executives:** Depending upon the size of your company and/or the partner company, your CxO suite may want or need to be engaged, if they weren't the ones to suggest it in the first place. Either way, a partnership is often executed "above the pay grade" of the DevRel team, even if the DevRel team is managing it and/or implementing it.

- **Legal:** If the Legal team hasn't looked over contractual details of any partnership agreement before the partnership is formalized, they will want to. In fact, in some companies, they will be the major blocker to a deal going through, at least until they've had the chance to weigh in. Although it can put the brakes on momentum building between the two firms, this is actually a good thing—partnerships have their own life cycles, and both sides will want clear and precise details for what happens if/when things grow chilly between the teams (even if they never do). Think of Legal's input as the safety belts of the partnership discussion—you buckle up, even knowing that 99% of the time, you'll never need them, because when that 1% happens, you'll really be thankful you did.

- **Marketing:** Some partnerships will want to engage in some joint marketing, where one side promotes the other side's products/services indirectly or directly. For example, if your company's product has a web

CHAPTER 22 PARTNERSHIPS

front-end, and your partner is an API-based content management system platform, the partner's marketing team will be looking for ways for your IDE to make developers aware of their CMS (perhaps in a project template, or by showing a status-bar advertisement for the CMS in places, and so on). Marketing folks can be particularly clever in thinking out of the box, so be prepared for some wild-eyed ideas that may need to be talked back to some form of executable reality.

- **Sales:** Similarly, yours or your partner's sales team may want to team up to help close some deals. Some of this may be in the form of **Customer Pre-Sales (223)** work, or perhaps their sales team would like your help in producing a joint **Case Study (151)** highlighting the two products in order to help win a big contract for both companies.

- **Technical Support:** One key question to bring up as part of the partnership discussion will be that of "who supports the customer when the issue is one between our two systems?" For example, if your company builds a plugin that integrates into a partner's platform, when a customer has a problem with your plugin inside their platform, which team takes lead on the support call? When your tech support team runs into a situation where it looks like the issue is in your partner's code, how can your team engage with theirs to resolve the issue?

Certainly the entire scope of the partnership can stretch well beyond that of the Developer Relations team, but in many companies, the DevRel team is "on point" for partner relationships, and often companies will use the DevRel team as the "first point of contact" for all partnership conversations. If the work gets to be too large, a separate organization will often get spun up to manage the business sides of the relationship, but that still leaves many or most of the technical side of the partnership to handle, and again, this often falls into the DevRel team's lap.

Implementation

Partnerships are born in the following ways:

- **Developer Relations-Initiated:** Developer Relations is constantly on the lookout for possible integration partners. The team is aware of their own product space and keeps that in mind as they meet other companies and hear of other products. Build relationships with Developer Relations professionals at other companies. As your network expands you'll increase your ability to create partnerships that will benefit your company. *Always be looking for companies to potentially partner with*. When there is a good match for a perspective partner, you will make connections either with the corresponding Developer Relations team or engineers. If your company also has Business Development or Partner teams you'll include them in the conversations as needed. They can help with business-related topics such as negotiating league contracts or written agreements for the two companies to work together.

- **Business Development/Partner Team-Initiated:** The Business Development/Partner teams are also looking to partner with third-party companies, but their aim is more focused on the business compatibility of the relationship. They may initiate the relationship and then pull Developer Relations in to help with the technical relationship. The Business Development team can help prioritize which partnerships are most beneficial or have the most potential from a commercial perspective.

- **Partner-Initiated:** Partners will also reach out to create partnerships. Have a process in place that your Developer Relations and Business Development teams follow to handle vetting and working with incoming partner requests. Evaluate how much of a lift the incoming partnership request will require and what benefits the relationship will bring to both parties.

- **Executive-Initiated:** Sometimes, the drive to partner comes from the C-suite directly, either yours or theirs, and sometimes both. Perhaps the CEOs were friends in college, perhaps the CTO found the other company from an article and connected to that company's CEO over LinkedIn, or even perhaps the boards share members. Whatever the reasons, there's a push from the executives to create a partnership—which can sometimes be long on intentions but short on details.

In each of these cases, chances are at some point the partnership will want or need to be reviewed by senior leadership in your company (and theirs) to make sure that it's aligned with larger strategic direction. Ideally, this will take place before too much work is put into the effort, as it's possible (likely, even) that the executives will have opinions (sometimes strong ones) on the details or proposal.

Be mindful of the motivation levels between partners and the level of value each partner will bring to a relationship. There are only so many resources—whether it's time, money, or people—to build and maintain partnerships. Consult with your Business Development team to prioritize which partners to put more time into and which partners to possibly do more of the lifting. Ideally, each company in the partnership would do the same amount of work in the relationship, but that's not always the case.

Sometimes your company is the smaller "scrappier" startup. If the decision falls to you or your team, don't spend all your time and resources going after companies larger than you; it will often result in your firm doing work to "keep big brother happy" that isn't directly relevant to your own bottom line. Build relationships with a fleet of equal-sized and smaller companies, in order to increase your reach and generate goodwill with the community. Working with smaller firms (or even individuals!) can also yield a surprisingly useful benefit, in that smaller firms are often more willing or tolerant to "process experiments" between you to make things more efficient and/or effective. This will help debug your internal processes and tooling, as well allow your team to gain experience "working out the kinks" between the partners, making integrations with larger partners flow more smoothly.

Sometimes your company is larger or more influential than the partner company. In this scenario, you will often have many partners, some or all of them smaller than you, and they will all be competing for resources for their partnership. In order to avoid negative outcomes (disappointment, bad PR, or even lawsuits), clear goals and expectations are paramount. Internally, have clear prioritization around projects and the time/effort commitment to each, so that the team is clear on who is working on what, at what effort level, for how long, and so on. Externally, to each partner, make sure they are clear on points of contact (is there an "account representative" who handles that partner?), technical resources available (do you have a website containing partner-specific documentation?), and any procedures that are required as part of the partnership (such as reporting bugs with your product/service).

CHAPTER 22   PARTNERSHIPS

No matter the size of the prospective partners, remember to be fair and respectful, but also remain aware of your team's bandwidth and, to some degree, your partner's bandwidth. If it feels like your partner isn't committed to the partnership, sometimes it's because they're not, it's better to back away rather than try to force it.

Metrics

- **Traffic on Partner Content:** When the partnership is focused on creating joint content, the goal is to increase the viewing audience of that content for both partners. The number of pieces of content—such as **Blog Posts (105), Articles (89)**, or **Recorded Videos (363)**—relates to this metric. However, the goal is to increase traffic. So, whether that's done with a single piece of content or a series is less important than the outcome of increasing the number of eyeballs on that content.

- **Usage of Integrations:** Partnerships that involve a technical integration between products should watch the traffic of the integration. The number of unique and returning visitors would be valuable metrics to indicate the success of the integration and partnership.

- **Sales numbers:** It is common that partnerships involve joint or referral sales, and so in those situations, any revenue that comes in through a partner should be tracked and attributed to the overall health of the partnership. This will require working with the Sales team to determine how they assign sales numbers—be prepared for the possibility of an emotionally laden conversation when bringing this up, as Sales teams often derive a significant amount of their compensation from commissions, and anything that remotely sounds like removing "their" sales and assigning it to a different group will be met with great resistance. In that conversation, emphasize that the DevRel team isn't out for commissions, just metrics.

Consequences

Healthy partnerships will provide value to both parties. That value can be categorized into three general areas: visibility, reputation, and product extension.

Visibility: Partners commonly amplify their joint message to their combined user bases, increasing visibility for both partners.

Reputation: Partnering companies share a portion of their reputation with one another. Smaller partners can gain credibility by partnering with larger companies. Larger companies can also break into new markets by partnering with companies in the new market space.

Product Extension: Partnerships will often result in a technical integration of the two products which will provide extended solutions for their users. If a partner has a marketplace for distributing or selling integrations, building an integration may also lead to being listed in that marketplace. Marketplace listings are a great way for users to discover your product, or at the very least discover that your product is compatible with the partner's product.

Risks: There are some risks to seeking out and establishing partnerships with other companies. Often, you or your team will be focused on establishing Partnerships with very specific companies and those companies may not be interested in partnering with you. Be careful

CHAPTER 22   PARTNERSHIPS

about spending too much energy and time chasing partners who may not be interested in creating a relationship. Definitely go for the ideal targets you want to partner with, but be prepared with alternatives that you would be willing to work with.

You may also get into a Partnership and realize that you and the partner may have different goals. If it's not possible to find a middle ground where both partners goals can be met, it's okay to walk away from a Partnership.

Every Partnership is a give-and-take relationship. If that balance doesn't exist, the Partnership will not last.

CHAPTER 23

Party

Topics: *Budget, Social*

A Party is a casual, community-focused event that brings developers, customers, and stakeholders together to build relationships, share knowledge, and celebrate milestones or product launches. These gatherings provide a relaxed networking and idea exchange environment, fostering goodwill and strengthening the connection between the company and its developer community.

CHAPTER 23   PARTY

Also Known As

Conference Mixer, Tech Conference After-party, Social, Event

Intent

Parties in the context of developer relations are multifaceted events designed to achieve several key objectives. These gatherings are not just about entertainment; organizations employ strategic tools to foster community, encourage collaboration, and share knowledge among developers.

One of the primary intents of hosting parties within developer relations is to build and strengthen community ties. These events provide a relaxed, informal setting where developers from various backgrounds and levels of expertise can mingle, share experiences, and form meaningful connections. This sense of belonging can enhance participants' commitment to the community and motivate them to contribute more actively by participating in discussions, sharing projects, or helping peers troubleshoot issues.

Parties, while primarily social, also serve as valuable educational platforms. Through workshops, demos, and casual conversations, developers can gain insights into emerging technologies, programming techniques, and industry trends. This learning aspect, which aligns with developers' intrinsic motivations to continuously learn and improve their skills, adds significant value to the event, making it more than just a social gathering.

Finally, parties are an effective tool for marketing and branding within the developer community. They provide a unique opportunity for organizations to showcase their culture, values, and commitment to supporting the developer ecosystem. Well-executed events can leave a lasting positive impression on attendees, enhancing brand loyalty and increasing the likelihood that developers will advocate for the organization within their networks.

Problem

You are looking to connect with customers and other developers in a highly interactive way, usually at a large gathering, such as a conference, that is not your own. You want to capture their attention and make sure they remember your company's presence at the gathering and/or create some connections with people at the gathering that you don't already have.

Context

You may want to differentiate between your loyal customers and those who are merely exploring your product or service without making a significant commitment. If you have branded **Swag (427)** to give away, you might not want to determine on the spot who receives premium items versus standard ones at the booth. Additionally, you may aim to build a reputation within the community as a company that appreciates and generously rewards those who are actively engaged. This approach could entice more people to become involved and strengthen their connection to your brand.

Moreover, hosting a party can serve as a way to celebrate important milestones, such as achieving a major open source release, launching a new product, or successfully concluding a **Hackathon (255)**. By framing the gathering as a celebration, you not only recognize the community's contributions but also foster a sense of shared ownership and pride in the accomplishment, making the event feel more meaningful and memorable.

Solution

Host an entertainment-centric event (a party), inviting either a select number of developers (customers or not), or opening the invite list to anyone who wishes to attend. Provide refreshments (food, drinks) and plenty of room for people to congregate and converse. There should be options for invited people and attendees to have non-alcoholic drinks. The purpose of the party is to have interactions, networking, and relaxation among conference attendees and not to inadvertently center the fun around the consumption of alcohol.

Hand out **Swag (427)** that is only to be had at this party, in order to create a little "FOMO" (Fear Of Missing Out) with those who were not able to attend (or were not invited to attend, whether because they didn't register in time, didn't choose to appear, or weren't a part of the invite list). Reference the party on the swag itself, either directly ("I went to Party, and got this lousy T-Shirt!") or simply note the date and year on the shirt someplace. The goal is to help individuals who are part of the "inner circle" community of those who were invited to the party to easily recognize one another—this invites them to talk with each other about stories emergent from the party, possibly enhancing the FOMO from the additional listers around them. This helps grow your reputation.

Participants

Like all parties, a gathering of this nature as a third-party event will require some up-front logistical support. **Event organizers** are the architects behind the scenes, responsible for the comprehensive planning, coordination, and execution of the event. They handle logistics, from venue selection to scheduling, and ensure the party progresses smoothly, providing a seamless experience for all attendees.

The **Developer Relations team** plays a vital role in a party or social event, serving as ambassadors for the company while maintaining a casual and approachable demeanor. Even in a relaxed setting, each member of the DevRel team continues to represent the company, engaging with developers and attendees in a way that fosters community building, trust, and positive relationships. They create meaningful connections by initiating conversations, answering questions, and offering insights into the company's products or services without being overtly promotional.

The **Attendees** themselves are vital participants; these conference-goers attend the social event to network, unwind, and immerse themselves in the relaxed, communal atmosphere, away from the formal confines of the conference.

Both introverted and extroverted attendees can benefit from a party in different ways. Extroverted attendees thrive in social environments, actively engaging in conversations, networking, and participating in group activities, making the most of the lively atmosphere to expand their connections. On the other hand, introverted attendees can benefit from smaller, quieter networking zones or one-on-one interactions where they can have meaningful conversations without feeling overwhelmed by the crowd.

Branding Teams play a strategic role, tasked with infusing the event with the company's identity. They ensure that the party not only entertains but also reinforces the brand's image and values through thoughtful placement of banners, swag, and other branded elements, maintaining a balance between subtlety and prominence.

Lastly, **Entertainment**, whether it be musicians, DJs, or other performers, contributes significantly to the event's ambiance, setting the mood and providing a backdrop that complements the networking and social interactions, thus rounding out the participant roles crucial to creating a memorable developer relations event.

Implementation

The initial phase of throwing a party involves defining the event's purpose and objectives. For developer relations, the intent might be to launch a new product, celebrate a milestone, or strengthen the community. This stage requires stakeholders to establish clear goals: Do they want to foster networking, showcase technological advancements, or boost morale? Answering these questions will guide the subsequent decisions about the event's scale, theme, and content.

CHAPTER 23 PARTY

Selecting the right venue is critical as it sets the tone for the event. The venue should align with the event's theme and be accessible to the target demographic. Factors such as location, capacity, availability of tech amenities (like high-speed Internet and audio-visual equipment), and layout need careful consideration. Additionally, choosing a date involves balancing several factors, including the availability of key participants, holiday schedules, and industry event calendars, to maximize attendance.

Once the venue and date are set, the focus shifts to how the event looks and feels. Branding elements, such as logos, color schemes, and thematic decor, should be consistently integrated to reinforce the organization's identity. Interactive elements can include technology demos, coding competitions, or collaborative workshops. These activities should engage attendees in hands-on experiences stimulating creativity and learning, making the event enjoyable and professionally enriching.

An essential aspect of party planning in developer relations is creating a safe and inclusive environment. This means implementing a clear code of conduct that outlines acceptable behavior and procedures for handling misconduct. Accessibility should be a priority, with the venue accommodating all participants, including those with disabilities. Efforts should also be made to welcome people from diverse backgrounds, promoting a culture of respect and inclusion through thoughtful communication and event programming.

Effective communication is vital to maximizing event attendance and engagement. This includes pre-event announcements, updates, and teasers that generate excitement and inform potential attendees about what to expect. Live updates and interactive content can keep the momentum going during the event. Post-event, sending out thank-yous, surveys, and content recaps helps maintain the connection with attendees, gather feedback, and set the stage for future events.

Evaluating the event's success against the initial objectives is crucial after the event. This involves analyzing attendance data, participant engagement, survey feedback, and social media activity. Understanding

CHAPTER 23   PARTY

what worked and what didn't helps refine future event strategies, ensuring continuous improvement in meeting the community's needs and strengthening the developer relations team with the community.

Metrics

Establishing a comprehensive approach to tracking metrics for a Conference Party is crucial. This approach should cover both quantitative and qualitative data, providing a solid foundation for effective evaluation and future planning.

- **Attendance:** This includes the total number of attendees and their demographic breakdown, such as roles, company size, and geographic locations. This helps understand who the event attracted and how well it aligned with the target audience.

- **Engagement levels during the event:** This can be assessed by observing how actively attendees participate in activities such as networking zones, interactive stations, or entertainment. This can be done by something as simple as an incremental "clicker" (much as joggers use to count laps while running). Tracking the number of interactions, such as conversations started, business cards exchanged, or social media mentions during the event, provides insight into the effectiveness of the networking opportunities provided.

- **Brand exposure:** This is measuring how often and where the company's branding elements were noticed or interacted with. This can include tracking the

325

distribution and use of branded swag, the visibility of banners, and mentions of the company in social media posts related to the event.

- **Feedback collection:** Another crucial metric, encompassing both formal and informal feedback from attendees, this can be gathered through post-event Surveys, on-the-spot interviews, or social media channels. Analyzing this feedback will help assess attendee satisfaction, the event's perceived value, and improvement areas.

- **Social media impact:** The team should track the number of posts, shares, likes, and comments related to the event, as well as any relevant hashtags. This helps gauge the broader reach and influence of the event beyond the physical attendees.

- **Cost-effectiveness:** This should be measured by comparing the total cost of the event against the tangible outcomes, such as the number of new leads generated, partnerships formed, or increases in brand awareness and loyalty.

- **Follow-up actions**, such as the number of attendees who engage with the company post-event, whether through continued social media interaction, participation in subsequent events, or conversion into customers or advocates.

Tracking these metrics will provide a holistic view of the event's success, highlight the return on investment, and inform strategies for future events. Each of these metrics should be documented in a detailed report, with data visualizations where applicable, to present clear insights to stakeholders and guide the planning of future parties.

Example

WidgetCorp decides to host "WidgetFest," a social event for developers, users, and enthusiasts, to strengthen their community ties in a relaxed, engaging environment.

Conceptualizing the Event: WidgetCorp's leadership decides to host "WidgetFest" to celebrate a successful product launch and reinforce the bonds within their developer and user community. The goal is to create an engaging, fun, and educational environment where attendees can connect over shared interests. The event is envisioned as a mix of social gathering and tech showcase featuring WidgetCorp's latest innovations. The planning team sets clear objectives to enhance community engagement, foster networking, and position WidgetCorp as a thought leader in the tech industry.

Venue Selection and Date: WidgetCorp decides to throw "WidgetFest" in conjunction with CascadiaJS, an annual **Developer Conference (179)** held in the Pacific Northwest, since the primary consumer of their WidgetPack are Javascript developers. They look at different options near the **Conference (179)** venue, and decide that WidgetFest will be set at a popular rooftop garden located a short walk from the main conference venue, chosen for its stunning city views and easy accessibility. The venue's open-air setup fosters a relaxed atmosphere, with ample space for attendees to mingle. The garden's aesthetic—equipped with ambient lighting and comfortable seating areas—perfectly aligns with WidgetCorp's intention to create a memorable, laid-back experience. To maximize attendance, WidgetCorp schedules "WidgetFest" during an evening where the conference has not scheduled an official event.

Designing Branding and Interactive Elements: WidgetCorp's marketing team develops a vibrant branding strategy for "WidgetFest," utilizing the company's colors and logo across all decorations, promotional materials, and digital platforms. The event features interactive tech demos where attendees can try out new products, participate in coding challenges designed to encourage collaborative problem-solving and attend workshops led by key developers from WidgetCorp. These elements are strategically placed throughout the venue to guide attendees through an immersive brand experience.

Safety and Inclusivity: To ensure "WidgetFest" is safe and inclusive, WidgetCorp establishes a clear code of conduct on the event website and at the venue. Signage and materials are designed to be accessible, with provisions for attendees requiring special accommodations. The event staff receives training to handle any issues sensitively and effectively. WidgetCorp also promotes diversity by featuring speakers and panelists from various backgrounds and offering discounted tickets to students and underrepresented groups in tech.

Engaging Participants Before, During, and After the Event: In the lead-up to "WidgetFest," WidgetCorp uses email campaigns, social media, and tech blogs to generate buzz. They provide sneak peeks of the tech demos and highlight keynote speakers to attract attendees. During the event, they encourage live social media posting and sharing with a custom hashtag, enhancing online engagement. Following "WidgetFest," attendees receive thank-you emails, access to event photos, and exclusive content recaps. WidgetCorp also sends out surveys to gather feedback and suggestions for future events.

Measuring Success and Gathering Feedback: Post-event, WidgetCorp analyzes the number of attendees, social media engagement metrics, and survey responses to measure the success of "WidgetFest." They track mentions in the press and on tech blogs and review feedback on the interactive elements and overall event experience. This data helps

WidgetCorp understand the event's impact on community engagement and brand perception, informing adjustments for subsequent events to meet community needs better.

Consequences

Many large vendor events will be in large cities with a number of party venues (restaurants, pubs, etc.) nearby; these will be snapped up quickly, likely within days of the date of the event being announced. If you are not able to secure a traditional venue in time, you may need to get creative with either the date and/or time of your event (perhaps consider a breakfast instead of an evening event, or perhaps an event the evening before the event starts as a "warm up" for the event's festivities), or with the location (perhaps a hotel will rent out its restaurant space, or perhaps an outdoor gathering in a nearby park if the event is held in a weather-friendly city and time of year).

It is likely that there will be competitors and/or partners who are looking to host a party at the event as well; consider partnering for your first party until you have a better sense of the costs and logistics of throwing a party of your own. If a competitor chooses to host a party the same night as your own, make no mention of it publicly. If you choose to host a party on the same night as a competitor, offset the time so that interested individuals can make both if they wish—and then provide a better experience than your competitor, so that next year, people will be drawn to your party over theirs should they conflict again.

Many individuals have food allergies and/or constraints, so make sure the refreshments are varied and offer a wide range of choices. If the group size is over 50, definitely provide options for those who are vegetarian, vegan, gluten-free, kosher, and halal. (If you're not sure what these options mean, consult with the venue for their options. If they have no such options, consider a different venue, and/or speak with the venue management about creative options.)

CHAPTER 23   PARTY

Keep in mind that negative stories from a party can do as much (or more) damage than positive stories can benefit you, so make sure you have solid contingency plans when someone at the party behaves badly (regardless of cause). If the party is going to serve alcohol or have any alcohol present, make sure your company personnel at the party do not drink to help keep an eye on the rest of the attendees' behavior and make sure all company personnel have details handy for taxis and rideshares in the event a partygoer has had too much to drink and needs a way back to their hotel or home. If the party involves any athletic or strenuous activity, have a plan in place should an attendee injure themselves. Venue hosts should be well-familiar with this, but remember, the party's reputation is tied directly to your company's reputation within the community, so anything that goes poorly reflects on your company, not the venue.

The Party pattern has distinct advantages and disadvantages that impact its execution and outcome. Advantages include providing a relaxed platform conducive to networking and community building, allowing individuals to form meaningful connections in a less formal environment than typical conference settings. This type of event also enhances brand appreciation by offering attendees a unique and memorable experience, associating the brand with positive, enjoyable interactions. Furthermore, parties provide an informal setting for feedback collection, where guests are more likely to share candid insights about the brand or products in casual conversations. However, there are disadvantages to consider. Such events require meticulous logistical planning and can be significantly resource-intensive, involving venue rental, catering, entertainment, and security services. They also present the potential for unforeseen issues, such as overcrowding, noise complaints, or other disturbances that could negatively impact the attendee experience and the company's image. Additionally, there's a risk that the brand messages may be diluted or lost if the event does not align well with the company's values or if the branding is too subtle or overwhelming, leading to mixed messages about the company's identity and core values.

Variants

Dinner: A variant of the party is a much more intimate event in which you invite a small number of selected guests to a nice dinner. Here, the goal is to provide opportunities to get to know your customer (or potential customer) much better, albeit in a casual setting. Dinners are a powerful way to cement relationships with individuals from the developer community, perhaps because you are looking to recruit them as **Ambassadors (71)**. Dinners are usually less-publicized so as to minimize hurt feelings of those who weren't invited, but often, the realization of not being invited turns into a determination to do what's necessary to score that invite—which is precisely the goal (greater engagement).

CHAPTER 24

Podcast

Topics: *Social*

A podcast, a series of spoken audio episodes focused on a particular topic or theme, is a powerful tool in the context of Developer Relations. It serves as a platform to share knowledge, discuss industry trends, interview experts, and provide insights into technologies, tools, and best practices. By tuning in, the audience stays informed and up-to-date, enhancing their understanding of the developer community. The convenience of podcasts, available for streaming or download through various platforms, allows listeners to stay connected, whether commuting, working, or relaxing.

CHAPTER 24   PODCAST

Also Known As

Vidcast

Intent

Create a deeper sense of connection with your developer audience by allowing them to see and hear you and/or guests discuss and/or demo your product/service, ideas related to the product/service, or just "interesting topics" that your community might find interesting. By doing so, you tap into developers' inherent desire to learn and grow in a high-reach fashion, but with a little more room for interactivity, particularly if the guests come from the community and/or your podcast encourages listeners to "send us your comments" (via email or other channels).

Problem

You want to improve the feeling of "connection" to your customers and provide a more "human" face to your product/service, company, or team, but in a relatively high-reach manner. Since most of your developers will never be within the same postal code as you or your company or your guests, you need a way to capture those conversations and release them out to the world, preferably through channels that developers are already using or at least aware of. Podcasts are particularly effective because they enable long-form conversations that delve beyond surface-level updates, offering nuanced discussions that shape opinions and influence the community. By featuring guests that developers already know and respect, such as thought leaders, peers, or even customers, you create a space where listeners feel like they're part of an authentic dialogue. This mix of accessibility and authority not only builds trust but also positions your company as a meaningful participant in the broader technical conversation.

Context

Reading a website has all the "human-ness" of staring at a billboard or reading a brochure, and often offers the viewer nothing in the way of culture or engagement. The phrase "putting a face to the name" (and, for that matter, even just knowing the name!) is a common one that indicates that the more humans can see other humans, the more we begin to feel a degree of connection or empathy to the company, team, or even the product/service itself.

Solution

Create a series of recordings (audio-only or audio/video) in which one or more members of your DevRel team host a variety of different individuals for an interactive conversation about one or more particular topics relevant to your product/service, your customers' concerns, or the larger technical domain in which your product/service exists.

Participants

To start, the podcast will need

- **Host(s):** Individuals responsible for steering the conversation, asking insightful questions, and maintaining a friendly and inclusive environment.
- **Guest(s):** Industry experts, community leaders, or notable personalities invited to share their insights and experiences.
- **Listeners:** The developer community who are the consumers of the podcast content.

- **Community Manager** (optional): Responsible for gathering community questions, feedback, and fostering community engagement.

- **Post-production Team** (optional): A group handling the technical aspects of recording, editing, and publishing the podcast.

- **Producer** (optional): Responsible for finding guests, scheduling times for recording, creating a backlog of episodes for steady release, and overseeing the process as a whole.

Hosts can often fill the Community Manager, Post-production, and Producer roles, but keep in mind that these jobs are all non-trivial, and the more hats a single individual wears, the more time they will need to put into the podcast.

In addition to the individual roles, various parts of the company will often have some insight, opinions, and interest in a company developer-facing podcast:

- **Legal:** If the podcast is company-sponsored, then the legal team is going to need to become involved at some point, if only to make sure that there is a firm framework in place to know what topics are "off-limits" for discussion and/or what an acceptable set of topics are. As a company-sponsored podcast, remember, any host(s) speaking with the company's voice could therefore be used as justification or citation in current or future legal proceedings against the company, so getting—and keeping—the legal team involved, even if only lightly, will be necessary to avoid accidentally putting the company in legal liability.

- **Marketing:** Partnering with the Marketing team will be useful when it comes time to promote the podcast, and the Marketing team will often have some ideas on how to gather metrics around the effectiveness of the podcast itself. They can often be a source of materials and information about the company's developer audience as well, if developers are the primary target for the product/service.

- **Recruiting:** Any time the company is hiring, the Recruiting team will want to have some window into whatever developer-facing activities are happening. In many cases, their involvement can be as small as "Could you please mention to people to look at our Careers page?" as part of the episode, or as large as having them on an episode to go into detail about the company's recruiting process, both as a subtle advertisement as well as a way to demonstrate to developers that yours is a company that is comfortable discussing its practices and processes.

- **Engineering:** The Engineering team will often be a source of potential guests for the podcast, so long as participation doesn't significantly take away time from development on the next feature. They may also be necessary as a "tech check" to make sure technical content mentioned in the podcast is correct, but generally podcast episodes avoid going too deeply into details, so this is not a hard requirement and can probably be handled on a case-by-case basis.

CHAPTER 24   PODCAST

Implementation

Creating a podcast will take a few steps, but keep in mind that the true appeal of a podcast is its regularity of episodes—no single episode will ever really create the benefits that a regularly scheduled and released collection of episodes will create.

To start with, the podcast must make several choices up front:

- **Goals:** What, exactly, is the podcast intended to do? Brand recognition by getting the company's name "out there" in the developer community? Or is it technical education, providing some developer-centric "additional material" on the topics that developers are struggling with? Or is the desire to help with sales, by providing a vehicle for advertisements to the developer audience, hopefully drawing them into sending an email or clicking on a form to formally start the sales process? Knowing the goals ahead of time, explicitly and concretely, will help immensely with many of the remaining decisions.

- **Theme/Topic:** Will the podcast be centered around a particular topic (however broad or narrow), or will it be centered around the podcast's guests? Going too broad risks not collecting enough viewers to form a "critical mass" of consumers, but being too narrow risks running out of topical material and/or "chewing the same old soup" over and over again, boring listeners.

- **Cadence:** How often do you want to release episodes? Releasing weekly creates a continuous connection between you and your developer audience but requires a significant time commitment to maintain that schedule. However, building up a backlog of pre-recorded episodes can help ease the pressure and ensure consistent releases. Releasing monthly requires less immediate commitment but results in less continuity and reduced interactivity with your audience. A backlog of episodes, regardless of the release frequency, provides flexibility and helps maintain engagement without gaps, especially during busier periods.

- **Format:** Will this be an audio-only podcast, or one that combines both audio and video? Traditionally, podcasts were audio-only at first, with audio/video called "vidcasts," but over time, the distinction has become lost. Audio-only is easier to capture, but video provides another dimension of capture, particularly with guests who are animated when they speak. Video does require greater bandwidth, however, both at time of capture and when being viewed, and keep in mind that many podcast consumers do so while doing other activities (driving to work, for example, or exercising) which preclude being able to watch what's happening on-screen. Video is also more complex to edit. If in doubt, consider doing audio-only at first, and if your audience starts agitating for video, or if there are reasons to support it (such as screen-sharing during the podcast).

- **Accessibility:** Keep accessibility in mind when making this decision. Deaf and hard-of-hearing developers will need either a transcription service or Braille translations of your audio, and a free-wheeling, everybody-talking-over-each-other format can often

CHAPTER 24   PODCAST

leave those listeners lost or confused. Blind or hard-of-sight consumers will have an equally difficult time consuming the video portions of the podcast.

- **Style:** Will this be an "ask me anything" between guests and listeners (who send in questions while the podcast is being recorded), or will there be a host who asks questions on behalf of the listening audience? Will the podcast allow guests to come with prepared messaging ahead of time? While many podcasts feel very informal, many have an underlying structure to them—podcast hosts will often send guests a list of questions ahead of time, for example, or at least go over two or three topics they plan to cover. Does your podcast want to stick to those questions, or will you allow the conversation to roam freely from point to point, possibly never discussing what you'd prepared ahead of time? Keep in mind, listeners often won't express a strong preference for conversation to be formal or informal, but the formality of the conversation will often subtly have an impact on how the viewers/listeners perceive the culture of the company. If, for example, the desire is to project a very formal and corporate-friendly culture (so as to be more attractive to more formal corporate environments, like financial services firms), then having a more scripted format helps present that. This may come as a "turn-off" to smaller, scrappier-culture companies (as in, startups), however, so a more informal, free-wheeling conversation can help project that image instead.

- **Hosting:** Will you do the podcast in person, with two microphones set up for the host and the guest, sitting at the same table across from each other, or will you use remote-communication tools (like Zoom) to have your discussion? Being at the same table—particularly if this is done at a conference—can allow for audience participation, which can make the conversation feel more "real" and "connected" to the audience, but has all the traditional problems of getting two people to the same table at the same time.

- Some podcasts are scheduled and held live (usually over a video chat platform) so as to facilitate open Q&A from audience members, and/or to allow for targeted questions from a certain user community. Doing so requires choosing a time, however, and that will often make live consumption uncomfortable for two-thirds of the time zones in the world. Noon PST, for example, which is easily accessible to individuals residing in North or South America, will be late-night in Europe and middle-of-the-night or pre-dawn in Asia. If your audience is global, consider varying the scheduled time for live participation to allow for participants from other regions. (Also, consider the guests' own time zones!)

- Another consideration around live podcasts is that of potential mistakes or liability from what is spoken; many guests, particularly if they represent large companies, will want to make sure there is an opportunity to edit out any accidental reference to topics that a large company does not want discussed on your podcast. You will also want to weigh the opportunity to edit the podcast to ensure it follows your company's code of conduct policies and/or meets your desired projected image against the increased interactivity of a live recording.

- **Logistics:** In addition to the hosting questions, equipment must be procured. While it's certainly possible to go with free solutions like using the free tier of popular teleconference software, or even recording the episode using a mobile phone, quality issues will often creep in very quickly and make things difficult on listeners.

- **Intro and Outro:** The music and welcome message at the beginning of a podcast are called "intros," while the messaging and music at the end of the podcast are similarly called "outros." While it is not necessary to hire professional voice actors or license a band to record the intro or outro, it will be seen as more professional to have both, and it can be a bit jarring to listeners to not have some consistent opening and closing, regardless of the quality. Although not necessary for a podcast, you may get tired very quickly of repeating the same opening and closing message while recording with the guest (and the guest may not realize when your intro has ended or your outro has started, which can disrupt the flow and require post-production editing).

Once the basic "feel" of the podcast has been established, each episode will often follow the same basic workflow:

- **Identify guests:** The lifeblood of the podcast are the guests you interview, so for any given episode, you will need to identify guests to interview. Guests can come from a variety of sources, ranging from company employees (the CEO and/or CTO being popular choices), to **Ambassadors (71)** from your community, to other conference speakers at either your **Conference (179)** or other 3rd-party industry events, to your company's **Partners (309)**. Finding guest participants will be a significant time commitment. While there are many, many people in the technology industry who are excellent podcast guests, you will want to find people who are somehow relevant to your product/service, and are willing to be a "friendly guest" (as in, someone that isn't a competitor or isn't going to subtly bad-mouth your product/service) on the show. You are not interested in "cross-examination" of a "hostile witness" on your podcast, you are interested in providing content that is both interesting and entertaining. (Leave the "shock jock" radio DJ antics to the radio.) Additionally, you will want to make sure your guest list is not exclusionary in any way, and often a podcast episode is a great way to give "new blood" a chance to get some "on-air" time, as a gentle way of seeing how well they perform "on a stage."

- **Schedule and logistics:** Once you have identified a guest, you will quickly want to set up logistics with them, primarily a date and time for the podcast to take place. Keep in mind you will want time both pre- and post-recording with the guest, so make sure to schedule accordingly—for a 30-minute podcast episode, reserve an hour's time slot, so you have a few minutes ahead of time before "going live." This cushion is necessary in cases where the guest(s) and/or host(s) are late,

CHAPTER 24   PODCAST

or there are tech issues. Even when everything flows exactly according to schedule, it is useful to revisit with the guest(s) the topic of the podcast episode (and any "no-go" topics that the guest(s) should not, cannot, or don't wish to discuss) before "going live." Make sure the host(s) and guest(s) all have a scheduled calendar invite with all the logistics (date/time, Zoom link or geographical location of the interview, topics, and so on) in it. Note that if the scheduled recording time is more than a month in advance, you may wish to send a quick note to the guest(s) a week or so ahead of time, to make sure something hasn't cropped up in the meantime, as does sometimes happen. Additionally, some episodes may need to be tied to external events, such as KubeCon or a major product launch, which requires careful planning of the release date. Work backward from that date to ensure you have enough lead time for recording, editing, and approvals, so the episode is ready to publish exactly when it will have the greatest impact.

- **Pre-recording:** As the guest(s) arrive, test to make sure their microphone is recording at an appropriate volume, and that they can hear you and others in the podcast. Record a short snippet and play it back, just to make sure the recording is coming through cleanly and with no background noise. Many professional podcasts will also record for 30 seconds with nobody on the podcast speaking, to capture the "room tone" so editing tools can help filter out hums, fans, static, or other recurrent background noises.

- **Recording:** This is the fun part! Here the host(s) will have the conversation with the guest(s) about the topics ahead of time, and—depending on the tone and format of the podcast's theme—either keep the conversation closely to the agreed-upon agenda or roam, free-wheeling, from one topic to another as the conversation takes you. The host(s) should make sure to keep the conversation flowing, ready with a follow-up question when the guest(s) end speaking, keeping an eye on the time to ensure the episode doesn't run too long or too short, and ensuring the guest(s) are all feeling comfortable during the conversation. If there is any audience participation, the host(s) should be the go-between, taking questions from the audience and repeating them to the host(s) (so they can be captured on the recording), and/or filtering the question if necessary to avoid topics the guest(s) have previously declared to be "off-topic." Keep in mind, the job of the host(s) is to make the guest(s) look good.

- **Post-recording:** After the record button has been stopped, the host(s) should (of course) thank the guest(s), but more importantly, ask if there were any segments that should be edited out or re-recorded. A guest should never be surprised by something in a podcast episode—this tends to spark bad feelings, and your guests will likely know one another and compare notes at some point.

- **Post-production:** Despite everyone's best efforts, it's highly likely that the recording will require some collation (certain recording tools will record locally on each participant's machine, then the localized audio and/or video streams are combined into one finished format), edit, potentially convert to different formats, upload/store the finished stream someplace publicly accessible, as well as write "advertising copy" to notify interested customers and/or other developers in the content. Some podcast platforms will do the notifications for you automatically, but you will also likely want to prepare notifications to go out in your **Newsletter (281)** and/or **Social Media (395)** channels.

- **Release:** Once finished with the post-production, upload the episode to your podcasting platform of choice. Podcast platforms also typically have some form of notification system in place, in which interested individuals can subscribe to receive notifications (and sometimes automatic download) of new episodes. This can also help draw more interested parties to your content, since most of these platforms have the ability to categorize ("tag") your podcast to certain kinds of audiences, or with certain keywords, or as being similar to other podcasts, and so on. The platform can then suggest your podcast to those who consume similar content. Most platforms will have a "release date" option for each episode, so that the episode will "go live" automatically at that date and time, and you will likely want to coordinate your Social Media notifications to go out at the same time the episode goes live. Make sure all the usual metrics systems are in place—number of times the episode was downloaded, listened, views, whatever is available on the platform—and review the numbers at some point after the release. In certain situations, it may be necessary to share the final recording with the guest and their company representatives for review and approval before publishing. This process helps ensure that any sensitive information is cleared, aligns the content with organizational guidelines, and prevents last-minute conflicts that could delay or jeopardize the release.

- **Community Engagement:** Involving listeners as active participants in the podcast, not just passive consumers. This can include soliciting feedback, incorporating listener-submitted questions, highlighting community stories, or inviting community members as guests. By making the audience feel included in shaping content, you strengthen their connection to both the podcast and the company, creating a two-way dialogue that fosters loyalty, trust, and a sense of shared ownership.

- **Feedback Loop:** Create avenues for listeners to share feedback and suggest topics.

- **Inclusive:** Foster an inclusive environment where every community member feels seen and heard.

- **Promotion:** "If you build it they will come" only exists in movies; in order to attract consumers, you will need to find ways to let developers know about your podcast. Sometimes this can take the form of asking your guest(s) to promote the episode on their **Social Media (395)** channels, but the lion's share of promotional work should be something you assume is yours to do. Look for ways to cross-promote, wherein you leverage other platforms and community networks to promote the podcast. SEO (Search Engine Optimization) will also be a key element for your podcast, so make sure to implement strategies that will improve its visibility and extend its reach.

CHAPTER 24   PODCAST

Keep in mind, each episode's workflow will overlap with other episodes, depending on the regularity you want your podcast to release. For example, if your podcast is releasing weekly, in a given week you will have just released episode 12, while at the same time you are responding to comments from episodes 10 and 11, recording episodes 18 and 19 this week, doing post-production on episodes 16 and 17, finalizing the guest lists for episodes 21 through 25, all while having episodes 13 through 15 "in the can" to release over the next three weeks.

Metrics

To document the metrics for tracking the performance of a Podcast, a thorough and multifaceted approach is necessary to capture various aspects of the podcast's reach, engagement, and overall effectiveness. The first metric to track is **listenership**, which includes the total number of downloads or streams per episode. This provides a baseline for understanding the podcast's reach and popularity. Additionally, tracking **subscriber growth** over time is essential to measure how the podcast's audience is expanding, indicating sustained interest and the effectiveness of promotional efforts.

Episode retention rates are another critical metric, reflecting how many listeners stay engaged from the beginning to the end of each episode. High retention rates suggest that the content is compelling and well-structured. At the same time, significant drop-off points indicate areas where the content may lose its appeal or where improvements are needed in pacing or delivery.

Audience demographics, including listener location, job roles, industries, and experience levels, should also be tracked. This data helps understand who the podcast is reaching and whether it aligns with the target audience. Additionally, tracking **listening platforms**—whether listeners are tuning in via Apple Podcasts, Spotify, or other platforms—provides insights into where the audience is most active and can inform platform-specific promotional strategies.

Engagement metrics are crucial for assessing how well the podcast resonates with its audience. These include the number of ratings and reviews the podcast receives on various platforms and the quality of these reviews. High ratings and positive reviews typically indicate that listeners value the content. Similarly, tracking **social media mentions** and using podcast-specific hashtags can gauge how the podcast is discussed and shared within the community.

Listener feedback is another important metric, which can be collected through direct surveys, social media polls, or feedback forms on the podcast's website. This qualitative data is not just a measure of the podcast's performance, but a testament to the audience's active role in shaping the podcast. Their feedback helps to identify what listeners enjoy about the podcast and areas where they feel improvements could be made. The feedback also provides ideas for future topics or guest speakers that could resonate with the audience, making them an integral part of the podcast's success.

Content effectiveness should be measured by analyzing which episodes perform the best in downloads, retention, and engagement. This can reveal trends in listener preferences, helping the team to refine future content planning. For example, if episodes featuring specific topics or guest speakers consistently perform well, it suggests that the audience has a strong interest in those areas.

Marketing and promotion effectiveness can be assessed by tracking metrics related to cross-promotion efforts, such as click-through rates on promotional emails, conversion rates from social media ads, and the impact of guest appearances on other podcasts or platforms. These metrics help determine which promotional strategies drive new listeners to the podcast and which might need adjustment.

SEO performance is also critical. Tracking the podcast's visibility on search engines and within podcast directories can provide insights into how well the podcast is being discovered organically. Metrics such as search rankings for relevant keywords, the number of backlinks to the podcast's website, and the effectiveness of episode titles and descriptions in attracting listeners are important to monitor.

Monetization metrics, if applicable, should also be documented. This includes tracking revenue from sponsorships, affiliate links, or listener donations and analyzing how these streams are performing relative to listenership and engagement levels. Understanding the financial aspect of the podcast can inform decisions on scaling, reinvesting in production quality, or exploring new revenue opportunities.

Finally, the **overall impact on brand perception** should be considered. The podcast is not just a performance metric, but a strategic tool that can significantly influence the company's reputation. It can be assessed through broader surveys or interviews with the developer community to gauge how the podcast influences their perception of the company or brand. This metric is more qualitative but is essential for understanding the podcast's strategic role in shaping the company's reputation and thought leadership within the industry.

All these metrics should be meticulously documented in a comprehensive report that includes quantitative data and qualitative insights. The report should be regularly updated, ideally after each episode or monthly, to track progress over time. Visualizations like graphs and charts communicate trends and highlight key findings. This comprehensive report, with its thoroughness and professionalism, will serve as a valuable tool for evaluating the podcast's success, guiding content and promotional strategies, and demonstrating the podcast's impact on stakeholders and the broader developer relations team.

Example

Diana, a new developer advocate at a company that provides an API-based content-management system (CMS), has been tasked with starting up a new podcast. When she asks about the goals for the podcast, she discovers that Marketing would like to increase the platform's brand recognition among developers, since the product is relatively new, and Product is eager to get some feedback from the developers who use the API, since much of that feedback loop currently goes through Support (and Product feels it is going through too many hands and is being watered down along the way).

Knowing this, Diana begins fleshing out the podcast. The theme will be around "developers and CMS," such as all the different ways developers can make use of a CMS even beyond the stock "build a **Blog (105)** or a news site" canonical example, as well as some of the ways developers can do traditional DevOps with a CMS, and even how to version-control the content of a CMS as part of a workflow her company's product supports.

She aims for twice-monthly releases to start, with a goal to have twelve episodes "in the can" for three months (that is, at the start of each month she has twelve episodes recorded and waiting for release) before going to the more aggressive weekly model (which Marketing would prefer). To keep it approachable by developers of all skill level, she's not going to go too technically deep in any one area, nor is she going to limit her pool of potential guests to any one technology stack—any programming language or platform for which the CMS has an SDK is a reasonable target. And in order to avoid any sort of requests by Marketing to include product demos, she's going to keep it audio-only, at least to start with.

Given her personal experience on the speech-and-debate team in college, she's comfortable being the Host, and until the podcast takes off, she'll act as the Producer and Community Manager as well. Fortunately, the company has an A/V team that will help with post-production edits,

CHAPTER 24   PODCAST

and their process already runs things past Legal, so she's squared away on that front. Fortunately, she already has a nice-quality standing microphone she's used for some **Webinars (469)** she's done for the company, and the Marketing folks don't want to lay out a lot of money for a travel budget for the podcast, so she's going to use Bluejeans, a popular podcasting SaaS, to record her podcasts.

Despite knowing that the CTO is itching to do an episode (actually, he's itching to do all of them, she's heard), Diana wants to get a little bit of a community following before she reaches out to people inside the company. Fortunately, the next week she's scheduled to be at KCDC, a popular technology-agnostic software developer conference in the Midwest United States, and she's on good terms with a number of the speakers there, many of whom are veteran podcast guests (and more than a few podcasters themselves), so she'll be able to kick off her podcast with guests who know what to expect as well as get some advice on how to better host.

While at the event, she talks about her upcoming podcast to the speakers, and over three dozen all eagerly volunteer. Elated, when she gets back to her hotel room she fires off emails to each of them to begin the logistical process. A few end up needing to decline (which is expected), but she ends up with a solid dozen episodes scheduled for recording in the next month. Many of those email conversations are similar to the one she has with Sarah, a developer advocate in the PHP space:

Diana: Sarah, I'm so excited that we're doing this podcast together. Thank you again! Are there any topics you'd like to discuss?

Sarah: OMG me too, I've always wanted to do one with you. Pretty much anything that's PHP is good for me. Does your company have a PHP SDK? Can we talk about how I could use it?

Diana: We've definitely got a PHP SDK! What if we start by talking a little bit about PHP and why it's so commonly used for CMS-based sites (gotta get that Wordpress elephant out of the room lol), then maybe we can branch out into other ways you've used a CMS in the past in your PHP work?

CHAPTER 24   PODCAST

Sarah: Oh, yeah, that's good! If we have time, can we shout out my company? Being consultants, we always look for the opportunity to maybe turn a few eyeballs and projects our way.

Diana: Of course!

The email conversation goes back and forth a bit more, and Diana makes notes to herself to make sure they save time at the end of the episode to ask Sarah if she wants to talk about her company for a bit, regardless of wherever else they go in the conversation. She puts together a schedule invite with a Bluejeans URL in it, including the agenda that they'd discussed, and fires it off.

Three weeks later, Diana is in the "waiting room" online in the Bluejeans app and Sarah logs in. They do a quick tech-check to make sure they can each see and hear each other and the recording is good, then Diana says, "OK, just a reminder, we can see each other but the recording is audio-only, so don't worry about your background or any of that. And it is all a recording, so if you need to back up and 'un-say' something, just stop and let me know and I'll edit it out before it goes live. You still OK with our agenda?"

Sarah looks a little nervous at that point and says, "Yeah, about that, actually, you know how we were going to shout out my company? They laid me off last week, so I don't really...."

Diana quickly jumps in, "Oh, no worries! We don't have to shout them out. Do you want to talk about you instead? Do you have a new gig yet? Are you actively looking? How can this help?"

Sarah brightens. "Well, actually, I was going to take this opportunity to go solo, so maybe we can do the shout out but for me as an independent consultant instead of the company?"

Diana grins, notes the change in her notes, and thumbs over the recording button, says, "Ready?"

Sarah's grin is huge. "Punch it."

CHAPTER 24   PODCAST

Consequences

Recorded Video (363) podcasts are commonly distributed on a platform such as YouTube podcasts, which provides the potential for extensive reach. However, YouTube has come under criticism in recent years for its suggestion algorithms, often leading viewers to content that may not be in keeping with your company's image or culture. Pay careful attention to any feedback your customers provide around any concerns or unpleasant experiences there.

Podcasts also are a great segue into or from **Live Streaming (273);** live-streams can find topical material from conversations had from a podcast, but podcast conversations can also be inspired from experiences had from a live-stream.

When selecting guests, podcasts often want to steer clear of anyone that could create either bad PR or legal liability or both—anything with the company logo on it, explicitly or implicitly, is "speaking with the company's voice," and could be cited in a court of law. The podcast host will want to have some guidelines from the Legal team about what is legally permissible to say and what to steer clear of, but guests are often unaware of the company's legal guidelines or concerns. Hosts, therefore, must either make the guests aware of those guidelines or concerns ahead of time, or else be prepared to edit out content that could create liability. In some cases, the entire episode will need to be thrown away and never released, which is another reason for the podcast to always have several episodes "in the can," so that other episodes can be shuffled around to replace the now-deleted one. It sucks when it happens, but it's better than costing the company millions in lawsuit settlements.

Podcasts offer a particularly low-cost (comparatively speaking) opportunity to allow the developer audience to "get into the head" of people who have influence or authority over the product/service. Rarely do developers get a chance to understand the thoughts or rationale behind a particular product or service's features (or lack thereof), so having the

Chief Architect or CTO on the podcast to discuss why those decisions were made—the state of the market at the time, underlying architectural considerations, future intentions, whatever went into the decision (that doesn't violate any NDAs, of course), all are interesting reasons to the developer community and help the developers better understand the product/service, and what to expect in the future.

Additionally, a podcast is a low-risk way to introduce new voices into the community, including members of the community that are looking to make the jump into doing more public speaking, such as at conferences. Whether these are voices coming from traditionally underrepresented groups, or voices from people who are just getting their career underway, or for any of a number of other reasons, it's to your interests to provide some space for "new blood," particularly because those voices will remember that you gave them the shot, and will often be among some of your most loyal return guests.

Variants

The **One-on-One Interview** is a variant of the podcast, in which the emphasis is on a guest, rather than on a particular topic, as an opportunity for your developer audience to find out more about the guest-as-person, rather than interacting with the guest-as-topic-expert. More emphasis is placed on the guest's history, perspectives, or thoughts, rather than on their perspective on a particular technical topic. Guest-centric questions often take the form of "you" questions, like "How did you get into tech?" "What made you interested in (the topic for which they are known)?" or "What advice do you have for beginners that you wish you had when you started?" are all good guest-centric questions. The emphasis and focus on the guest provide a humanizing view of the name developers recognize, and often is a good way for guest(s) to improve their personal brand recognition. For this reason, it is often common for company-sponsored

CHAPTER 24   PODCAST

podcasts to do 1-on-1 interviews (also known as the "Ask Me Anything" or "AMA") with people at the company that the developer community might not normally get to know on a personal level, like the CEO, CTO, and/or various leadership figures around the product/service used by the community, such as the organization's VP of Engineering, VP of Product, Chief Architect, or similarly senior individual.

CHAPTER 25

Product/Service Development

Topics: *Code*

DevRel works on integration endpoints (à la APIs) for connecting or extending the core product/service.

CHAPTER 25   PRODUCT/SERVICE DEVELOPMENT

Also Known As

Extensions; Providers

Intent

Certain aspects of the product/service are not easily accessible (or accessible at all) to the community, and the company has deemed it necessary that they should be. Engineering arguably should be focused on providing this, but can't due to constraints (time, budget, bandwidth, etc.).

Context

Ideally, many of the extensions or integrations discussed can and should be written by third parties outside the company, to avoid the maintenance burden that would come with developing them "in-house." But for whatever reason, third parties haven't built those extensions or integrations, either because they lack access (the product/service is tucked behind the firewall and the code is not public), knowledge (they do not know the integration or extension points exist, or how to use them), or rationale (they do not have reason to build them).

Solution

From the Developer Relations perspective, the solution for a product development pattern involves the DevRel team stepping in. They create integration endpoints, such as APIs, CLI apps, framework templates, or other extensions, to bridge gaps between the product/service and the community. By prioritizing accessibility and usability, DevRel ensures that developers can easily connect or extend the core product. Their focus on

CHAPTER 25 PRODUCT/SERVICE DEVELOPMENT

showcasing what's possible not only addresses the developer community's immediate needs but also encourages third-party contributions and fosters trust in the ecosystem.

Participants

In product development, the creators are primarily the DevRel team, which includes Developer Advocates, Technical Writers, and Community Managers. They collaborate to design and deliver integration points like APIs or extensions. They often work closely with engineering teams for technical guidance, product managers to align efforts with business objectives, and marketing teams to ensure the resulting tools reach the right audience. Participants include external developers, partners, and the broader community, whose feedback is not just important but integral to the process. They use these integrations to build on the core product and provide feedback, shaping the future of the product.

Implementation

Implementing product development involves a structured process where the DevRel team takes ownership of identifying, designing, and delivering developer-centric solutions. This begins with gathering insights from the community to pinpoint specific gaps or challenges in accessing or extending the core product. The team then prototypes integrations, APIs, or extensions, leveraging lightweight and agile methodologies to ensure quick iteration. Collaboration with internal stakeholders ensures alignment with technical and business goals, while thorough documentation and developer-friendly resources accompany the launch to maximize usability. Post-release, the team actively monitors adoption,

CHAPTER 25 PRODUCT/SERVICE DEVELOPMENT

gathers feedback, and iterates on the solution to maintain relevance and effectiveness, creating a sustainable ecosystem that empowers both the company and its developer community.

Metrics

To document the metrics for product development, focus on measurable outcomes that reflect both developer engagement and business impact. Track adoption rates of the integrations or APIs created, such as the number of developers using the extensions or the volume of API calls. Measure developer satisfaction through surveys and emphasize the significant role of community contributions in the product's success, such as the number of third-party integrations developed after the initial release. Business-oriented metrics like increased product retention or direct revenue influenced by these integrations further highlight the impact. Finally, gather qualitative feedback through case studies and testimonials to contextualize the quantitative data.

Example

The fictitious DevRel team at StreamFlow, a company specializing in real-time data streaming services, noticed a recurring issue in their developer community: customers needed help integrating StreamFlow's platform with popular cloud-based analytics tools like Tableau. While the core engineering team focused entirely on building new platform features, the DevRel team recognized an opportunity to address this gap. By leveraging feedback from **Forums (233)**, customer support tickets, and **Hackathon (255)** events, the team designed and developed a pre-built integration API specifically tailored for Tableau. They created **Detailed Guides (243)**, **Code Samples (387)**, and even a live demo application to showcase how to use the integration effectively.

One early adopter, a mid-sized retail company named ShopSphere, used the integration to combine StreamFlow's real-time customer data streams with Tableau's analytics dashboards, providing their marketing team instant insights on customer behavior. The DevRel team worked closely with ShopSphere, providing technical support and gathering feedback to refine the integration further. As ShopSphere's marketing campaigns improved due to the new insights, they publicly praised StreamFlow's developer resources in a case study. The resulting buzz increased interest in StreamFlow's platform, leading to a 20% increase in new customer sign-ups.

Consequences

If the integration is connected to something internal that must remain internal (such as internal services or databases), chances are that maintenance of this integration will need to be continued and upheld by the DevRel team until such time that it can be handed off to Engineering to own. (And it should be handed off!) Note that Technical Support will be needed on it, so the sooner it can be "folded in" to the larger product/service offering, the better, particularly as customers make more and more use of it.

If the integration or extension is built as part of a customer or partner deal, expectations for long-term stability and support are even higher. What begins as a quick DevRel solution to unblock adoption can quickly become mission-critical for the customer. This creates both opportunity and risk: the integration may strengthen the relationship and showcase the product's flexibility, but it also ties the DevRel team to ongoing support obligations that may not align with their core mission. Without a clear plan to transition ownership to Product or Engineering, DevRel risks becoming a shadow engineering team, stretched thin and unable to focus on community engagement. On the positive side, these integrations can serve as prototypes that inform the product roadmap, providing concrete evidence of demand and accelerating the case for official support within the core platform.

Variants

API Gateway: For larger companies with siloed internal services that have little to zero commonality or standardization to their endpoint description or implementation, it sometimes falls to the DevRel team to build a single point of access for customers to integrate against, providing a standardization layer before "farming out" the API call elsewhere into the collection of internal services. Often, this Gateway is built to be accessible over HTTP, although any distributed protocol could work: HTTP, gRPC, GraphQL, or a messaging tool. In these cases, DevRel is taking on more of an Engineering role, because until the Gateway can be re-homed into an Engineering org, DevRel will need to treat the Gateway with all the rigor and discipline that any Engineering product would demand: on-call support, bug triage, version (and revision) management, and so on.

CHAPTER 26

Recorded Video

Topics: *Presentation*

A video or series of videos (in a channel on YouTube) or Social Platforms or company website.

You want to have a closely collected group of video content that's easily accessible to your customers, but with some curation and high "reach" thanks to search engines.

CHAPTER 26   RECORDED VIDEO

Context

Video content is hard to search effectively. Search engines have yet to reach the level of sophistication necessary to pick out spoken words or identify the contents of images present in the video to be picked up. Any search engine result is generally either tied to metadata about the video or keyed perhaps to the content of any caption or comments on the video.

Large Language Models (LLMs), such as Google Gemini, are becoming a reliable source for parsing video, helping developers understand and summarize videos much faster.

Additionally, hosting video is not always easy, particularly if there is a desire to retain ownership of the video itself. Simply putting a video file on a web server makes it accessible to the world, but it also makes it vulnerable to "right-click, download," allowing visitors to your website to capture the video for their own purposes (benign or otherwise) and reducing their "stickiness"—their desire or need to remain on your website.

Solution

Take any videos you create or capture and post them to YouTube, ideally captured as part of a YouTube channel tied to your company and/or product/service. Provide informative captions, and make sure to link to other videos that directly relate to (or are talked about within) your video.

Participants

Videos produced by Developer Relations teams are focused more on the content and less on the high polish of Hollywood quality finishing and effects. Much of the time videos are fully produced—recorded, edited, and published—by a single person. The participants listed here are the roles required to produce recorded video. The size of your team will dictate whether individuals take multiple responsibilities.

- **Writer:** Videos need a plan, whether it's fully scripted or follows a vague outline; a writer will need to organize thoughts into a cohesive story for the video to follow.

- **Presenter:** This is the on-screen talent. You want someone who brings a lot of energy and communicates clearly. Developer Advocates who regularly get in front of physical and virtual audiences to speak tend to have the right skillset.

- **Editor:** Editors polish out the rough edges of a video and prepare it for publication. Sometimes that's as easy as trimming off the beginning or end of a single video clip and uploading it to YouTube. And other times, the Editor may spend hours splicing together multiple takes into a single presentation.

- **Publisher:** This person is in charge of publishing the video on the appropriate platform with the correct title, thumbnail, description, and metadata. They track comments and address them if there is a need.

Implementation

There is a wide range of ways to implement recorded video. Whether you produce a coding demo with a simple voiceover or a more formal production showing the face of a presenter on screen next to slides, how you implement recorded content depends largely on the needs of your company and the strengths of your team.

CHAPTER 26   RECORDED VIDEO

Planning a video begins by writing an outline or storyboard of the material you want to record. Figure out the scope of the information the video will show. Then, organize the information into a story that flows smoothly and leads the viewer to a call to action. For the duration of the video, you're taking the viewer on an educational journey where they will learn the video's message by the end. When outlining the story, keep the viewer focused on the main points and any essential related information that's needed to grasp those points. The outline will help you stay on target and not get distracted by meandering into deep technical details related to the topic that aren't needed to complete the task and would be better consumed as documentation or in a separate video.

With an outline in place, the next step is to write a script for the presenter. Not all presenters like reading from a script, as they may struggle to keep their speech natural as they read. Recording from a script is not imperative for every recorded video. However, it does provide a team the opportunity to quality check the message before it's recorded, making sure all the needful details are covered. And, if you're recording multiple takes when capturing the video or capturing each scene in asynchronous order, using a script will keep the talk track consistent, making the editing process that much easier.

Depending on the nature of the video, it may be easier to record the screen capture first with no sound and then go back and record the audio narration separately. That way, the presenter doesn't have to worry about performing the demonstration and talking at the same time.

Screen Capture When capturing a screen recording, keep the focus entirely on the subject you want the viewer to observe. Remove distractions and other clutter from the screen. If it's code, maximize the window of the code editor to cover the desktop. Increase the font size to be large enough to show the code being talked about without a lot of unrelated code on the screen.

Avoid moving fast around the screen, whether with lots of quick scrolling or frequently jumping between windows. This is likely the viewer's first time seeing this information, and they may become easily disoriented. Make sure the narration talks through what is on the screen and then talks the viewer through changes in the scene.

Presenter Recording: Presenters in a recorded video should have their face centered on the screen, with a small amount of space between the top of their head and the top boundary of the video. Make sure the presenter is well-lit with direct lighting to reduce shadows. The camera should ideally be at the eye level of the presenter. The background should not draw attention away from the presenter. Lighting, objects, or decorations in the room, and camera angles should all be chosen to bring the viewer's eyes back to the presenter's face.

Developer advocates tend to want to wear clothes with their company logo in recorded video, similar to when they go on stage at a conference. However, keep in mind that most camera angles that focus on a presenter's face cut off just below the shoulders, which hides any logos on the presenter's clothing.

Post Production: After the content is captured, it's time to edit the shots into a cohesive story for the video. Add any additional audio or screen effects, and then publish the video.

Video Length: Some recorded videos will only need to be a few minutes—like quick announcements or short demonstrations. In comparison, others will require more depth and time. Keep in mind, attention spans are short. Long videos of deep technical dives rarely keep viewers' attention.

Decouple Platform Ownership: When creating accounts on platforms such as YouTube, be sure to document the email address used to create the channel. And, if possible, use a service account to decouple that email from a single person in the company. In some cases, such as YouTube (at least, as of this publication), if that email account is deleted, the YouTube channel will go with it.

CHAPTER 26   RECORDED VIDEO

Metrics

- **Views:** The most basic metric to measure the success of recorded video content is views. Every video platform should be able to report the number of views a video has received. And, looking at viewership numbers will help tell the story of what type of content is resonating with viewers.

- **Time spent in video:** To get even more granular with the number of views a video has, some services may allow you to see how much time viewers spend watching a video and even which segments of a video are more viewed than others. The more granular you can get your viewership data, the more specific you'll know what your viewers want to see.

- **Call to Action:** A recorded video should lead the viewer to a specific action—installing something, creating an account, signing up for something like a newsletter, or building something new. Measure the number of times this call to action is fulfilled.

Example

The High Flying AI Company is revolutionizing the air travel industry with an LLM for building travel itineraries. Their customers are delighted with the platform's ease of use and the accuracy of the results. On the backend, High Flying AI is revolutionizing how partner travel companies can train the High Flying models to include the latest travel information. The Developer Relations and Documentation teams have written **Reference Documentation (373)** detailing the specifics for the APIs that partners can

CHAPTER 26   RECORDED VIDEO

use to train the models. They've also written Tutorials that show step-by-step instructions for getting started using the endpoints. Now they need some recorded video to augment the documentation and **Tutorials (451)**.

Kerim is a developer advocate for High Flying with a knack for creating informative and engaging videos. He arranged a meeting with an engineer and a product manager responsible for the public API to get their input on which features to cover. Kerim had a good idea of what he wanted to cover in the video already, but wanted to get everyone's thoughts to make sure they agreed with the expected outcome. He went into the meeting with a first draft of his outline already completed, so that he could keep the meeting brief for everyone involved.

During the meeting, Kerim also walks through the code he's going to demonstrate during the video. The demo shows how to authenticate with the High Flying API, how to structure the body of a POST request, and how to handle the response of making a GET request. He plans to take the viewer through the whole process in around three minutes.

After receiving the needed feedback on the outline and demo, Kerim writes up a script he plans to follow during the recording and shares it with the group for one last approval. All of this preparation work gives Kerim confidence to produce the video according to the plans agreed on by the team without the fear of any major revisions or reworks.

Kerim records the video in the format of a live coding demo where his face is visible on screen for the duration of the program. His camera is positioned just above his eyes, framing his face at the center of the picture. He sets up additional lighting behind the camera to illuminate his face and positions an external microphone close to his mouth. The mic is attached to a swing arm so Kerim can have both hands on the keyboard. Kerim leaves the camera running as he walks through his script and demo. He records each step in the demonstration with a pause in between. That way, if he makes mistakes, he can make edits beginning and ending at the pauses. When Kerim notices he made a mistake, he pauses, restarts the segment, and continues with the presentation.

Once the recording is captured, Kerim goes back over the footage and removes the small segments containing mistakes.

Before publishing the finished video to YouTube, Kerim asks a designer at the company to create some titles and thumbnail graphics for publication.

After publishing the video, Kerim posts announcements to High Flying AI's various social media channels with links to the video.

Consequences

YouTube has a couple of recommended practices regarding videos uploaded to their site, including creating a unique thumbnail, creating descriptions that match search engine keywords that you'd like to trigger a link to your video, including relevant tags, and choosing the right category for your videos. If you want to make it easily consumable by customers (who don't always have time to watch a long video), consider breaking the video up into smaller, linked videos or separating the one video into chapters.

A variety of data can be helpful to store as metadata to make a video more searchable. Consider using a video's show notes or links as metadata. Also, publishing a video's transcript can make it more understandable to LLMs.

Channels imply a continuous stream of content, and encourage viewers to "subscribe," thus receiving notifications when new videos are posted. The other side of this subscription, however, is an unwritten commitment on the part of the video publisher (that is to say, you) to continue to publish new content every so often. Consider making it clear when subscribers can expect new content ("Thanks for watching, everybody, and stay tuned for next week's installment, when we...."), and then fulfill that promise.

CHAPTER 26 RECORDED VIDEO

YouTube channels also often have extensive threaded comments, and failing to engage with commenters can often make your channel look either stale or aloof. Consider dedicating some time from your team to respond and answer to those comments (perhaps as part of their larger **Social Media (395)** duties), posting links to **Samples/Examples (387)** or Gists for larger code samples, if necessary.

Blog Posts (105) and **Social Media (395)** can also be used to draw attention to new content on the YouTube channel, increasing your draw. Additionally, **Newsletters (281)** can also be used to draw those more interested in video content to your YouTube channel, and vice versa. Do not, however, automatically sign up YouTube subscribers to your newsletter, or vice versa—developers always need to opt-in to whatever subscription you are offering, or you risk turning them off to your product/service and company entirely.

YouTube channels can attract advertising and/or sponsors. Still, in general, your emphasis should be on finding like-minded or friendly partners who are willing and interested in cross-linking between your various reach-based efforts (video or otherwise).

Variants

Recorded Video is arguably a variant of **Webinar (469)** and/or **Live Streaming (273)**, as well as a tool for recording **Office Hours (289)** and making them available to others, so, in many ways, this could be a variant of each of those patterns. In fact, the main reason this is a stand-alone pattern is because of YouTube's versatility, in that it can be used for a variety of these activities, and all can be gathered under the same YouTube channel.

- **Short-Form** video is when you create small clips that are 60 seconds or less. They're designed to be distributed on platforms such as YouTube Shorts or

CHAPTER 26   RECORDED VIDEO

TikTok. The clips can either be highlights extracted from previous Long-Form videos, such as **Webinar (469)** and/or **Live Streaming (273)**, or they can be stand-alone productions. Keep in mind, they're meant to be viewed in a vertical orientation, such as on a phone. So they should be produced with something close to a 9x16 aspect ratio. Short-form video provides you with an additional avenue to extend your reach and connect with an audience that doesn't have an appetite for a longer, more in-depth video.

CHAPTER 27

Reference Documentation

Topics: *Code, Writing*

Precise documentation about the API, interfaces, classes, or whatever makes up the "surface area" of the product/service with which developers interact.

CHAPTER 27   REFERENCE DOCUMENTATION

Also Known As

Docs, guide, release notes, reports, user manuals

Intent

Customers using your product/service will need to know all the possible configuration, parameters, types, and effects that your product/service uses or depends on. While they could crawl through the source code to figure out the implications and ramifications (assuming your product/service is open source), doing so is extremely labor-intensive and always subject to change with each passing revision or pull request.

Context

Customers will want this information to be handy, searchable, and, in some cases, integrated with as many of their developer tools as possible; at a minimum, it will need to be something that can be linked publicly, so that it can be referenced from either internal or external **Forums (233)**, **Articles (89)**, **Tutorials (451)**, and **Blog Posts (105)**.

Developers need comprehensive information that is the "final word" on what your product/service does, aside from running the code. If your product/service is not open-source or is cloud-hosted, this will be the only way customers will know how your product/service behaves without painful and time-consuming experimentation/trial and error.

Reference documentation explains each class, module, function, argument, and parameter in isolation. However, describing how various objects work together to accomplish a certain task would be more appropriate for **Tutorials (451)**.

Solution

Create a set of documentation that is publicly accessible, possibly derived from the codebase itself, that is comprehensive and complete. Reference documentation should focus on the "what" of every publicly accessible aspect of your product/service.

Participants

The most ideal authors of reference documentation are technical writers who work directly with the engineers who wrote the code or the product manager responsible for defining the specifications of the feature. If the team doesn't have such writers available then other developer relations professionals could jump in. Or, the engineers or product managers themselves should write the documentation for their code.

Implementation

Many modern programming languages have libraries for generating reference documentation based on function signatures and comments in the code. Java has javadoc, Go has Go Doc, and for APIs there is the OpenAPI Specification (OAS) which provides a set of guidelines for building APIs and also offers reference doc generation. Your first instinct should be to see if there is a library available for your technology stack.

When none of these libraries are available, here are the things to include when manually writing reference documentation. Start with the most macro of objects, whether that's a class, module, or function, and work toward the most micro. With each element include a name, short description, all of the available arguments that can be passed in, each of the values that can be returned, and any of the error types the object could throw. An example or two of the object signature in action may also be helpful.

CHAPTER 27   REFERENCE DOCUMENTATION

Accuracy is paramount for reference documentation, especially with example code snippets. Have processes in place to validate example code each time there are changes in the product.

Metrics

Coverage: The percentage of the application or system that is covered by reference documentation. Every function, method, argument, and response that a user can experience should be covered in the reference documentation.

Bug SLA: The amount of time it takes to address a bug in the docs. Bugs will happen, especially as products evolve and are updated. Your team should be prepared to fix bugs as they are reported. Measure the time it takes to push out these fixes.

Support tickets created: A direct benefit of good reference documentation is a reduction in Support tickets. Users should be able to find answers to their questions in those docs and not need to interact with a human. This is one of those metrics that's like a golf score. The lower the number the better.

Example

The developers at ReallyCoolGameWorlds have developed an API for interacting with their world-building engine. The API provides access to all the objects in the engine, including maps, characters, and pick-up items. Before releasing their API, the Developer Relations team at ReallyCoolGameWorlds publish documentation that describes all the endpoints, available methods, and properties for each of the resources for the API. They organize the documentation by each action that can be taken with the API.

376

CHAPTER 27   REFERENCE DOCUMENTATION

For each action, they begin with a short **description** and then list the `HTTP method` and `endpoint` path of the action. Next, they provide a table of the `parameters` that can be passed as arguments to the endpoint, followed by the possible **response** codes users might expect. Then, they list a full `curl` command showing an example **request** that could be copied and pasted right in the terminal for the users to try, followed by an example of the JSON **response** users could receive. Lastly is a list of the possible **errors** users could encounter while working with the action.

Altogether, the documentation for the createCharacter action would look like this:

createCharacter

Description

Creates a new character in the world-building engine with customizable attributes.

HTTP Method: POST
Endpoint: `/api/v1/characters`
Parameters

Name	Type	Required	Description
`name`	`string`	Yes	The name of the character to create
`class`	`string`	Yes	The class of the character (e.g., "knights radiant")
`level`	`int`	No	The starting level of the character (default: 1)
`attributes`	`string`	No	Key-value pairs for custom attributes

Response

- **201 Created**: Successfully created the character. Returns the character ID and details.

- **400 Bad Request**: Missing required parameters or invalid data.

377

CHAPTER 27 REFERENCE DOCUMENTATION

Example Request

```
curl -X POST https://api.reallycoolgameworlds.com/api/v1/characters \
-H "Authorization: Bearer YOUR_ACCESS_TOKEN" \
-H "Content-Type: application/json" \
-d '{
  "name": "ArcherQueen",
  "class": "archer",
  "level": 5,
  "attributes": {
    "strength": 12,
    "agility": 18,
    "intelligence": 10
  }
}
```

Example Response

```
{
  "id": "12345",
  "name": "ArcherQueen",
  "class": "archer",
  "level": 5,
  "attributes": {
    "strength": 12,
    "agility": 18,
    "intelligence": 10
  }
}
```

Errors

- **400**: If name or class is missing.
- **401**: If the API token is missing or invalid.
- **500**: Internal server error.

CHAPTER 27 REFERENCE DOCUMENTATION

Consequences

Reference documentation is often a large undertaking, and will require a great deal of time and energy to create, update, and maintain. Keep in mind that automatically generated documentation can only go so far, and will be dependent on the developers' willingness to document the code extensively. (For example, the `javadoc` documentation-generation tool can build documentation from the names and structure of Java classes and methods, but cannot infer anything beyond the names.)

Where reference documentation focuses on the "what" of your product/service, consider using **Guides (243)** to explain the "why" or the "how," as appropriate.

Have a third party review your reference documentation, and file issues or bug reports against insufficient documentation or documentation that doesn't tell developers anything further than the name of the thing in question.

Consider open-sourcing your documentation, such as hosting the documentation as a GitHub project, such that others outside your company has access. This will allow others (such as **Ambassadors (71)**) to find incorrect or incomplete elements of the documentation and submit changes or pull requests to correct it.

Keep in mind that reference documentation plays a key role with language learning models. It's important to keep the documentation accurate with the current version of the product. That way AI models can be trained on the most accurate information.

Variants

- **Knowledge Base:** Often, after a product/service has been out for a while and has gathered a fair amount of experience in its Technical Support, it's easy to find patterns of questions and problems that customers are having. The larger the customer base, the quicker those patterns will emerge. In an effort to try and provide a high-reach/low-interactivity customer support option, put together (and continue to update and curate) a formalized collection of questions or topics into a website or queryable database, called the knowledge base, and make it available online. (In many respects, services like Stack Overflow or Reddit are community-curated knowledge bases. The benefit of those is that they're created and hosted by an external service. And, they're largely maintained by the community. Read more about these external services in **Forums (233)**).

- **Glossary:** A dictionary of terminology related to your product or platform. Many products have their own lingo or definitions for common words that differ outside the context of the platform. Take, for example, the definition of a Service in Kubernetes. The Kubernetes documentation defines a Service as, "a method for exposing a network application that is running as one or more Pods in your cluster."[1] While in the context of Service Oriented Architecture, a service represents, "a repeatable business activity with a specified outcome."[2] A glossary is a place to define these terms so that users can reference their meaning and not get confused when using your platform.

---

[1] https://kubernetes.io/docs/concepts/services-networking/service/.
[2] https://en.wikipedia.org/wiki/Service-oriented_architecture.

CHAPTER 28

SDK

Topic: *Code*

A Software Development Kit (SDK) is a library of code intended to be used "as-is" as either the sole means or a helpful abstraction (layer on top of HTTP APIs) when using the company's software.

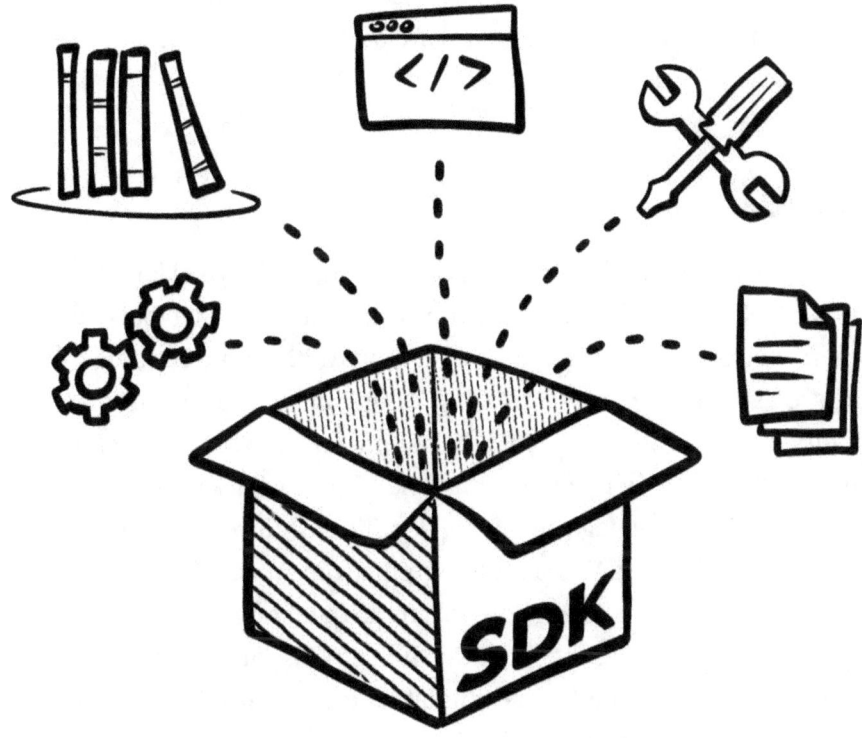

CHAPTER 28 SDK

Also Known As

API Client Library, devkit

Intent

Your product/service is an API or other protocol-based service (like a database), using a protocol as its primary form of communication with customer code. Like all HTTP APIs, it is loosely typed and can accept a wide range of values for each part of the HTTP request, but many (if not most) of the possible range of values will yield errors or incorrect results. Getting the requests correct is often an exercise in frustration and time as developers struggle to ensure they are passing the right data in the right places.

Context

Developers, particularly those working with statically typed languages (Java, C#, Kotlin, Swift, and so on), are accustomed to using tools that generate errors at compile-time, rather than waiting until runtime to discover that things aren't working. Additionally, it takes time and multiple lines of code to marshal the parameters into something HTTP can transport, and then to unmarshal the response back into the native data types of the language, including handling any errors indicated by the return value. Most API calls also require some form of authorization, usually in the form a token. Those tokens are generated after the user of the API authenticates their identity. If the API is called frequently throughout the customer's code, this all represents additional code that customers must debug and maintain for the length of the project.

Additionally, when exploring a new product/service, developers experimenting with the product/service want (dare say need) the quickest way to get started with the product/service, in order to be able to ascertain if it is of use or how to use it.

Because of its loosely coupled nature, working with HTTP from code requires more attention to detail (headers, status codes, methods, and payload structures) than using native constructs (classes, functions, modules, whatever the language uses as first-class citizens), adding to the learning overhead.

Solution

Even though the API (HTTP-based or otherwise) technically is accessible from any language that speaks HTTP (which is to say, all of them), provide an SDK that encapsulates the details of making those HTTP calls into something that is language- or platform-friendly.

Participants

SDKs are usually built and maintained by **Engineers** familiar with the API. They may be the same engineers directly responsible for building and maintaining the API itself or simply consumers of the API. Both approaches have their advantages. The API developers will have the most intimate knowledge of the API and be aware of every feature and limitation, even the ones not publicly documented. These teams can also take advantage of libraries that automatically generate SDK if their API follows standards such as OpenAPI. The advantage of having other engineers—say Developer Experience or Developer Relations Engineers— build the SDKs with only the publicly available API documentation as a resource allows teams to "dog food" their own APIs and documentation, ensuring a quality developer experience.

CHAPTER 28   SDK

Implementation

The level of effort needed to build and maintain SDKs depends on how the corresponding API is built. If the API adheres to the OpenAPI standard, then SDKs can be generated with tools like openapi-generator. Otherwise, SDKs can be built in various languages—Java, C#, Python, Go, JavaScript, etc.—to handle common API operations, carry out each CRUD operation on every API endpoint, as well as serialize and deserialize data for each native language.

SDKs should be treated as production-level code, complete with automated tests, code reviews, **Reference Documentation (373)**, **Guides (243)**, **Tutorials (451)**, **Recorded Video (363)**, and **Samples/Examples (387)**.

The library will likely be open source and as such its life cycle will be managed in a public repository. That repository needs to provide a way for users to submit issues and feature requests. The SDKs will need to be updated regularly to keep up with changes in the API and address customer-reported issues. Be mindful of breaking changes when making those updates.

Metrics

- **Repository Stars:** Stars on the SDK repository provide a public metric that not only your team can track but it communicates to the community the popularity of the SDK.

- **SDK Traffic:** SDK traffic can be measured by including a **User-Agent** with every API call. The header should identify which SDK and version is making the request. Such a header might look like User-Agent: Golang-SDK-v.1.10.0.

- **Bug SLA:** The amount of time it takes to address a bug in the docs. Bugs will happen, especially as products evolve and are updated. Your team should be prepared to fix bugs as they are reported. Measure the time it takes to push out these fixes.

Example

Rachel is an engineer tasked with building the first version of a public API for her company's work management platform. During the design phase of the project Rachel decides to follow the OpenAPI specification. This helps her define the structure of the API so that she can automatically generate documentation and SDKs with the help of tools such as openapi-generator. Then, whenever she makes changes to the API she can also generate those changes for the documentation and SDKs.

Consequences

This SDK can be open sourced, adding to the company's open-source profile, which, for some companies, will also be a gentle introduction to doing more open-source work in general. This also provides the company an opportunity to explore how to use open-source development practices more fully without taking undue risk with the code or processes around the product/service.

Variants

Software enablement tools created by Developer Relations teams often come in multiple forms, depending on the goals, platform, and target developer audience. One variant is a **platform integration toolkit**, which provides the components developers need to build for a specific operating system, device ecosystem, or runtime—such as Android, iOS, or Web Assembly. These usually include libraries, headers, compilers, testing environments, emulators, and usage documentation.

Another common variant is a **language-specific developer package**, which tailors APIs and helper functions to be idiomatic for a specific programming language such as Python, JavaScript, or C#. These variants aim to reduce friction by abstracting platform-specific requirements and exposing functionality in a way that aligns with the language's conventions and developer expectations.

There are also **service integration kits** that streamline access to cloud services or APIs. These may bundle authentication helpers, usage patterns, and utilities for observability, retries, and error handling. Some variants are designed to be **lightweight components** optimized for edge devices or low-resource environments, minimizing dependencies and binary size. Others may take the form of **UI toolkits or drop-in widgets** designed to integrate branded user interface elements into applications, such as payment flows, authentication forms, or real-time chat interfaces. Lastly, **extension frameworks** exist to allow third-party developers to augment an existing application or platform through plugins or custom modules—common in the context of IDEs, browsers, or CMS platforms.

CHAPTER 29

Sample/Example

Topics: *Code*

Fully executable code but single-focused for third-party developers to use as a learning exercise

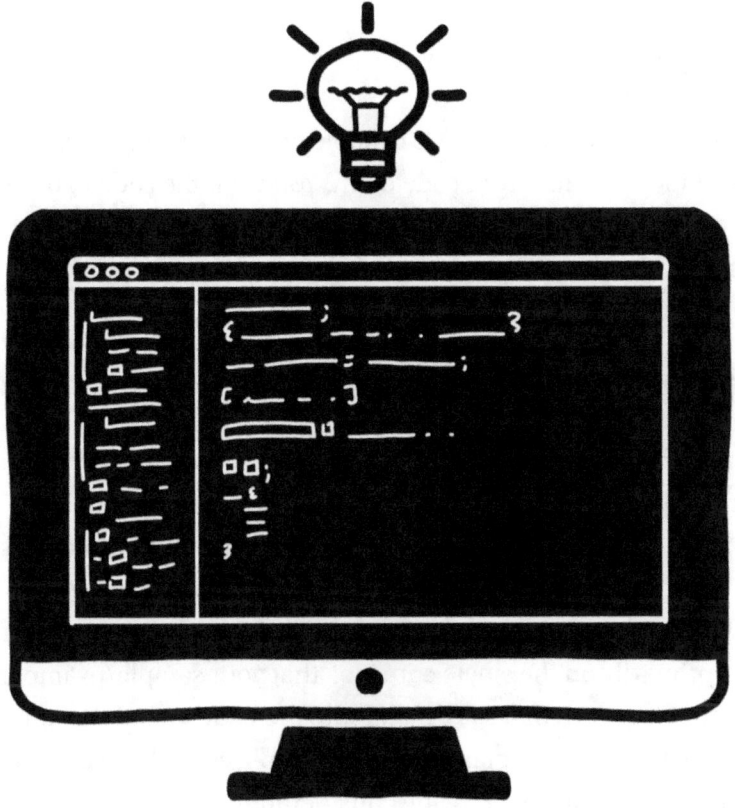

CHAPTER 29 SAMPLE/EXAMPLE

Also Known As

Demo

Intent

You want to show developers how to use your product/service, but there are enough details and/or need for precision that human language isn't sufficient to get the point across. You want developers to be able to see how to use your product/service from code.

Context

The product/service is one that is callable or usable from code, and is one that developers will use from code often. You want the code to be visible to as many developers (customers or otherwise) as possible, maximizing its reach.

Solution

Write code that illustrates a particular aspect, point, or element of your product/service. Keep it as simple as possible and only include the elements that are needed to demonstrate the feature and still allows the code to run. Unless they're necessary for your demo, leave out things like validation, security, edge-case handling, and so on—so as to focus primarily on the single core idea that your sample/example is looking to solve. With that said, make sure the code includes comments or documentation that explains how the sample could be used in a production-level solution. Provide considerations for security, resilience, and performance.

CHAPTER 29   SAMPLE/EXAMPLE

Place that code someplace widely accessible (such as a public version control system like GitHub or GitLab). You should also reference the samples in your **Guides (243)** or **Reference Documentation (373)**, or your **Forums (233)** so that developers can discover the code as they learn more about your product/service.

A good sample/example can also provide the solid base for building other pieces of content like **Blog Posts (105)**, **Live Streams (273)**, **Webinars (469)**, or **Conference Sessions (197)**. Which leads to the point that each audience learns in their own way. Some would prefer to read through samples, following along with the steps, and building on their own. Others would rather a video describe the sample/example and show the results of each step taken. And still others want to sit in a conference and watch a demonstration of a sample/example and then take that information and go explore on their own. You want to cater to as many audiences as possible. So, when you create a sample/example you should consider supplementing it with these other pieces of content as well.

It's also highly advantageous to include **Partner (309)** companies/products in your sample/example. Creating a sample/example that includes a partner company/product not only shows your users how to integrate with the partner company/product, but the sample/example can increase the visibility of your product/service as the partner refers their audience to the sample/example. You help your users and theirs.

Participants

Typically, a sample/example needs one code author, but the sample should always have another—ideally multiple people—to review the code before publication.

The reviewers can insure the code is accurate and the explanations complete. Reviewers can include other members of the developer relations team or engineers who work on the product or feature being sampled.

389

CHAPTER 29   SAMPLE/EXAMPLE

Including members of the Engineering team adds the benefit of having those engineers work directly with someone building working with their product. The sample author can provide feedback into the product while the engineers provide feedback on the sample.

Engineering teams often spend so much time on the "inside" of the product that having a periodic reminder of what it looks like from the "outside" will be constructive and help identify potential awkwardness in its use ahead of time.

AI is also proving to be increasingly more reliable as a code review tool, and could serve as an additional set of "eyes" to review a sample. However, don't let it replace all human review cycles.

Although not formally a part of the sample/example's implementation, sample/examples are often paired with **Conference Sessions (197)**, **Workshops (477)**, **Articles (89)**, **Reference Documentation (373)**, and **Blog Posts (105)**, and it is common for review of the presentation/prose to happen at the same time as that of the code. In these cases, it will be helpful to have an editor or copyeditor on hand to review the presentation/prose while engineers review the code.

Implementation

Quality samples come from viewing your product, documentation, and resources through the eyes of your users—especially new users. Those who are digging into the product, or a particular feature, for the first time. By viewing things with that perspective you'll be able to see the potential pain points and how to build the right samples or examples to address them.

Key points to keep in mind when writing good samples:

- Write the code so that it's easier to read and understand.

- Comment the code so that the code file could stand alone as its own teaching resource.
- Write a README that explains the context of the problem and solution the sample solves.
- Include links for further information in the README.
- Save the sample in a public repository that can be linked to and is easy to find with public searches.
- Easy to download/check out and run.

As with all software, every sample should have a plan for being maintained. Put processes in place to evaluate and address bugs, assign work, test changes, and roll out improvements.

Metrics

- **Stars on the Repo:** This can be seen as a vanity metric, but it does indicate the number of users who looked at the sample project and found it helpful.
- **Sample Usage:** Track the number of times a sample is invoked by the community. This usage can be measured by including a User-Agent inside the sample when it makes calls to your API. The request header on the API call should identify the name and version of the sample making the request. Such a header might look like User-Agent: Golang-TeamSetup-Sample-v.1.10.0. Tracking usage also provides a clearer story about whether the community is using the sample and how much attention should be given on keeping the code up-to-date.

- **Bug SLA:** The amount of time it takes to address a bug in the docs. Bugs will happen, especially as products evolve and are updated. Your team should be prepared to fix bugs as they are reported. Measure the time it takes to push out these fixes.

Example

Emil notices a trend in Stack Overflow where several users posted questions related to the syntax of the configuration file used when running his company's agent CLI. Each of the fields available in the configuration file are listed in his company's **Reference Documentation (373)** but Emil sees from the series of questions—and more importantly, his nearly identical answers for each—that an example posted to a public repository would be helpful to his user base and cut down on the work of repeatedly answering those questions.

Using the answers he posted to Stack Overflow, Emil creates a sample configuration file that highlights and clarifies the areas in question. He writes a detailed README.md that explains in detail what the sample solves and the steps for how to use it. He also explains the problems or questions the sample is solving. And finally, Emil writes a Blog post explaining the context of the problems this particular configuration solved, and links to the sample project in the post.

Consequences

The sample/example needs to be small enough to illustrate a single point only, or you run the risk of developers being overwhelmed with too many details and losing track of what's going on. For this reason, while samples/examples are executable, they typically do exactly one thing and nothing more.

CHAPTER 29   SAMPLE/EXAMPLE

The choice of technology stack can be important in the creation of a sample/example—if the product/service is aimed at a particular segment of the market identified by technology stack (".NET developers," "Front-end Web developers," etc.), then the sample/example should come from stacks that are closely aligned to the target market's choice. However, if the product/service is platform-agnostic (such as an HTTP API service), then samples/examples should be spread evenly across all the target markets, and/or ported to each platform as time and budget allows. When porting to other platforms, make sure to use idioms and approaches that are mainstream for that platform—Python and Java code are both object-oriented, for example, but each has particular ways it approaches software implementation, and doing a line-for-line direct conversion from Java to Python will feel strange to Python developers.

Note that developers are fond of taking samples/examples and using them "as is" for their own work, changing only those elements which are necessary to get it working inside their own applications. This often means that if the sample/example contains no validation or security, then the developer will also often leave out validation or security. Make sure Legal drafts a disclaimer for all sample/example code reminding developers that this code is not production-ready.

Variants

- **Gallery:** "Kitchen Sink" Demo. You want to provide customers with a wide range of samples/examples, but you also want them to be able to see what each looks like from the user perspective and don't want developers to have to build each sliver of a feature in order to see it. By gathering all of the samples/examples into a single executable application, where each sample/example is its own selectable option within the Gallery, you keep the sample/example code isolated enough to allow customers to easily focus in on the single sample/example, while still keeping it to a single executable application.

- **Reference application:** A reference app is one that is intended to be more of a complete/comprehensive demonstration of the product/service, solving a (often fictitious) problem or providing capabilities to a (fictitious) company. Here, the code can do many of the things that are left out of samples/examples—such as validation and security—because the reference application is more about how all the parts fit together, rather than just examining any single part. In fact, in many cases, the reference application is one that has too many parts, and is over-engineered to have more features or capabilities than is strictly needed for the problem described.

- **Gist:** Smaller than a sample/example, designed to demonstrate a very specific snippet of code, such as a single method, part of a class, or short REPL session. A GitHub Gist is a stand-alone snippet of code often used in conjunction with other artifacts, such as linking in a **Forum (233)** or **Social Media (395)** post or embedded inside a **Blog Post (105)**.

Note that several tools (like Visual Studio Code or the JetBrains suite of tools) have extensions or plugins that know how to work directly with the Gist API, making it easier to create and share them.

CHAPTER 30

Social Media

Topics: *Social, Writing*

In order to keep a steady flow of minor news and announcements to your community, keep a regular routine of posting to the various social media channels, pointing out your other activities both online and in-person, and just keeping people "in the know" of what's going on around your company and/or product/service.

CHAPTER 30   SOCIAL MEDIA

Also Known As

Platforms, Channels, Networks, (Online) Groups, Facebook, Twitter/X, LinkedIn, Mastodon, BlueSky, YouTube, Twitch, TikTok, Discord, Telegram, Weibo

Intent

Keeping developers' attention is never easy, considering all the different tools and technologies vying for their focus. You want your product/service to stay "top of mind," even after adoption, because greater usage means more feedback and (potentially) more community activity. To achieve this, it's important to maintain a moderate but consistent level of interactivity with customers (and potential customers) across social channels. These platforms shouldn't just be treated as push-based notification feeds, though. They're also powerful tools for **listening and learning**. Effective social listening can reveal valuable insights into developer needs, pain points, and emerging trends, while also enhancing customer satisfaction by demonstrating that the team is attentive, responsive, and engaging in genuine two-way conversations.

Context

While you could always make use of a **Newsletter (281)**, many developers already receive too much email in their inbox, and refuse to add to the pile, even for tools they use every day. It's possible, with enough budget, to purchase billboards and highway signs, but these are fairly low-"hit"-rate options, since there's no guarantee that developers will drive past them or even recognize them when they do.

While social media channels have not created the utopia their adherents imagined when they debuted more than a decade ago, they have become an important medium for communication between organizations and the communities that surround that organization (such as customers, press, observers, and so on). As the most recent form of communication media, many of "the rules" around social media are still being developed organically as different organizations and entities engage with it, but it also represents the most convenient means to reach a broad swath of your target audience at a relatively meager cost.

Solution

Make use of the various Internet social media platforms that developers already use to notify them of **Conference Sessions (197)**, to come visit the **Booth (137)** at an upcoming event, interesting **Blog Posts (105)**, **Sponsorships (405)**, published **Articles (89)**, the official welcome to your new **Ambassadors (71)**, and so on. Use the posts as opportunities to draw some greater interactivity by following all of the current social media suggestions, like asking open-ended questions and generous re-posting of related responses, particularly from your customers.

Participants

Before anything else, social media accounts must have **posters**, individuals who have the credentials (and tools) to post messages on the social media platform. While it goes without saying that most or all of the DevRel team's developer advocates will be posters, there may be others around the company that will be contributing to DevRel activities, and it would be convenient (if not outright necessary) for them to have access as well.

Regardless of who is responsible for the social media account(s) and its content, the Legal team will want to be involved, at least at first, for the same reasons it looks to be involved in any public-facing content-creation endeavor: to try and keep the company from being sued over something

CHAPTER 30   SOCIAL MEDIA

avoidable. In the world of social media, however, where the window to respond to a post is measured in hours rather than weeks, the Legal team may need to either provide guidelines of topics to avoid, or have a representative handy to approve drafts the same day they are drafted.

You may want to connect with your Marketing or Brand team, who are generally the keepers of graphics (in various formats and sizes) of the official company logos and color schemes. More importantly, they will often have "brand guidelines" around the kind of messaging that the company as a whole looks to put forward (online and in the real world) to the world. Working with them to make sure your account follows—or at least doesn't directly contradict—those guidelines can go a long ways toward building a happy "middle ground" between the two groups (and their respective social media accounts!). More importantly, the Marketing or Brand team will often have already gone through the "what can and can't we say" with the Legal team, so you can benefit from their experience.

Because many social media platforms have the ability to capture a collection of responses (a survey) from followers, you may find that your Product team will periodically want to create a survey around potential new product features or to gauge consumer feedback on the product/service's newly released features. This will often come when the social media account has demonstrated a high degree of engagement, and should be seen as a sign of success.

Implementation

The larger the company, the more likely that it already has one (or more) social media accounts on a variety of platforms. Before any DevRel activity can take place in social media, you will need to ascertain your relationship to these accounts within your company—is DevRel a part of the "space" that account occupies? Or is DevRel substantially different from the messaging that account provides? Talk with the owners of those accounts to find out what their goals are, and who they imagine their audience to be. Have a deep look at the posts on that account for the past three months. Are those posts intended for a developer audience? Look at the responses. Do they appear to be coming from developers? If so, this account may be the correct place from which you should post.

If no existing account seems to fit with the mission of DevRel, then it will be necessary to create a new suite of accounts on the various platforms you choose to use. Since these accounts are often tied to an email address, work with your IT team to create a special-purpose email alias ("twitter@yourcompany.com" or "facebook@yourcompany.com") if they don't exist, instead of tying them to a particular individual's email. (When that individual leaves, and the email address is retired, you will lose your ability to recover passwords.)

Once the account is created, spend a nontrivial amount of time considering what the account's profile should contain and look like. Avoid personal photos—this isn't an account for an individual, but your team as a whole. If the company has a logo, look at using some variation of that. If the DevRel team has a mascot, use a logo of that. Avoid anything that might spark controversy if you can help it, as this avatar and profile could end up being the first impression developers have of you.

After the profile is up and running, decide explicitly what your post cadence will be—will you look to post once a day, once an hour, or once a week? Like **Blog Posts (105)** and **Newsletters (281)**, maintaining a consistent cadence is vastly more important than what the actual period of the cadence is. Social media generally encourages a faster cadence than blogging or email (social media platforms were originally called "micro-blogging sites"), but social media also is more forgiving of cadence "misses" than other media.

Writing posts is generally a quick-turnaround effort, as the best posts will generally still conform to the original 140 character limit. (Twitter/X has since abandoned this limit, but the vast majority of participants on the platform refuse to pay for the privilege of writing longer-form posts.) Keep them short and sweet, and make copious use of hyperlinks to other online artifacts **(Blog Posts (105), Articles (89), Webinars (469)**, press release announcements, and so on). The hyperlinks will help drive consumer eyeballs to your other online activities and/or the activity your people are doing in the real world (such as **User Group (457)** talks or **Conference Sessions (197)**).

Metrics

Of all the media available to DevRel teams, social media is often one of the most metricized, since the social media platforms often make volumes of numbers available for analysis. It's easy, in fact, to drown in so many metrics. Regardless of which metrics your team chooses to select as foci, keep a few metric concepts in mind:

- **Filtered follower counts:** In the early days of social media, a huge amount of emphasis was placed on the number of followers a given account had, on the grounds that the more followers, the more humans were seeing your posts. Subsequent insight has led us to realize that given the larger number of "bots" and automation that surrounds social media (not to mention the unscrupulous "social media influence peddlers," who provide thousands of follower accounts for your account, for a price), the simple follower count isn't reflective of actual consumption anymore. Look for metrics that provide some reasonable assurance that the followers are actual humans.

- **Engagement:** While it's easy to generate thousands upon thousands of posts, shouting into the void doesn't really advance the company's mission at all. How often do followers respond to posts by sharing (also known as reposting or retweeting) with their own networks? How often do they react (such as an "upvote" or a "like") to the post? Most of all, how many post some kind of comment? Having one million followers doesn't mean much if a major release only generates twenty-three "likes." On the other hand, if that major release notice generates a thousand "likes" from your two thousand followers, you have a very active and engaged social media account.

Example

When the tech product "CodeRanger," a powerful AI-driven coding assistant, was mentioned on a wildly popular YouTube channel, "Tech Titans," the Developer Relations team saw a unique opportunity to amplify the buzz. The host praised CodeRanger in the show for its ability to instantly refactor legacy codebases, calling it "the developer's dream tool." The mention sparked an immediate uptick in traffic to the product's website and numerous inquiries on social media. The Developer Relations team quickly capitalized on the momentum by posting a clip of the shoutout, tagging the host, and including the hashtag #CodeRangerRevolution. The tweet went viral, gaining thousands of shares and likes within hours, with developers sharing how CodeRanger could help solve real-world coding challenges.

To build on this surge of interest, the team encouraged user engagement by posting interactive content like polls ("What's your biggest coding pain point?") and retweeting developers sharing their experiences with CodeRanger. They also hosted a live Q&A session on LinkedIn Live, where engineers answered questions and demonstrated live use cases of the tool. The combination of real-time engagement, visibility from the YouTube mention, and authentic interaction bolstered CodeRanger's reputation in the developer community. Within a week, the company reported a significant boost in sign-ups and a noticeable shift in online sentiment, with many developers hailing the tool as a must-have in their workflow.

Consequences

Deliberately choose your target social media platforms. No one social media platform is without its issues: Facebook/Meta groups and Twitter/X have historically been popular, but recent shifts in public perception of their corporate leadership have led large numbers of developers away from using those platforms. Instagram and TikTok are more popular with younger generations, but each has run into its own particular brand of difficulty. Developers often ignore LinkedIn until they are looking for a job. And so on. Keep in mind that each has its own demographics and its own "culture," and choose those which most closely match that of your target persona and your company's brand and culture. Legal should be consulted on any corporate concerns or restrictions around posts.

Note that it is extremely likely (and desirable!) that individuals on the DevRel team will have their own personal Social Media accounts. Resist the temptation to ask the DevRel team to "be" the social media for the company, and instead create "corporate" social media accounts on each social media platform of interest. That said, personal and professional identities are never fully separable online. Disclaimers in bios don't change the fact that team members are seen as representatives of their employer. If someone chooses to maintain a more casual or edgy persona, they need to recognize that their behavior and tone will still reflect on the company, for better or worse.

Remember that much, if not most, of the goal of social media is interactivity, which means responding to others' social media commentary and comments as much as posting your own. While the DevRel team can certainly add "checking the feed" to their list of responsibilities, it will feel much more responsive if this is a part- or full-time commitment on the part of somebody within the DevRel team. They do not need to be

CHAPTER 30   SOCIAL MEDIA

a full Developer Advocate; in fact, it can often be a nice "half step" for a junior/associate DevRel team member to take on managing the social media community. Content (posts, etc.) can be created by others, then "pipelined" for release (just as with **Blog Posts (105)**).

Follow (and amplify) the posts of those the DevRel team (and the company as a whole) interacts with: **Partners (309)**, **Ambassadors (71)**, the **User Group Network (457)**, and **Sponsored (405)** Organizations. In particular, make sure to draw attention to the DevRel team's activities such as **Articles (89)**, **Conference Sessions (197)**, **Webinars (469)**, **Hackathons (255)**, any **Books (121)**, and so on. This is precisely the kind of content that social media emphasizes, and it is largely expected across most corporate social media accounts.

Keep in mind that many developers find a more "tongue-in-cheek" tone to corporate social media more attractive than formalism, so look for ways to "have a little fun" with the account without losing sight of the purpose (interactivity). Many social media accounts have found they have gathered great traction from taking subtle yet pointed jabs at their competition, although doing so always runs the risk of coming out "in second place" in the exchange if the competition turns out to be wittier. However, some brands have found that some "good-natured ribbing" back and forth between the two creates more engagement from both communities, and in particular, if the participants aren't direct competitors, it can generate positive reactions for all parties involved.

If your Social Media activities are successful, your customers will begin to rely on the channel as a way to contact the company, possibly even bypassing other (more formal) communication channels. This can allow for a greater "organic" level of communication, but might also lead your customers to bypass those channels (such as those for Technical Support, for example) in favor of the more informal world of social media. You will need to work ahead of time with the other teams inside your company to decide how you will "feed" messages from social media into their

403

respective processes—for example, if a customer Tweets and claims to have found a bug, how will that Tweet be turned into a ticketed bug report?

It's also important to note that the more successful your social media channels become, the more interest other parts of the company may express. For example, if your CTO finds that your social media channel is gathering a lot of engagement, they may want to start posting their own thoughts to the channel. This can be both amazing and dangerous—the CTO will often be looking to create references and/or impressions about themselves personally, whereas ideally the account will be tied to no particular person at the company. (Even CTOs leave from time to time.) It may be desirable to encourage the CTO to create their own social media accounts and amplify their messages from the DevRel account, rather than have the CTO post "as themselves" from the DevRel account.

Periodically, a post will generate commentary that creates less-than-positive responses. This can create angst for the company and/or various groups inside the company, particularly within the Marketing or Branding team.

Variants

- **Corporate Account:** The official company/product presence, brand-guided and legally reviewed.

- **Community Account:** A developer/community-focused channel (**DevRel, Ambassadors (71)**) with a more authentic, conversational tone.

- **Personal/Advocate Accounts:** Individual team members posting in their own voice; high authenticity but tied to the company by association.

- **Closed Groups/Communities:** Semi-private spaces (Facebook Groups, Discord, Slack, LinkedIn Groups) that emphasize peer-to-peer interaction over broad reach.

CHAPTER 31

Sponsorship

Topics: *Budget, Social*

Sponsorship is a strategic approach where a tech company supports events, conferences, open-source projects, or individual developers through financial backing, resources, or expertise. This not only builds goodwill, strengthens relationships, and enhances the company's reputation within the developer community but also provides significant benefits to the developers themselves. By aligning with initiatives that resonate with their audience, developer Relations teams can foster trust, demonstrate genuine commitment to the ecosystem, and amplify their brand's visibility.

CHAPTER 31   SPONSORSHIP

Also Known As

Conferences; User Groups; Technology Advocacy Groups (Java User Groups, IASA, INETA, etc.)

Intent

Sponsorship is a strategic initiative that aims to establish and strengthen meaningful connections within the developer community. It does so by providing support that aligns with their values and needs, while subtly promoting the sponsoring company's brand and offerings. The developer Relations teams play a crucial role in this process, fostering goodwill and building trust. They also play a key role in demonstrating the company's unwavering commitment to the community's success. This approach not only enhances the company's reputation but also creates opportunities to increase product awareness, drive adoption, and indirectly contribute to sales by positioning the company as a trusted and integral part of the developer ecosystem.

Context

The sponsorship context involves a competitive and dynamic environment where tech companies aim to connect with developers who are often skeptical of overt marketing efforts. Developers value authenticity, community involvement, and tools or services that genuinely support their work. In this setting, sponsorship allows Developer Relations teams to engage with the community by funding or supporting initiatives such as **Conferences (179)**, **Hackathons (255)**, meetups, **Open-Source Projects (297)**, or individual contributors. This community involvement is not just a strategy but a value that the company shares with developers. By doing

CHAPTER 31   SPONSORSHIP

so, the company can demonstrate its commitment to the ecosystem, build positive brand associations, and gain visibility among key stakeholders while contributing to its reputation as a collaborative and developer-focused organization.

Solution

Sponsorship is strategically identifying and supporting opportunities that align with the interests and needs of the developer community while showcasing the company's value. This involves allocating resources to sponsor events, projects, or individuals that significantly impact developers, such as **Conferences (179)**, **Workshops (477)**, **Hackathons (255)**, **Open-Source (297)** contributions, or educational initiatives. By actively participating in these efforts, Developer Relations teams can foster authentic relationships, amplify brand visibility, and establish the company as a trusted and integral part of the community. The sponsorship should be thoughtfully executed to ensure it delivers value to developers, reinforces the company's reputation, and creates opportunities for developers to explore its products or services organically, indirectly driving adoption and sales.

Participants

On the company side, sponsorship players include Developer Relations teams, marketing departments, and senior leadership. The Developer Relations team serves as the primary driver, identifying relevant opportunities and managing the sponsorship relationship, while marketing ensures alignment with broader branding goals and measures impact. Senior leadership often provides strategic direction and budget approvals. Their involvement ensures sponsorship efforts align with the company's long-term objectives and priorities. These participants collaborate to design sponsorships that resonate with developers, balancing community value with company benefits.

Community participants include event organizers, project maintainers, educators, and developers who attend or benefit from the sponsored initiatives. These individuals or groups interact with the company through Developer Relations **Office Hours (289)** by sharing their needs, providing feedback, and exploring collaborative possibilities. Office hours are an open channel for fostering dialogue, allowing the community to propose sponsorship ideas, clarify expectations, and build trust with the company. This interaction strengthens relationships, ensures the sponsorship aligns with real-world developer needs, and creates mutual value for both the community and the sponsoring organization.

Implementation

Sponsorship involves a structured process to identify, evaluate, and execute sponsorship opportunities that align with both the company's goals and the developer community's needs. This begins with researching and selecting events, projects, or initiatives that resonate with target audiences, followed by clear communication with organizers or stakeholders to define the terms of the sponsorship. Contracts and deliverables are established, ensuring both parties understand expectations, such as branding placement, speaking opportunities, or product demonstrations. Throughout the sponsorship, the Developer Relations team actively engages with the community by attending events, participating in discussions, or providing technical support to maximize visibility and impact. Post-sponsorship, the team evaluates the outcomes, gathering feedback from the community and measuring success against predefined goals, such as increased product adoption or improved brand perception, to refine future sponsorship strategies.

Metrics

Establishing metrics for sponsorship involves defining clear, measurable objectives that align with the goals of the company and the developer community. Key metrics include community engagement levels, such as attendance at sponsored events, participation in sponsored initiatives, or the number of meaningful interactions during and after the sponsorship. Metrics should also track brand visibility, including impressions from branding at events, mentions in social media or community discussions, and any increases in website traffic or social media followers directly attributable to the sponsorship. These metrics provide a quantitative view of the sponsorship's reach and resonance with the target audience.

In addition to engagement and visibility, measuring the impact of sponsorship on product adoption and developer sentiment is critical. This includes tracking metrics like the number of developers who try or adopt the company's products during or after the sponsorship period, downloads or signups attributed to the initiative, and developer feedback from surveys or interviews about their perception of the company's role in the community. Long-term metrics, such as the retention of sponsored project users or sustained mentions in the community, offer insight into the sponsorship's lasting effects. These data points should be collected systematically and presented in reports that tie sponsorship outcomes back to broader Developer Relations and business goals, ensuring transparency and continuous improvement in strategy.

Example

Imagine a fictitious tech company, CodeLink, specializing in developer tools for cloud-native applications. The Developer Relations team at CodeLink, led by Sarah, identifies the annual "Cloud Innovators Summit" as an ideal sponsorship opportunity to connect with their target audience of cloud developers. The team collaborates with the marketing department to secure a platinum sponsorship, ensuring prominent branding at the event and a keynote speaking slot for Sarah to showcase CodeLink's newest product—a Kubernetes debugging tool. The DevRel team plans a hands-on workshop during the summit to make the sponsorship impactful, allowing attendees to try the tool in real-world scenarios.

At the event, the Developer Relations team doesn't just promote the product—they engage directly with the developer community. Sarah's keynote highlights real-world challenges developers face with Kubernetes debugging and how CodeLink's tool addresses them, striking a chord with the audience. During the workshop, developers use the tool in a controlled environment, gaining firsthand experience and providing feedback that helps the team refine the product. Meanwhile, marketing leverages the event to collect video testimonials, social media buzz, and signups for a free trial of the tool. The interactive approach creates a sense of collaboration and positions CodeLink as a community-focused innovator.

Post-event, the DevRel team follows up with attendees, sharing resources and continuing the dialogue through office hours and community forums. The sponsorship leads to a measurable spike in product trials, positive social media mentions, and requests for deeper integrations with CodeLink's tool. The feedback collected helps improve the tool and informs future feature development. CodeLink's sponsorship investment boosts adoption and sales.

Consequences

Sponsorship requires budget, and will likely require somebody from the DevRel team to act as liaison between the event and your Legal and Accounting teams. Accounting will want an invoice to pay against (and information about who they are paying, addresses, etc.), and Legal will likely want to review any agreements to be signed. This can take longer than you expect, particularly if the event or group is new to your company and they want to see some due diligence beforehand.

Make sure your **Social Media (395)** point out the sponsorship—this brings some additional attention to the organization/event and creates a more symbiotic relationship between the organization and the company.

Note that conference sponsorship does not prevent or assume having a **Booth (137)**; where sponsorship flexes on Reach, the Booth focuses on interactivity.

Variants

Ambassador Sponsorship: At times your team will find it difficult to be present at an event or user group, either because you lack the bandwidth or the event is simply not a high enough priority in your planning to justify the time. In these situations, it can be helpful to present the opportunity to one of your **Ambassadors (71)**: by covering their travel and expenses ("T&E") to go speak at the event, you help build their brand while at the same time bringing an expert to that group without sending one of your own people.

CHAPTER 32

Survey

Topics: *Budget, Social*

A survey is a structured method of collecting information or feedback from individuals, typically through predefined questions. In the context of Developer Relations, surveys are used to gather insights from the technical community about their experiences, preferences, and challenges. The goal of a survey is to capture quantifiable data that can be analyzed to inform decisions, improve engagement strategies, or understand the community's needs. Surveys can be distributed through various channels like email, social media, or in-app prompts. They may include multiple-choice, rating scale, or open-ended questions to gather various responses.

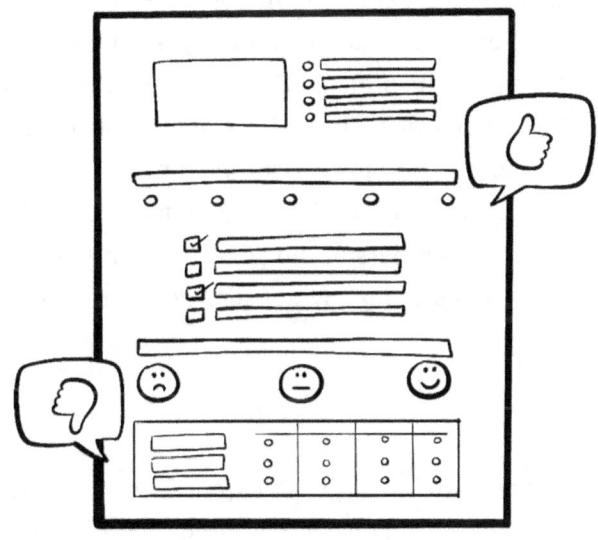

CHAPTER 32   SURVEY

Also Known As

Other names for a survey include **questionnaire**, **feedback form**, **poll**, **assessment**, **evaluation**, **inquiry**, and **opinion** form. In Developer Relations, these terms can be used interchangeably to describe tools or methods to gather information or opinions from a technical community. Each name may imply slight variations in focus or formality, but all serve the purpose of collecting structured data or feedback to inform decision-making and improve community engagement.

Intent

A survey in Developer Relations is a coordinated process that aims to systematically gather feedback, insights, and data from a technical community. This process helps to understand their needs, preferences, experiences, and challenges better. A well-structured survey allows organizations to identify trends, measure satisfaction, evaluate the effectiveness of programs or tools, and uncover areas for improvement. The detailed intent behind conducting a survey is to create a direct line of communication between the organization and the technical community, enabling data-driven decisions. These decisions enhance engagement, improve product offerings, and foster a stronger relationship with the community. By capturing quantitative and qualitative data, surveys help provide a comprehensive understanding of the community's perspectives, driving strategic initiatives aligned with users' needs and expectations.

Context

The context for a survey in Developer Relations involves understanding when and why this tool should be used to gather feedback from the technical community. Surveys are typically employed when there is a need

CHAPTER 32 SURVEY

to collect structured, reliable data to inform decisions about developer/user engagement, product features, community programs, or overall satisfaction. They are often used after specific events, product launches, or campaigns to assess impact, but can also be deployed regularly to track ongoing user sentiment and trends. The context includes

- Recognizing the importance of timing
- Choosing the proper distribution channels
- Ensuring the survey is relevant and accessible to the target audience

It's also about considering the survey's scope, such as whether it is a quick pulse check or an in-depth assessment. Additionally, the context involves striking a balance between the need for detailed information and respect for the community's time, ensuring the survey doesn't feel burdensome or intrusive. The ultimate goal is to gather actionable insights to improve the developer experience and foster a stronger, more engaged community.

Beyond internal feedback, surveys can also serve as thought leadership tools, designed not only to collect insights but to share them back with the broader community. These surveys establish credibility by producing benchmark reports, uncovering industry trends, and offering developers valuable comparisons to their own practices. When executed transparently and shared widely, they position the organization as a trusted expert and help shape conversations across the developer ecosystem.

Solution

The solution for a survey in the Developer Relations context involves designing and distributing a structured set of questions that effectively capture the insights and feedback needed from the technical community. This begins by **defining clear objectives** for the survey, such as

CHAPTER 32   SURVEY

understanding user satisfaction, gathering feedback on a product, or evaluating the success of an event or program. The survey should be **thoughtfully constructed** to include a mix of question types, such as multiple-choice or open-ended questions. This mix ensures a comprehensive understanding of the technical community's feedback, as it gathers both quantitative and qualitative data.

Once the survey design is complete, the next step in the solution is to determine the **best channels for distribution**, ensuring it reaches the intended audience. This might involve sending the survey via email, embedding it in a developer portal, promoting it through social media channels, or including it as in-app notifications. Timing is also critical, as surveys should be sent when developers are most likely to respond, such as immediately after a product release, event, or significant interaction with the community. Another effective opportunity arises when you have a captive audience at a conference session, meetup, or hackathon, when developers are already highly engaged and more inclined to provide thoughtful feedback on the spot.

To increase response rates and the quality of feedback, the survey should be kept concise, relevant, and respectful of the technologist's time. Clearly communicating the value of their participation is key. Incentives, such as offering small rewards or exclusive content, can further encourage participation.

Finally, the solution includes **analyzing the collected data**, interpreting the results to extract actionable insights, and following up on the findings. The impact of your participation in this survey can be significant, as it might involve making changes to programs, addressing identified pain points, or communicating the results back to the community to show that their feedback has been heard and acted upon.

CHAPTER 32   SURVEY

Participants

The survey participants in the Developer Relations context are members of the technical community who interact with a product, platform, or program. These participants may include active users of a development tool, contributors to **Open-Source Projects (297)**, attendees of technology events, or individuals engaged in the community through **Forums (233)**, **Social Media (395)**, or developer advocacy programs. Depending on the survey's focus and the target audience, they can range from beginner developers to seasoned professionals.

Participants interact with the survey by responding to structured questions designed to gather their feedback or insights. This interaction typically happens through digital platforms, such as an online survey form, an email invitation, or a link embedded in a developer portal or app. Depending on how the survey is distributed, participants may engage via desktop, mobile devices, or within the product.

The interaction begins with the invitation to participate, which may be voluntary or triggered by specific actions, such as after attending a workshop, completing a tutorial, or using a new feature. Participants are usually guided through a series of questions that may include multiple-choice, rating scales, or open-text responses. The survey design should ensure that the interaction is smooth, intuitive, and accessible, making it easy for participants to complete the survey without taking too much time.

In most cases, participants expect that their responses will be handled respectfully and anonymously and that their feedback will be considered in future decisions or improvements. How they interact with the survey and their willingness to provide meaningful input often depend on their perception of the survey's relevance and their trust in the organization requesting the feedback. Offering transparency around the purpose of the survey and how the data will be used can also enhance engagement and the quality of their interaction.

CHAPTER 32 SURVEY

Implementation

A more detailed survey implementation in the Developer Relations context involves a step-by-step process that ensures the survey is designed, distributed, and analyzed effectively to gather actionable feedback from the technical community. The implementation begins with clearly defining the survey's goals, such as understanding user satisfaction, measuring the impact of a new feature, or gathering insights on community engagement. These goals are crucial as they guide the entire survey process and ensure that the feedback collected is relevant and useful.

Next, the survey is designed to align with these goals. This involves crafting well-structured questions that are clear, unbiased, and relevant to the developers. The survey should include a variety of question types, such as rating scales, multiple-choice questions, and open-ended responses. This diversity in question types is essential as it allows for a comprehensive understanding of the technical community's perspectives and experiences, ensuring that no aspect is overlooked.

There's also a real science to writing effective survey questions, and it's worth investing time in researching best practices. For example, value-based trade-off questions like "Would you rather have feature A or feature B?" tend to generate more actionable insights than no-cost questions such as "Would you like better performance?" (to which the answer is almost always yes). To improve the quality of the responses, keep the survey concise and ensure that each question adds value to the survey's overall objective.

Once the survey is designed, the next step is determining the best timing and channels for distribution. Timing is crucial, as the survey should reach participants when they are most engaged, such as shortly after an event or product interaction. Distribution methods may include

- Sending the survey via email
- Posting it in **Community Forums (233)**

CHAPTER 32   SURVEY

- Promoting it through **Social Media (395)** channels
- Embedding it within a product interface or developer portal
- Capturing responses from engaged audiences at **Conferences (179)**, meetups, and **Hackathons (255)**

Each channel should be selected based on where the technical audience is most active and responsive.

To increase participation, it's essential to provide context about why the survey is being conducted and how the feedback will be used. This not only helps to increase user participation but also ensures that the feedback received is relevant and useful. Offering incentives, such as access to exclusive content, entry into a raffle, or early access to new features, can also motivate developers to take part. It's also essential to ensure the survey is easy to complete across devices, allowing developers to respond via desktop or mobile platforms, and to provide options for accessibility.

As responses come in, the data must be gathered and analyzed systematically. Using statistical tools to measure trends, patterns, and averages for quantitative data. For qualitative data, such as open-text responses, use text analysis tools or manual review to identify recurring themes, pain points, or suggestions. This step often involves segmenting the data by categories like experience level, region, or type of engagement to gain deeper insights into specific groups within the technical community.

After the data is analyzed, the next stage involves reporting the findings to key organizational stakeholders. This could include generating visual reports, dashboards, or summaries highlighting the most important trends, opportunities for improvement, and actionable recommendations. The emphasis here is on transparency, ensuring that all stakeholders are fully informed and involved in the process. Transparency with the technical community is equally important. Sharing the survey results—whether

CHAPTER 32   SURVEY

through **Blog Posts (105)**, **Newsletters (281)**, or **Community Forums (233)**—demonstrates that their feedback is valued and encourages ongoing participation in future surveys.

Finally, based on the findings, actionable steps are taken to address the feedback. This might involve implementing changes in the product, improving developer programs, or addressing specific pain points raised in the survey. To close the loop, communicate any changes made as a result of the survey back to the technical community, reinforcing the idea that their input directly influences the evolution of the product or community initiatives. This end-to-end process ensures that the survey captures valuable insights, leading to meaningful improvements and more robust user engagement. It's important to remember that this process is iterative, and continuous improvement is a key part of the survey implementation.

Metrics

Documenting the metrics for a survey that a developer relations team would create and publish is a crucial task. It involves identifying the key performance indicators (KPIs) that will measure the effectiveness of the survey and the insights gathered from the technical community. These KPIs are not just numbers, they are the compass that guides us in our mission to engage and understand the technical community, underscoring the significance of our role. The first set of metrics would focus on the survey participation rate, which includes the number of users who received the survey, the number of respondents who completed the survey, and the overall response rate. These metrics help assess the survey's engagement and whether it reached the intended audience.

The next important metric is the completion rate, a key indicator that tracks how many participants finished the survey compared to those who started it. This metric is not just a number, it's a call for continuous improvement, emphasizing the need for ongoing enhancement. It helps us evaluate if the survey was too long, unclear, or disengaging at any point. If the completion rate is low, it's a signal that the survey needs to be streamlined or improved for better clarity. It's a reminder that we can always do better.

Response quality, a critical metric that includes analyzing the depth of open-ended responses and the consistency of ratings or answers in multiple-choice questions, is not just about the data. It's about the value of the work we do, measuring how seriously participants took the survey and the value of the data collected. Tracking the average time to complete the survey ensures it aligns with expectations and does not overwhelm participants.

Quantitative metrics such as average satisfaction scores, Net Promoter Score (NPS), and rating distribution across key questions are essential for identifying trends and overall sentiment. These numbers help the developer relations team gauge satisfaction levels or gather feedback on specific products, features, or community programs. The distribution of responses across different segments, such as developer experience level, region, or engagement type, should also be tracked to provide context to the data and identify trends within specific subgroups.

Another important metric is engagement with follow-up questions or post-survey interactions. This includes tracking how many participants opted into further research or expressed interest in participating in future surveys, which measures the community's ongoing engagement.

After the survey data has been collected and analyzed, the impact of the findings is a key metric. This involves tracking changes made to products, developer programs, or communication strategies based on the feedback and then measuring whether those changes improve developer satisfaction or engagement in future surveys or interactions. This metric is crucial as it measures the effectiveness of the changes made based on the survey feedback.

Finally, it's important to document any learnings related to survey distribution, timing, or format. This includes which distribution channels were most effective, the optimal timing for sending out the survey, and any adjustments needed in the structure or wording of the survey for future iterations. These operational metrics help the team refine their approach for future surveys to maximize participation and data quality.

Example

The developer relations team at DevTech, a fictional tech company, proactively noticed a growing interest in their new cloud development platform, CloudBuilder. To better understand how developers use the platform, identify pain points, and gather insights for future improvements, the team decided to create and publish a survey targeting CloudBuilder users. They aimed to measure user satisfaction, gather feedback on key features, and explore how developers use the product in real-world scenarios while learning what enhancements developers would like to see in future updates.

The team began by designing the survey, starting with demographic questions to capture the respondents' background, such as their experience level, region, and the type of projects they work on. These details allowed the team to segment the responses and gain a deeper understanding of the diverse needs within the developer community, demonstrating the DevTech team's dedication to understanding and meeting their specific needs. The survey then moved into multiple-choice questions that asked developers to rate their overall satisfaction with CloudBuilder on a scale of 1 to 10, alongside questions to gauge their experience with specific features like deployment automation and cloud resource management.

In addition to these structured questions, the survey included open-ended prompts where developers could provide detailed feedback. Questions like "What is the biggest challenge you've faced while using CloudBuilder?" and "What features would you like to see added or improved in future releases?" aimed to capture qualitative insights that could guide the platform's future development. These open-ended responses were crucial in identifying challenges and opportunities that might not have been anticipated by the DevTech team.

After designing the survey, the developer relations team distributed it through multiple channels, including email, the CloudBuilder dashboard, and DevTech's community forum. They timed the release of the survey two weeks after a major CloudBuilder update, allowing developers to explore the new features before giving feedback. They offered a small incentive to encourage participation by entering respondents into a raffle to win DevTech swag while emphasizing that developer feedback would directly shape the next phase of CloudBuilder's development.

Once the survey closed, the team analyzed the results. They found that while developers were generally satisfied with the platform, there were recurring complaints about the complexity of the deployment automation feature. Developers also suggested improvements to the documentation, noting a need for advanced use cases. Based on these findings, the DevTech team prioritized improvements to the automation feature, enhanced the documentation, and created a roadmap for integrating additional third-party tools. They followed up by sharing the survey results with the developer community, reinforcing that their feedback was valued and acted upon, demonstrating our commitment to transparency and accountability. Finally, the team reflected on the lessons from the survey, making notes to refine future surveys to drive further engagement and improve CloudBuilder.

Consequences

For the Developer Relations team, the potential positive outcomes of a well-executed survey are significant. It can provide valuable insights into the technical community's needs, preferences, and pain points. This data allows the team to tailor their outreach efforts, improve engagement strategies, and foster a stronger relationship with developers. The team's efforts can lead to a better understanding of how the community interacts with the company's products, guiding future communication, events, or initiatives, and thereby increasing user satisfaction and loyalty.

However, if the survey needs to be better designed, has unclear objectives, or fails to capture meaningful data, it can lead to negative consequences. Low-quality data or low response rates can provide a skewed or incomplete understanding of the technical community, leading the Developer Relations team to make misguided decisions that don't truly address the needs or issues of the users. Furthermore, surveys are too frequent, lengthy, or do not show clear follow-up actions based on the feedback. In that case, developers may feel tired or disillusioned, reducing trust in the organization and its willingness to listen. This disengagement can damage the relationship between the technical community and the company.

For the broader organization, the potential positive outcomes of a well-executed survey are significant. When survey results are used effectively, they can inspire growth and innovation by helping prioritize feature development, address common complaints, and guide the overall direction of a product based on real user feedback. This can lead to more efficient resource allocation, better product-market fit, and higher satisfaction among the user base.

Moreover, survey results can influence the company's reputation in the technical community. Positive results, if shared publicly, can enhance the company's standing, showing that it values user input and is responsive to their needs. On the other hand, negative feedback or a lack of follow-up on survey responses can harm the company's image, leading to distrust or disengagement from key segments of the technical community. Therefore, the consequences of a survey are wide-reaching, affecting not only the Developer Relations team but also the company's ability to innovate, grow, and maintain a loyal user base. This underscores the team's integral role in the company's success, making them feel valued and integral.

Variants

A survey can take different forms in the developer relations context depending on the objectives, audience, and timing. One common variant is the **satisfaction survey**, which gauges developers' happiness with a product, service, or event. These surveys typically ask developers to rate their experiences, often using metrics like Net Promoter Score (NPS) or Likert scales to capture overall satisfaction and likelihood of recommending the product.

Another variant is the **feature feedback survey**, designed to gather targeted feedback on specific features, tools, or functionalities within a product. This type of survey is often used after launching a new feature or making significant updates, asking developers for detailed feedback on usability, effectiveness, and any improvements they would like to see. It helps the team understand the adoption and impact of a particular aspect of the product.

Event-based surveys are another variant, typically conducted after developer events like hackathons, conferences, or webinars. These surveys capture feedback about the event's organization, content, speakers, and overall experience. The goal is to evaluate how the event met developers' expectations and gather suggestions for improving future events.

A pulse survey is a shorter, more frequent variant designed to collect quick insights regularly. It usually contains a few questions and monitors ongoing trends or sentiments within the developer community. Pulse surveys help track developer engagement or satisfaction changes over time without overwhelming participants with a lengthy questionnaire.

Another variant is the onboarding survey, typically sent to developers after signing up for a new product or service. The purpose is to gather feedback on their initial experience, ease of use, and any challenges faced during the onboarding process. This variant helps to identify any friction points early in the user journey and improves the onboarding experience for future developers.

CHAPTER 32 SURVEY

Exit surveys are used when developers stop using a product or service, aiming to understand the reasons behind their departure. These surveys focus on identifying dissatisfaction or unmet needs that led to the exit, providing valuable insights into how the organization can improve retention and address critical issues.

Finally, the community engagement survey focuses on understanding how developers engage with the broader community. This variant gathers insights on how often developers participate in forums, events, or discussions and what motivates their involvement or disengagement. It helps assess the community's health and shape strategies to foster deeper connections among members.

Each variant serves a different purpose but shares the goal of capturing meaningful data to inform decisions and improve the developer experience.

CHAPTER 33

Swag

Topics: *Budget*

Swag refers to branded merchandise or items given away to developers and community members as part of engagement strategies. By offering practical, high-quality, or creative swag, a DevRel team can foster goodwill, enhance the company's reputation, and build loyalty.

CHAPTER 33 SWAG

Also Known As

T-shirts; Fidget Spinners; Flash drives; Flying Monkeys, Merchandise, Freebies, giveaways, promotional products

Intent

Swag intends to create memorable, positive interactions that resonate with developers and the broader tech community, reinforcing the company's brand and values. The team can enhance visibility, build trust, and indirectly drive product adoption and sales by strategically distributing swag through sponsorships, events, or partnerships.

Context

Constantly sending a developer communication, particularly if it is not initiated by the developer, is quick to "turn them off" to your company and/or product/service. Developers are also often excited by novelty (sometimes childishly so), and will often share their experiences with a novelty item found at a conference across social media for some period of time.

Solution

Provide a giveaway item—either a novelty item or something that has some level of utility to the developer in their daily life—that has the company or product/service logo branded on it, and hand them out (or ship them) to developers who express interest.

Participants

Team members involved in swag from the company side include the Developer Relations team, marketing specialists, and community managers who design, order, and distribute swag with strategic goals. From the community side, participants include developers, influencers, and event attendees who engage with the company during conferences, booths, or other interactions.

Implementation

Implementing swag involves designing and producing items that align with the company's brand identity and developer interests, such as apparel, stickers, or functional tools like USB drives or notebooks. The swag is ordered and distributed strategically through channels like conferences, meetups, virtual events, or as rewards during office hours. This process includes selecting items that provide value or spark interest, managing logistics for timely delivery and creating opportunities for meaningful interaction, ensuring the swag is a catalyst for building connections and boosting the company's presence within the developer community.

Metrics

Metrics for swag should capture both quantitative and qualitative impacts on engagement, reputation, and sales. These include the number of swag items distributed, event attendance, and participation linked to swag campaigns. Additionally, tracking metrics such as leads generated, developer retention rates, and survey feedback can provide insights into the effectiveness of swag in fostering goodwill and driving product adoption.

CHAPTER 33 SWAG

Example

At CodeSphere, a tech company focused on cloud development tools, the DevRel team collaborated with marketing to create a unique piece of swag: a set of custom-designed, reusable cable organizers shaped like miniature clouds, each branded with the company logo and a QR code leading to free tutorials. The idea emerged during a brainstorming session where the team aimed to produce a practical yet affordable item that resonated with developers. These cable organizers, lightweight and easy to ship, were introduced during CodeSphere's community office hours and handed out at local meetups, alongside opportunities to learn about the company's latest product updates.

Consequences

Swag is almost always present at any **Booth (137)**. It is also not uncommon to see swag being given away at **Conference Sessions (197)**, sometimes even with some kind of small "contest" or "test" attached to it. ("Answer a question and win a free T-shirt!" is one way to artificially boost Q-and-A/participation in a session.)

Swag is often obtained by purchasing through one of the many "swag vendors" who are accomplished at putting logos and/or messages on standardized items. Pens/pencils, notebooks of all shapes and sizes, USB flash drives, T-shirts, sweatshirt/hoodies, all are usually easy to obtain by going through the vendors' website and providing the appropriate shipping destination and a credit card. Larger companies may even have internal processes for obtaining swag, rather than dealing with an external vendor directly.

Novelty swag can sometimes backfire and create negative branding, particularly if it accidentally annoys a developer group or creates issues for conference organizers. T-shirts, for example, have long been handed out in men's sizes, which often alienates women; for any swag item, make sure to get a diverse set of opinions on it before committing to something.

Variants

Practical swag includes functional items like notebooks, pens, USB drives, or laptop stickers that developers can use daily. These items are cost-effective and keep the brand visible during the recipient's regular work routines.

Digital swag involves non-physical rewards such as free software licenses, exclusive templates, digital art, or access to premium learning content. This variant is ideal for virtual events or global audiences where shipping physical swag is impractical.

Experiential swag focuses on creating memorable moments, such as offering free event tickets, private workshops, or virtual one-on-one mentoring sessions. These provide lasting value and deepen relationships between developers and the company.

Eco-friendly swag emphasizes sustainability, such as reusable water bottles, bamboo tech accessories, or organic cotton apparel. This variant aligns with values-driven developers and enhances the company's reputation for social responsibility.

CHAPTER 34

Technical Support

Topics: *Code, Writing, Social*

Technical support involves providing timely and practical assistance to developers using a company's products or platforms, addressing their technical issues, questions, and feedback.

CHAPTER 34   TECHNICAL SUPPORT

Also Known As

Developer support, customer support, technical assistance

Intent

Customers using your product/service are inevitably going to find issues (or what they think are issues), and as the connection between developers and your company, you will be a first point of contact they will use to communicate with your company when they are stuck or believe they have found a bug or issue. Your customer is running into issues of one form or another with your product/service: Either it is not doing something it should, or it is doing something it shouldn't, or at least is behaving in a manner that is unexpected. It may be as simple as simply being "down," and they cannot correct the problem themselves.

Context

Formal technical support teams often have a formalized process by which they triage and handle (or escalate) technical support requests (tickets), in order to help that team focus on fixing the biggest-impact smallest-effort-required bugs. Each tech support team triages their tickets in a different manner, according to their policies and OKRs, and anyone looking for ways to circumvent this process often earns the wrath of the senior management of the technical support team.

Depending on the nature of your product/service, the technical support team may not be well qualified to handle developer technical support requests; for example, if your product/service is consumer-facing (like a cloud-based accounting system or an online gaming platform), the technical support team will likely be much more focused on working with end user consumers, and not your developer-customers.

CHAPTER 34   TECHNICAL SUPPORT

Solution

Dedicate some portion of your team's bandwidth to acting as a first-tier technical support team, either handling the issue entirely or passing it on internally to others better able to track the problem down. Continue to act as the point-of-contact for the customer, taking ownership of the communication and acting as their advocate in meetings about the issue. Ensure that they receive an answer (even if it is one they don't care for or want to hear).

If the product/service is geared toward end user consumers, you may need to create an informal (or formal) developer tech support team to support those folks directly.

Participants

Technical support participants from the company side include support engineers, product teams, and developer advocates who collaborate to address technical challenges faced by users. From the community side, participants include developers, technical influencers, and community moderators who share insights, report issues, and contribute solutions. In the Developer Relations technical support pattern, these participants interact by exchanging feedback, identifying trends in developer needs, and co-creating resources like documentation, FAQs, or example projects.

Implementation

Implementing technical support involves creating structured channels for communication, such as dedicated forums, chat platforms, ticketing systems, and live coding sessions. It requires establishing clear workflows for issue triaging, escalation, and resolution, focusing on quick and transparent responses. Developer Relations teams play a central role by leveraging their technical expertise and product knowledge to liaise between the company and developers, ensuring that feedback loops inform product improvements. Effective implementation also includes monitoring support metrics, identifying common pain points, and providing proactive resources like tutorials, troubleshooting guides, and code samples to empower developers and reduce repetitive inquiries.

Metrics

To document metrics for technical support, focus on capturing data that reflects both the effectiveness of support and its impact on developer satisfaction and product adoption. Key metrics include response time, resolution time, and the volume of issues handled, which indicate efficiency and reliability.

Example

A fictitious Developer Relations team at TechFlow, a company specializing in real-time data streaming platforms, noticed an uptick in support requests from developers needing help integrating the company's API with their existing applications. Developers expressed frustration about incomplete documentation and inconsistent error messages. The DevRel team, led by Tom, collaborated with the product and support teams to address the issues systematically. They hosted a series of live debugging sessions tailored to specific use cases, walking through common problems developers were facing and providing immediate solutions. Tom personally followed up with key participants after these sessions, gathering deeper insights into their challenges and documenting additional feedback.

Armed with this feedback, the DevRel team worked closely with the product team to improve error handling in the API and rewrite the documentation, adding clear examples and edge-case scenarios. They released a public roadmap to show developers the planned changes, fostering transparency. Within weeks, TechFlow saw a 30% reduction in API-related support tickets, and social media buzz about the improvements attracted new developers to the platform.

Consequences

Any form of contact with your team can be the entry point to an informal technical support request: feedback on an **Article (89)**, one of your **Ambassadors (71)** having an issue themselves, **Forums (233)**, **Social Media (395)**, even somebody walking up to you at a **Conference Session (197)** are all prime candidates for a customer's opening line, "Do you have a moment? I've run into something weird, and I could use your help...."

Developer technical support is often more intricate and complex than end user technical support, since software development is often more subtle and more "open-ended" than what users are capable of doing. This means that developer technical support is often a more time-intensive task (on a per-ticket basis), and it requires personnel who are at least somewhat proficient at writing code. If the company currently does not have a developer technical support team, your team will need to step into that role, and own any developer technical support requests that come in. This is an enormous time commitment if your product/service becomes at all popular, so while your DevRel team members may be able to serve in this role for a time, you will quickly reach a point where your available bandwidth is exceeded and a dedicated developer technical support team will need to be hired. (This team can be either a part of DevRel or a part of Engineering—there's solid arguments for both.)

CHAPTER 34   TECHNICAL SUPPORT

Having the DevRel team involved at some level in developer technical support can help generate additional feedback about the product/service, and in particular the places where either the documentation needs to be improved (perhaps the **Guides (243)** need to have deeper details about a complex topic) or fixed (perhaps the **Reference Documentation (373)** doesn't accurately reflect how the product/service works) or extended (perhaps a new **Sample/Example (387)** helps demonstrate how to avoid a common bug).

Variants

Onboarding Support: Focused on helping new users get started with the product effectively. This can include tailored guides, interactive walkthroughs, and personalized assistance during the initial stages.

Dedicated Developer Support: Offers premium or specialized support for enterprise customers or key accounts, including features like guaranteed response times, priority handling, and direct access to product experts.

CHAPTER 35

Training

Topics: *Presentation, Code, Budget*

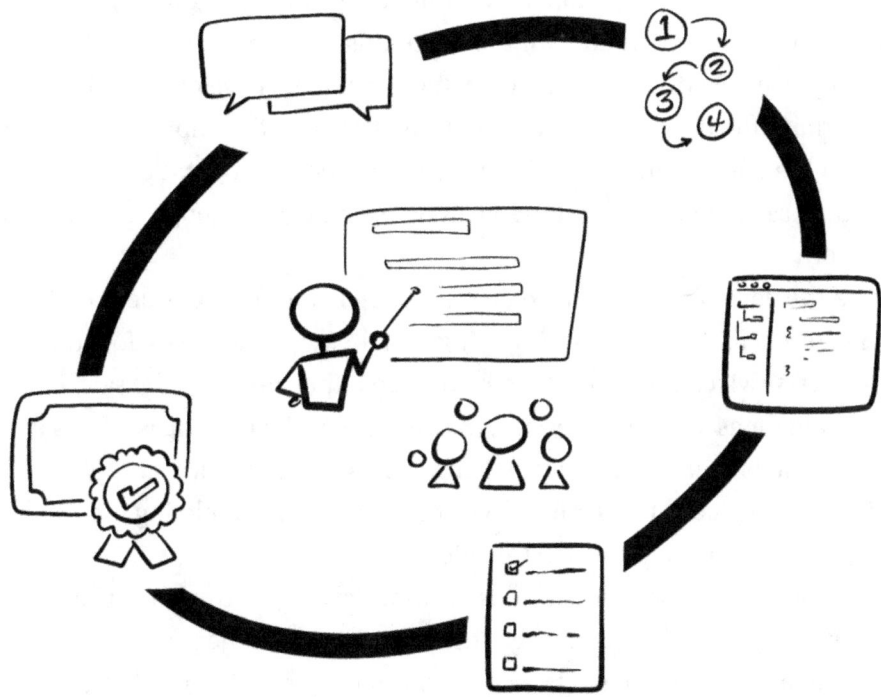

Also Known As

Tutorials, certification, upskilling, courses, workshops, off-sites, learning retreat

CHAPTER 35 TRAINING

Intent

You want to teach developers how to use your product so they are able to make use of your product/service.

Context

Your product/service is complex enough, or feature-rich enough, that there is concern that developers will not be able to learn how to use it from written documentation or presentations. Perhaps there are complex concepts involved, or new concepts that developers have not seen before, or perhaps the configuration of the product/service is complicated due to a high level of dependency or interaction between configuration settings. In some cases, just getting started can be complicated enough to merit concern.

If the developers looking to be trained on using your product/service are external to the company, implying that their company paid for your product/service, the training can be offered either as part of the sale, or else paid for as a separate service. In some cases, the training is a formal part of establishing credibility in using your product/service, complete with a fancy piece of paper to convey the success in completing the training—this is often called a Certification.

If the product/service is extensive, new developers working at your company may want or need to go through training on the product/service themselves. These classes may want to be held internally and without external participants present, so that potentially sensitive company decisions or implementation details can be discussed without violating NDAs.

Solution

Provide training classes, ranging in length from half-day (four hours) to full weeks (40 hours or more), in which an instructor (an expert in your product/service, such as a member of your DevRel team, or perhaps one of your Ambassadors) provides a presentation describing some part of the complexity, then monitors the room for questions and provides support while the attendees do some hands-on exercises ("labs"). This cycle can run once or twice in a half-day class, or may run three or more times per day in a full-day or multi-day format.

Participants

In any training class, the principal participants are the **instructor**, who leads the training, and the **students**, who are there to learn and practice the topic. The instructor is responsible for the bulk of the work during the training's time frame, doing the lecture and taking questions from the students, then taking questions and providing assistance during the labs.

In some training scenarios, if the demand is significant enough, the course materials may be written by a third party, such as another instructor, or even an individual specifically designated (and trained) as an educational content creator. Alternatively, if the training class is taught by multiple instructors, it can be useful to designate a **course author** who is responsible for both the quality of the course and keeping it up-to-date with the latest changes in the product/service. This course author can sometimes come from a background in formal education, but usually must have some depth of knowledge on the topic.

Although not required, many training class materials benefit greatly from a quality-check of the materials, including a copyedit on any written materials and a QA/implementation check of any code that goes with the labs. This task is often given to the course author as part of their preparation of the materials, but like all content creation benefits greatly from a "second pair of eyes" doing a review.

Coordinating the logistics for a training class is often done by a **course coordinator** or **scheduler**, who assumes responsibility for logistics, including drop-shipping any necessary physical materials to the course site. This individual may also be responsible for selecting the instructor for the course, and confirming schedules with students.

Implementation

Training class implementation comes in phases:

Inception: First, the course must be outlined and fleshed out. What collection of topics "hangs together" well enough to be something that feels whole and complete without being too overcomplex and cognitively burdensome? Some of this will be driven by the amount of time the stakeholders want the class to be—shorter classes are easier to fit into schedules and are easier on the students' mental faculties but cannot convey as much material or complex concepts.

Creation: Once the rough outline and time frame is known, the course can be fleshed out. If this is a "lecture-lab" style class, then a matching set of lectures and exercises must be created for each "module" covered in the class. Many training materials authors will claim that it is easier to work on the labs first (essentially writing the solution) before attempting to work on the lecture materials, but this is a topic that has as many different perspectives as any other content-creation topic.

One important but often-overlooked training course topic is that of the setup requirements. What software must be on students' computers in order to work against the lab exercises? What steps are required to prepare the computer for this work? If the students are going to be working against a service "in the cloud," then either students must be prepared to sign up for the cloud service during the class, or must come with pre-existing service credentials. Note that if the students are working against a shared multi-tenant service instance, care must be taken to ensure that students' work does not conflict with one another, or with any other work being done on that instance. (For this reason, it is often useful to create a stand-alone instance used specifically for course use.)

Validation: Like all products, the training course can benefit from an "external" (to the course author) review, ideally by having someone sit through a beta-test run of the course. This can prove quite time-consuming, however, so many course authors need to be satisfied with a "materials review" by subject matter experts, in which they read over the materials, examine the exercises, and provide feedback. Because of the importance of the exercises, it is highly suggested that review efforts focus more on the exercises and the length required to complete them, than on reviewing the lecture materials. As a rule of thumb, it will take 2 to 3 times longer for a student to complete a particular exercise than one who is already familiar with the material, and 3 to 5 times longer than the course author (who doesn't have to parse the instructions to know what they are trying to do with this exercise). Thus, if the lab period wants to be 30 to 45 minutes long, the course author should make sure they can complete the exercise—with no shortcuts, like cutting-and-pasting from the solution—in 10 minutes or less.

Logistics: Before the class can be taught, it must be scheduled and logistics arranged. Typically a class of up to 25 (30 at the most) students can be taught by a single instructor. If the class is larger than 25, it will require additional instructors, or there may be students who cannot get questions answered during a particular exercise period. Students must be able to fit comfortably into a room for long stretches of time, with a decent view of an overhead projector as well as enough "elbow room" to be able to work on their lab exercises without disturbing their neighbors. This often means finding a conference room that can be occupied for the length of the training class (plus an hour on either end, for the instructor to set up and clean up, respectively). Typically a good Internet connection is a necessity (since most product/services require it), and if the students' machines should have software preinstalled, it will be up to the logistics coordinator to make sure that message reaches the students prior to their arrival for the class. (Note that it's common for students to either not see that message, ignore it, or simply not have the time to do the preinstalls, so the Internet connection should be sufficient to allow for each student to be downloading large binaries simultaneously, or some students may have a sub-optimal experience.)

Execution: On the day (or days) of the course, the instructor delivers the lectures and assists with any questions during the corresponding lab. Despite whatever logistical support may or may not be coming from the company, the instructor is typically the first point-of-contact for any student issues or concerns, and as such the instructor should be familiar with all of the logistical details (meals, snacks, networking, etc.) and/or know whom to contact in the event of an issue outside of their control. The instructor must be prepared to be "on" all day, lecturing and then answering questions, often with no time for breaks or even lunch.

Review: Periodically, the course needs to be reviewed for accuracy and correctness, as changes to your product/service and/or the surrounding context (new programming language versions, new programming languages, shifts in the market, and so on) may conspire to affect either the accuracy of the material or the efficacy of how it is presented. In some cases, it may seem worthwhile to rewrite the course entirely, or, if the situation merits it, close it down and strike it from the training offerings.

Metrics

Metrics for training classes can include

- **Student surveys:** The simplest way to track the success of a training class is to ask the students via some kind of Survey. This can be as simple as a half-dozen ratings-

CHAPTER 35 TRAINING

style questions with a score attached, or more complex (more questions, open-ended questions that yield no score rating, and so on). If the training class is its own economic activity (purchased from your company apart from the original sale of the product/service itself), then it will likely be a necessity to include some kind of student survey, and the results shared with the students' management.

- **Participation:** Another means to track training is to track the number of students that have completed the training. Keep in mind, however, that a decline in student participation numbers may not be a direct correlation to the skill of the instructors or the quality of the materials; in tight economic settings, training budgets are often the first to be slashed, but the drop could equally be due to a major rewrite (and simplification or clarification) of the product/service's documentation and guides. Of course, the opposite is true, as well: if the documentation begins to lose its utility, that can trigger a surge in training numbers.

- **Follow-up surveys:** One tactic less often used is that of the follow-up survey: six months to a year after the course's completion, the students are emailed a survey asking their feedback on the course and its ability to help them in their daily work routine. Note that this survey runs two risks: the follow-up rate (of students taking the survey) is likely to be much lower.

445

Example

The story of the DevRel team at CodeSphere shows how effective training can improve adoption of a product. CodeSphere offers a complex cloud-based platform for processing data. After launching their product, the marketing team noticed that, despite initial interest, many developers found it difficult to get started. To address this issue, the DevRel team created a two-day training course that included lectures and hands-on labs.

They designed the course to help participants navigate the platform's tricky setup steps, build small projects, and use reusable code samples. The marketing team advertised this training as a special benefit for early customers. During the sessions, DevRel instructors encouraged questions, helped participants with debugging, and offered advice tailored to each person's needs.

As a result, customers who completed the training reported quicker project launches, fewer support requests, and a greater sense of loyalty to CodeSphere. The marketing team shared stories of these customer successes, enhancing the company's reputation as an innovator and a supporter of developers.

The sales team also gained from this initiative, as prospects felt reassured that choosing CodeSphere meant getting not just software but also the training and support needed to succeed. Overall, the training became a key part of the DevRel strategy, improving the company's image, building community trust, and contributing to revenue growth.

Consequences

Training is expensive in terms of time and expense, both to the customer and to the provider (you), particularly for in-person training. (Virtual training is only slightly less expensive since there is no travel and associated expenses, but many companies find virtual training to be less engaging than in-person.)

On the provider side, materials must be developed and calibrated, to ensure that there's not too much material to cover in the allotted time, or that the labs for the students to do are within an acceptable range of time to carry out. In a typical 8-hour business day, three lecture/lab pairs are common—lecture for 45-60 minutes (sometimes as much as 90 minutes) followed by a lab on that same subject for 30-45 minutes. Three of these, plus lunch and a few breaks, makes for a full day. (If you shorted lectures to 30-45 minutes each, you can often get four in, two before and two after lunch.)

If your team is responsible for the logistical support for classes (finding a venue and/or a conference room in which to conduct the training, organizing attendee signups, sponsoring guests on the company network, and so on), strongly consider dedicating one person on the team to coordinating all of this, particularly if the training class is going to be repeated and/or become a staple of your team's offerings. While it may seem efficient to let each instructor handle their own logistics, one person taking care of the logistical burden can often have some efficiency benefits as that individual learns "tricks of the trade" and builds relationships with other logistical sources.

Note that effectively supporting attendees during training means there is a hard limit on the number of attendees—in general, companies that provide training set this number at 25-30 people per instructor. This limits the reach, but maximizes interactivity. Note that if your team is looking to increase its reach without hiring new team members, consider Ambassadors conducting training on your company's behalf.

When calibrating labs, keep in mind that what takes you (an individual experienced with the product/service) n time will take participants usually $2n$ or $3n$ time; thus, if it takes you 10-15 minutes to write the lab (from scratch, no cutting/pasting from prepared files), then it will take your audience 30-45 minutes, minimum.

CHAPTER 35   TRAINING

Note that it's often possible to take the labs from a training class and release them as Hands-On-Labs, albeit with some form of "lecture" to go along with it (either a **Recorded Video (363)**, **Guide (243)**, or perhaps in conjunction with an **Article (89)**). Alternatively, feedback from your customers about your Hands-On-Labs may lead you to conclude that offering a training class is necessary.

Variants

- **Internal Training:** The most common variant of this is for your DevRel team to organize and provide logistical support for training of your Engineering team, both by conducting training themselves and by organizing training from other sources (such as from industry luminaries and/or established training companies). In this scenario, the DevRel team is taking on more of a "talent development" role, and will often want to conduct surveys of both Engineers and Engineering Managers to identify gaps in current knowledge, and/or upcoming projects that might use new technologies. DevRel is uniquely positioned to be able to do this well, given that they will often be at conferences (and therefore know personally highly qualified individuals to conduct the training), understand what trainers would need (because they often are doing the same thing), and/or are constantly "on the lookout" for what is new and/or just a fad (and therefore can assist in topic selection).

- **Certification:** One way to help customers self-identify (and silently promote your brand) as being experts in your product/service is to offer up a formal, branded certificate that offers your company's endorsement of the customer's skillset once the customer has completed one or more of the Hands-on-Labs successfully. If your product/service is broad enough or deep enough, offer several different certifications, each with an associated examination (that verifies the developer has learned the appropriate material) that developers must go through (successfully) to claim. Rather than hold a formal classroom event, greater scalability can be achieved by having the interested developers learn the material from other sources (classroom training, books, or hands-on experience), and the company provides one or more examinations that seek to test the developer's knowledge on a particular topic. Known as "certifications," this is often an attempt by the company to help level-set what knowledge is reasonable to expect of a developer who claims familiarity with your product/service. Ambassadors will frequently be expected to have a significant number of these certifications, and it is not uncommon for the company to look to publish **Books (121)** on the material specific to the examination—as a matter of fact, if the company doesn't publish one, it's highly likely that a third-party will do so. The value of these certifications is the subject of much debate within the industry, but the existence of certifications tends to suggest a degree of maturity around and popularity of the product/service.

CHAPTER 36

Tutorial

Topics: *Writing, Code*

A Tutorial is a step-by-step instructional resource designed to guide developers through solving specific problems or implementing features using a company's product or technology. Tutorials help bridge the gap between documentation and real-world applications, making it easier for developers to learn and adopt new tools. By providing clear, actionable guidance, Developer Relations teams can enhance the developer experience, showcase product value, and build trust, ultimately boosting the company's reputation and driving product adoption.

Also Known As

How-To, Walkthrough, Hands-On Example

CHAPTER 36   TUTORIAL

Intent

Your product/service is complex, with a large number of possible ways to get started, or large feature set. Developers find it difficult to get started, and/or make use of features. You might have **Reference Documentation (373)** or one or more **Guides (243)**, but these are not sufficient to get developers using your product/service or certain features of the product/service.

Context

Getting developers started is not a one-time exercise. Any developer that wants to learn your product/service is going to be coming at it "brand new," and it is irrelevant how long your product/service has been around—every developer is new to your product/service the first time they begin exploring it. Therefore, it is important that whatever solution you use to help them has a long longevity to it, and is easily reusable.

Developers are accustomed to being able to "do" rather than just "sit and listen." Psychological studies are mixed on whether different people have different "learning styles," but in general the adage "tell me and I forget; show me and I might remember; have me do and I remember" seems to hold for many if not most developers.

Every single developer will need to go through learning how to use your product/service (particularly as the number of features increase), so unless the company's business model assumes or relies on a small customer base (or a large DevRel team!), this must be a high-reach activity.

Solution

Create a tutorial that takes a developer from a well-defined "point A" to a well-defined "point B," with step-by-step instructions (and code) that developers can exercise and run for themselves. The steps taken should be concrete, clear, and comprehensive, so that developers understand what they are doing and why they are doing it.

In order to minimize the amount of research a developer must go through to get started with a tutorial, consider providing a **Live Playground (265)** for developers to use.

Participants

While tutorials can technically be written by a single author who has enough expertise on the subject matter and knows how to construct understandable prose, it is ideal to have a reviewer go over the content for editorial clarity and technical accuracy. In most cases, that would require one editorial reviewer and one technical reviewer.

Implementation

Provide clear instructions for getting a developer from a well-defined "point A" to a well-defined "point B." The instructions should be clear enough to remove all friction from getting started to following each step. Explain any prerequisites or dependencies that need to be installed before the tutorial can begin. If possible, provide a starter project that contains the required resources to begin the tutorial, or even a **Live Playground (265)** where you can control the surrounding infrastructure of the tutorial.

The instructions of the tutorial should provide just enough information to accomplish the task and then link to **Reference Documentation (373)** or a **Guide (243)** for additional context on that aspect of the system.

A tutorial is a chance for developers to get their hands on your software and try it out. Make sure the journey the instructions walk through are doable but also showing enough of the product to get developers excited about its possibilities.

CHAPTER 36 TUTORIAL

Metrics

- **Page hits:** Traffic to a tutorial page shows how many people are viewing and potentially going through the tutorial.

- **Completion rate:** The number of times a tutorial is completed.

- **Usage of feature:** Effective tutorials should inform and educate users on a particular feature and usage of that feature should increase.

Example

Amber is a developer advocate for a company that develops a low-code tool for developing cross-platform applications. The team already has plenty of educational material for getting started with their product. What they need now is more content that goes beyond "Hello, world" and shows users how to build more robust solutions. Amber decides a good place to start is to describe how to connect a project to a live datasource, read data from that source, and print it to the application window.

She begins the tutorial by explaining to the reader that they should already be able to create a basic "Hello, world" application, linking to that tutorial. Next, she gives step-by-step instructions for setting up a MongoDB database and adding a collection so there is data for the application to pull. Then, she gives instructions for how to create a connection between the application and the database. Amber includes screenshots of the low-code configuration screens, highlighting the areas where the database connection happens, so the reader can see what it's supposed to look like. And, finally, she lists instructions for querying the database and printing the results to the application window.

CHAPTER 36   TUTORIAL

Consequences

Unless your product/service is particularly small or has a small developer-facing "surface area," just one tutorial will not be enough. It is very likely that with each new feature developed in the product/service, a new tutorial showing how to use that feature will be useful if not necessary. New tutorials will be needed as new features are released.

Tutorials will also need to be updated regularly as the product/service modifies some of its existing features or functionality. The more tutorials, the more time and effort will be required to keep them up-to-date. This is a useful activity for the more junior members of the DevRel team (to help them get practice debugging against your product/service as well as help them learn the product/service more comprehensively).

Because it is difficult to predict ahead of time where developers will get stuck, consider providing the "answers" (completed tutorial) as a **Sample/Example (387)** for developers to consult.

It is common to use material from a tutorial for a **Workshop (477)** at a conference, providing some in-person lecture in front of the hands-on work, rather than relying on prose. Similar results can be achieved by combining a **Webinar (469)** with a tutorial, creating greater reach but sacrificing some interactivity.

If there is a large number of tutorials, and there is demand for a higher-interactivity approach, tutorials can be combined with in-person (or virtual) lectures and turned into **Training (439)**.

Variants

- **Step-by-Step Tutorials**: These traditional, linear tutorials break down a task or feature into small, manageable steps. They are ideal for beginners or developers unfamiliar with the technology, providing a clear, guided pathway to achieving a specific goal.

455

- **Scenario-Based Tutorials**: These tutorials focus on real-world use cases or problem-solving scenarios, allowing developers to learn in a context that mirrors their challenges. They are particularly effective for demonstrating the practical application of a tool or technology in specific industries or workflows.

- **Interactive Tutorials**: Delivered through platforms that allow developers to write and execute code within the tutorial, these tutorials provide immediate feedback. They are highly engaging and suitable for developers who prefer hands-on, trial-and-error learning experiences.

- **Video Tutorials**: These offer step-by-step guidance in a video format, often accompanied by narration and visual demonstrations. They are great for visual and auditory learners and can include screen recordings, diagrams, and animations to enhance understanding.

- **Live Tutorials**: Conducted in real time, such as during **Webinars (469)** or live coding sessions, these tutorials enable direct interaction between the facilitator and participants. Developers can ask questions, clarify doubts, and receive instant feedback.

- **Gamified Tutorials**: These introduce game-like elements such as challenges, rewards, and progression tracking to make the learning experience more engaging and enjoyable. Gamification is particularly appealing for developers who thrive on achieving milestones and overcoming challenges.

CHAPTER 37

User Group Network

Topics:

A user group is a collection of people who share a common interest with a desire to connect with others, exchange ideas, and learn more on the topic.

CHAPTER 37   USER GROUP NETWORK

Also Known As

Meetup Group, Special Interest Group (SIG)

Intent

Your product/service is out and available, and has some popularity, but there doesn't feel like there is much "community" around it: It's difficult to identify individuals who are using it as opposed to those who just examine it. It feels like there are people out there who could benefit from finding one another and gathering periodically to discuss it, but the community remains entirely online.

Context

You want to increase the interactivity and reach simultaneously, but conferences occur too rarely to meet regular interactivity goals. (Most conferences run once or twice a year, and you're looking for monthly interaction.) Additionally, you want to improve the interactivity between the members of the community ("side-to-side"), not just between your company and customers ("top-down"). No existing user group community or network exists. You have significant budget, and significant organizational bandwidth.

Solution

Create, sponsor, and organize one (or more) user groups in geographic regions (most often large cities) that gather individuals who are interested in the company or product/service for discussions and camaraderie. Use a tool like Meetup.com to organize and advertise. Find or provide venue space.

Find or provide speakers. Provide **Swag (427)**. Connect **Ambassadors (71)** to UGs. After some period of time (years, most likely), look to hand off the administration of each group to a local leader within each group.

Participants

- **Group organizers:** Also known as group managers, organizers are the ones running the show when it comes to logistics surrounding the group and meetings. They schedule speakers/topics, meeting spaces, and refreshments. And they make sure all relevant information is communicated to the group via the group website, social media, mailing lists, platforms such as Meetup.com, and/or chat tools like Discord. Each of these tasks can be delegated. In fact, delegation is encouraged so that no one person is overburdened. However, it's the organizer who orchestrates and is responsible for completing the tasks.

- **Speakers:** Speaking at user group meetings is very similar to giving a talk at a **Conference Session (197)**. If possible, attend a meeting before giving the presentation to get a feel for the group vibe so that you can tailor your talk to the situation. In many cases, user group meetings are more casual than conference sessions, which may allow for speakers to be more experimental with their presentations. Not all speakers need to be experts, and people of all experience levels can provide insight that can benefit the group.

CHAPTER 37   USER GROUP NETWORK

Implementation

The lightest lift for engaging with user group communities is to sponsor existing groups in related topic areas. For example, if your product is something JavaScript developers would be excited about, find a local JavaScript group. Discover what the group needs—food/drink, venue, speakers—and offer to provide what's needed in exchange for getting a chance to talk to the group and hand out Swag.

Starting a user group takes more effort but gives you more control over all aspects, especially the overall theme of the group. The main concerns are finding a suitable venue, coordinating speakers, providing food and drink, and advertising.

Venue: Select a venue easy to access with either convenient parking or close proximity to mass transit stations. For companies with physical offices, hosting meetings in their own spaces can be ideal. Everyone in attendance will learn where the company offices are and leave with a vivid impression of their workspace. Other options for suitable venues are meeting spaces inside a co-working space, or some restaurants and bars offer meeting spaces with access to screens for presenting.

Inside the venue, arrange the meeting space with comfortable seating that allows attendees to easily hear the presenters and see the presentation screen. Depending on the size of the group and layout of the room, attendees could be arranged in a semi-circle facing the presenter to encourage discussion and interaction.

Meeting Format: Presentations are normally the main draw to user group meetings, and are what distinguish one meeting from the next. When a meeting is advertised, the call to action is usually "Join us on February 4th as Shallan Davar will present her talk, 'Not Losing Your Mind (and Your Work) in a Sea of Revisions.'" The talk is the draw and the main event of the meeting. How you package the rest of the meeting around the presentation(s) depends on your goals and group size. Consider some of these options:

- Provide time for the group to gather, eat, and connect. The two main purposes of user groups are sharing information and connecting with other like-minded people. Let the people connect.

- Recognize any sponsors who provided a space for the meeting, food, speakers, or other resources. Give the sponsors time to pitch their product or project to the group.

- Allow time to let anyone stand up in front of the group and advertise job opportunities.

- Let folks get up for a minute or two and share a project they're working on.

- Give people a chance to introduce themselves. This might not make sense if your group is large. But, if time permits, it's great for everyone to get to know each other and network.

Speakers: Arranging speakers can be the most time-consuming task of running a user group, but also the most rewarding. While it's a given that talks should at least be tangentially related to the overall topic of the group, be open to experimenting with topics and speakers. User groups are an ideal place for new speakers to gain experience, as local groups are less intimidating than cavernous conference rooms. Encourage new speakers and provide opportunities for them to try presenting. Keep in mind that audiences have differing experience levels, and no one person knows all the things about all the things. Everyone who has a desire to speak has something they can share.

Talks for future meetings need to be arranged no later than the previous meeting. That way, speakers have time to prepare, the group has time to advertise, and attendees have a chance to clear their schedules.

CHAPTER 37   USER GROUP NETWORK

Food/Beverage and Swag: User groups love **Swag (427)**. And pizza. (Or other easily delivered food options; consider breaking away from the mold and providing Thai food or tacos, just to be different. Anything that can be served "family style" is a good candidate.)

Advertising is vital when starting a new group and essential to maintain healthy attendance going forward. Lean heavily into your company's **Social Media (395)**, as well as the networks of your team—throughout the company. Identify where developers of your chosen topic congregate—Discord, Slack, etc.—and make announcements on those platforms as well. A healthy pattern of messaging should be one month out, then two weeks, and then a few days before the event.

Metrics

- **Attendance:** One of the first questions management will ask surrounding any event is how many people attended. This gives an idea of the reach the user group has on the community and on the popularity of the speaker and topics.

- **Calls to Action:** Whether your company gives a talk, hosts, or sponsors, there should be a call to action. Invite the group to visit your site, sign up for an account, or subscribe to your newsletter. Whatever the action is, track it.

CHAPTER 37   USER GROUP NETWORK

Example

RadiantCloud is a popular API management platform looking to connect with its developer community near its headquarters in downtown Seattle, WA, to drive sign-ups for its new Slack Workspace for the RadiantCloud community. The DevRel team at Radiant has organized a user group to gather at their offices near King Street Station. The company works out of a co-working space that offers a large meeting area with projectors, screens, and ample seating. The team invites Kaladin Stormblessed, a RadiantCloud Ambassador from a Seattle-area gaming studio called BridgeFour, to deliver a talk about his team's experience migrating to RadiantCloud entitled, "Journey Before Destination: BridgeFour's Magical Migration to RadiantCloud."

Goals: The goal for the evening is to get RadiantCloud users in attendance to connect with one another in person and also register for the community Slack Workspace. With over 100 attendees registered, the team has a goal of 60 people actually attending. And, of those, they expect 30 to sign up for the Slack Workspace. That would give the Workspace a jumpstart of chatter that will make the Workspace more inviting than an empty set of Slack channels.

Advertising: The meeting is advertised on RadiantCloud's **Social Media (395)** channels, in the company newsletter, as well as a banner displayed on each user's dashboard when they sign in to the platform. Syl, RadiantCloud's social media manager, also prepares copy for employees to post to their personal social feeds. Account managers also send personal invitations to their customers in the greater Seattle area. All advertisements invite attendees to register for the meeting so the team can have an idea of how many people to plan for.

Logistics: Tress runs events for RadiantCloud and will handle the logistics for the meeting. Before the day of the event, she creates signs to be placed in their building, directing meeting attendees to the RadiantCloud offices. She also gets a couple of volunteers to help attendees with the

CHAPTER 37　USER GROUP NETWORK

elevator and getting into the locked office space. Tress gathers chairs and arranges them facing the screens where Kaladin will be presenting. She asks Adolin, one of Radiant's recruiters, to set up a table near the entrance of the office to greet everyone as they enter.

Dalinar, a Developer Advocate for RadiantCloud, prepares a slide deck with an agenda, announcements, an invitation to register for the Slack Workspace, and a bio slide for the speaker. The agenda for the evening was as follows:

- 6:00 pm —Eat/Drink/Mingle
- 6:15 pm —Announcements
    - RadiantCloud Community Slack Workspace
    - Demo recently released RadiantCloud features
- 6:30 pm —*"Journey Before Destination: BridgeFour's Magical Migration to RadiantCloud,"* by Kaladin Stormblessed.

Running the meeting: On the day of the event, Tress orders catering for a taco bar to be delivered 15 minutes before the meeting begins. Tress greets Kaladin and shows him around the meeting space, and introduces him to Dalinar, who helps Kaladin perform a "tech check" to make sure his laptop is compatible with the projector. Once everything is connected, Dalinar invites Kaladin to get some food and mingle while the other attendees arrive. The bulk of the crowd arrives just before 6:00 pm. They are greeted by Adolin, who gives each person a nametag and a special RadiantCloud t-shirt on their way in. Adolin's table is also covered with a variety of RadiantCloud stickers for everyone to choose from as they pass. The attendees gravitate to the food counter, where they fill their plates and find open seats. The agenda slide is on. The crowd isn't naturally talkative, but Dalinar and Tress work their way through the room, making introductions and sparking conversations.

CHAPTER 37   USER GROUP NETWORK

Right at 6:15 pm, Dalinar steps up to the podium and welcomes everyone to the meeting. He walks through the agenda and progresses into the announcements, where he invites everyone to join the Slack Workspace. On his invitation slide, he has a QR code that allows everyone to register for the Workspace right there in the meeting. Dalinar then moves into a brief demo of the latest RadiantCloud features before introducing Kaladin.

After Kaladin's talk, Dalinar closes the meeting by announcing the time and topic of the next meeting and gives one last invite to join the Slack Workspace.

Follow Up: The following day, Nichole, the Marketing Operations specialist at RadiantCloud sends out a follow-up email to everyone who registered for the meeting. The email recaps the announcements, along with links for joining the Slack Workspace and documentation for the new RadiantCloud features. And, the email closes with an invitation to register for the next user group meeting in a month.

The team gathers for an internal meeting to evaluate the night's activities. They discover the meeting is a success! They counted 75 attendees present and 35 new users in the Slack Workspace. They even found that some of the users were already chatting inside the Workspace.

Consequences

The creation of a User Group network is no small undertaking—it will require significant investment in time, money, and bandwidth. The larger the network desired, the more people required to organize, and it may be beneficial to have company employees somewhat local to each region in which the network is being created, at least to time zone/continental levels. (Encourage those employees to regularly attend the user group meetings to maximize interactivity and connection.)

At some point, the User Groups will need to be supported organically, or they will die off over time. Chances are strong that some will in certain areas anyway, no matter how much support your company puts into them. From the start, look to identify individuals within each region who are willing and able to handle the organization and administration of the user group; many such individuals are often willing to do so, so long as there is some level of financial and marketing support from the company.

User groups are a fantastic way to identify **Ambassadors (71)** within the community.

Variants

- **Guilds. Centers-of-Excellence:** When focused internally, DevRel can often organize internal user groups the same way it does external user groups, for much the same purpose: to provide a space in which the community of like-minded individuals can gather, share information, and mutually benefit from the conversation and support. In earlier business terminology, this was often called a "center of excellence," but the term fell out of use when it didn't turn out to be the panacea businesses expected it to be; more recently, the term "guilds" has come more to the fore. Resist temptations to make these organizational units (divisions, teams, etc.), instead preferring to keep them informal, open to anyone, and cross-organization—doing so will often encourage others who aren't currently working in that space to attend a meeting or two "just to see what it's all about" and create better communication between different roles within the company.

CHAPTER 38

Webinar

Topics: *Presentation*

An online presentation that is live and contains a limited element of interactivity between the audience and presenters.

Also Known As

Webex, Webcast, Vidcast, Web event, Virtual workshop

CHAPTER 38   WEBINAR

Intent

You have information that you want to disseminate to a large group, so you want to maximize reach, as well as collect the contact information for everyone who attends.

Context

This may be a part of your company's sales cycle to try and draw potential customers into the "top of the funnel" (as the Marketing types say), or it could be a series of videos designed to keep your users informed on the latest product features. In either case, keep your desired audience in mind.

For the sales-focused presentations, you often want your presentation to be more formal and "professional," similar to what might be seen in a more formal setting. It may be desirable to hold this presentation private to a particular customer, or a group of closely related customers (such as in a particular business domain your product/service is attempting to support or break into). These are often "gated," where registration is required to attend, and the registration information is passed to the Sales team as potential leads.

Solution

Hold a live **Webinar (469)**, an online presentation by a member of your DevRel team (or perhaps one of your **Ambassadors (71)**) at a scheduled time. Prepare a presentation topic, with or without demos as desired, and optionally record it for later viewing on a video platform such as YouTube or Vimeo. Read more about those videos in the **Recorded Video (363)** pattern.

If gathering leads is a priority, you may consider keeping the recording "gated" for a given amount of time before releasing it to the general public.

Participants

The host of the webinar is the guide of the show. They can either present alone or have guests. Having one or more guests will allow for the presentation to be a more natural conversation between the presenters, making the experience more comfortable for presenters and viewers alike. If the video is part of a series, bring in a variety of guests from inside and outside the company to offer varying perspectives on the topics.

Guests from inside the company will be experts on particular features of the product. They will provide valuable insight on the inner workings of those features because they were involved in the process of building them.

External guests are particularly valuable when the topic of the presentation is about how your product integrates with theirs. The webinar will likely benefit the guest as well and is a great **Partnership (309)** activity. The guest can talk in detail about their product and then both the host and guest will discuss how the two products combine to better serve users.

The third type of external guest is an industry expert that is brought on to the show to discuss a particular topic. The idea is that this expert would likely have a large following and that following would come watch the live video. This gives your product exposure and your company credibility, being associated with the expert.

Some webinars, if broadcast live, will look for audience participation, sometimes in the form of typed messages (chat), other times in the form of specific times for questions asked by the audience over voice.

Implementation

Producing and broadcasting webinars requires hardware and software for capturing and broadcasting video. Built-in cameras are usually sufficient for producing live webinars. Although, you should use an external microphone to clearly capture your voice and cut down on echoing. You

CHAPTER 38   WEBINAR

also want to make sure you have ample lighting shining on the presenter from the front, and minimize light in the background behind the speaker.

To broadcast the webinar, you'll need an account with a service that will capture and broadcast the video. Depending on whether you want to capture leads, you'll want to make sure the service supports attendee registration so you can capture contact information of the webinar attendees. Keep in mind that some marketing operations teams need to have that attendee information to sync with your company's CRM—such as Salesforce or HubSpot. Check with your marketing operations or sales teams to make sure the platform you choose integrates with your company's CRM product.

Metrics

- **Live Viewers:** The point of webinars is to inform with the intention of influencing viewers to action. For the viewers to act on the content of a webinar, they need to first be in attendance. The number of live viewers also informs you about the relevance of guests and/or webinar topics.

- **Recorded Viewers:** Webinar recordings can live on as video assets that can be useful for viewers who weren't able to attend live. Due to the format of webinars being closely related to a prepared presentation with slides, the viewing experience for watching the recording can provide a similar value to viewers as watching the live presentation. Recording viewers don't get to interact or ask live questions, but interactions are more the focus of **Live Stream (273)** presentations and not webinars.

CHAPTER 38   WEBINAR

Example

Julie's company provides a service that helps teams respond to incidents. She wants to provide a webinar that teaches organizations about the importance of establishing psychologically safe environments to allow for more effective incident response practices. Her marketing and sales departments agree that such content would be extremely interesting to their customers, and help Julie set up HubSpot to connect to Zoom so that it captures attendees' contact information as they register for the event which will be held in Zoom.

They schedule a date and time for the webinar and then write the copy of a social media post that everyone in the company can copy and paste into their networks to get the word out. They also plan on posting from the company's social media account several times before the event. The marketing operations team adds an announcement about the webinar in the company newsletter.

For content, Julie plans on piecing together slides from a couple of talks she gives at conferences, as well as including some insights from some research she's been doing on psychological safety.

On the day of the webinar Julie asks her teammate George to monitor the chat for questions. In case there are no questions from the audience, Julie also gives George a couple he can post to help get the Q&A section of the webinar going.

Consequences

Scheduling the webinar for a time that is most conducive to your target audience is critical; alternatively, consider scheduling the webinar multiple times, at times that are friendly to a particular segment of your audience (noon Central European time for your European customers, then noon Central Standard Time for US developers, for example). Taking that

471

CHAPTER 38 WEBINAR

little bit of extra effort to meet your customers where they are will go a long way in gaining their trust.

Webinar presentations are often very similar to a **Conference Session (197)** or a presentation given to one of your **User Group Network (457)**, and usually materials from one can be used here and vice versa. Keep in mind that no matter where the material is used, it takes time and practice before a presenter is "smooth" delivering the material, so consider holding the same webinar several times in order to get the material to a point of confident delivery.

Interactivity over a webinar is often not great, limited to questions through the "chat" functionality of most videoconferencing platforms. More recently, platforms have provided options for participants to signal using "gestures" (hand raised, thumbs-up, thumbs-down, etc.), but these usually imply that the participant is a full participant, and can voice questions; this may be undesirable for a webinar since you generally have little to no control over who can sign up for the presentation. (During the pandemic, several stories of "Zoom bombing" made the headlines, in which public Zoom presentations were "crashed" by individuals who would shout or display offensive things to the participants before they could be booted.) You may prefer to use a platform with a little less interactivity options for your audience to reduce the risk of these "bombers."

Webinars are generally more conceptual in nature, and often make for a strong tactic as part of the sales funnel or **Customer Pre-Sale Meeting (223)**. While nothing prevents the creation of a webinar that pairs well with, say, a **Guide (243)**, historically, these are rare.

Keep in mind that most low-interactivity high-reach activities are often consumed by developers without their full attention. (This is part of the problem with most online **Training (439)**, unfortunately.) The webinar is therefore not the best place to put high-detail information such as lists of configuration settings or syntax. Leave those minute details for **Reference Documentation (373)** and focus on the high-level concepts for the webinar.

CHAPTER 38   WEBINAR

Your goal for the webinar is to get the developer's attention on a certain topic and then direct them to one of your other resources such as a **Blog (105)**, **Reference Documentation (373)** or a **Guide (243)**.

Variants

- Live streams are the more casual, interactive sibling of webinars. They tend to be less scripted and less structured programs. The audience is usually encouraged to interact more with the panel, and the panel will normally prioritize addressing the questions and comments from the audience over sticking strictly to an agenda.

- Online workshop is an interactive event that covers a single topic. The format is similar to an in-person **Workshop (476)**, where the content and instructors guide attendees through a series of **Tutorials (451)** on a single topic. The difference is the presenter carries out the workshop over a webinar or streaming platform such as StreamYard or Zoom.

- Online conference is an online event consisting of multiple sessions that may cover various topics, much like a regular **Conference (179)**. While it's possible to present the conference over a simple webinar tool such as Zoom, usually online conferences are delivered over event platform services like RingCentral Events. These tools have features that allow for sessions to be scheduled and run concurrently. There are also areas for sponsors to connect attendees in virtual exhibit halls.

CHAPTER 39

Workshop

Topics: *Presentation, Code*

A workshop serves a specific purpose. It's not just about learning new skills or understanding a specific topic. It's about applying that knowledge in a practical setting. Participants engage in coding tasks, live demos, and problem-solving activities to learn how to use a product, tool, or technology. The workshop's emphasis on active participation and real-time feedback allows attendees to apply what they've learned and ask questions as they go. The goal is to provide practical knowledge and foster a deeper connection with the showcased technology or product.

CHAPTER 39   WORKSHOP

Also Known As

Hands-on lab, training session, bootcamp, tutorial session, interactive session, skills lab, learning lab, technical deep dive, developer training, and practical session

Intent

A workshop is more than just a learning session—it's an interactive and immersive experience. It's a place where participants, particularly developers or technical professionals, can engage in practical exercises and gain hands-on experience with a specific technology, tool, or product. This hands-on approach is a key feature of workshops, distinguishing them from passive learning methods like listening to presentations or watching demos. The goal is to move beyond passive learning and instead engage attendees in practical exercises that allow them to apply their learning in real time. Workshops are designed to help developers or technical professionals build new skills, solve real-world problems, and deepen their understanding of how a product or technology works. The workshop's interactive and immersive nature empowers participants to become more confident and proficient in using the technology being showcased, offering guided, step-by-step instruction combined with opportunities for experimentation and direct feedback. Ultimately, the intent is to foster a stronger connection between the participants and the product or technology, increasing the developer community's adoption, engagement, and trust.

Context

The context for a workshop typically involves a focused, hands-on learning environment where developers, engineers, or technical professionals come together to gain practical experience with a specific product, tool, or

CHAPTER 39 WORKSHOP

technology. Workshops are usually part of more significant events such as **Conferences (179)**, **Hackathons (255)**, or **User Group (457)** meetings, or they can be stand-alone sessions offered by a company or organization. They are designed to address the needs of participants who want deeper, practical engagement instead of just theoretical knowledge or high-level overviews. Workshops are structured to provide real-time guidance and support, often led by subject matter experts or Developer Relations team members. The highly interactive sessions allow attendees to work on coding challenges, solve problems, and explore use cases that mirror real-world scenarios. Participants often expect to leave the workshop with tangible skills they can immediately apply to their work or projects. The context also includes creating an environment where developers feel comfortable asking questions, experimenting, and troubleshooting to foster a collaborative and immersive learning experience.

Solution

The solution for a workshop is to create a well-structured, hands-on session that allows participants to actively engage with the specific product, tool, or technology being taught. This involves designing a detailed curriculum that breaks down complex concepts into manageable tasks, guiding participants step by step through practical exercises that help them apply what they're learning in real time. The workshop should include demonstrations, live coding, and interactive problem-solving, allowing attendees to experiment with the technology and troubleshoot challenges as they arise.

The workshop should be tailored to the audience's skill level, ensuring that the content is accessible to beginners while still providing depth for more advanced users. It's important to offer clear, concise instructions and provide support throughout the session, either through direct guidance from the instructor or with the help of additional staff who can assist

477

participants. This hands-on, interactive approach reinforces learning by encouraging active participation and immediate application of the concepts.

The environment should be collaborative, fostering a sense of community with opportunities for participants to ask questions, receive feedback, and share their own insights. By the end of the workshop, attendees should have a stronger understanding of how to use the product or technology in their own work, along with a sense of confidence in applying the practical skills they've learned. The workshop solution aims to leave participants with practical, usable knowledge and a positive, engaging experience with the product or tool, fostering deeper connections within the developer community.

Participants

The participants in a workshop typically include the **instructor** or **facilitator**, the **support staff** or **co-facilitators**, and the **attendees**. The instructor is usually a subject matter expert or a member of the Developer Relations team who leads the session. They are responsible for guiding the attendees through the workshop, explaining concepts, demonstrating the use of tools or technologies, and leading hands-on exercises. The instructor interacts with the attendees by answering questions, providing real-time feedback, and ensuring everyone can follow the material.

The support staff or co-facilitators play a complementary role by offering additional assistance to attendees who may need help troubleshooting issues, setting up their development environments, or understanding specific aspects of the workshop. They circulate the room or engage with participants online in virtual workshops, ensuring no one falls behind. Their role is crucial for maintaining the pace of the workshop while allowing the instructor to stay focused on delivering the main content.

The attendees are developers, engineers, or technical professionals looking to gain hands-on experience with the product or technology being taught. They actively engage by following along with the exercises, asking questions when encountering difficulties, and collaborating with the instructor and fellow participants. Attendees might share their insights or experiences, contributing to a collaborative learning environment. The interaction between the instructor, support staff, and attendees creates a dynamic, interactive session where participants can learn by doing and get immediate feedback on their progress. This fosters a productive learning experience and strengthens the connection between the participants and the technology being explored.

Implementation

A workshop begins with **careful planning and curriculum design**. The first step is identifying the specific product, tool, or technology that will be the workshop's focus, ensuring that it addresses a relevant need or challenge within the developer community. The workshop should have a clear set of learning objectives outlining what participants should be able to achieve by the end of the session. The content is meticulously designed to be hands-on, focusing on real-world applications, so participants can directly apply what they learn during the session to their projects, empowering them with practical knowledge.

Next, the **workshop structure** is created, usually broken into distinct sections such as a brief introduction, live demonstrations, hands-on coding exercises, and a closing Q&A or review. The introduction provides context for the technology or product, explaining why it's valuable and how it fits into broader industry trends or challenges. The live demonstrations offer a step-by-step walkthrough of key concepts, tools, or workflows, giving participants a visual and practical understanding of the technology's work. The workshop's core is the hands-on exercises, where participants follow guided instructions to apply the concepts they've learned. These exercises should gradually increase complexity, allowing participants to build confidence with each task. Throughout the workshop, attendees should be encouraged to experiment, ask questions, and troubleshoot issues as they arise.

The **technical setup** for the workshop is crucial. Before the event, participants should receive instructions on setting up their development environments, including any necessary software, tools, or resources they will need to follow along. Participants should have access to products or cloud resources, such as sandboxes, that enable them to work with the services they are learning about. Instructors should ensure that all the technical requirements are communicated and that support is available to help participants get set up. During the workshop, additional facilitators or support staff should be present to assist with technical issues, ensuring that the instructor can maintain the session flow without interruptions. This may also include providing pre-configured environments, such as cloud instances, Docker containers, or virtual machines, to simplify the setup process and reduce participant friction.

Once the workshop is in progress, **active engagement** is key. The instructor should use interactive elements such as polls, live coding, or group activities to keep participants engaged. There should be regular pauses for questions and clarification to ensure that everyone is keeping up with the material. The instructor, always understanding the diverse learning paces, must remain flexible, adapting the pace of the workshop based on the feedback and progress of the participants. It's essential to foster a collaborative atmosphere, where participants feel comfortable asking questions and offering insights. This not only encourages participation but also fosters a culture of knowledge sharing.

After the main content has been covered, the workshop concludes with a **Q&A session and a recap** of the material. This is a pivotal part of the workshop as it allows participants to ask any remaining questions and solidify their understanding of what they've learned. Instructors should provide additional resources, such as links to documentation, sample code, or follow-up tutorials, so participants can continue to explore the technology on their own. A post-workshop survey is also a valuable tool for gathering feedback from participants, helping the Developer Relations team improve future workshops.

Finally, **post-workshop support and follow-up** are crucial to ensure continued engagement. After the workshop, the Developer Relations team should make the session materials available, including recordings, slides, and code examples. They should also encourage participants to reach out with additional questions or issues through dedicated community channels or follow-up office hours. This follow-up helps strengthen the relationship between the company and the developer community, ensuring that the workshop has a lasting impact beyond the event itself.

Metrics

To document the metrics for a workshop, it is essential to track both quantitative and qualitative data that measure the workshop's success, engagement, and impact. The first metric to consider is **attendance**, including the number of registered participants versus those who attended. This helps gauge the level of interest in the topic and the effectiveness of pre-event promotion. Alongside attendance, tracking the **drop-off rate**—how many participants leave before the workshop ends—provides insight into the engagement and quality of the content. High retention rates suggest that the workshop was engaging and well-paced, while significant drop-offs may indicate areas for improvement.

Engagement during the workshop is another critical metric. This can be measured by how actively participants engage with the content through asking questions, participating in polls, or completing hands-on exercises. For virtual workshops, tracking metrics like the number of chat interactions, questions submitted, or activity on collaborative tools such as shared code repositories or live demos will give a clear view of how interactive and engaging the session was. The engagement can be tracked for in-person workshops through facilitator feedback and observing how many participants actively participate in coding tasks or discussions.

Post-workshop feedback is crucial to understanding the effectiveness of the session. Attendee surveys, immediately following the workshop or a few days later, can provide valuable qualitative data on how well the content was understood, what was most beneficial, and what areas need improvement. Survey questions should cover the instruction's clarity, the exercises' quality, and whether participants felt they had gained valuable skills they could apply to their projects.

Completion rates for hands-on exercises or coding challenges provide insight into how well the material was absorbed. Tracking how many participants completed all exercises versus those who struggled or gave up can indicate whether the difficulty level was appropriate and whether the support during the session was sufficient.

Follow-up actions should also be tracked. This includes the number of participants who continue to engage with the company or product post-workshop, such as by joining community channels, downloading related resources, or signing up for follow-up events. Tracking how many attendees become active users of the product or service featured in the workshop is an essential metric for determining the workshop's long-term impact.

Finally, **overall satisfaction**, collected through post-event surveys, helps quantify how likely participants are to recommend the workshop to others, clearly indicating the workshop's success and its value to the community. These metrics should be documented in a comprehensive report that includes numerical data and qualitative insights. Charts and graphs can be used to visualize trends, and a summary section should provide recommendations for improving future workshops based on the data collected.

Example

Imagine a developer relations team at CloudTech, specializing in cloud infrastructure services, planning to create and publish a workshop titled "Building Scalable Microservices on CloudTech's Platform." The workshop aims to teach developers how to deploy and manage microservices using CloudTech's specific tools and infrastructure. The workshop is aimed at intermediate-level developers with experience in cloud computing and containerized applications.

The first step is **planning**. The Developer Relations team collaborates with CloudTech's product engineers to establish clear learning objectives, such as grasping microservices architecture principles and mastering the deployment, scaling, and monitoring of microservices on CloudTech's platform. They craft a hands-on curriculum that features step-by-step exercises, enabling participants to set up a microservices environment, deploy their services, and utilize CloudTech's monitoring tools to assess performance. The workshop, designed to be approximately three hours long, includes live demonstrations by the instructor and coding exercises for participants, providing a unique hands-on learning experience.

Once the content is ready, the team moves into **promotion**. They create a landing page for the workshop on the CloudTech website and promote it via **Social Media (395)**, **Newsletters (281)**, and **developer forums (233)**. The workshop is open to 50 participants, and registrations fill up quickly due to the topic's relevance. Attendees receive an email a week before the workshop with instructions on preparing, including downloading necessary software and setting up their development environments.

On the workshop day, the instructor starts with an engaging introduction, elucidating the significance of scalable microservices and how CloudTech's platform can efficiently manage them. Following the introduction, the instructor guides the participants through the process of deploying their first microservice, offering explanations and presenting live demos. Participants actively follow along, completing the exercises on their own machines. The **support staff**, comprising CloudTech engineers, are on standby via chat to assist participants in resolving any issues. The workshop unfolds seamlessly, with the instructor frequently pausing for Q&A sessions to ensure everyone is on track, fostering an interactive and engaging learning environment.

At the workshop's conclusion, participants successfully deployed and scaled their microservices on CloudTech's platform. The instructor wraps up with a recap of the key takeaways and encourages participants to join CloudTech's developer community, offering them a platform for continuous learning and support. All workshop materials, including the code examples and video recordings, are shared with attendees after the session, along with a survey to gather feedback. This commitment to post-workshop support, including access to the developer community and free trials of the platform, underscores CloudTech's dedication to the participants' ongoing learning and professional growth.

Following the workshop, the Developer Relations team documents the event's success. **Metrics** are collected, including the number of participants who attended versus those who registered, engagement during the session (measured by questions and exercises completed), and post-workshop survey results. Feedback is overwhelmingly positive, with many participants praising the hands-on approach and the immediate applicability of the content. Some attendees suggest adding advanced exercises for future sessions, providing valuable insights for the team's next workshop. The team also tracks **follow-up actions**, such as how many participants joined CloudTech's community channels or signed up for free platform trials.

Based on the success of this workshop, CloudTech's Developer Relations team plans to run a series of workshops with a similar format. The team will use the feedback and data gathered from this session to refine their approach and ensure that future workshops continue to provide valuable, hands-on learning experiences for the developer community.

Consequences

The consequences of a workshop impact both the Developer Relations team and the company or organization. For the Developer Relations team, a successful workshop strengthens their credibility and reputation as effective educators and community leaders. It allows them to build stronger connections with the developer community by offering valuable, hands-on learning experiences that address real-world challenges. A well-executed workshop can increase developers' trust, engagement, and loyalty, positioning the team as a reliable resource for learning and problem-solving. However, if the workshop is poorly executed—whether due to technical difficulties, unclear content, or lack of support—it can harm the Developer Relations team's reputation, leading to frustration among participants and a loss of trust in the team's ability to deliver high-quality educational experiences.

For the company or organization, the outcomes of a workshop can have both immediate and long-term effects. A successful workshop can increase product adoption by providing developers with the skills and confidence to use the company's tools and technologies effectively. It can also drive positive word-of-mouth, leading to greater visibility and interest in the company's offerings within the developer community. Additionally, workshops allow the company to gather feedback on their products, identifying potential areas for improvement based on participants' experiences. On the other hand, if the workshop fails to deliver value, it can result in negative perceptions of the company's products or services, potentially causing developers to disengage or look for alternatives. A poorly received workshop may also negatively affect the company's ability to support and educate its users, which could impact current customers and future prospects.

Overall, workshops carry significant consequences for both the Developer Relations team and the company. A well-executed workshop can build strong relationships, increase product usage, and enhance the company's standing within the developer community. Conversely, a poorly executed workshop can damage trust, reduce engagement, and negatively affect the perception of both the team and the company.

Variants

The variants of a workshop can take several forms, each tailored to different learning objectives, audience sizes, and levels of interaction. One common variant is the **in-person workshop**, which takes place at conferences, meetups, or company-hosted events. These workshops offer an immersive experience with face-to-face interaction, direct engagement, and hands-on support, making it easier for attendees to ask questions and collaborate with others in real time. While they are limited by location and the number of attendees who can participate, the engagement and connection they provide are unparalleled.

Another variant is the **virtual workshop**, conducted online through Zoom, Microsoft Teams, or other webinar tools. Virtual workshops are accessible to a global audience and provide flexibility for participants who cannot attend in person. These workshops often include interactive elements like breakout rooms, shared code environments, and real-time chat for questions and feedback. While they offer convenience and a broader reach, virtual workshops can face challenges with maintaining engagement and troubleshooting technical issues for participants in remote environments.

Hands-on labs are a more technical variant of a workshop where participants work on a predefined series of tasks or challenges, often in a sandboxed environment. These labs focus heavily on skill-building, allowing participants to learn at their own pace. Step-by-step instructions with minimal live instruction typically guide them, and support is available as needed. Hands-on labs are ideal for technical deep dives where participants must explore complex tools or workflows.

Another variant is a **hackathon-style workshop**, where participants are given more freedom to work on creative or open-ended projects related to the technology being showcased. These workshops often focus on problem-solving, collaboration, and innovation, with participants working in teams or individually to build solutions within a set time frame. This variant encourages experimentation and creativity but requires clear structure and support to guide participants toward achieving their goals.

Lastly, there are **tutorial-based workshops**, which are more structured and instructional. These workshops typically focus on teaching a specific skill or technology through a detailed, step-by-step approach. The instructor leads participants through a series of exercises or lessons, with frequent pauses for questions and feedback. Tutorial-based workshops effectively introduce new technologies or concepts and ensure participants leave with a solid foundational understanding.

Each variant serves different purposes, and the choice of which to use depends on the specific learning objectives, the audience's needs, and the logistical considerations of the event. The adaptability of these variants empowers Developer Relations teams to flexibly plan workshops in various settings, ensuring that participants gain practical, hands-on experience in ways that best suit their learning preferences and goals.

Index

A

Abstractions, 67
Accessibility, 324, 334, 339, 358
Accountability, 423
Accuracy, 376
Active engagement, 480
Activity pattern documentation
    consequences, 13
    context, 10
    example, 12
    implementation, 11
    intent, 10
    metrics, 12
    participants, 11
    pattern name, 9
    resources, 10
    solution, 11
    variants, 13
Activity patterns, 7–9
    catalog, 8, 22
Adoption metrics, 302
Advertising, 462, 463
AMA, *see* Ask Me Anything (AMA)
Ambassadors, 37, 40, 42, 47, 50, 70, 71, 134, 190, 209, 235, 253, 286, 331, 343, 379, 403, 411, 437, 447, 449, 458, 463, 466
    communications, 84, 85
    conference booth, 73
    content, 72
    developer relations teams, 72
    Engineering team, 85
    forums, 73
    marketing and sales departments, 88
    participants, 73
    to product/service, 72
Ambassadors program
    acceptance criteria, 82
    activities, 74, 80
    announce, 77
    announce program, 75
    DCom, 81
    evaluate candidates internally, 76
    healthy feedback loop, 79
    identify potential Ambassadors, 76
    news and information, 78
    organizational access, 74
    periodically review and call, 77
    review program size, 78
    "touch" rate, 80
    turnover, 79

Ambassadors program (*cont.*)
    waiting list, 80
    work out benefits, 75
API, *see* Application programming interface (API)
Application programming interface (API)
    Client Library, 382
    developers, 360
    endpoints, 358
    integration points, 359
    internal services, 362
    product/service, 357
App Store, 30
Article Editor, 91
Articles, 38, 50, 112, 122, 130, 135, 390, 397, 400, 437, 448
    authors, 95, 96
    cancellation clause, 92
    citation rate, 97
    click-through rate, 97
    content-management systems, 97
    copyedit review, 96
    cross-system reader tracking, 98
    CTA, 98
    deadline, 93
    "Dev" than "Ops", 99
    engineering team, 91
    final editing, 92
    free trials, 98
    internal notifications, 100
    "introductory", 101
    iterate, 95
    legal team, 92
    length, 93
    marketing, 100
    marketing team, 92
    online magazine publisher, 99
    outcomes, 101
    outline/story, 94, 95
    product/service, 101, 102
    reference rate, 97
    semi-direct, 91
    target audience, 93, 94
    voice, 94
    Webpack, 99
    web views, 97
    white papers, 103
Ask Me Anything (AMA), 290, 356
Assessment, 414
Attendance, 481
Attendees, 323, 478
Audience demographics, 114
Audio-only podcast, 339
Authority, 334

B

Backlinks, 114
Bandwidth, 305
Blog Post pattern
    author(s), 107, 108
    company or organization, 107, 108
    developer community, 107, 108
    editor(s), 107, 108

INDEX

Blog posts, 14, 16, 24, 30, 38, 50, 61, 69, 102, 105, 135, 177, 246, 310, 371, 389, 390, 392, 394, 397, 399, 400, 420
- aims, 106
- around thematic periods, 109
- audience demographics, 114
- author, 106, 115
- Backlinks, 114
- bounce rate, 113
- cadence, 109
- citation rate, 114
- click-through Rate, 112
- comments and discussions, 113
- content, 106, 107
- content planning, 109
- content planning phase, 115
- context, 107
- conversion rate, 114
- CTR, 114
- editing and review phase, 110
- editor for review, 116
- interview, "ask me anything," or Q&A, 120
- metrics, 112
- opinion pieces, 120
- page views, 112
- participants, 107
- personal blogs, 111
- post-publication engagement, 110, 114
- post-publication phase, 117
- product announcement, 119
- publishing and promotion, 110
- publishing phase, 116
- reference rate, 113
- reference traffic, 113
- roundup posts, 120
- schedule, 109
- SEO, 114
- social shares, 113
- synonymous, 106
- technical tutorial, 119
- thought leadership posts, 119
- time on page, 112, 113
- topic selection, 108
- unique visitors metric, 112
- visual aids, 107
- writing phase, 110, 116

Blogs, 85, 122, 287, 292, 301, 374
BlueSky, 396
Book of the Runtime (BotR), 136
Books, 69, 86, 102, 118, 121, 253
- as Articles, 135
- as Blog posts, 135
- compensation and licensing, 124
- contract, 128
- customer commitment, 134
- deadline, 125
- DevRel team, 134
- diagrams, 133
- documentation, 122
- draft ready, 128
- e-books, 135
- guide, 122
- handbook, 122
- internal book, 136

INDEX

Books (*cont.*)
   layout, 124
   length, 125
   long-form writing, 123
   manual, 122
   manuscript, 129
   material, 122
   metrics
      downloads, 129
      draft-ready, 131
      giveaways, 130
      mentions, 130
   .NET developers, 136
   outline/story, 127, 128
   participants
      author(s), 123
      copyeditors, 124
      developmental editors, 123
      technical reviewers, 123
   playbook, 122
   proposal, 124
   publication on topic, 134
   publisher, 128
   reviewers/copyeditors, 129
   as Swag, 135
   target audience, 125, 126
   voice, 126, 127
   writing cost, 134
Booth, 40, 86, 130, 135, 182, 208, 262, 397, 411, 430
   act professional and approachable, 144
   attendee information, 142, 148
   bold branding, 148
   at conference, 138
   conference event, 140
   demonstrations, 141
   design, 140
   engagement activities, 142, 148
   feedback mechanism, 142, 148
   interaction with target audience, 149
   materials, 144
   metrics, 145
      adoption count, 147
      follow-up count, 146, 147
      live product demos, 146
      swag count, 146
      traditional, 146
      visitor count, 145
   non-trivial time commitment, 143
   number of attendees who watch each demo, 146
   participants
      Attendees, 140
      Booth Staff, 139
      Demo Presenters, 139
      Logistics Team, 139
   pit crew, 149, 150
   position, 141
   post-event report, 144
   product/service, 149
   setup and teardown, 141
   staff training, 143, 148
Bots, 400
Brand exposure, 325
Branding, 320, 327

INDEX

Branding elements, 324
Brand perception, 350
Brand team, 398
BrightLedger, 269, 270
Budget, 17
Budget-based patterns, 19
Bugs, 376, 385, 392
Bug triage, 362
BuildFlow, 285
Business impacts, 302

C

Cadence, 339
Call to action, 277
Call-to-Action (CTA), 98
Campaign, 24, 25
Careful planning, 479
Case studies, 26, 61, 72, 151, 177, 360
   aims, 152
   biased/unconvincing, 164
   challenges, 154
   consequences, 163, 164
   content creation phase, 161
   context, 153
   data analytics, 162
   Developer Relations team, 163
   implementation
      content creation phase, 157
      identify suitable candidate, 156
      information gathering phase, 156
      initiate contact, 156
      monitored and evaluated, 158
      publication and distribution phase, 157
      review and approval process, 157
      visual design, 157
   implementation phase, 154
   implementation process, 161
   interviews, 161
   as marketing tool, 164
   market presence and reputation, 163
   metrics, 158
      backlinks, 159
      bounce rate, 158
      conversion rates, 159
      engagement time, 158
      feedback and interactions, 159
      internal feedback, 159
      lead generation, 159
      overall ROI, 159
      page views or downloads, 158
      social shares and referral traffic, 159
   narrative approach, 154
   participants, 155
      audience or readers, 155
      collaborative process, 156
      customer, 155

INDEX

Case studies (*cont.*)
    developer relations
      team, 155
      product or service team, 155
  performance, 162
  as powerful narrative, 151
  publication phase, 162
  results section, 154, 161
  review process, 162
  ShopEase, 160
  solution, 153
  story begins, 160
  variants, 166
    comparative case study, 165
    industry-specific case
      study, 165
    multi-customer case
      study, 165
    problem–solution case
      study, 166
    success story, 165
    technical deep dive, 165
    video case study, 166
  visualizations, 160
Case Study pattern, 153, 163, 165
Centers-of-excellence, 466
Certification, 439, 449
Champions program, 83
Channels for distribution, 416
CI/CD movement, 33
Citation rate, 114
C++ legacy libraries, 28
Click-through rates (CTR), 114, 284
CloudBuilder, 422, 423

CloudConnect, 303–305
CloudForge, 260, 285
CloudTech, 483, 484
Code, 18
CodeFlow, 115
  developer blog, 116
  social media channels, 116
CodeForge, 293
CodeFusion, 269
Code Gym, 266
CodeLink, 409, 410
Code-of-conduct, 279
CodeRanger, 401
Code reviews, 167, 263,
    264, 290
  collaborative, 168
  community-focused, 167
  consequences, 176, 177
  context, 169, 170
  example, 175, 176
  implementation, 172, 173
  intent, 168, 169
  internal code review, 177
  metrics, 173, 174
    business influence
      metrics, 174
    community engagement
      metrics, 174
    participation metrics, 173
    quality improvement
      metrics, 174
  participants
    developer Relations team
      members, 171

INDEX

external developers and engineers, 171
internal software engineers, 171
product owners, 171
sessions/webinars, 173
solution, 170
tool, 390
CodeSphere, 284, 285, 430, 446
Coding, 29
Coding demo, 365
Codist, 26–28, 33, 51, 55, 61, 66
   executive team, 27, 28
   launch, 33, 34
   Product team, 26
Co-facilitators, 478
Communication, 304, 324, 414, 424, 434, 435
Communication strategies, 421
Community, 21
   contributors, 300
   engagement, 307, 336, 347
   engagement survey, 426
   growth, 302
   hours, 290
   roundup, 287
   survey, 292
Company, 21
Company or organization, 118
Competitors, 305
Completion rates, 482
Conferences, 85, 179, 262, 274, 405, 406
   booth, 73

"call for proposals" (CFP), 190
CodeStream Solutions, 187
consequences, 193, 194
create "buzz", 181
DevOps-centered, 190
fierce debate and discussion, 188
high-interactivity event, 180
implementation
   community engagement strategies, 183
   content planning, 183
   logistics front, 183
   post-conference actions, 183
"lounge area", 189
metrics, 183
   attendee feedback, 184
   brand visibility and exposure, 185
   deal acceleration, 186
   networking activity, 185
   overall attendee satisfaction with the event, 186
   registration and attendance, 184
   ROI, 185
   session attendance, 184
   sponsorship effectiveness, 186
Mixer, 320
participants, 182
   attendees, 182
   organizing team, 182
   speakers, 182
   vendors and partners, 182

INDEX

Conferences (*cont.*)
    party, 325
    preparation, 188
    "quiet zone", 189
    solution, 181
    staff members, 191
    StreamCon, 187
    team, 188, 191, 193
    TechReady, TechWeek, 195
    themes and content, 190
    website, 192
Conference sessions, 24, 27, 40, 63, 72, 86, 101, 102, 117, 130, 149, 177, 182, 193, 197, 198, 208–210, 226, 261, 286, 310, 389, 390, 397, 400, 430, 437
    aims, 205
    brief introduction, 205
    communication channel, 208
    complex information, 199
    effectiveness, 208
    implementation
        content creation, 201
        delivery, 202
        engagement strategies, 202
        financial and logistical requirements, 203
        rehearsing, 202
    metrics, 203
        audience retention, 204
        content sharing, 205
        engagement levels, 203
        overall attendee satisfaction, 205
        post-session follow-up engagement, 204
        quality of content delivery, 204
        session attendance, 203
        social media impact, 204
        speaker performance, 204
    participants
        Audience, 200
        Company Stakeholders and Management Leadership, 200
        Conference Organizer, 201
        Event Staff, 201
        presenters, 200
        Session Moderators, 200
    Q&A segment, 207, 208
    rehearsals, 207
    solution, 199
    surface area, 199
    validation, 206
    variants
        Beta/Buzz Talk, 209
        Meetup Session, 209
        Sponsored Conference Session, 210
Conference Talk, 13, 16, 17
Confidentiality agreement, 35
Content-creation endeavor, 397
Content effectiveness, 349
Content-management systems (CMS), 97, 249, 351
Content planning, 115
Context, 5

INDEX

Conversion rate, 114
Copy Editor, 91
Core contributors, 300
Cost-effectiveness, 326
Course author, 441
Course coordinator, 442
createCharacter, 377–379
Creation, 442
Curriculum design, 479
Customer, 21
Customer check-in, 24, 59, 61, 213, 290
    active listening and empathy, 215
    CodeSpark, 218, 219
    consequences, 219, 220
    consistent and intentional process, 215
    essential, 214
    implementation, 216
        conferences, 216
        conversation, 216
        feedback, 217
    intent, 214
    legal, 220
    metrics, 217
        bugs filed, 218
        diversity of customer profiles, 217
        feature requests submitted, 218
        frequency, 217
        long-term impact, 218
        number of check-ins, 217
        resolution tracking, 218
        surveys, 218
    participants
        collaborative and conversational, 216
        Community Manager, 215
        decision-makers, 215
        Developer Advocate, 215
        developers, 215
    partner meeting, 221
    virtual meeting, 218
Customer Pre-Sale Meetings, 135
Customer pre-sales, 38–40, 43–45, 49, 63, 223
    consequences
        direct, 229
        indirect, 230
        significant risk, 230
    customer engagement, 224
    decision-making process, 225
    DevRel's role, 225
    evaluation phase, 225
    implementation, 227
    metrics, 228
    participants
        level of participation, 226
        marketing, 226
        product managers' involvement, 227
        sales, 226
    pre-sale approach, 224
    process, 224
    technical advocacy, 224
    at TechNova, 228, 229

INDEX

Customer pre-sale (*cont.*)
    variants
        Architecture Review Pre-Sale, 231
        PoC pre-sale, 231
        Technical Workshop Pre-Sale, 231
    visibility, 226
Customer support, 434

D

DataForge, 160
DCom, 26, 58
    Champions, 81–84
    executive team, 26–28
    Social Media, 64
    team, 28–31
    VP of Developer Relations, 26
DCom-related activities, 82
Decouple platform ownership, 367
Dedicated developer, 438
Designing object-oriented software, 2
Developer-focused organization, 407
Developer Relations team, 118
Developers, 283, 367, 379, 382, 388, 452
    advocates, 20, 283
    audience, 1, 281, 284
    clinics, 294
    community, 282
    digest, 287

    experience, 415
    office hours, 291
    relations, 414
    relations team, 20, 300, 301, 306, 322, 436
    support, 434
DevRel, 29, 34, 285, 311, 312, 335, 357–359, 397–399, 427, 436, 438, 446, 448
    campaign, 25, 26
    engineers, 7
    Q3 Planning Meeting, 50, 51, 58–66
    team, 2, 20, 29, 269, 274, 291, 292, 360, 361, 399, 400, 402, 403, 410
    team Q1 planning, 36–41
    team's Q2 planning meeting, 41–47
DevTech, 422, 423
Digital swag, 431
Direction, 15
Disclaimers, 402
Discord, 396
Distribution methods, 418
Docker, 271, 272
Documentation, 445
Drop-in widgets, 386
Drop-off rate, 481

E

E-books, 135
Eco-friendly swag, 431

e-commerce, 278
Ecosystem, 300
Edge-case handling, 388
Edge-case scenarios, 437
Editing, 344
Editors, 116, 365
End-to-end process, 420
Engagement levels, 325
Engineering team, 337
Engineers, 283, 383
Enterprise-level features, 307
Entertainment, 323
Entertainment-centric event, 321
Entire product trials, 269
Error users, 377
Evaluation, 414
Event-based surveys, 425
Event organizers, 322
Examples, 43
Execution, 444
Executive meeting, 33, 62
Executive team's H2 review and planning, 48–58
Exit surveys, 426
Experiential swag, 431
Expert Q&A Sessions, 294
Extension, 358
Extension frameworks, 386

F

FAANG companies, 30
Facebook/Meta, 396, 402
Facilitator, 478

Fear of Missing Out (FOMO), 75, 181, 322
Feature feedback survey, 425
Feedback, 416
    collection, 326
    form, 414
Fidget spinners, 428
Final editing, 92
Flash drives, 428
Flexibility, 339
Flying Monkeys, 428
Follow-up, 481
    actions, 482
    meetings, 185
    surveys, 445
Forces, 8
ForgeEdge, 260
Forums, 73, 74, 85, 192, 234, 253, 290, 292, 374, 380, 389, 394, 437
    Ambassadors, 242
    "Code of Conduct", 239
    Code Reviews, 242
    company's participants, 239
    conversations, 238
    extensions/providers, 242
    Guides/Reference Documentation, 242
    hosting forums, 241
    implementation, 237–241
    legal, 238
    metrics, 240
        post-response time, 241
        posts, 240

INDEX

Forums (*cont.*)
    post views, 240
    upvotes, 241
  participants
    authors, 236
    moderators, 236
    operations staff, 236
    readers, 236
  platforms, 241
  pre-built ("turnkey") packages and services, 236
  samples, 242
  SDKs or Samples/Examples, 242
  solution, 234, 235
  Technical Support, 242
  Tech Support team, 242
  variants
    developer portals, 242
    Jira, 242
    wiki, 242
Freebies, 428
Frequency of use, 268

G

Gamified tutorials, 456
Gang of Four (GoF), 5
  book, 24
  pattern language, 24
  patterns, 20
Gateway, 362
GDE program, 30
Gist, 294, 394
GitHub, 301, 304, 379, 389, 394
GitLab, 301, 389
Give-and-take relationship, 318
Giveaways, 428
GiveCamp, 261
Good-natured ribbing, 403
Google, 56
GraphQL, 362
Group organizers, 459
Guest-centric questions, 355
Guests, 469
Guides, 66, 134, 194, 243, 270, 379, 384, 389, 445, 448, 452, 453
  acceptable quality, 248
  Ambassador, 253
  Articles, 253
  Conference Sessions, 253
  documentation, 253
  domains, 246
  in draft state, 247
  implementation, 247, 248
  intent, 244
  metrics, 249, 251
    audience demographics, 251
    bounce rate, 251
    citation rate, 251
    click-through rate, 250
    page views, 249
    reference rate, 250
    time on page, 250, 251
    unique visitors, 249
    visualizations, 251
  newsletter, 250
  participants
    author, 246

INDEX

copyeditor, 246
editors, 246
technical reviewer, 247
technical writer, 246
reference documentation, 253
solution, 245, 246
at TechNova, 252
variants
    API Integration Guide, 254
    Best Practices Guide, 254
    Comprehensive Tutorial, 254
    Migration Guide, 254
    Quick Start Guide, 254
    Troubleshooting Guide, 254
Guilds, 466

H

Hackathon, 67, 193, 195, 211
    code review, 263, 264
    communication, 257
    community of developers, 256
    creativity and innovation, 258
    developers, 260
    get-to-market, 256
    infrastructure and sponsorship, 258
    metrics, 259, 260
    participants, 257
    participation, 261
    products/services, 256
    sponsors, 258
    time frame, 257
    tools, 258, 259
Hackathon-style workshop, 487
Hands-on experiences, 324
Hands-on-labs, 67, 448, 486
High Flying models, 368
Host, 321
Hostile witness, 343
Hosting, 341
Hosting video, 364
H1 planning meeting, 31
HTTP method, 377
HubSpot, 470
Hyperlinks, 400

I

IDE integrations, 31
In-person Office Hours, 193
In-person workshop, 486
Inquiry, 414
Instagram, 402
Instructor, 441, 478
Integration, 358
Interactions, 277
Interactive elements, 328
Interactive tutorials, 456
Interactivity, 14, 472
Internal conference, 211
Internal training, 448
Internet, 444
Investment, 268
Iterators, 3

INDEX

J

Java and C# developers, 55
Java community, 21
JavaScript developers, 31, 460
JetBrains, 394

K

Kansas City Developer Conference (KCDC), 40, 46, 47
KCDC announcement, 83
Kerim, 369
Key performance indicators (KPIs), 420
Kitchen Sink, 393
KPIs, *see* Key performance indicators (KPIs)
Kubernetes, 410

L

Language learning models, 379
Language-specific developer package, 386
Large language models (LLMs), 364
Leadership, 283
Learning retreat, 439
Lightweight components, 386
LinkedIn, 396, 402
LinkedIn Live, 278, 401
Listener feedback, 349
Listenership, 348
Lists, 3
Live coding, 278, 279
Live playground
    capabilities, 265
    coding sessions, 267
    configuration, 266
    consequences, 270, 271
    creators, 267
    environment, 267
    hosting costs, 268
    infrastructure, 268
    installing, 266
    metrics, 268, 269
    pre-configured scenarios, 266
    product features, 267
    resource, 271
    user session, 268
    variants, 271, 272
Live streaming, 275, 287, 294, 354, 371, 372
    coding, 278, 279
    DevRel team, 274
    emotional connection, 274
    participants, 275
    sample/example, 274
Live streams, 389, 473
Live tutorials, 456
Live viewers, 277, 470
LLMs (*see* Large language models (LLMs))
Logistical support, 447
Logistics, 342, 343, 443, 444, 463, 464
Logistics management, 262
Long-term effects, 485

INDEX

Long-term metrics, 409
Long-term relationships, 297
Long-term sustainability, 305

M

Marketing, 283, 311, 320, 349, 398
    department, 2
    team, 337
Mastodon, 396
Meeting format, 460, 461
Meetup Group, 458
Merchandise, 428
Metadata, 370
Meta-patterns, 3
Micro-blogging, 399
Microphone, 344
Mobile toolkit, 58, 59
Monetization metrics, 350
MP3 players, 56
Multiple-choice questions, 421
Multi-tenant service, 443
MVP program administration, 30

N

.NET community, 21
Net Promoter Score (NPS), 421, 425
Networking zones, 323
Newsletter, 38, 40, 42, 43, 61, 85, 97, 112, 147, 185, 190, 191, 293, 396, 399, 420
    communication channel, 281
    content, 284
    copyeditor, 286
    developers, 282
    gap, 282
    mechanisms, 284
    pattern, 283
    product/service, 283
Noise complaints, 330
Non-disclosure agreements, 26
Novelty swag, 430
NPS, *see* Net Promoter Score (NPS)

O

OAS, *see* OpenAPI Specification (OAS)
Object-oriented adoption, 3
Object-oriented software, 2
Office hours, 371, 408
    customer's environment, 290
    developer-focused channels, 292
    developers, 289, 291
    follow-up actions, 292
    hands-on support, 295
    recording, 294
    sample/example, 290, 294
    scheduling, 290
    time-consuming, 293
Off-sites, 439
Often-overlooked training, 442
Onboarding support, 438
Onboarding survey, 425
On-call support, 362
One-on-one interactions, 323

INDEX

One-on-one interview, 355
Online conference, 473
Online sentiment, 402
Online workshop, 473
OpenAPI, 383, 384
OpenAPI Specification (OAS), 375
Open hours, 290
Open rates, 284
Open-source projects, 405
    career-building, 306
    collaborative
        contributions, 298
    collaborative ecosystem, 301
    community-driven, 298
    community engagement, 300
    consequences, 305
    context, 299
    developer feedback, 301
    developer relations, 297, 304
    dual-licensed, 307
    feedback and contributions, 299
    high-quality tools, 299
    initiatives, 297
    library, 303
    metrics, 302, 303
    multi-region deployments, 304
    resource-intensive, 305
    software ecosystem, 306
    solo-maintained project, 307
Open-text responses, 417
Opinion, 414
Opinion pieces, 120
Overall satisfaction, 482
Overcrowding, 330

P

Partner, 389
Partnerships, 88, 185, 190, 469
    bandwidth, 316
    business development, 313
    developer relations, 313
    equal-sized, 315
    executive-initiated, 314
    executives, 311
    formal relationships, 309
    healthy relationship, 310
    legal agreement, 311
    motivation levels, 314
    partner-initiated, 314
    product extension, 317
    risks, 317
    sales, 312, 316
    team-initiated, 313
    technical integration, 309, 316
    technical members, 310
    technical resources, 315
    technical support, 312
    time/effort commitment, 315
    traffic content, 316
Party, 40, 46
    attendance, 325
    casual conversations, 320
    community-focused, 319
    community's contributions, 321
    company's presence, 321
    competitors, 329
    developer relations, 320
    dinners, 331

INDEX

entertainment, 320
event strategies, 325
follow-up, 326
logistical planning, 330
loyal customers, 321
participant's commitment, 320
pattern, 330
planning, 324
refreshments, 329
strenuous activity, 330
technological advancements, 323
vendor events, 329
venue, 324
Patterns, 4, 5
   activity patterns, 7–9
   art-and-science, 4
   building blocks, 17–19
   context/solution, 5
   documentation, 8
   language, 5, 6
   name, 9
   physical building, 4
   preoccupation, 4
   quick reference, 19
   software development, 4
   tags, 68
Peer-to-peer interaction, 404
Pit Crew, 208
Platform integration toolkit, 386
Podcast, 30, 49, 287, 348
   audience demographics, 348
   connection, 334
   conversations, 352
   culture/engagement, 335
   developer-facing, 336, 337
   dozen episodes, 352, 353
   engagement metrics, 349
   episode retention rates, 348
   feedback, 347
   goals, 338
   guests, 335, 342
   host, 335
   intros and outros, 342
   legal liability, 354
   liability, 341
   listenership, 348
   listening platforms, 348
   logistics, 342, 343
   long-form conversations, 334
   low-risk way, 355
   "no-go" topics, 344
   post-production, 345
   post-production team, 336
   post-recording, 345
   powerful tool, 333
   pre-recording, 344
   producer, 336
   product/service, 334, 343
   promotion, 347
   recording, 345
   regularity, 338
   releasing, 346
   schedule, 343
   SEO performance, 350
   theme/topic, 338
Podcast, 38
Point-of-contact, 444

INDEX

Poll, 414
Posters, 397
Post-production, 345, 367
    engagement, 114
    phase, 117
Post-recording, 345
Posts, 374
Post-session surveys, 292
Post-sponsorship, 408
Post-survey interactions, 421
Post-workshop feedback, 482
Post-workshop support, 481
Pre-recording, 344
Pre-Sales, 209
Presentation, 18
Presenters recording, 367
Producer, 336
Product Announcement, 119
Product-market fit, 424
Product/service, 22
Product/service development, 357
    constraints, 358
    long-term stability, 361
    relevance and effectiveness, 360
    structured process, 359
    third parties, 358
    third-party contributions, 359
Product/service integrations or extensions, 221
Product trials, 269
Promotional products, 428
Promotion efforts, 349
Proof-of-Concept (PoC) Pre-Sale, 231
Proofreading, 286
Prototype/factory method, 5
Prototype objects, 24
Prototypes, 362
Prototyping Lab, 266
Public forums, 237
Publisher, 365
Publishing phase, 116
Pulse survey, 425
Python, 393
Python community, 21

Q

Q-and-A style interaction, 234
Q&A sessions, 202, 480
QR code, 430
Quantitative metrics, 421
Questionnaire, 414

R

RadiantCloud, 463, 464
Reach, 14
ReallyCoolGameWorlds, 376
Recorded video, 17, 280, 354, 384
    audio narration, 366
    call to action, 368
    coding demo, 365
    developer relations, 364
    documentation, 366
    duration, 366
    narration, 367
    opportunity, 366

physical and virtual
audiences, 365
samples/examples, 371
social platforms, 363
time, 368
video content, 364
viewership, 368
writer, 365
Recorded Videos, 38, 64, 67, 226
Recorded viewers, 277, 470
Recording, 344, 345
Recruiting team, 337
Reddit, 380
Reference, 66
Reference documentation, 270,
293, 368, 373, 375, 384, 389,
392, 452, 453
coverage, 376
createCharacter, 377–379
developers, 376
developer tools, 374
errors, 379
Java classes, 379
JSON response, 377
labor-intensive, 374
open-sourcing, 379
parameters, 377
participants, 375
products/services, 374, 379
programming languages, 375
response, 377, 378
task, 374
Reference Documentation,
61, 85, 194

Release notes, 374
Repository stars, 384
Reputation, 241, 317
Reputation management, 307
Return on Investment (ROI),
159, 185
ROI, *see* Return on
Investment (ROI)
Roundup posts, 120

S

Safe Zone, 266
Salesforce, 470
Sample/example, 45, 64, 86, 90,
177, 287, 310
code author, 389
companies/products, 389
developers, 388
engineering teams, 390
gallery, 394
guides, 389
Java code, 393
perspective, 390
presentation/prose, 390
product/service, 388, 394
quality samples, 390
reference application, 394
reference documentation, 389
reviewers, 389
single-focused, 387
software, 391
technology stack, 393
usage, 391

INDEX

Sample/example (*cont.*)
    validation, 393
    vanity metric, 391
Sandbox, 271
Satisfaction scores, 421
Satisfaction survey, 425
Scenario-based tutorials, 456
Schedule, 343
Schedule conversations, 234
Scheduler, 442
Screen capture, 366, 367
SDK, *see* Software development kit (SDK)
Search engine rankings (SEO), 114
Security, 307
Self-explanatory, 90
Semi-private spaces, 404
SEO, *see* Search engine rankings (SEO)
Service integration kits, 386
Session duration, 268
SIG, *see* Special Interest Group (SIG)
ShopEase, 160
ShopSphere, 361
Short-form video, 372
Singletons, 3
Slack channel, 304
Social, 18
Social media, 64, 75, 85, 102, 117, 185, 190–192, 276, 282, 287, 293, 301, 326, 346, 371, 394, 396, 409–411, 413, 437, 471
    accounts, 403
    activities, 403
    announcements, 395
    commentary, 402
    communication channels, 403
    communication media, 397
    community activity, 396
    consumer feedback, 398
    consumption, 400
    corporate account, 404
    engagement, 400
    influence, 400
    less-than-positive responses, 404
    listening and learning, 396
    mentions, 349
    online, 395
    part-or full-time commitment, 402
    personal/advocate accounts, 404
    push-based notification, 396
    quick-turnaround effort, 399
    special-purpose email, 399
Social Media, 64, 85, 102, 117, 185, 190–192
Social platforms, 363
Software design, 3
Software development kit (SDK), 177
    abstraction, 381
    API documentation, 383
    customer code, 382
    data types, 382
    extension frameworks, 386

INDEX

HTTP, 382, 383
life cycle, 384
native constructs, 383
open-source profile, 385
participants, 383
platform integration
    toolkit, 386
product/service, 383
samples/examples, 384
tools, 385
UI toolkits, 386
Speak at conferences, 118
Speakers, 459, 461, 462
Special Interest Group (SIG), 458
Sponsoring, 141
Sponsoring company, 210
Sponsors, 256, 258, 261
Sponsorship, 46, 60, 149, 186, 208,
    258, 261, 262, 397
accounting, 410
ambassador, 411
authentic relationships, 407
context, 406
description, 406
event organizers, 408
initiatives, 405
marketing, 407
metrics, 409
opportunities, 407, 409
product awareness, 406
real-world developer, 408
relations teams, 407
structured process, 408
Stack overflow, 380, 392

Stakeholders, 359, 407, 408,
    419, 442
Step-by-step instructions, 369
Step-by-step tutorials, 455
Streamers, 279
StreamFlow, 360
StreamYard, 473
Students, 441
Student surveys, 444
Style, 340
Subscriber growth, 284
Subscription, 370
Support tickets, 376
Survey, 186, 360
    channels for distribution, 416
    clear objectives, 415
    collected data, 416
    demographic questions, 422
    developer experience, 415
    enhancement, 420
    feedback, 419
    goals, 418
    metrics, 420
    open-ended responses, 418, 421
    operational metrics, 422
    participants, 417
    questions, 418
    sentiment and trends, 415
    statistical tools, 419
    strategic initiatives, 414
    technical community, 413,
        414, 424
    thoughtfully constructed, 416
    timing, 418

INDEX

Sustainability, 307
Swag, 72, 262, 460, 461
   community members, 427
   description, 428
   designing and producing, 429
   developer communication, 428
   functional items, 431
   marketing specialists, 429
   opportunities, 429
   quantitative and qualitative impacts, 429, 430
   utility, 428
   vendors, 430
Swag, 47, 86, 128, 136, 138, 140, 143, 146, 149, 182, 185, 208
System of forces, 5

T

T&E, *see* Travel and expenses (T&E)
Tech Conference After-party, 320
TechFlow, 437
TechMo, 29
Technical assistance, 434
Technical decision-makers, 283
Technical support, 380
Technical setup, 480
Technical support
   company's products, 433
   first-tier, 435
   metrics, 436
   moderators, 435
   participants, 435

point-of-contact, 435
product knowledge, 436
product/service, 434, 437
smallest-effort-required bugs, 434
troubleshooting, 436
Technical tutorial, 119
Technical writers, 20, 283
Technology Advocacy Groups, 406
Technology demographic, 90
Tech support, 290
Tech Titans, 401
Telegram, 396
Third-party-hosted forum system, 234, 235
Thought leadership posts, 119
TikTok, 372, 396, 402
Tokens, 382
Tongue-in-cheek tone, 403
Tracking, 326
Tracking completion rates, 269
Training, 287, 455
   attendees, 447
   conference room, 443
   configuration, 440
   credibility, 440
   execution, 444
   follow-up surveys, 445
   hands-on exercises, 441
   in-person, 446
   lecture/lab pairs, 447
   logistics, 443, 444
   participants, 441, 442
   participation, 445

product/service, 440
review, 444
Training, 61
Transparency, 307, 423
Travel and expenses (T&E), 411
T-shirts, 428
Tutorial-based workshops, 487
Tutorials, 270, 284, 287, 369, 374, 384, 439
completion rate, 454
developers, 453
instructions, 453
low-code tool, 454
one-time exercise, 452
page hits, 454
product/service, 452, 455
sample/example, 455
step-by-step, 451–454
technical accuracy, 453
usage, 454
Tutorials, 39, 40, 43, 45, 119, 194, 247
Tweets, 404
Twitch, 275, 276, 278, 396
Twitter/X, 278, 396, 402
Twitter/X posts, 82

U

Unsubscribe rates, 284
Upskilling, 439
Usability, 358
User-agent API, 384

User group, 274, 400, 406
attendance, 462
call to action, 462
employees, 465
follow up, 465
food/beverage, 461
geographic regions, 458
goal, 463
interactivity, 458
logistics, 463, 464
meeting format, 460, 461
network, 287, 403, 411
organizers, 459
product/service, 458
speakers, 459, 461, 462
venue, 460
User Group Network, 61, 86, 130
User manuals, 374

V

Validation, 388, 443
Variants, 271, 272
Venue selection, 327
Vidcast, 334, 467
Video length, 367
Video tutorials, 456
Viewership, 368
Virtual workshop, 467, 486
Visibility, 317
Visualizations, 350
Visual Studio Code, 32
VSCode integration, 32

W, X

Webcast, 467
Web event, 467
Webex, 467
Webinars, 38, 274–276, 280, 301, 310, 352, 371, 372, 389, 400, 455
   broadcasting, 469
   contact information, 468
   goal, 473
   high-reach activities, 472
   marketing and sales, 471
   online presentation, 467, 468
   presentation, 469, 472
   sales cycle, 468
   scheduling, 471
   viewers, 470
Webpack, 99
Weibo, 396
White paper, 103
WidgetCorp, 327, 328
WidgetFest, 327, 328
Wiki, 242
Workshops, 15, 17, 67, 130, 193, 270, 390, 439
   consequences of, 485, 486
   context, 476, 477
   engagement, 481
   engagement during, 481
   follow-up actions, 484
   goal, 476
   hands-on approach, 476
   hands-on session, 477
   learning session, 476
   metrics, 484
   opportunities, 478
   participants, 478, 479
   planning, 483
   problem-solving, 477
   promotion, 483
   step-by-step instruction, 476
   structure, 479
   support staff, 484
Writing, 19
Writing phase, 116

Y

YouTube, 364, 367, 370, 371, 396, 401
YouTube channels, 30, 49

Z

Zoom, 473
Zoom presentations, 472

GPSR Compliance

The European Union's (EU) General Product Safety Regulation (GPSR) is a set of rules that requires consumer products to be safe and our obligations to ensure this.

If you have any concerns about our products, you can contact us on

ProductSafety@springernature.com

In case Publisher is established outside the EU, the EU authorized representative is:

Springer Nature Customer Service Center GmbH
Europaplatz 3
69115 Heidelberg, Germany

www.ingramcontent.com/pod-product-compliance
Lightning Source LLC
LaVergne TN
LVHW021954060526
838201LV00048B/1575